TRADITIONS OF CIVILITY;

Eight Essays.

BY

SIR ERNEST BARKER

"CIVILITY: *the state of being civilized:*
freedom from barbarity"
DR JOHNSON

ARCHON BOOKS
1967

First published 1948
Reprinted 1967 by permission of
The Cambridge University Press

Library of Congress Catalog Card Number: 67-28551
Printed in the United States of America

CONTENTS

*The Frontispiece is a reproduction of the Creation of Adam
by Michelangelo in the Sistine Chapel, Rome*

PREFACE

With one exception (the essay on Oliver Cromwell and the English People, which appeared originally in the *Cambridge Miscellany* in 1937 and is now out of print), the essays in this book are all new and hitherto unpublished. This is not to say that their origins do not, in most cases, go back for a number of years; but further reading and fresh reflection have enlarged, and even enriched, their original substance. The last four years, 1943-7, during which the essays have been composed in their present form, have been a time of harvest in which crops have been gathered and stored from seeds sown long ago. That is a benefit of retirement and the autumn of life.

Civility is defined in Dr Johnson's *Dictionary* as 'the state of being civilized'. That sense of the word, according to the modern dictionary, is now archaic. But to my mind civility is a better term than civilisation; and accordingly I have given to this book (which may be described as a series of studies in the history of culture and civilisation) a title suggested by two lines of Coventry Patmore:

> The fair sum of six thousand years'
> Traditions of civility.

Such is the thread which runs through all the essays—the continuous thread of what Dante calls *humana civilitas*.

The first five essays, though written independently and on different occasions, seem to me, as I look at them in retrospect, to be united by the common theme of the legacy of Greece. The last three essays stand by themselves. Their matter is English— or 'Anglo-Saxon'. The essay on Cromwell, based on a lecture originally delivered in Hamburg at the end of 1936, speaks for itself. The essay on Paley is based on a lecture originally delivered (but in a much shorter form) as one of a course of Lowell Lectures in Boston, Massachusetts, in the spring of 1929; and so, too, is the final essay on Natural Law and the American Revolution.

The arrangement of the essays is chronological; and the reader will find himself carried from ancient Greece, through the Middle Ages, to the century of the Renaissance and Reformation, thence to the century of the Puritan Revolution, and so to the century of William Paley and the Declaration of Independence. Perhaps the chronological sequence conceals a 'fault' or cleavage between the first five essays, which are all, in some sense, Greek, and the last three, which are not, except incidentally, concerned with Greece.

But the theme of tradition, and the key-note of continuity, are common to all the essays. With the concurrence of my wife, to whose suggestion the third essay is entirely due, I may perhaps be permitted to set these words at the end of this preface:

Liberis nostris
Haec nobis tradita tradimus
Posteris invicem tradenda.

E. B.

September 1947

I

GREEK INFLUENCES IN ENGLISH LIFE AND THOUGHT

I

'Except the blind forces of Nature, nothing moves in this world which is not Greek in its origin.' The words have often been quoted. They are not those of a zealot for Greek. They are the words of Sir Henry Maine, who held chairs of law both in Oxford and in Cambridge [1] and was one of the first (at any rate in England) to apply the historical method to the study of laws and institutions. That method carried him back to the Greek origins of our modern civility; and he repeated the thought of Lucretius:

> Humana ante oculos foede cum vita jaceret...
> Primum Graius homo mortales tollere contra
> Est oculos ausus primusque obsistere contra.

The words which Maine used (in his Rede Lecture of 1875 on 'Village Communities') are an obvious exaggeration. They forget —or rather *he* forgot—Judaea. His contemporary Matthew Arnold held a juster balance when he wrote, in a passage in *Culture and Anarchy*: 'Hebraism and Hellenism—between these two points of influence moves our world.... Hebraism and Hellenism are, neither of them, the law of human development;...they are, each of them, contributions to human development.' Nor was it Judaea only that Maine forgot. He also forgot, or at any rate he omitted, the general contribution of Asia—the ancient origins of civilisation which germinated on the banks of the Nile and by the waters of

---

[1] Maine (a Scholar of Pembroke College, and afterwards Fellow and Master of Trinity Hall, in the University of Cambridge) was Senior Classic in 1844. He held, during his long and distinguished career, the Regius chair of civil law, the Corpus chair of jurisprudence (at Oxford), and the Whewell chair of international law.

Babylon; the old civility of Persia and the seeds scattered (even among the Greeks themselves) [1] by the mythical 'Zoroaster'; the metaphysical subtleties of Indian thought; the ancient and suave culture of China.

But if the saying of Maine, like most other sayings which cut deep in the mind, has too narrow an edge to be generally just or exactly true, it has its truth; and before we turn to our particular theme of Greek influences in English life and thought, we are bound to pay a just measure of homage to the general influence of Greece on the general life of our Western world during the last two thousand years. There is an undying stream of Greek ideas— ideas about man's social life and political order; ideas about the human good and the virtues of man's moral nature; ideas about exact demonstrable truth and the canons of poetic and artistic beauty—which is the source and the inspiration of most of the thoughts we think in the ordinary discourse of our minds. Issuing into Rome and the Roman world, and thus assuming a Latin tincture which made it Greco-Roman, the stream flowed down the thousand years of the Middle Ages; and from them it has flowed in turn, with an undeviating continuity, through the five hundred years of our modern history. This is the classical heritage, or the Greco-Roman legacy; and even Roman law itself, specifically Roman as it may seem to be, is a part of that general legacy.

For all its continuity, the stream of the classical heritage has varied in its course; and it has varied in two ways. There has been, in the first place, a variation in the volume of its waters, and in the mass of the deposit—the fertilising silt—which the waters have carried. There have been periods or parts of the course of the Greco-Roman legacy in which the stream has run thin and shallow, trickling as it were along a dry bed in an almost invisible current

---

[1] Professor Jaeger, in his *Aristoteles* (pp. 133–8), has suggested that Plato's Academy was deeply interested in Zoroaster and the teaching of the Magi; and he has argued, on the evidence of ancient references to his lost treatise περὶ φιλοσοφίας, that Aristotle, too, was acquainted with the doctrines of Persian dualism. See the writer's article on 'Some Foreign Influences in Greek Thought', in *Greece and Rome*, Vol. v, no. 13, October 1935.

(there was such a period or tract, for example, during the three centuries between the fall of the Western Empire in 476 and the accession of Charlemagne in 768); and then there have come, in turn, periods or tracts in which—aided by some new conformation of circumstances or swollen by some new influx—the stream has again reappeared, 'brimming and bright and large', with a 'renaissance' of its waters and a 'revival' of all their deposited learning. But the word 'renaissance', so often and so vaguely applied to the periods of a larger volume of waters in the stream of the classical tradition, is a dubious and even a misleading word. It is a modern word in our language,[1] which only goes back for a century (the term 'revival of learning' has a more respectable antiquity); and even if it had a longer warrant, and a more precise significance, it conveys an erroneous idea. It suggests that something has died, and has had to be reborn. There never was any death of the classical heritage. The process of its transmission was a continuous process; and if it had ever stopped, civilisation itself would have stopped. If we confine the word to the simple sense of revival—a revival which, on the secular plane, is parallel to religious revivals, when an old and undying and continuous belief is kindled into a bright and large flame—we shall reduce it to the measure of truth. In that limited sense we may well confess, and even profess, that there have been a number of renaissances—not one renaissance, but many—the Carolingian renaissance about 800; the twelfth-century renaissance of the School of Chartres, of the teaching of Abelard, of the recovery of Aristotle's *Posterior Analytics*, and of the beginnings of the University of Paris; the thirteenth-century renaissance of the recovery of Aristotle's *Ethics* and *Politics*, and of the teaching of St Thomas Aquinas; and finally (but not only) the 'Italian' renaissance—which was French, Spanish, German, Dutch, and English, as well as Italian—the renaissance of the recovery of Plato, of Homer, of the general body of Greek literature, but, above all, of the Greek New Testament, as published in Erasmus's edition of 1516 and Cardinal Ximenes's Complutensian Polyglot of 1522.

[1] See below, p. 80.

There is a second sense in which the stream of the classical heritage has varied in its course. There has been a variation not only in the volume of the waters, but also in the language in which they murmured as they flowed. For long centuries—we may even say for a thousand years, from the fall of the Western Empire in 476 to the fall of the Eastern in 1453—the language was Latin. The heritage itself might be Greek as well as Latin, or Greek even more than Latin; but the language in which it was expressed was Latin. The logic of Aristotle (one of the greatest of all the instruments of European education) survived and was studied in Latin translations for all those thousand years; and even when St Thomas commented on Aristotle's other treatises, and built a philosophy which reconciled the *fides* of the Church with the *ratio* of the Lyceum, he did it upon the basis of Latin translations prepared for his use. It was a great variation and a sweeping change in the course of the stream of the classical heritage when Greek thought began to be studied in the Greek—the original Greek itself, from which the Latin had flowed. This was the achievement and the significance of the 'Italian' renaissance; and in this sense that renaissance, even if it was one among many, was also unique and distinctive. It was a revival in a deeper sense than any of the previous revivals. It was more than the return of Greek influence in the medium of the Latin language: it was the return, at long last, of the direct, clean impact of Greek influence *in the original Greek*. The truth which the generations had garbled, without wishing to do so or even knowing that they did, was re-uttered; and the Greek tradition once more stood clear in its own Greek self. This was not merely a literary event; it was also a renaissance of philosophy and a reformation of religion. In philosophy, thinkers went back behind the Latin translations to the authentic text of Aristotle; and they recovered the original Greek of Plato, who counted even more than Aristotle with men such as Marsilio Ficino and Thomas More. In religion, divines went back behind the Latin Vulgate to the Greek text of the Gospels and Epistles; and this was the way in which a revival of learning passed into a reformation of religion, carrying men back

4

through the centuries to the original image of the Founder and the original teaching of His disciples.[1]

We may therefore hold the belief—but we must hold it without forgetting the legacy of Judaea—that the mind of Europe has largely lived, in spite of some interruptions and many variations, on the substance of the Greek heritage. This is the common European inheritance; and we may therefore also hold that community in the Greek heritage is one of the bases—and not the least—of any unity which Europe possesses. If ever we attain a United States of Europe, this community in the classical heritage—a heritage which was originally Greek, and has always remained fundamentally Greek—will be largely its spiritual foundation. That is the profoundest reason, and perhaps the only really cogent reason, for continuing to maintain the tradition of a classical education. It is a perpetual reminder to the nations of Europe of the common fibre of their minds and the common substance of their ideas. Their philosophic terms, their political vocabulary, the language of their sciences, and the words of their literary and artistic criticism, have all a common Greek origin. It is the fact that the Greek heritage has been wrought into history, rather than the fact (which is perhaps also a fancy) of its own superior excellence, which is the strength of its claim upon our allegiance. It is the process of its historical transmission, among the nations and through their generations, rather than the product itself, which matters. The wise votary of Greek studies will defend them more for their historic significance than for their canonical authority in matters of truth and taste. The essential argument in favour of Greek studies is not their superiority: it is the simple fact that, so far as Europe is one, it is one in virtue of sharing in a single *paideia* (or, as the Romans called it, *humanitas*)—and the ancient mother of this single *paideia* is ancient Greece.

If we look at the matter from this point of view, we may

---

[1] Erasmus wrote of the Greek New Testament, in 1516: 'Hae (litterae) tibi sacrosanctae mentis illius vivam referunt imaginem, ipsumque Christum loquentem, sanantem, morientem, resurgentem; denique totum ita praesentem reddunt ut minus visurus sis si coram oculis conspicias.'

perhaps avoid an ancient danger which has vexed the progress of human thought. This is the danger of making the Greek heritage the absolute canon of truth and taste, and of imposing it as a yoke on man's living and growing mind. If the Greeks themselves had always observed the rules, the canons and the 'unities', which have been deduced by the moderns from their example, they would never have gone very far. We can learn more from the Greeks if we observe their way of going about things than if we observe and follow the paths they actually trod. Their real lesson is the lesson of a fresh curiosity, engaged in wondering and therefore able to arrive at philosophy, the child (as Plato said) of wonder: it is the lesson of a zest for observing and understanding the facts, and for finding, on that basis, an explanation which, as they said, 'saved the facts'. In a word it is their general method which matters more than their results; and if we imitate at all, our wisdom will lie in imitating their method in order to improve their results. Euclid is a typical—perhaps the most typical—expression of 'the Greek genius and its meaning to us' (more typical even than Sophocles, and far more typical than Sappho):[1] but the results

---

[1] The writer recently unearthed, by accident, some words which he wrote, as long ago as 1913, in a review of Sir Richard Livingstone's book on *The Greek Genius and its Meaning to us*. (The words had the honour of being quoted by Sir Thomas Heath, in a paper on Greek Mathematics and Science, printed at Cambridge in 1921.) They are as follows:

'To be a Greek was to seek to know; to know the primordial substance of matter, to know the meaning of number, to know the world as a rational whole. In no spirit of paradox one may say that Euclid is the most typical Greek: he would fain know to the bottom, and know as a rational system, the laws of the measurement of the earth. Plato, too, loved geometry and the wonders of numbers; he too was essentially Greek, because he was essentially mathematical....No doubt the Greek genius means many things. To one school (perhaps a prevalent school in Oxford to-day) it means an aesthetic ideal, somewhat variegated and diversified by anthropological survivals and outcrops. To others, however, it means an austere thing, which delights in logic and mathematics; which, continually wondering and always inquisitive, is driven by its wonder into philosophy, and into inquiry about the why and wherefore, the whence and whither, of tragedy, of the State, indeed of all things. And if one thus finds the Greek genius in Euclid and the *Posterior Analytics*, one will understand the motto written over the Academy—"Let no man enter here without geometry". To know what the Greek genius meant you must (if one may speak ἐν αἰνίγματι) begin with geometry.'

6

of Euclid himself can be, and have been, improved by modern geometry. Greece was too much and too unreflectingly flattered for many centuries; and men's minds allowed themselves too readily to become the dazzled slaves of her light and leading. Philosophy, science, and the drama itself, were subjugated to the authority of Aristotle; and hence in growing ages of thought, such as the age of Bacon and Descartes, we find men claiming a right of resistance to what had become a mental tyranny—a tyranny never intended by its own original author, but a tyranny, none the less, which was forged for him by his interpreters.[1] Dryden expressed the just spirit of revolt which animated his age:

> The longest tyranny that ever swayed
> Was that wherein our ancestors betrayed
> Their free-born reason to the Stagirite
> And made his torch their universal light.

There is truth in Dryden's accusation. Our human life—mental, moral, and even physical—is an oscillation or tension between tradition and initiative, continuity and novelty. We need both. If we remember only continuity, we fall into stagnation; and we lose our human right, which is a duty as well as a right, of liberty and the progress which comes from liberty.

II

When we consider the influence of Greek political theory on the modern theory of the State, we are apt to think only, or at any rate to think primarily, of the influence of Plato's *Republic* and

[1] Another and very different form of this tyranny has been studied by Miss E. M. Butler (now Professor) in her work on *The Tyranny of Greece over Germany*. Examining the influence of 'Winckelmann's Greece' on the development of German poetry since the end of the eighteenth century—from Goethe and Hölderlin to Stefan George—she argues that if 'Greece has profoundly modified the whole trend of modern civilisation...Germany is the supreme example of her triumphant spiritual tyranny' (p. 6). Speaking of the German Hellenists in the field of poetry, she concludes (pp. 335-6) that 'they wished to seize and possess Greek beauty, and make it their own; or to outdo it; or failing that to destroy it; or to drag it violently into the present....Small wonder... that the history of German Hellenism has such a painfully sensational side.'

Aristotle's *Politics*. But Greek political theory is not only the theory of the *polis*, which engaged and absorbed the attention of Plato and Aristotle; it is also the theory of the *cosmopolis*, which engaged the attention, and even attracted the devotion, of the Cynics, the Stoics, and the later eclectics such as Posidonius of Apamea—that last great Greek who put together in the University of Rhodes, during the first century B.C., the *summa philosophiae* which was presented to Christianity and influenced the thought of St Paul.[1] The modern theory of the State has been affected by both of these two phases of Greek political theory—not only by the classical theory of the *polis*, but also by what may be called the post-classical theory of the *cosmopolis*; and, of the two, it is possible to argue that the latter has exerted, through the centuries, a greater and more pervasive influence.

In some respects Plato and Aristotle go together in the field of political theory, and their influences converge: in other respects they stand apart, and their influences diverge. Taking them together, we may fairly say that both of them are the apostles of the necessity of the *polis* to the individual, of the priority of the *polis* to the individual, and of the general claim and call of the *polis* upon the individual. They are both the prophets of community; and the community of which they are prophets is a totalitarian community, touching everything and laying its hand on the whole of the life of its members. 'Cette Cité grecque qui comprend tant de choses ne saurait manquer d'être un État touche-à-tout.' When modern theory has sought to emphasise the claim and the call of the community, it has gone back to Plato and Aristotle—and more especially to Plato. Rousseau and Hegel may both be cited in evidence. Rousseau was not a believer, as his interpreters have too often assumed, in the sovereign individual or the natural rights of man: he was a collectivist who believed that the life of the individual could only be fulfilled in the common life of the community, and who held that it was 'l'état civil qui, d'un animal stupide et borné, fit un être intelligent et un homme'. In the strength of this belief he naturally went back to Greek

[1] See the second essay, pp. 42–3.

political theory; and he even advocated the old Greek practice of the small community, where all the citizens could gather together directly, in a primary assembly, to elicit and express a general will, where 'none was for a party', and 'all were for the state'. Hegel, like and yet unlike Rousseau, found his new Hellas in the system of Prussian monarchy. Believing that the state 'carries back the individual, whose tendency it is to become a centre of his own, into the life of the universal substance' (the phrase is almost an echo of the earlier phrase of Rousseau), he too went back to the Greek philosophers of the fourth century B.C.—and more especially to Plato—to corroborate his theory of the totalitarian and yet liberating community. In the very spirit and almost in the language of Plato, he proclaimed that the unity of the State—'the free power that interferes with subordinate spheres', assigning to each its specific function—must be expressed 'in an actual individual, in the will of a decreeing individual, in monarchy', which is thus identified with philosophy (the power that 'thinks things together' and assigns its place to each) and enthroned as philosopher-king.

But Plato and Aristotle, if they sometimes converge, have none the less exercised different influences on the course of political development. Aristotle could say, as he does in the beginning of the eighth book of his *Politics*, that 'we must not regard any citizen as belonging to himself, but all as belonging to the state'; but the saying is an echo, and almost a quotation, of a passage in Plato's *Laws*, and there is much in the theory of Aristotle which runs in a different direction. The trend and influence of the theory of Plato has been in favour of the expert: it has been in favour of political experiment and innovation; it has been in favour of a new social order, running to the length of a controlled (or controlling) communism. Plato was little of a Fabian: he had an ardent idealism which would not stop at solutions of the *interim*, or proceed by the method of *pedetemptim*; but we may none the less trace his influence in the theory of modern Fabianism, with its belief in the scientific expert, its trend towards scientific experiment, and its movement towards a new social order imposed on the errors and confusion of the past. The thought of Aristotle, and its permanent influence, are of a different order. His political philosophy has a curious English quality; we may almost say that it is Whig; at any rate it shows a Whig sense of the value of time and tradition, and of the wisdom of human co-operation with the working of time and tradition.[1] He is in favour of the collective judgement of ordinary men, and their 'general bank and capital' of good sense, rather than the expert's 'private stock of reason': he is in favour of the steady rule of law, rather than experiment and innovation; he is in favour of private property and the existing social order, as the products of a natural evolution, rather than the metaphysical symmetry of a new social dispensation. Burke, who expounded the same general philosophy, was not ignorant of Aristotle, or of his great commentator St Thomas Aquinas; and he echoes and even quotes the *Politics* in his *Reflections on the Revolution in France*.

The classical scholar, trained in the classical texts of the fifth and fourth centuries B.C., is perhaps too apt to forget the post-classical theory (for which the texts are far more exiguous) which passed into the Roman Empire and into the Christian Church. But the survival and the influence of Stoicism are facts of the first order of importance. Absorbed by the Roman lawyers, and incorporated in their scheme of *jus naturale*—penetrating the Christian Fathers, and expressed in their general theory of society—Stoicism became a continuous thread in the living cloth woven by human thought. In the Stoic theory of the *cosmopolis* the rational faculty of man was conceived as producing a common conception of law and order which possessed a universal validity, transcending alike the cities of the Greeks and the nations of the Gentiles; and according to Stoic thought—already anticipated in action by the policy of Alexander—this common conception included, as its three great notes, the three values of Liberty, Equality, and the brotherhood or Fraternity of all mankind. This common conception, and its three great notes, have formed a European set of ideas for over two thousand years. It was a set of ideas which lived and moved

[1] See the introduction to the author's translation of the *Politics*, p. xxxi, and his *Essays on Government*, pp. 223-4.

in the Middle Ages; and St Thomas Aquinas cherished the idea of a sovereign law of nature, imprinted in the heart and nature of man, to which kings and legislators must everywhere bow. It was a set of ideas which lived and acted with an even greater animation from the days of the Reformation to those of the French Revolution, during the epoch of the School of Natural Law, when thought, escaping from theological trammels, evolved, and elaborated in detail, the notion of a secular natural law, based on the pure reason of man, which should control his states and their governments, both in their external relations and in their domestic conduct.[1]

We may ascribe two major results to the speculation and teaching of this School of Natural Law. The first was the development of the modern system of international law to control the external relations between states. From Gentilis at Oxford (c. 1590), Grotius in Holland (c. 1620), and Pufendorf at Heidelberg and Lund (c. 1670), down to Vattel in Switzerland (c. 1760), a steady succession of thinkers drew out the continuous Stoic thread of the law of nature into a law of nations which should be a *jus belli et pacis*. The second result was even greater. In the days of the French Revolution the School of Natural Law, which had already spoken through the mouth of Locke to justify the English Revolution of 1688, and had recently served to inspire the American Revolution of 1776, proclaimed its ideas to a listening Europe. They were ideas of the proper conduct of states and governments in the area of internal affairs. They were ideas of the natural rights of man—of liberty political and civic, with sovereignty residing essentially in the nation, and with free communication of thoughts and opinions; of equality before the law, and the equal repartition of public expenses among all the members of the public; of a general fraternity which tended in practice to be sadly restricted within the nation, but which could, on occasion, be extended by

[1] The writer would ask permission to refer to the introduction of his translation of Gierke's chapters on *Natural Law and the Theory of Society, 1500 to 1800* (§ 3, on the law of nature, pp. xxxiv–l), and, for what is said in the last paragraph of this section (p. 12), to Troeltsch's lecture on *The Ideas of Natural Law and Humanity in World Politics*, translated in Vol. I, pp. 201–20, of that work.

decree to protect all nations struggling for freedom. It is a long road from Zeno, the founder of Stoicism, to the explosion of the French Revolution; but it is a continuous road.[1]

It is one of the curiosities of history—but, even more, one of its tragedies—that Germany, whose thinkers had played no small part in elaborating the doctrines of natural law during the seventeenth century and much of the eighteenth, deserted the tradition of Stoicism—and, with it, a Christian tradition—almost at the very time when that tradition was flowering and budding in North America and Western Europe. One of the most fateful happenings in the world—for revolutions of thought can also be fateful happenings—was the triumph on the east of the Rhine of a different, and indeed almost opposite, set of ideas about the year 1800. Romanticism came, and ascribed divinity to the separate people or *Volk*, with its own folk-music, its own folk-songs, its own folk-lore, and its own general *Volksgeist*. Hegel came, and did obeisance to a deified State, which was the incarnation of 'the universal substance' of a sadly particular and tragically localised 'objective mind'. A new school of historical law arose, which rejected the idea of a universal law of nature, and preached in its place a folk-law, or *Volksrecht*, developed by the particular evolution of each people, separate for each people, and finally sovereign for each people. The conception of a common law controlling states and their governments, both in their external relations and in their domestic conduct, thus disappeared in the rolling clouds of a folk-philosophy; and a gulf emerged between Western Europe, with its old Stoic inheritance, and a Germany possessed by its new Teutonic conception of the sovereign Folk and its sovereign nebulosity. One of the great problems of our day is to bridge that gulf, and to bring Germany back from her long and voluntary exile into the spirit of the ancient classical heritage.

[1] 'There is certainly a line of descent from his (Alexander's) prayer at Opis, through the Stoics and one portion of the Christian ideal, to that brotherhood of all men which was proclaimed, though only proclaimed, in the French Revolution.' (W. W. Tarn, in the *Cambridge Ancient History*, Vol. VI, p. 437.)

III

It is natural, after this summary account of the influence of Greek ideas of politics—and also of law, for politics and law were hardly divided in the thought of Greece—to turn to the influence of Greek ideas of economics. Plato's theory of communism has exercised a long influence (but often in garbled or imperfect versions, which have failed to reckon with its dominant political purpose and the restriction of its scope to the governing classes of his ideal state): there is a line of connection which runs from the *Republic* to More's *Utopia*; and a socialist writer of our time has noted 'the continuity of communist and socialist thought, from its germ in More's *Utopia*, to its full maturity in the theory and practice of Lenin'.[1] But it is the general theory of economics set out in the first book of Aristotle's *Politics* which has perhaps had the most abiding and the profoundest effect. Agrarian in his view, and mainly interested in the production and use of the kindly fruits of the earth, Aristotle frowned on exchange for profit, as a source of improper gain and the origin of an 'acquisitive' commercial class. He had some sympathy with the primitive method of barter, which satisfied men's natural wants in terms of their mutual needs; and he was clear that wealth must be limited and controlled by the dominant purposes of family and civic life, to which it was only a means, and which would be defeated rather than served if it were turned into an end and thus accumulated in excess of men's just and proper requirements. He had, indeed, a balanced view of the origin and function of a money currency; but he had also a clear conviction that currency existed merely to facilitate exchange and to remedy the imperfections of barter, and not to breed interest at usury.

This general theory—or, as it may perhaps more justly be called, this general set of ideas—became an inheritance of the Middle Ages. Adopted and expanded by St Thomas Aquinas, it also affected the canon law of the medieval Church. Against the conduct of exchange for profit the Church set up the idea of the *justum*

---

[1] John Strachey, *The Theory and Practice of Socialism*, p. 277.

pretium, which was generally held to be the price that enabled the trader to maintain his family at the recognised standard of his time and place; and as the medieval trader was usually also a craftsman, who had produced the goods in which he traded, this idea of the just price entailed in effect an idea of the just wage. Against the practice of usury the Church similarly erected a set of principles defining the cases and the conditions in which interest could legitimately be charged—either because the lender participated with the borrower in risk, or because by lending he suffered the loss of a chance of legitimate gain which he might otherwise have made. The idea of the just price, and the set of principles about interest, were not merely aspirations or pronouncements of the Church: they were adopted in actual commercial law, and incorporated in the town ordinances followed by the courts of medieval towns.

No doubt there are other reasons—reasons more practically cogent than the authority of Aristotle, even when backed by that of St Thomas Aquinas—which also serve to explain the teaching of the Church, and the general adoption of its teaching, during the latter half of the Middle Ages. But whether their share was great or small, Greek ideas of economics still counted for something in that period. A change came in the sixteenth century. The system of Church economics, with its covering sanction of classical authority, might suit an age of agrarian producers interspersed with town tradesmen who were also craftsmen. It was less suited to a new age of mercantile capitalism; of the enclosure of land by great landlords; of a disturbed currency and rising prices. It was still less suited to the still newer age of industrial capitalism which arose on the basis of mercantilism, and proceeded to oust its predecessor in favour of a regime of free trade, free competition, and the unlimited pursuit of illimitable wealth under the banner of *laissez-faire*. Yet even in an age of industrial capitalism we may trace a return, by way of reaction, to old Greek ideas. From the middle of the nineteenth century onwards, as the age of enlightenment passed into an age of disillusionment, there were thinkers who began to proclaim that the Greeks had seen economics more steadily because they had seen all life as a whole. One of these thinkers was Ruskin. He went back even beyond Aristotle for his view of economics: he returned to the *Republic* of Plato and the *Oeconomicus* of Xenophon. He wished, as they, in a simpler age, had wished, to subordinate economics to ethics; he would have had it again become what it originally meant to the Greeks— a science of household management, with happy family plots, and happy domestic industries, all serving the purposes of ethical—and also aesthetic—development. By his foundation of St George's Guild, and still more by his teaching in books such as *A Joy for Ever* and *Unto this Last*, he sought to put wealth in its place, where it would be controlled and limited by considerations of welfare. Bringing the inspiration of Greece to stir the Victorian age, he made his interpretation of the Greek view of economics a nursing mother of English socialism; and though he was not himself a socialist—he may be called more justly the prophet of an aesthetic authoritarianism—he helped to give working men and their leaders a vision of Greece (too long and too much confined to the wealthier and more fortunate classes) which lightened the way of many who became authentic socialists. The light of Plato was reflected in him, if it was also refracted: he had a Platonic zest for the education of the citizen in 'the perfect exercise and kingly continence of body and soul'; and like Plato he urged men to turn their eyes from getting and spending to the building of the life beautiful in the light of an idea of the good.

IV

Education, as well as economics, is a sphere in which the tradition of Greece has exerted an influence on English life. The educational ideals of the sixteenth century, as they are expressed in Elyot's *Book of the Governor*, or in Castiglione's *Il Cortigiano*, not only include a knowledge of Greek authors, and particularly of Plato; they are also built on the old Greek model in the spirit they are meant to produce and in the curriculum which they suggest for the production of that spirit.[1] The effort of the Renaissance was not only an effort for the introduction of Greek into the studies pursued in grammar schools and other places of education; it was also an effort to achieve a general revolution, which should 'set Dunce in Bocardo' (or in other words send Duns Scotus and the medieval schoolmen packing) and substitute the arts of beauty for the art of dialectic. But we may also trace in our own age, and in the educational development of the seventy odd years since 1870, a return of Greek conceptions; and we may trace that return in two notable directions.

The first direction is that of public elementary (now called primary) education. There may seem, at first sight, to be little that is Greek in the elementary school—though the writer remembers being grounded in Euclid (and Euclid after all is Greek) in his old elementary school. But there is a document dealing with the purposes and function of the elementary school which is well worth consideration. It takes the mind back to a 'tradition of civility' which is as old as Aristotle. The document is 'The Introduction to the Code'—the code of regulations for public elementary schools—as it appeared from 1904 onwards. 'The purpose of the public elementary school', it is there declared, 'is to form and strengthen the character, and to develop the intelligence ...with this purpose in view it will be the aim of the school to train the children carefully in habits of observation and clear reasoning, and afford them every opportunity for the healthy development of their bodies.... And, though their opportunities are but brief, the teachers can yet do much to lay the foundations of conduct...implant in the children habits of industry, self-control and courageous perseverance...teach them to reverence what is noble...foster a strong sense of duty, and instil in them that consideration and respect for others which must be the foundation of unselfishness and the true basis of all good manners.'

These are indeed words which take the mind back. Character comes first, and with it the laying of the foundations of conduct:

[1] See Essay V on 'The Education of the English Gentleman in the Sixteenth Century', and especially pp. 135, 148.

intelligence comes next, and with it a training in the habits (ingrained in the ancient Greeks) of observing the facts and reasoning clearly on the basis of the facts; finally comes the body, and the healthy gymnastic of the body. Is not this Greek, and has it not an Aristotelian ring? This training of character by 'habituation' in early youth; this notion of an ethical along with a mental discipline: this remembering of the importance of the development of healthy bodies—all these things are to be found in the last two books of the *Politics*. Was the writer (or the writers) of the words which have just been quoted aware of the analogy? And was there even, perhaps, affiliation as well as analogy? A vivid memory of a conversation with Sir William Anson, who had been Parliamentary Secretary to the Board of Education from 1902 to 1905, may supply something of an answer. He had, he said, himself been trained in the classical course at Oxford. Sir Robert Morant, Permanent Secretary of the Board of Education from 1903 onwards, had been similarly trained. It might well be that they had remembered their training. The Greek tradition flows in many channels, like the irrigation waters among the vineyards on the terraces of Italian hills; and it may fertilise government departments.

The other direction in which we may trace a return of Greek conceptions of education is the growing emphasis laid in our time on the idea of leisure. The word leisure comes to us, through the French, from the Latin *licere*, and it suggests—or used to suggest— the idea of being able to do as you please. It is defined in the dictionary as 'the state of having time at one's own disposal, time which one can spend as one pleases, free or unoccupied time'. But this is an old and libertarian sense, which has been slowly altering during the last twenty or thirty years—and altering, it may fairly be suggested, under Greek influence. Many of those who are thinking and writing and planning to-day about 'the uses of leisure' have really in their minds not the French word *loisir*, but the Greek word *scholē*, which is commonly translated by our word 'leisure'. There are many, for instance, who feel that education in adolescence should be largely directed to developing tastes, eliciting capacities, and encouraging hobbies, which will help to fill the leisure of later years with positive activities. There are many, again, who feel that there is room for a large development of adult education, in the years of grown manhood, which will occupy leisure with studies—studies not only of history, economics, and politics, but also of the works of nature and the creations of art. Indeed, there is now a growing conviction—we may almost call it a philosophy of life—that though work and vocation matter, and matter very profoundly, as our Puritan and our Victorian ancestors thought, there is also something else which matters, and matters at least as much, or possibly even more. In an age of mechanical production, producing so much so quickly, the work of man's hands recedes; leisure descends upon him: he is thrown back on the use of his mind; and if he would avoid what the Middle Ages called the sin of 'accidie'—the sin of sloth, or torpor of the faculties—he must add to work and vocation, now reduced to the half of life, the active practice of the uses of leisure.

Under these influences thought turns back, consciously or unconsciously, to the ideas of the Greeks. The old negative or libertarian conception of leisure, as a 'licit' period of non-occupation in which a man may do as he likes, begins to be coloured and tinged by the active and ordered notions implicit in the Greek conception of *scholē*. That conception, expounded by Aristotle at the end of the seventh book of the *Politics*, has two main implications.

In the first place, *scholē* is not regarded as contrasted with activity, or as being a time or state of inaction: on the contrary, it is regarded as being itself activity, and indeed the highest form of activity—and this for the two great reasons (which are really a single reason), first that it engages and sets in motion the speculative part of man's soul, and secondly and consequentially (since the motion of the speculative part of the soul is an end in itself) that it issues in a form of activity which is pursued for its own intrinsic sake, and not for the sake of an object extraneous to itself. *Scholē* is thus the exercise of the mind, in its highest reach, for its own pure sake;

and what is contrasted with it is not activity in general (for it belongs itself to that sphere), but the particular activity of 'work', or *ponos*, which engages only the lower reaches of the mind and engages them only for an ulterior object.

In the second place, *scholē*—the highest form of man's activity—is not only contrasted with 'work': it is also contrasted with 'recreation', or *anapausis*, which is at once the negation of work and its complement and corollary. Recreation is rest from the labours of work, but it is also a preparation for new and similar labours; and in both of these aspects—that of rest no less than that of preparation—it is in its nature the inseparable companion of work. *Scholē* stands by itself, in its own independent right: it is not the shadow of work, but the light which shines above work. And if we ask ourselves the question, 'What is the content of *scholē*, and what is the nature of its activity?' the answer is to be found in one of the commentators on Aristotle. 'It is employment in work desirable for its own sake—the hearing of noble music and no doubt of noble poetry: intercourse with friends chosen for their worth; and above all the exercise, in company or otherwise, of the speculative faculty.'[1]

It will be seen that Aristotle operates with three notions—*scholē*, *ponos*, and *anapausis*—leisure, in the high Greek sense; work, or vocation; and rest, or recreation. We have still to operate, in our own day, with these three notions. Indeed, it may be said to be the problem of our modern civilisation that we should find and maintain a right proportion between these three elements—work, play, and the use of leisure. The greatest of the three is the use of leisure. To give it its proper place (and, as Aristotle would say, its proper 'equipment') is partly a matter of voluntary action by social forces, and partly a matter of public action by the political community. The voluntary action of social groups and agencies can do much. Indeed, it is already doing much in the creation of community centres by community associations (acting on the basis of neighbourhood units) which seek to adorn the leisure of their members by drawing them together, not only for games and

---

[1] W. L. Newman's edition of the *Politics*, Vol. III, p. 442.

recreation, but also for the hearing and performing of music, for the acting and even the writing of plays, and for the exercise of the speculative faculty at lectures and in discussion groups. But there is also room for the public action of the political community in the adorning and equipping of leisure. The State has already done much in the way of libraries, galleries and museums. There is more that may still be done in the way of national theatres, national concert halls and national opera houses. It has been calculated that at the popular festivals of Athens, in the fifth century B.C., there were produced, in theatres or halls furnished by the State, at least 2,000 plays and from 4,000 to 5,000 dithyrambs. We need not expect so great a crop: indeed, it would perhaps confuse us. But we are none the less entitled to expect that our great State should do something—all the more when the sun of private patronage is setting—as foster-father and patron of the liberal arts of leisure.

V

The argument has hitherto turned on the influence exercised by Greek theory—political, economic, and educational—on the course of modern life. It may now turn to Greek history and the record of the Greek past. It is not only the *theory* of Greece which still lives and acts upon us. It is also the *history* of Greece—the remembered record of what happened to men and their states in the Greek past, the surviving memory of Greek achievement, Greek heroisms, and Greek flaws—which, like all the memories that live in our minds and colour their nature, is still a part of our life and an influence on our action.

The remembered record, the surviving memory, which we call Greek history, has two modes of operation. One mode of its operation is subtle, but it is also direct. It is the mode by which Greek history acts as it were of itself, simply by virtue of being there, and because it is in the air—the mental air we are always breathing. The other mode of its operation is simpler, but it is also indirect. This is the mode by which Greek history acts in our minds as a part of our education and a subject of the curriculum.

It is a matter of the operation of Greek studies, and particularly the study of Greek history, on the thought of those who pursue these studies. In the first of the senses here described Greek history is a general influence, acting on all alike—at any rate all who are susceptible to historic influences. In the second sense Greek history is a special influence, acting on a small and separate class.

It may seem a vague nebulosity to speak of Greek history acting 'of itself, by virtue of being there, and because it is in the air'. It may clarify the matter if we use two phrases about the past. The first is 'the Living Past'. The past is not dead, as we often assume: it never dies, so long as it is remembered; and even if it is not consciously remembered, it may survive in something that still lives in our minds as an unconscious heritage. At any rate the *remembered* past still lives—in us and in our minds. We have inherited it with the mental air we breathe: it is a part of the substance of living minds; and it is living because they are living. It cannot be dead, because it is in us—and we are not dead. The second phrase is 'the Changing Past'. The past is not static or fixed, as again we often assume. Because it lives in our minds, it also changes with them; it assumes new forms from age to age; and it does so because what we feel towards it, and what we can draw from it into ourselves, is something that undergoes change with the changing generations. This idea of 'the Changing Past' may seem a bewildering paradox; and we may repeat to ourselves the words of the Greek poet, quoted by Aristotle in the *Ethics*:

> For this alone belongs not even to God,
> To make undone the things that have been done.

But the sense of the phrase is simple, and as true as it is simple. It is a simple truth that the past changes in us, as the view which we take of its nature changes. From this point of view we may think of the past as describing an orbit round the present; and we may thus regard any given period of the past—say the period of the fifth and fourth centuries before our era—as sweeping in a circle of change which places it in different relations to each successive present. Sometimes the Greek past may recede in its orbit, as it did in the age of Pope Gregory VII, who was not Greek-minded, or in that of Dr Johnson, who was Roman rather than Greek, if indeed he was anything other than English. Sometimes, again, the Greek past comes close: it shines with its original light: it invigorates a whole generation with the warmth of its first splendour. This was so in the age of the Italian Renaissance, and of the revival not only of Greek letters but also of the Greek spirit. It was so in the age of Winckelmann, and of the return to the art of Greece at the end of the eighteenth century. Perhaps it is so again, in this first half of the twentieth century.

A particular past may always swing into a particular congruity with a given present: and when that happens to some past in its orbit, it will give light and warmth to the present with which it swings into congruity. The writer cannot but feel that he has himself experienced a congruity between the Greek past and the present in which he has lived since he went up to Oxford, half a century ago, in the last decade of the nineteenth century. No doubt this congruity—if indeed it exists, and is more than an 'idol' in the mind of the classical student—is partly a web of connection spun by the genius and industry of scholars. It is the product of Jowett's Plato and Murray's Euripides: of Butcher and Jebb and Burnet, of Myres and Livingstone and Zimmern, and of all the translators and interpreters *qui lampada tradiderunt*. But it is also due to another cause which goes far deeper. There is a real congruity, as well as a web of connection spun by scholars, between our own age and that of the fifth and fourth centuries B.C. Both may be justly described as ages of rapid movement, or ages of transition, such as sometimes come, like the flowering of the aloe-tree, in the growth of the human spirit. Both may justly be said to be vexed by similar problems—the problem of making democracy good against the personal dictator or *tyrannos*, on the one hand, and on the other against the danger of class-conflict and proletarian dictatorship; the problem of the proper distribution of wealth, which vexed the Greeks as it vexes us: the problem of the relations of the sexes and the position of women, which engaged the attention of Euripides and Plato (not to mention Aristophanes) as it still continues to engage the attention of novelists, poets and thinkers to-day; the problem of foreign policy and a just order of relations between independent states, which set Plato thinking of the institution of a *jus belli* in the fifth book of his *Republic*, and Isocrates preaching a pan-Hellenic symmachy (or 'united states of Greece') in his *Panegyricus*, as it still sets thinkers and statesmen to-day to plan a new league of nations or a new charter of the united nations. Above all, perhaps, the democrats of our own age go back to the age of Greek democracy with an eager interest in the parallel which it offers and the lessons and warnings which it suggests. Here the great text—greater than anything to be found in Aristotle's calm and yet critical appreciation of democracy: greater than the plays of Euripides which discuss and proclaim the virtues of free speech and a free polity [1]—is the Funeral Speech of Pericles, as recorded by Thucydides. The writer still recalls a day, now thirty years ago, when being in Preston on some business of the war of 1914–18 he saw with delight some words from the speech carved on the front of the Public Library. 'The whole earth is the tomb of famous men'—so the inscription began; and on it went round the building. Must there not be some congruity between the age of Thucydides and our own when the Library Committee of a Lancashire town (it is true that the town is 'proud Preston') has his words set on high before the eyes of its townsfolk? [2]

We may therefore say, as Croce has said, 'Dead history revives, and past history again becomes present, as the necessity of life demands them.' We may also add, as Professor Sir John Myres has added: 'I would go even further and submit that it is in great part to renewed need of such standards of behaviour and of criticism [as the Greeks set], in our period of unavoidable and rapid

---

[1] Milton placed a quotation from the *Supplices* of Euripides at the beginning of his *Areopagitica*:

> 'This is true liberty, when free-born men,
> Having to advise the public, may speak free.'

[2] The Harris Library and Museum at Preston, 'a massive building in the Greek style', was erected in 1893, the year when the writer went up to Oxford.

transition, that we may ascribe the revival of interest in these ancient attempts to solve fundamental and eternal problems; and that the forms actually taken by some current attempts to solve those problems afresh under present conditions are in some degree —and I think in increasing measure—due to their unexhausted value as inspiration and guidance.' The living past and the changing past are always living and changing, to meet the necessity of life and the renewed need of standards, and to furnish new help (which is very old) in the solution of eternal problems.

The history of the Greek past not only acts on the present as a force which moves in an orbit round it, and may swing into congruity with it. There is also the other mode of its action, as a part of education and a subject of the curriculum. We may therefore turn to Greek studies, and particularly the study of Greek history, as they act in education; as they influence statesmen and men of affairs who have been trained in and by them; and as they issue into the forum and politics by way of the school and the University.[1] We owe one great debt to the Italian Renaissance of the fifteenth century, which spread into our country (as it also spread into the rest of Western Europe) during the course of the sixteenth. This was the reception of Greek as a current subject of education in schools. New schools arose among us which gave a warm welcome to the new subject. Conspicuous among them was St Paul's School, founded by Dean Colet early in the reign of Henry VIII, with William Lily, a pioneer of Greek studies, as its first high master. But St Paul's School, if it was the first, was not the only English School which turned to Greek in the sixteenth century. The grammar schools (such as Manchester Grammar School, founded in 1515 by Hugh Oldham, Bishop of Exeter, who knew Dean Colet and corresponded with Foxe, the Bishop of Winchester, on the foundation of his new Renaissance College

---

[1] This theme has been handled by Sir Richard Livingstone in a contribution to the lectures of the Warburg Library, for the session 1930-1, entitled 'The position and function of classical studies in modern English education'. The reader is also referred to Essay V in this volume on 'The Education of the English Gentleman in the Sixteenth Century.

of Corpus Christi in Oxford)—the grammar schools, as their very
name indicates, generally made provision for the teaching of the
two grammars, Greek as well as Latin, and sometimes even for
the teaching of Hebrew grammar in addition to complete the
triad of classical languages.[1] Nor was it only the grammar schools
which taught Greek as well as Latin grammar. The new endowed
schools of the sixteenth century—Harrow and Westminster,
Christ's Hospital and Merchant Taylors—were generally humanistic schools; and the school statutes of Harrow (1590) gave
specific directions for the teaching of the texts of some of the
Greek orators and historians.

The tradition of Greek was thus established in English schools;
and with the tradition of Greek there was also established, at the
same time, the tradition of Greek history. It was not only the
Greek language which entered into the curriculum: it was also,
and along with it, the great figures, events, and principles of the
history recorded in the language. Nor was the knowledge of
classical history—Roman as well as Greek—confined to the pupils
of the grammar schools and the other endowed schools who could
study original texts. The sixteenth century and the early seventeenth
century was a great period of translators and translation—from
Italian, Spanish and French, as well as from Latin and Greek. The
translations of the period from the Greek carried Greek history,
and even Greek thought, to the people at large—to Shakespeare
in the theatre, to the country gentleman in his study, and to the
merchant in his counting house. Few of them, perhaps, translated
directly from the Greek; but Philemon Holland, 'the Translator
Generall in his age', went straight to the original in his versions

[1] Grammar schools were defined in trust deeds and school statutes of the
sixteenth and seventeenth centuries as meaning schools in which Latin, or Greek
and Latin, and occasionally also Hebrew, were taught. A judgement of Lord
Eldon in 1805 gave this definition legal validity; and the Grammar School Act
of 1840 specifically enacted that a grammar school should mean a school for
the purpose of teaching Latin and Greek, or either of them, whether Latin and
Greek were expressly described or generally indicated by the word 'grammar'.
See *The Education of the Adolescent* (a Report of the Consultative Committee
of the Board of Education, 1926), pp. 268–9.

of Xenophon's *Cyropaedia* (1632) and Plutarch's *Moralia* (1603). Often, however, the translators made their versions from French versions of the original. It was in this way that Thomas Nichols, a goldsmith, translated the whole of Thucydides from Seyssel's version in 1550; and it was in this way, too, that Sir Thomas North (who perhaps studied at Peterhouse, Cambridge) made his translation of Plutarch's *Lives* from Amyot's version in 1579. North's Plutarch, above any other book, has given to thousands of Englishmen, from Shakespeare downwards, their picture of the Greek past; and his 'Lives of the noble Grecians and Romans', as the title runs, 'compared together by that grave reverend philosopher and historian Plutarch of Chaeronea', has been perhaps the greatest vehicle of the Greek past in our language.

Whether trained in the reading of Greek historians at school (be it at Harrow or elsewhere), or conning Greek history in their study through the medium of Plutarch, the statesmen at Westminster and the Justices of the Peace who governed the countryside in their quarter sessions had generally some inkling of the Greek past. Indeed, they knew ancient history—Roman as well as Greek—perhaps more than they knew the history of their own country, and certainly more than they knew the history of Europe at large. Nor was this as foolish as it may seem. They would have done better to know something more of English and European history. But they were not doing amiss in cherishing some knowledge of the history of a culture and civilisation which (as it was argued at the beginning of this essay) forms a continuous thread and a common substance in the general tradition uniting the different nations of Europe. It was not only the orators in the eighteenth-century House of Commons who cited precedents in ancient history and evoked the shadows of its great figures. It was also the orators of the French Revolution. There was something, after all, in this evocation of antiquity, and it was more than an oratorical parade of learning. The French Revolution was going back to Greek ideals—ideals as old as the Stoics. And even our English statesmen of the age of Dr Johnson, un-Hellenic as that age may have been, had strands of Greek feeling in their minds as well as Greek tags on their lips. 'If you take English political thought and action from Pitt and Fox onwards,' Professor Gilbert Murray has written, 'it seems to me that you will always find present...strands of feeling which are due—of course amongst other causes—to the germination of Greek influence; an unquestioning respect for freedom of life and thought, a mistrust of passion,...a sure consciousness that the poor are fellow-citizens of the rich, and that statesmen must as a matter of fact consider the welfare of the whole state.'

In any consideration of the influence of Greek history on English life and development it would be an injustice and an ingratitude to omit some mention of the old English Universities. Regius Professorships of Greek were established at both Universities by Henry VIII. Cambridge produced, in Bentley, a Greek scholar who left a profound impression on the college of which he was Master and the whole of his University. But the trend of the studies of Cambridge was particularly influenced by Newton; the Senate House Examination, on which the degree of Bachelor of Arts was given, had indeed become, by the end of the eighteenth century, an admirable and searching examination, but it was almost exclusively mathematical. When a Classical Tripos was eventually instituted, in 1822, it was made an examination to which only those who had already obtained honours in the Senate House Examination were admissible; and it was not till some thirty years later that candidates were allowed to take the Classical Tripos and to obtain the degree of Bachelor of Arts without passing any other examination.[1] The Classical Tripos at Cambridge is thus an examination of a comparatively recent growth; and while it has produced a fine edge of accurate and delicate scholarship, and a succession of classical teachers perhaps unparalleled in any other University, it has not lain so much at the heart of University studies, or attracted so many students, or passed so much into

[1] Except 'the Previous Examination', instituted in 1822, which may be termed the equivalent of Responsions at Oxford and regarded as of the nature of an entrance examination. The history of the institution and extension of the Classical Tripos is set out in D. A. Winstanley's *Early Victorian Cambridge*, pp. 65–71, 216–18.

national life, as the parallel but older course of Literae Humaniores at Oxford.

The masters of classical studies at Oxford include no names of the magnitude of Bentley or Porson. The genius of Oxford has generally run less to the individual than to the group or sodality of scholars engaged in a common subject of study, whether the subject were the philosophy of Aristotle or the theology of the Oxford Movement; and it may almost be said that Aristotle himself, as the common bond of a group of scholars, has been the great master of classical studies at Oxford. Archbishop Laud already confessed him as his 'master *in humanis*'; but it was not till the beginning of the nineteenth century, from 1807 onwards, that the school of Literae Humaniores—with Aristotle and Plato as its core, but with Greek and Roman history closely surrounding the core—began to be planted and watered. For almost the whole of the nineteenth century this school held the primacy at Oxford; and even when other schools arose, for example in History and Law, their teachers were largely drawn from men who had been trained in the curriculum of Literae Humaniores. The examination statute of 1830 admirably illustrates the basis and nature of the school. It is to include 'not only the Greek and Latin tongues, but also the histories of Greece and Rome, *that is, those which are considered ancient*,...and the sciences of morals and politics also, in so far as they may be drawn from the writers of antiquity, still allowing them occasionally, as may seem expedient, *to be illustrated by the writings of the moderns*'.[1] A study of the Greek and Latin past, considered as a living past, and thus pursued in relation to the present—this was the essence of Literae Humaniores. It was

[1] The definition is quoted from the article by Sir Richard Livingstone mentioned in a previous note. The two passages printed in italics (the italics are those of the writer) are both significant. The histories of Greece and Rome, it is implied, are only to be 'considered' ancient: they are really modern, in the sense that they are a living past congruous with modern life; and hence Dr Arnold (who published an edition of Thucydides) could speak of 'what is miscalled ancient history, the really modern history of the civilisation of Greece and Rome'. In the same spirit the teachings of ancient writers on morals and politics are to be 'illustrated' by modern writers: they, too, like ancient history, are regarded as having an essential congruity with the present and its problems.

a noble conception, though it was a conception which may also be criticised. There are differences as well as analogies, between the past and the present; and to concentrate attention largely on analogies is to sacrifice the core of scholarship and science which consists in a precise sense of differences. But the school of Literae Humaniores succeeded with a great pragmatic success. It was the school taken by Gladstone in 1831, as it had been taken by Peel before him in its early and inchoate form in 1807: it was the school taken by Asquith, Bryce, Morley, Milner and Curzon. But the civil servant, at any rate in our modern days, matters almost as much as the statesman; and it is perhaps a fact of at least equal importance that after the days in which Jowett turned the attention of Balliol and Oxford to the civil service in England and India, some hundreds of civil servants were trained in the school of Literae Humaniores. It is largely in this way that the Greek past, for nearly a century, has poured into the English present. The results are with us. Something has already been said of their nature under the head of education. But they are part of our general life as well as of our education. The writer still remembers hearing Mr Asquith say, at the height of his power, in a speech at a dinner in the hall of New College given by Mr Fisher (then a Fellow of the College): 'It was in this hall, from Alfred Robinson's lectures on the *Republic*, that I learned such lessons of statesmanship as I have since tried to carry into effect.' It was a generous, perhaps too generous, tribute to his old lecturer. But it had its kernel of truth. *Jampridem in Isim defluxit Ilissus.*

VI

It does not belong to the scope of this essay, which is concerned with Greek influence on English life and thought, to treat of Greek influence in the higher reaches of the arts—in architecture, for example, or again in literature. Yet some few words may be said in conclusion on the theme of Greek influence in English poetry. The English metaphysical poets of the seventeenth century, and particularly Donne, were indebted to the Platonic doctrine of love and the Platonic theory of ideas, which had already inspired

Edmund Spenser's Hymns 'in honour of Love' and in 'honour of Beauty' and some of the sonnets in his *Amoretti*.[1] Henry More, of Christ's, the Cambridge Platonist, had fed in youth on Spenser, and in his *Platonick Song of the Soul* he was a confessed disciple of Plato; with him was gathered a group of Cambridge Platonists (one of the few Cambridge 'groups') which included Cudworth, the Master of More's college, and Whichcote, the Provost of King's College, from whose teaching the group began.[2] Some six years senior to More at Christ's was Milton, a scholar so versed in Greek that he could play on every stop of Greek music—the epic; the tragic (in the perfection of his final poem of 1671, *Samson Agonistes*); the pastoral (in *Lycidas*); and the lyric, as in the Pindaric splendour of the poem *At a solemn music* or the perfect beauty of the last song of his *Arcades*,

> Nymphs and Shepherds, dance no more
> By sandy Ladon's lilied banks.

The most consummate poet of England, Milton was also the most penetrated by Greek—far more penetrated than his Cambridge contemporary Cowley, whose *Pindarique Odes*, it has well been said, 'may be odes, but are not Pindaric'. But what a century of the influence of Greece in English poetry was the seventeenth century. Dryden felt it, if afar off, in *Alexander's Feast*; and the learned Jonson, often too learned and too stiff, could at times use his learning to write pure Greek lyrics. 'Drink to me only with thine eyes' is an exquisite cento from the *Letters* of the Greek sophist Philostratus; and the hymn to Diana ('Queen and huntress chaste and fair') might be a lyric from the *Hippolytus* of Euripides.[3]

[1] See Professor Sir Walter Raleigh's introduction to Hoby's translation of Castigliano's *Book of the Courtier*.

[2] On the Cambridge Platonists, see below, p. 120.

[3] Shakespeare, as Matthew Arnold wrote, is 'free of our questions'. One can only wonder what was the inspiration of some of the great sonnets, such as

> 'What is your substance, whereof are you made,
> That millions of strange shadows on you tend?'

or of the mysticism of *The Phoenix and the Turtle*. A great mind can draw into itself, by a sort of divination, what is in the air. There is something of Plato's *Symposium* here, as there is in Spenser and Donne. How it got there is another question.

In the eighteenth century, Thomas Gray was in the succession of scholar-poets (Spenser, Milton, Crashaw and others) who have lived in the University of Cambridge; but the inspiration of Gray was Norse and Old English studies as well as the classical heritage. It was with Shelley and Wordsworth that a pure Greek influence returned in force into English poetry. Shelley recaptured the Platonic tradition of some of our seventeenth-century poets. He not only translated the *Symposium*: he also wrote, in his *Epipsychidion*, a poem inspired by its teaching. In his *Adonais* he captures a strain of the purest Platonism, and in his *Prometheus Unbound* he marries the teaching of Plato and the inspiration of Aeschylus to the 'perfectibilitarianism' of his father-in-law William Godwin. Wordsworth (who also, at one time, came under the influence of Godwin) was a calmer Platonist, who drew on Plato in his great *Ode on the Intimations of Immortality*, and continued to draw on him in his later sonnets.[1] Nor was Wordsworth only a Platonist. He had also studied Greek history, in Plutarch and other writers; he had been fascinated by the story of Dion and Timoleon, to which he turns more than once in the *Prelude*, and to which he devoted a poem, full of reminiscences of Plutarch, in his later years.

Browning, Swinburne, Matthew Arnold (what could be more Greek than *Sohrab and Rustum*?), and Robert Bridges—the Greek tradition lives in them all. It has never been a 'tyranny' for English poets, as it may be said to have been for German poetry: on the contrary it has married itself happily (marriage, not tyranny, has been its note) with native instincts and wood-notes. Words-

[1] The Sonnet called *After-Thought*, of 1820, occurs to the mind.
'Still glides the stream, and shall for ever glide:
The Form remains, the Function never dies;
While we, the brave, the mighty, and the wise,
We Men, who in our morn of youth defied
The elements, must vanish.'
There is much of Greek philosophy, from Heraclitus to Plato, in those lines; and the third line is a literal translation of a line in Moschus's lament for Bion:
ἡμεῖς οἱ μεγάλοι καὶ καρτεροί, οἱ σοφοὶ ἄνδρες.
Wordsworth had studied his classics deeply at St John's, Cambridge, and afterwards. (Dr Inge, in his lectures on *The Platonic Tradition in English Religious Thought*, discusses the Platonism of Wordsworth, pp. 69–74, 78–9.)

worth was as English as any poet who ever wrote, a poet of the English earth and the English temper; and if Greek came from his muse, it was just because Greek was an integral and accepted part of the English tradition he knew. This brings our argument to an essential quality of English humanism where it touches Greek. It has not been something academic—a rare scholarly vintage which might go to the head and unbalance the poet or thinker. It has had, like many things English, an easy and amateur quality. The love of the classics and of Greek has not been confined to the classical scholar. Homer could interest prime ministers like Mr Gladstone and Lord Derby, as well as English scholars (if there were such) of the type of Wolff and Lachmann. Scholarship might suffer as a result: the culture of the nation profited.[1] One realises this quality of English humanism when one talks with a continental scholar. The writer remembers some days of talk with a continental professor of Greek who happened to be his guest. The professor's interest was engaged in the permeating quality of English humanism—the way it flowed into conversation, politics, and literature. Why, he asked, had we written no book on this remarkable subject? He did not want to learn about the history of classical scholarship in England, in the technical sense of the term: that he knew; he wanted to learn about the humanism which penetrated life—which could send a civil servant or a banker (Mackail or Leaf) deep into the Greek Anthology; which might make a principal clerk in the War Office a student of Plotinus; which could even make the untaught Keats write an *Ode to a Grecian Urn*. It is indeed a story which deserves to be told— Greek in the vicarage, the bank, the civil service, the Prime

[1] Professor Dibelius, in his book on England (English translation, p. 160), notes that 'in so far as Humanism means general classical education and the rounding off of the human personality, no people has been so strongly [inter-] penetrated by it, in its ruling classes, as the British'. But he adds: 'On the other hand, but a faint echo is to be found of the even more important humanistic ideal of life, which means, over and above even classical learning, some definite individual intellectual achievement, the adoption of a personal angle to some great general human problem. There has been no Goethe and no Nietzsche in England.' Perhaps England may be content to have had Wordsworth and Matthew Arnold in lieu of Goethe and Nietzsche.

Minister's study, or the Viceroy's Lodge in India. A captain serving in Burmah will write to you to ask for a plain text of the *Republic*; and T. E. Lawrence could carry the *Odyssey* into strange places.

VII

Much has been said about Greece and Athens in this essay. But there is also a Hebrew tradition; and there is also Jerusalem. Athens and Jerusalem have both been great factors in English life. Athens with its sweetness and light (however widely diffused) has appealed, in the main, to the upper and professional classes, who have hitherto been the governing classes. Jerusalem, with its power and profundity, has appealed to the English middle and working classes—the classes of the Puritan and Nonconformist tradition; the classes of industry and commerce. It is impossible for us to understand our country unless we remember Jerusalem as well, and as much, as Athens. Indeed, it may well be said that the greatest thing in our life—in our education, our literature, and the whole set of our minds—has been Jerusalem, and the Authorised Version of the Bible. It has been the Hebrew tradition which has inspired much of our poetry, from the time of our Anglo-Saxon forefathers and 'Caedmon'; which has done much to make our social and political ideas, and not least our general idea of the personal responsibility of every individual; which has helped so largely to nerve men for service and mission, at home and abroad, in the cause of the prisoner, the slave, and all who were 'desolate and oppressed'; which, in a word, has been *Il Penseroso* in so much of the play of our minds. It would be a poor compliment to Hellenism, and it would only argue that we had forgotten its lesson of the duty of facing and 'saving' the facts, if we forgot the great complement and corrective of Hebraism which stands by its side.

Matthew Arnold's words were quoted in the beginning: 'Hebraism and Hellenism—between these two points of influence moves our world.' At the end it is not inapposite to quote some stanzas from a poem written by another English poet, his contemporary, who for thirty years was a classical master at one of the

English public schools which have always cherished Greek, without forgetting Jerusalem. The poet is T. E. Brown: the poem is his *Israel and Hellas*.[1] It begins with the words: 'I sometimes wonder of the Grecian men'; it moves, as it draws to an end, to a comparison of 'the Grecian men' with the Hebrew.

> And was it possible for them to hold
> A creed elastic in that lightsome air,
> And let sweet fables droop in flexile fold
> From off their shoulders bare,
> Loose-fitting, jewel-clasped with fancies rare?
>
> For not as yet intense across the sea
> Came the swart Hebrew with a fiery haste;
> In long brown arms entwined Euphrosyne,
> And round her snowy waist
> Fast bound the Nessus-robe, that may not be displaced.
>
> Yes, this is true; but the whole truth is more:
> This was not all the burning Orient gave;
> Through purple partings of her golden door
> Came gleams upon the wave,
> Long shafts that search the souls of men who crave;
>
> And probings of the heart, and spirit-balm,
> And to deep questionings the deep replies
> That echo in the everlasting calm—
> All this from forth those skies,
> Besides Gehenna fire and worm that never dies.

[1] T. E. Brown, a Fellow of Oriel College, Oxford, from 1854 to 1858, was afterwards Second Master at Clifton College, from 1864 to 1893. It should be added here that though the poem holds Hellenism and Hebraism in the balance, the last words go in favour of the Greek:

> 'Who, seizing one world where we balance two,
> From its great secular heart the readier current drew.'

II

CYCLES OF CHANGE IN THE ISLAND
OF RHODES

Rhodes is the name both of an island and of a city. The island is a lozenge-shaped island, tilted from the south-west to the north-east, which lies a few miles from the south-west corner of Asia Minor, and looks across to the mountains of the mainland. It has an area of some 500 square miles, and a population of some 50,000. The city stands on the northern tip of the island. It was famous in antiquity for its commerce, its art, and its learning; but that epoch has left few visible traces. It was famous again in the Middle Ages as the home of the Hospitaller Knights of St John of Jerusalem; and it still bears the marks to-day of their fortifications and architecture.

The island and the city of Rhodes form part of the Dodecanese. 'The Twelve Islands' (actually fourteen, but two of them are so small that they cover an area of less than ten square miles) have more than one title to fame. Besides Rhodes they include the island of Cos, the home of Hippocrates and the birth-place of Greek medicine, and the island of Patmos, where St John 'heard a great voice as of a trumpet'. The islands of Rhodes and Cos are still famous, as they were in antiquity, for their grapes. There is still, as there was in antiquity, a busy coming and going of sailing-vessels. The exports still go, as they did in antiquity, very largely to Egypt. The human stock is still, as it was in antiquity, Greek in its blood and its way of life. Many things change; but geography and race are generally constant.

There are two great flowering ages in the history of Rhodes. One is the Hellenistic age. This lasted, in its noonday glory, for the century and a half between 305 B.C., when the city successfully withstood a siege by the Macedonian Demetrius (afterwards called Poliorcetes or 'the Besieger'), and 168 B.C., when it was humbled and deprived of its mainland possessions by Rome. But the glory of Rhodes, like the glory of Venice in a later age, had a long sunset. The city withstood another great siege, by Mithridates of Pontus, about 88 B.C.; later still, it served as a place of education for the republican orators and statesmen of Rome, such as Cicero and Julius Caesar; and under the Empire it was still a university, and a rival of Athens, even if it had ceased to be a state and had been merged into the dominions of Rome. The other great flowering age was the medieval, from A.D. 1310, when the city and the island were conquered by the Hospitallers and wrested from the Byzantine Empire, down to 1522, when the Hospitallers yielded to the Turks and withdrew to the island of Malta. The Hospitallers of Rhodes, like the ancient Rhodians before them, knew what it was to be besieged. They had withstood three sieges before the last and victorious siege of 1522. If Demetrius, for failing in a siege, was called 'the Besieger', we may justly call Rhodes itself the 'Well Besieged'

I

The first beginnings of the ancient splendour of Rhodes go back to the year 407 B.C.—three years before the fall of Athens and the end of the Peloponnesian War—when the other cities of the island were federated with, and incorporated into, the city-state of Rhodes.[1] Rhodes the city henceforth included Rhodes the island, as Athens the city included Attica. The new city-state was still politically dependent, during the fourth century, now upon this power and now upon that; but in the new world which followed the conquests of Alexander, and among the turmoil of the disputes which raged between his successors, Rhodes achieved independence—an independence which soon became a position of pre-eminence in all the seas of the Eastern Mediterranean. At first she had to steer a cautious course between the Macedonian kings in the North and the Egyptian Ptolemies in the South. On the whole

---

[1] The writer is indebted, in this section, to Professor Rostovtzeff's chapter on 'Rhodes, Delos, and Hellenistic Commerce', in the *Cambridge Ancient History* (Vol. VIII, p. 420).

her commercial interests, and with them the balance of her policy, inclinèd in the direction of Egypt. Once, it is true, she fought one of the early Ptolemies, and defeated his fleet in a naval action off Ephesus; but this was a passing enmity, and it hardly broke the permanence of a friendship which was marked by the frequent erection of civic monuments in honour of the Egyptian kings. Towards Macedonia her policy was more distant. There was the memory of the siege of 305, commemorated by the colossal statue of Apollo (the famous Colossus of Rhodes) which stood at the entrance to her harbour: there was the general Macedonian policy, which seems to have been constant during the third century, of keeping a hold on the northern Aegaean and promoting the prosperity of Delos, as a centre of trade and a clearing-house of business, in opposition to Rhodes. But though Macedonian opposition, especially when it allied itself with the Cretan pirates to the south-west who were always a menace to Rhodian trade, was not without its dangers, it hardly affected the steady progress of Rhodian power. The city conducted a great commerce, sustained by a great navy, from Egypt to the Crimea, and from Cyprus to the south of Italy; she stood for the freedom of the seas and the cause of free trade; she forced the citizens of Byzantium, about 220 B.C., to abandon the tolls which they sought to impose on ships passing through the Bosphorus. Perhaps her greatest age came in the early years of the second century B.C. The advancing majesty of Roman power had moved against Macedonia, and broken the Macedonian army at Cynoscephalae in 197 B.C. Rhodes was allied with Rome: Rhodes indeed had invoked Rome, after she had herself declared war against Macedonia (once more allied with the Cretan pirates) in 202 B.C. The fall of Macedonia was the opportunity—alas, an opportunity all to brief—for the zenith of Rhodian power. For some thirty years, from 197 to 168 B.C., she had a period of glory parallel to the great period of Athenian glory in the fifty years between the end of the Persian and the beginning of the Peloponnesian War. She was president of an island league, and the chief power in the Aegaean; she extended, by the grace of Rome, her mainland territories in the south-west of Asia Minor: she ruled both Caria and Lycia. Her hand was heavy on the pirates who preyed on her trade: her navy was ubiquitous: her governors visited the cities of the league to defend their interests and compose their quarrels. Her far-stretched power carried her to the Scythian corn-lands of Southern Russia: her wine found many markets; her standard of coinage spread over the Aegaean to the Dardanelles. This glorious age soon passed; but before we come to the story of its passing, we may pause to take stock of the general character and achievement of Rhodes from the time when she built her Colossus, about 300 B.C., to the time when Rome withdrew her grace and favour after 168.

The city itself was counted the most beautiful of the Hellenistic age. It was a walled city (as it still is, though the present walls are those of the later Middle Ages), descending like an open fan from the hills to the sea and the docks. Legend, embroidering the truth, ascribed the planning of the city to Hippodamus of Miletus, the architect of Pericles. Nature, rather than art, was responsible for the city's beauty; but there was one work of art which brought it abiding fame, the Colossus, or gigantic statue of Apollo, one hundred feet high, which perhaps stood on the site of the present Fort St Nicolas, at the end of a spit of land projecting into the sea, and caught the eye, like the sky-scrapers of New York to-day, as ships approached the land. The Colossus had only a brief history: it collapsed in an earthquake, after some sixty years, about 250 B.C. But it permanently impressed the imagination of the Greeks; and it counted, along with the Pharos of Alexandria, the Tomb of Mausolus in the neighbouring Halicarnassus, and the Temple of Diana at Ephesus, among the seven wonders of the world.

Rhodes was a great commercial and financial city—an ancient Venice; we may even say an ancient London. Perhaps the staple of her commerce was corn—especially the corn of the Nile valley, which, like the steppes of South Russia, was one of the granaries of the Greek world. The supply of corn acquired a new importance in the new economic conditions of the Hellenistic age; and the function of Rhodes as the middleman of its supply was the chief cause of her rise to greatness. She also dealt in the metal of Cyprus, the source of copper, and indeed the source of its name: she dealt in the linens and dyed garments of Egypt and Syria: she dealt too, in her own wine—not, it is said, a very good wine, but easily exported in a general cargo, and so widely exported that Rhodian wine-jars, with the Rhodian stamps (mostly of the period 225–150 B.C.), may be found not only in Egypt and Syria, but also in Sicily and even Carthage. Lying close to Asia Minor, a great source of the supply of slaves for the ancient world, Rhodes was also largely concerned, as our own English city of Bristol was till the latter half of the eighteenth century, in the conduct of the slave-trade. On the basis of this varied commerce—corn, metals, textiles, wine, and slaves—there naturally arose a developed system of finance and banking. Rhodes became a clearing-house and an exchange-centre for the Hellenistic world. Her merchant princes were also great bankers, with their branches in many commercial centres. The State itself made political loans; its citizens managed private banks of deposit. There is an epitaph to the memory of a Rhodian citizen which runs: 'For three decades he kept on deposit gold for foreigners and citizens alike with purest honesty.' The London of its age, with the same ramifications and the same reputation of financial probity, Rhodes spread the vogue of its currency as London has spread the vogue of sterling. The standard of coinage which she introduced soon after the unification of 407 was diffused not only over the Aegean, but also beyond.

The commerce of Rhodes entailed a large mercantile marine, and that in turn entailed a navy for its defence. The Rhodians were experts in shipbuilding: they were masters of the art of dock-construction: they were also skilled siege-engineers, just as were also, at a later date, the sailors from the Italian maritime cities who aided the Crusaders in the conquest of the coast-towns of Palestine. The navy of the Rhodians was famous and powerful: the great fighting ships, some of which were rowed by five banks of oars, were built in emulation by wealthy citizens, by way of a 'liturgy' or voluntary offering to the state; and competitions between the ships were the peculiar form which athletic rivalry assumed in Rhodes. The marines were citizens: so too, perhaps, were the sailors and oarsmen. The navy of Rhodes policed the neighbouring seas, in the same sort of way as the navy of England sought to police the seas of the world during the nineteenth century. Rhodes, in her great age, had a θαλασσοκρατία; but she sought to use it not only for her own benefit, but also for the general advantage. She opposed the imposition of tolls and duties. She sought to keep the pirates of Crete and the east Mediterranean in check: one of the consequences of the reduction of her power by Rome, after 168, was a new vogue of piracy, which ultimately became so serious that Rome was forced to the extraordinary measure of making Pompey generalissimo-in-chief against the pirates in 67 B.C. But the main achievement of Rhodes on the high seas, and one of her great titles to enduring fame, was the work which she did in the cause of maritime law. She tried to secure, in virtue of her pre-eminence, and on the basis of common agreement with other seafaring cities, a set of uniform rules for the conduct of maritime commerce. She codified, in fact if not in form, the best practice of the law of the sea. The achievement of Rhodes passed into the practice of Roman law. The *Lex Rhodia de jactu*, the Rhodian law of jettison, is mentioned in a passage of the *Digest*; and we are told, in connection with this mention, that one of the Antonines ordered the law of the Rhodians to be taken into account in maritime cases where it did not conflict with the law of Rome.

The government of Rhodes, following a tendency which is perhaps natural in great commercial cities, and which was also illustrated in medieval Venice, was in the nature of a benevolent mercantile aristocracy. The form was democratic: the reality was that of an aristocratic tutelage of the *demos*. Power was vested in the *Boulē*, or Senate, rather than in the popular assembly. One of the most important officials, as we might expect from the position of the navy among the Rhodians, was the High Admiral. He had something of the position of a doge: at any rate he was charged with the conduct of foreign policy. Foreign policy and diplomatic representation were matters of primary importance to Rhodes, just as they were to Venice: her commercial prosperity largely depended on the wise management of external relations. It was here

that she made her great error, at a crisis of her fate: the meteoric
Greek temper had not the same shrewd and subtle tenacity as the
Venetian; and a sudden and explosive defiance to Rome, in 169 B.C.,
was the proximate cause of Roman enmity and Rhodian decline.
The social life of the island, during its great age, was rich and
varied. Civilian merchants and bankers were predominant; but
there was also a large naval and military flavour. Many of the
ancient monuments attest this flavour: they were erected in honour
of naval and military exploits; and associations of ex-service men
who had served together on the same ship are one of the peculiar
features of the Rhodian records. The population was mixed in
blood and origin. By the side of the aristocratic native families
who managed the State, there were many metics, or resident
aliens, who had come to Rhodes from various quarters of the
Greek world. They too had their associations, which took the form
of religious guilds. There was also a large population of slaves, who
intermarried, in their higher ranges, with the resident aliens. Some
of them were natives of the island; many had been brought from
Asia Minor; some had come from as far afield as Macedonia and
the Crimea. A general standard of comfort seems to have been
maintained. The Rhodian government, controlling a great trade
in corn, was able to give *panem et circenses*—or rather, as we shall
see, something higher than *circenses*—to the masses. Strabo cele-
brates the provision which was made for the people. 'They are
rationed', he says, 'with corn, and the well-to-do support with
provisions those in need according to ancestral practice.'

But there was more than corn to be had, and more than competitions of ships to be seen, in Rhodes. It was a city of education
and culture and art—a second Athens. In the spirit of Plato's
Laws, where the state-provision of schools by a minister of education is already advocated, the Rhodians had officials, called *epistatai*,
who were charged with the care of public education; and the rich
were expected to meet the cost, in the same way as they were
expected to provide ships, by means of 'liturgies'. There were also
public libraries: in culture, as well as in material civilisation,
Rhodes was a well-equipped city. Nowhere was this equipment

more conspicuous than in the field of statuary and sculpture. From 300 B.C. onwards there flourished a Rhodian school of artists in bronze and marble. The Colossus of Rhodes was made of bronze (the metal of the fallen statue, weighing 20 tons, was ultimately sold, about A.D. 650, to a Jew who carried it away on the fabulous number of 980 camels); and its vogue led to the erection of many other works in bronze. But it is by its marble statuary that Rhodes is still known and remembered. It was a Rhodian sculptor who carved the famous Victory of Samothrace, about the middle of the third century B.C., and critics have remarked a naval note in the figure of Nikē, represented as poised on the deck of a ship and straining forward against the winds of the sea. But the most famous monument of Rhodian sculpture, which comes from the end of the second century B.C., is the Laocoon, which was carved by three natives of Rhodes. Is it just a triumph of technique, or the world's great masterpiece of sculpture? Perhaps we may safely call it the glory of ancient baroque; and we may compare it, as such, with the almost equal glory of another monument of Rhodian sculpture, the Farnese Bull or the punishment of Dirce, of which a Roman copy survives in the museum of Naples.

There is still another title to fame which ancient Rhodes might justly boast; and to some of us it may almost seem the greatest of all her titles. She was one of the great Universities of the ancient world: she was a home both of oratory and of philosophy. In the days of her material decline she attained her greatest spiritual height: it was in the latter part of the second century, and during the first, that she became a place of intellectual resort for the Mediterranean world. The great Stoic teacher Panaetius, who took his philosophy to Rome about the middle of the second century B.C., was a member of a prominent Rhodian family. Even greater, though an adopted and not a native son of Rhodes, was Posidonius of Apamea, who settled in Rhodes in 95 B.C. and died there some forty-five years later. He is in some ways the greatest intellectual figure of his generation. He was a historian: he was a traveller and a geographer; above all he was a philosopher, whose lectures were attended by Cicero and who was twice visited by Pompey.

He presented, and indeed we may say that he made, the Greek view of the world which was current when Christianity appeared: he prepared the intellectual seed-bed in which Christianity struck its roots. That is his importance: his writings, as Dr Edwyn Bevan has said, 'expressed with unique completeness the general mind of the Greek world at the Christian era: he focused it and made it conscious of itself'. He was not an original philosopher: he was rather a syncretist or eclectic, who fused Stoicism with Platonism. But the amalgam which he made was none the less important; it was the *summa philosophiae* which Christianity found: it was the body of belief with which St Paul, a citizen of the same quarter of the Mediterranean world as Posidonius, had to make his reckoning a century after Posidonius's death. In the words of a German scholar, Paul Wendland, we may call Posidonius the last great Greek, the systematiser of the whole of the product of Greek culture, the controlling genius of the last phase of Greek thought in the last days of Greek autonomy. By his side the Rhodian rhetorician, Apollonius Molon, who taught Cicero, and even the adopted Rhodian poet, Apollonius Rhodius, who wrote his *Argonautica* at the court of the Ptolemies about 250 B.C., are hardly to be reckoned.

Such was Rhodes in her noon-day, from 305 to 168: such was she even in her afternoon and sunset, from 168 to 50 B.C.—the year in which Posidonius died and the Civil Wars were beginning which destroyed the Roman Republic and inaugurated the Roman Empire. Her decline after 168 was material rather than spiritual; and even on its material side it was not overwhelming. Her appearance of defection from Rome and her intrigues with Macedonia during the early years of the Third Macedonian War, when Rome was temporarily unsuccessful, were an aberration of policy which involved her in retribution after the Roman victory at Pydna in 168. Perhaps Rome was the more anxious to inflict retribution because she had some measure of jealousy for the prosperous commerce and the wide influence of the greatest of contemporary Greek city-states. At any rate the axe descended. Rhodes lost her control of Caria and Lycia, and therewith a

43

revenue which she counted at 120 talents a year: she had to see Delos erected into a free port, and made a rival centre of commerce (especially for the slave-trade), with the result that her own harbour-dues were reduced from 1,000,000 to 150,000 drachmae. But if the island fell to a lower plane, it did not fall irreparably; and Rome was a frowning friend rather than a hostile foe. The pity was that Rhodes had no longer the power to police the seas or to repress the pirates, who now became more rampant than ever, and connected themselves closely with slave-raiding and trading. The commerce of the whole Eastern Mediterranean, and that of Rome herself, suffered heavily as a result. But Rhodes still clung to Rome: she withstood a siege by Mithridates, the enemy of Rome, in 88: her navy aided Sulla in his campaigns against Mithridates afterwards: it aided Pompey in his war against the pirates in 66. The first serious blow which befell Rhodes came with the Civil Wars, when Cassius—the Cassius of the lean and hungry look—plundered the city for refusing to submit to his exactions, and reduced it to desolation for the time being. It continued, however, to be a free city: it revived under the peace of Augustus: it was the only city which did not take advantage of the permission which Augustus gave to the cities of Asia to cancel their debts; and it was still celebrated, as a city of wealth and culture, by the Greek writers of the first half of the second century A.D. But a great earthquake came in A.D. 155: Rhodes passed from the pages of history; it ceased to be a free city, and it was hence-forth a little and unknown island engulfed in the vast expanse of the Roman Empire. It was an earthquake which had ruined the Colossus about 250 B.C.; it was another earthquake which, some four centuries later, marked the final ruin of the great free city over which the Colossus had towered, in which the law of the seas had been digested, and where a final summary of Greek thought had been achieved by the last great Greek.

II

Twelve and a half centuries passed, after the earthquake of A.D. 155, before Rhodes made a resounding re-entry into the pages of history.[1] During all those centuries the island had been a part of the Roman Empire—first of the undivided Empire ruled from Rome, and then, from A.D. 400 onwards, of the East Roman Empire ruled from Constantinople. Little is recorded of the island during the revolving years of a whole millennium and more of history. It was attacked by the Arabs during the early ardour of their conquests: they fell upon it about A.D. 650, and they besieged the well-besieged island again in 717 and 718, at the same time that they were also beleaguering Constantinople. But it was not till towards the close of the eleventh century that the development of the West began once more to draw Rhodes into the general current of history. On the one hand the Italian maritime cities, and more especially Venice, were now feeling their way to the trade of the East, and finding that Rhodes, as it was in antiquity, and is becoming again in our own day, was a natural trading station; on the other hand the Crusaders, moving eastward by sea to the Holy Land, began to touch at Rhodes on their way. But neither the commercial nor the crusading movement affected Rhodes deeply before 1310. There were other commercial stations which interested the Italian cities more; and the Crusaders were occupied, down to the fall of Acre in 1291, on the mainland of Syria and Palestine. Rhodes continued to remain in the direct allegiance of Constantinople until 1204, when the Latin Crusaders conquered the city; and even afterwards, during the thirteenth century, it was under the control of princes who acknowledged their vassalage to some Greek emperor who claimed to be the inheritor of Constantinople.

But the fortunes of the Western Crusaders in Palestine were destined eventually to carry them to Rhodes, and to weave the history of Rhodes into the fabric of the Crusades. The crusading

[1] In this section the writer is chiefly indebted to Baron de Belabre's *Rhodes of the Knights* (Oxford: the Clarendon Press, 1908).

kingdom of Jerusalem, established in A.D. 1100 at the end of the first Crusade, had collapsed before Saladin in 1187. Some relics still survived; but the surviving relics found themselves compelled to recoil to the West, and to seek in the islands of the Southern Aegaean the safety which they could not find on the mainland. One of these relics was the order of the Knights of St John of Jerusalem. The Knights Hospitallers had by this time developed from military almoners, managing a hospital in Jerusalem for poor and sick pilgrims, into an international club or corporation, drawn from the aristocracy of Europe, possessing a corporate property scattered over the West, holding its castles and pursuing its policy in the Holy Land, and even interesting itself in the transport of pilgrims, the conduct of commerce, and the business of international exchange and finance. At the beginning of the fourteenth century they were confronted with two grave problems. In the first place, after the fall of Acre, there was no foothold left on the mainland of Asia. Temporarily the Order established its headquarters in Cyprus, which our English Richard I had conquered during the Third Crusade, and which had become the home of a Latin kingdom, under the Anglo-French dynasty of the Lusignans, during the thirteenth century. Was the Order to remain in Cyprus, or was it to move still further afield to some independent basis? This was one problem. But its solution was bound up with a second and even graver problem. While the Hospitallers were lingering in Cyprus, their great brother-Order, that of the Templars, with which they had collaborated and quarrelled for the last two centuries, was undergoing a grave period of tribulation at the hands of Philip IV of France. The tribulation attained its height in 1307: it threatened, and in 1311 it ultimately involved, the dissolution of the Order. If the Hospitallers were to escape a like fate, they must seek some new *raison d'être*, find some new basis of operations, and justify themselves to the world by some new and permanent form of achievement.

The solution was found in the conquest of Rhodes from the vassal prince who held it in allegiance to the Palaeologi, the dynasty of emperors who recovered Constantinople from the Latin

Crusaders in 1261. The Grand Master of the Hospitallers was armed not only with the blessing and authority of the Pope, but also with papal funds and the aid of a crusading fleet: the city of Rhodes was captured by the middle of August 1310; the rest of the island was brought into submission within a few years. The Order had thus acquired what had long been a home of piracy (a disease endemic in the Levant); it had also acquired a great strategic centre, from which it could wage war against the pirates of the other islands and the Asiatic coast, and thus renew the ancient tradition of the old Rhodian city-state. The way for the coming and going of Christian pilgrims was henceforth eased; and illicit trading between the Christian West and the Moslem of Egypt, which the Popes of the fourteenth century sought to forbid, could now be policed and checked. The Order had thus found a new mission, which was at the same time an ancient tradition—the mission of policing the seas, repressing piracy, and imposing once more a *Lex Rhodia* on the commerce of the waters of the Levant. History repeated itself even more curiously when about 1340 the Hospitallers became members of a maritime league (just as the ancient Rhodians had been presidents of an island league) which was formed under the aegis of the Pope for the security of seafarers and the suppression of Turkish pirates. By 1350 the Knights of Rhodes had acquired a commanding position. They had annexed the islands of the Dodecanese: they had gained, with the aid of the Maritime League, the possession of Smyrna, which they held until it was captured and sacked by Tamerlane about 1402; and with the revenues acquired from these possessions, from trade, and from the properties of their Order in the West, they maintained a permanent and powerful fleet, which burned to the water's edge, in 1347, the bulk of a Turkish fleet of 150 sail.

For more than two centuries, till the days of Luther and Henry VIII, the Knights of Rhodes were one of Europe's bulwarks against the Ottomite, more faithful and more constant than the Venetian Republic of which Byron sang in *Childe Harold*. During those centuries they kept back the growth of a Turkish fleet: they policed the seas: they established consuls in Egypt and Jerusalem to defend the interests of Christian pilgrims: true to their name, they maintained a great hospital in Rhodes, with physicians and surgeons and nurses, for the aid of sick Christian wayfarers. They were not, indeed, always at war, nor did they always play the part of the gallant defenders of a Christian outpost: they traded as well as fought, and they were ready, in the fifteenth century, to negotiate treaties of commerce with the Turk. They lived a life of amenity, and even of luxury, on the island; they had fine palaces and gorgeous silver plate in the city of Rhodes: they had pleasant villas and happy retreats in its lovely environs. But they were always set among war and rumours of war: they stood three sieges (in 1320, in 1444, and in 1480) before they went down, with their colours flying, in the last and great siege of 1522; and again and again they fought sea-battles against Moslem fleets.

The Order not only changed its function when it settled in Rhodes: it also changed its organisation. The habit of the Order remained the same: the Knights wore a black dress marked with a white cross of eight points—the cross which was later, when they moved to Malta, named the Maltese Cross. But from being a cosmopolitan club predominantly tinctured by France they became—perhaps in order to escape from the too close interest of the French monarchy, which had proved fatal to their brother Templars—an international federation of eight branches or Tongues. France still supplied three of the Tongues: Spain had two: England, Italy and Germany were each represented by one. Our English tongue counted only sixth in the order of importance; and no Englishman was ever Grand Master of the Order. Each Tongue had its head or 'pillar', who also held one of the great offices of the Order: the head or pillar of the English Tongue held the office of Tureopolier, and in that capacity commanded the cavalry and the coastguard. The pillar of each Tongue controlled the priories, and under them the commanderies, in the country connected with his Tongue: the pillar of the English Tongue was master of the grand prior in London and of the fifty-five commanderies under him. Each Tongue was responsible for one of the eight sections of the walls of Rhodes: the English

Tongue had a section of some 450 yards in length, at the back of the city, away from the sea and towards the hills. The walls of the English section, as they now stand, were built about 1460, during the Wars of the Roses. Their defenders, headed by John Burke and William Weston and Nicholas Hussey (it is good to think of such English names in Rhodes), played a gallant and glorious part in the final siege of the city.

The city of Rhodes was rebuilt, and indeed remade, by the Knights. They found, when they captured it, nothing of the old classical city, but only a Byzantine city which had been built, after still another earthquake in A.D. 515, on the site where the classical city had stood. The Byzantine city was largely in ruins when it was seen by the English Crusaders, under Richard I, in 1191: they compared it, for that reason, to Rome. The new influx of commerce and a cosmopolitan population which followed on the entry of the Knights, coupled with the need for better defence against Turks and Egyptians, led to an entire replanning and reconstruction. It was this replanning and reconstruction which left Rhodes what it remained until Italy became its temporary mistress in 1912. New walls of the Western type, renewed and improved during the two centuries of occupation by the Knights, were carried all round the city, including the harbour-front. Near to the sea, and forming the heart and centre, stood the *collachium* or inner city, which contained the Knights and their quarters. The remainder or outer city—outer only in the sense that it stood outside the *collachium*, but inner in every other sense—was the burgh or town, occupied by a various civilian population of Western Europeans, Greeks, and Jews. The Greeks were in a majority, and their language predominated; but French was also common; Italian and Spanish and German might be heard; and there were also Englishmen who, after their kind, probably spoke little else but English. The *collachium* and the burgh must both have been multilingual places; but no doubt they helped to form, and to ease human intercourse by forming, that *lingua franca* which still survives in the Levant.

The great artery of the *collachium* was the street of the Knights.

This ran from the outer wall to the waters of the great harbour. At the end which abutted on the outer wall, to the north, stood the prior's palace and the church of St John, both ruined in 1856 by an explosion of some powder which had been left in the crypt of the church: along the street were ranged the auberges or head-quarters of each of the eight Tongues: at the end of the street which touched the harbour there stood, and still stands, the great hospital. There are two relics of England in the *collachium*, both near to the harbour-end of the street of the Knights. One is a fragment of the auberge of the English Tongue—a vaulted hall, with two round columns supporting an archway. The other is a little square chapel on the walls, in the top of the tower of St George, which contains, on the wall facing the altar, a fresco of the saint on horseback, carrying the shield of the Order, and in the act of killing a dragon.

There is another relic, or rather a whole set of relics, not in the city of Rhodes, but scattered all round the island, which may still remind us of dead and gone Englishmen who gave their lives to the service of the Order. The 'pillar' of the English Tongue, as we have already had reason to notice, was the captain of the coastguard of the island. An elaborate system of coastguard stations, or castles, now mouldering in ruins, was built in an irregular ellipse on projecting points of the coast or on lofty hills in the interior. There were seventeen of these castles: they were connected by watch-towers: they served as centres of protection, and in case of need as centres of refuge, for the surrounding peasantry. Each castle was the stronghold of a district or *castellania*; their garrisons, and the coastguard patrols which connected them, were composed of Rhodian Greeks. It is good to think of the English captain surveying and controlling the work of the coastguard stations and their patrols in Rhodes, in much the same way as a coastguard officer still does along our own English coasts to-day. It was a natural office for an islander to discharge. There are still English names—Bell, West, Allen, de Winton—scratched on the walls of a little underground chapel near one of the coastal castles.

The Ottoman Turks could not permanently endure the possession of Rhodes by the Knights. The island lay on the route between Constantinople and Alexandria: it threatened the vital line of Turkish communication: it had to be reduced. The Sultan Solyman the Magnificent gathered his forces in August 1522: Rhodes the well-besieged stood a five months' siege with gallant fortitude:[1] it was forced to capitulate five days before Christmas Day: and the Knights were given the space of twelve days to prepare for their evacuation. The Sultan entered the city two days before the end of the year: he paid a surprise visit to the Grand Master in his palace; he found him busily engaged in the homely office of packing. Early in the morning of New Year's Day, 1523, the trumpet of the Knights sounded for the last time in Rhodes; their fleet of thirty-one ships, with the refugees on board, put out to sea. The great carrack, or warship, of the fleet was commanded by William Weston, the 'pillar' of the English Knights, and the last of the English Turcopoliers in Rhodes.

The fleet, sailing westward, went to Crete. The Emperor, Charles V, was told the story of the siege. 'Nothing in the world', he said, 'has been so well lost as Rhodes.' There was no attempt to recover the lost island; but in 1530 Charles V gave to the Hospitallers the island of Malta in lieu of the island they had lost. There they established themselves, and there their eventual heir was England. Their inheritance in Rhodes remained with the Turks for nearly four centuries, from 1522 to 1912. Then came the Italians, and, with them, the establishment of an Italian University in the city in which Posidonius had taught, and the building of an Italian quarter and monuments on the northern side of the walls built by the Knights. So Rhodes, like all places and things in our

---

[1] The siege was celebrated, long afterwards, in an heroic play, in two parts, by Sir William D'Avenant, entitled *The Siege of Rhodes*. The first part was produced in 1656: it was sung in recitative, and it marked the beginning of English Opera. It was also notable in that it was marked by the first use of regular scenery in England, and by the first public appearance of a woman on the stage. A second part was added to the first for the new production of 1661. Two famous musicians, Henry Lawes and Matthew Locke, wrote most of the vocal music; and Henry Purcell, the father of the famous Purcell, acted one of the parts.

human world, has run along the grooves of change. The island which Pindar celebrated in the Seventh Olympian, as a domain assigned to the Sun-god Apollo for ever, has always turned its face to the sun, and has always remained bright Rhodes—*clara Rhodos*, the island of sunshine and roses[1]—in a constant climatic allegiance. But under the constant sun there has been a changing cycle of masters. First the Roman; then the Byzantine; then the Frankish Hospitaller; then the Turk; and last the Italian, seeking to vindicate, after long centuries, the memory and the succession of Rome. Now, at long last, the wheel is coming full circle: the island is returning to its ancient allegiance as a member of the society of Hellas; and Greeks will again walk freely in the streets of the city of Rhodes, as their forefathers did in the centuries between the age of Demosthenes and the age of Cicero.

[1] The roses have given the island its name.

III

DANTE AND THE LAST VOYAGE
OF ULYSSES

I

There is a passage in the *Inferno* of Dante's *Divina Commedia* which runs (in Laurence Binyon's fine translation) as follows. The speaker, it should be premised, is Ulysses, whose voice comes to Dante and his guide from 'the horned flame' of fire in which he and Diomed are wrapped and 'tormented for old guile'—the two who had sinned together being thus punished together in hell for their crimes of deceit and fraud before the walls of Troy:

The greater horn of the ancient flame was stirred
　　To shudder and make a murmur, like a fire
　　When in the wind it struggles and is blurred,
Then tossed upon a flickering crest yet higher,
　　As it had been a tongue that spoke, it cast
　　A voice forth from the strength of its desire,
Saying: "When I from Circe broke at last,
　　Who more than a year by Gaeta (before
　　Æneas had so named it) held me fast,
Not sweet son, nor revered old father, nor
　　The long-due love which was to have made glad
　　Penelope for all the pain she bore,
Could conquer the inward hunger that I had
　　To master earth's experience, and to attain
　　Knowledge of man's mind, both the good and bad.
But I put out on the deep open main
　　With one ship only, and with that little band
　　Which chose not to desert me; far as Spain,
Far as Morocco, either shore I scanned.
　　Sardinia's isle I coasted, steering true,
　　And the isles of which that water bathes the strand.
I and my crew were old and stiff of thew
　　When, at the narrow pass, we could discern
　　The marks that Hercules set far in view

53

That none should dare beyond, or further learn.
  Already I had Sevilla on the right,
  And on the larboard Ceuta lay astern.
'Brothers', I said, 'who manfully, despite
  Ten thousand perils, have attained the West,
  In the brief vigil that remains of light
To feel in, stoop not to renounce the quest
  Of what may in the sun's path be essayed,
  The world that never mankind hath possessed.
Think on the seed ye spring from! Ye were made
  Not to live life of brute beasts of the field,
  But follow virtue and knowledge unafraid.'
With such few words their spirit so I steel'd,
  That I thereafter scarce could have contained
  My comrades from the voyage, had I willed.
And, our poop turned to where the Morning reigned,
  We made, for the mad flight, wings of our oars,
  And on the left continually we gained.
By now the Night beheld within her course
  All stars of the other pole, and ours so low,
  It was not lifted from the ocean-floors.
Five times beneath the moon rekindled slow
  The light had been, and quenched as oft, since we
  Broached the hard issue we were sworn to know,
When there arose a mountain in the sea,
  Dimm'd by the distance: loftier than aught
  That ever I beheld, it seemed to be.
Then we rejoiced; but soon to grief were brought.
  A storm came out of the strange land, and found
  The ship, and violently the forepart caught.
Three times it made her to spin round and round
  With all the waves; and, as Another chose,
  The fourth time, heaved the poop up, the prow drowned,
  Till over us we heard the waters close."

That is the story which Dante tells in Canto XXVI of the *Inferno*.
It is a new and splendid imagination, 'voyaging through strange
seas of thought', as it makes Ulysses himself do. It leaves the

Homeric story entirely out of account: indeed, Dante had no knowledge of Homer (when he cites Homeric passages, he is citing passages which he found quoted in Aristotle's *Ethics*); and it would thus be more accurate to say that his story of the end of Ulysses leaves the Homeric story unnoticed because it was *res ignota*. There is therefore no 'Return'. Ulysses never goes home; never slays the suitors; never sees Penelope again. He goes straight from Circe—of whom Dante knew from references in the Latin classics, though it is not clear that he did not confuse her with the Sirens, or at any rate suppose her to be one of the Sirens[1]—through the Pillars of Hercules to the far seas and death. An invincible curiosity spurs him on in his wanderings to follow the quest of knowledge—*seguir virtute e conoscenza*; and he follows it—to the end.

Before we examine, and seek to interpret, the new and splendid imagination of Dante, it may be well to look before and after—to consider first the old Greek versions of the end of Ulysses, and then the modern version created by the fancy of Tennyson. Indeed, it may even be worth our while to go still further afield, and before considering the old Greek versions or Tennyson's modern version to look at a figure which in various shapes has haunted the minds of men—the figure of 'the Wanderer'. There is no need to reflect on the shape of this figure called 'the Wandering Jew'—except to note that it is at least as old as Matthew Paris, the chronicler of St Alban's Abbey in the middle of the thirteenth century. More germane to our theme—because, like Ulysses, it belongs to the sea—is the shape which is called 'the Flying Dutchman'. This is a shape of the figure of the Wanderer which is later than the age of Dante. It belongs, at the earliest, to the Age of Discovery; and it belongs to the tempestuous waters of the South Atlantic, round the Cape of Storms, which we now know, by a euphemism, as the Cape of Good Hope. In the *Lusiads* of Camoens (himself a wanderer in far seas), the spirit of the Cape, Adamastor, is made to appear to Vasco da Gama in a vision, and to threaten all mariners who dare to venture into his seas. A sailor's

[1] See below, note on p. 61.

legend arose in time of a spectral ship, sailing for ever about the Cape, under a captain condemned for his blasphemy, or for a murder committed on board, to voyage on in an unending endeavour to make an impossible port. The idea of the spectral ship and 'the ancient mariner' recurs again and again in poetry. It is not only present in Coleridge. It is present in the *Bateau Ivre* of Arthur Rimbaud:

> Je sais les cieux crevant en éclairs, et les trombes
> Et les ressacs, et les courants; je sais le soir,
> L'aube exaltée ainsi qu'un peuple de colombes,
> Et j'ai vu quelquefois ce que l'homme a cru voir.

It is present again in a contemporary poet of South Africa; it appears in Roy Campbell's volume of verse, *Adamastor*, especially in the poems called *Rounding the Cape* and *The Albatross*. It is curious that this South African dream of the wandering ship and the wandering mariner should eventually have taken a Homeric shape and connected itself with the name of Ulysses. That happened in an article in *The Times*, some twenty years ago. Mr L. S. Amery, lover of Homer's *Odyssey*, imagined himself, in that article, suddenly meeting, on a steamship in South African seas, the much-travelled far-wandering Ulysses. An albatross soared past as he suddenly appeared. He spoke much of men and their cities, and of the secret springs of politics. Challenged with the question, 'Tell me thy name', he answered, 'Ulysses the son of Laertes'; and as he answered he was instantly gone—and once more an albatross soared past.[1]

---

[1] The article here mentioned, which was first published in 1927, forms the first essay in the volume *The Stranger of the Ulysses*, published in 1934. The volume contains some other variations on the theme of Ulysses—notably the essay entitled 'The Last Voyage of Ulysses', in which he is made to go eastward, through the Black Sea and up the Borysthenes, to become the ancestor of the great Gothic kings of a later day. The reader is also referred to Mr Amery's presidential address to the Classical Association on the *Odyssey* in 1936, published by John Murray.

There is also an essay on Ulysses, under the title of 'The Eternal Wanderer', in the late G. M. Sergeaunt's *Classical Studies*, published in 1929. Mr Sergeaunt refers to the passage in the *Germania* of Tacitus, c. III, in which he mentions— but refuses to confirm or refute—the story of Ulysses having been carried,

There is little, however, of the wandering mariner in the story, or rather the prophecy, of the last days of Ulysses, which is told by Homer in a passage of the eleventh book of the *Odyssey*. When Ulysses goes to the bounds of the Ocean to raise the spirits of the dead, and offers them blood to drink in order that they may speak, he is visited by the spirit of Teiresias, the prophet of Thebes, holding a golden sceptre. Teiresias drinks and speaks. He prophesies the return of Ulysses to Ithaca, and tells him what he is to do, and what will befall him, after he has returned and slain the suitors. He is to go from Ithaca with an oar on his shoulder to the land of a people who know not the sea or ships; and when he meets the sign of the wayfarer who says, 'You have a winnowing fan on your shoulder', he is to fix the oar in the ground and to make a sacrifice to Poseidon. Then he is to go back home to Ithaca, and to offer hecatombs to all the gods of Olympus. 'And to thyself', Teiresias ends, 'death shall come off the sea, a death so exceeding gentle, to take thee away when thou art weary in the ripeness of old age; and thy people shall be blessed around thee: this is the truth that I tell thee.'[1]

There is still, it is true, some touch of the sea and its waters about the story. There is the oar which Ulysses carries: there is the death that shall come off the sea. But the prophecy of Teiresias leaves a shadow of mystery. We can guess, indeed, why Ulysses must go, after slaying the suitors, across to the mainland and far up-country, carrying an oar on his shoulder. He has to go far from the sea, by a kind of inverted atonement, in order to placate the god of the sea under whose wrath he lies, and to assoil himself there of blood. That is why he must carry an oar to the land of *longo illo et fabuloso errore*, as far as the North Sea, and having visited the soil of Germany and founded and named the town of Asciburgium, near the Rhine, 'where an altar dedicated to Ulysses, with the name of his father Laertes added, is also said to have been once discovered'.

[1] This passage comes in the *Odyssey*, XI, 119–37. Ulysses repeats the prophecy to his wife in XXIII, 247–84. In repeating it he adds to it. 'We have not yet come to the end of all our troubles', he tells Penelope; 'there will still be infinite labour to come, great and grievous, which I must accomplish;...he bade me go to cities of men exceeding many.' Perhaps this hint of *later* wanderings among many cities may have helped to inspire the *Ulysses* of Tennyson.

a people who know not the sea or ships, and must sacrifice there to Poseidon. But what is the death that eventually comes to him off the sea, in a ripe old age? Later Greek epic provided an answer in a poem, now lost, called the *Telegonia*, of which the argument has been preserved in the *Chrestomathy* of a late Greek writer Proclus. According to this argument, Telegonus, the son of Ulysses and Circe, when he was grown to manhood, came to Ithaca in search of his father. Practising the old trade of reiver or pirate, as Greek seafarers so often did, he ravaged the island and killed his father. That was the death which came to Ulysses off the sea; but it was hardly a death 'so exceeding gentle'. The *Telegonia*, in a spirit of romantic sentiment very different from that of the *Odyssey*, then proceeded to a happy ending. Telegonus, discovering what he had done, repented bitterly. At his prayer, and by the intervention of his mother Circe, Penelope and Telemachus her son were made immortal. Telegonus married Penelope: Telemachus married Circe; and they all lived happily ever afterwards.

Tennyson, in his *Ulysses*, true to the English spirit of compromise, steers a middle course between the Homeric version and the story told by Dante. Following Homer, he makes Ulysses return and settle in Ithaca. But he imagines him chafing 'among these barren crags...an idle king...match'd with an aged wife'; and having built this bridge of transition he proceeds to follow Dante.[1] Ulysses becomes again the Wanderer, who 'cannot rest from travel':

> I am become a name:
> For always roaming with a hungry heart
> Much have I seen and known; cities of men
> And manners, climates, councils, governments.

But he not only becomes the Wanderer; he also becomes something more. He becomes—and here Tennyson quotes or paraphrases Dante—the Seeker,

> yearning in desire
> To follow knowledge like a sinking star
> Beyond the utmost bound of human thought.

[1] But, as has already been mentioned in a previous note, there is a hint towards the end of the *Odyssey* which Tennyson may also have followed.

Wanderer and Seeker, he assembles his crew, old like himself, for one last voyage to the West—it may be to perish, washed down in the gulfs; it may be to 'touch the Happy Isles and see the great Achilles'. Written in compromise, the poem of Tennyson ends in uncertainty: 'it may be' or it may not be. A compromise, a cento, the *Ulysses* of Tennyson has the uncertain music of a variation on a double theme.

II

Against this background we may now study the story told by Dante of the last voyage of Ulysses to the far West. It is a story entirely new-minted. There is no hint of it in the classical sources; there is no hint of it in the post-classical writers about the legend of Troy—the writers who go by the name of Dares Phrygius and Dictys Cretensis—whose fanciful embellishments contributed so much to the handling of 'the matter of Troy' by medieval writers. The one thing which Dante may possibly have derived from the *Historia de excidio Trojae* of Dares Phrygius is the association of Ulysses and Diomed: the rest is his own invention. No doubt his invention may have derived some spur, or drawn some elements, from old traditions and contemporary happenings in the Mediterranean. There was an old tradition, for example, about the city of Lisbon, which in the Middle Ages was called Lyxobona, or Ulixbona, or Olysipona, or Olyssipo. A verbal consonance, combined with a habit of finding some classical founder for the cities and towns of the Mediterranean, readily suggested that Lisbon was the city of Ulysses, founded by him on a voyage to the West in his later days. This may have been one spark which fired the imagination of Dante. Another, and a greater, may well have been the contemporary voyages of Genoese navigators, in search, it is said, of a Western continent—voyages which form the prelude of that of the Genoese Columbus in 1492. Almost exactly two centuries before that voyage, in the year 1291, such an expedition started; but no man ever returned to tell where it had penetrated or what its fate had been.[1] Dante may have heard of the expedition; and he may, it has been suggested,[2] have combined its memory with the popular notion, common in the Middle Ages, of the Mountain of Loadstone by which ships were attracted and drawn to their ruin—the 'mountain in the sea, dimm'd by the distance', out of which came the storm that 'found the ship, and violently the forepart caught'.

But these are only elements or rudiments—pieces of raw stuff which may have been used by the imagination of the poet, and which may help to explain the genesis of his idea, without explaining in any way the significance of that idea. What are we to say of the idea itself, which moves with a motion unexplained by any of its elements? What was Dante's conception of the mind and motives of Ulysses? And what, in particular, was his conception of the purpose and meaning of what we may call 'the Search of Ulysses'?

The picture which Dante draws of the mind and motives of Ulysses is based on classical sources which can readily be traced. One of these sources is a passage in the *De Finibus* of Cicero.[3] Speaking of the delight of liberal studies and arts, for which men will neglect their health and their household, 'enduring all things because they are caught by the zest of pure understanding and knowledge', Cicero remarks that Homer's fable about the songs of the Sirens shows some inkling of this truth. The fascination of the Sirens was that they professed to have knowledge; what drew men to them was the desire of learning. Cicero proceeds to translate some lines from the *Odyssey*—the lines of the invitation which the Sirens address to Ulysses. (It is in Cicero's Latin hexameters,

---

[1] E. J. Payne, in the *Cambridge Modern History*, Vol. I, pp. 18–19, dates the voyage in 1281. He notes that the two Genoese vessels may have been making for islands in the West (of which there were various medieval legends—Arabic, Spanish, Welsh, and Irish); 'but the better tradition is that they merely proposed to circumnavigate South Africa'. It is the way round Africa which Dante makes Ulysses follow.

[2] E. Moore, *Studies in Dante*, Vol. I, p. 264, n. 2.

[3] v, c. xviii, §§ 48–9. The writer owes his knowledge of these passages to the commentary of Scartazzini on the *Divina Commedia*.

as well as in the renderings of Homeric quotations in the medieval Latin translations of Aristotle, that Dante read such verses of Homer as he knew.) The man who listens to us, they promise,

> variis avido satiatus pectore musis
> Doctior ad patrias lapsus pervenerit oras.

We know the whole story of the Trojan War—and then a greater bait follows—

> Omniaque e latis rerum vestigia terris.

The moral of the story of Ulysses and the Sirens is then drawn by Cicero in these words: 'Homer saw clearly that the story he told could gain no credence, if he depicted this great man as caught and held in the toils merely by petty ditties. The Sirens promise knowledge: no wonder that a man who desired wisdom should prefer *that* even to his country. Curiosity has a passion for knowing all sorts and descriptions of things; but great minds must be considered as drawn, by the contemplation of greater things, to the desire of knowledge itself.'

Here is one clear and obvious source from which Dante may have drawn his conception of the mind and motives of Ulysses. We can see now why it is possible that Dante confused Circe with the Sirens, or perhaps regarded her as one of the Sirens: the Circe who had 'held him fast' was a Siren who had caught and held him in her toils by the promise of knowledge, and from whom he 'broke at last' to prosecute the search for the knowledge she had promised.[1] We can see, too, in Cicero's phrases cues for some of the lines in Dante's poetry. In Cicero the man desirous of knowledge will neglect *res familiaris*: in Dante neither son nor father nor even the love of his wife can conquer the hunger of Ulysses for knowledge. In Cicero's Latin hexameters the Sirens speak of

---

[1] A passage in the *Purgatorio* (xix, 19–24) seems to make it clear that Dante regarded Circe as a Siren. Here Dante has the vision of the Siren, 'the sweet Siren', who tells him that she had 'turned Ulysses from his wandering way unto her song'. The Siren in the singular, who turned Ulysses from his way (as the Sirens in the Homeric story failed to do, because the ears of his crew were stopped to their song), must be Circe.

knowing 'all the tracks of things that lead from earth's wide bounds': in Dante Ulysses seeks to become 'del mondo esperto', and refuses to renounce the experience of following the sun ever westward in order to discover the uninhabited hemisphere in the Atlantic. The echoes in Dante may, of course, be pure coincidence, and not responses to the suggestion of anything he had read; but, even so, the echoes remain.

Another source which Dante may possibly have had in his mind is a passage in one of the *Epistles* of Horace.[1] Here Ulysses is made to figure as a type of the power of virtue and knowledge:

> quid virtus et quid sapientia possit
> Utile proposuit nobis exemplar Ulixen.

(To Dante too *virtus* and *sapientia* are the notes of his character; and his motto is *seguir virtute e conoscenza*.) The word *exemplar* in Horace is significant. It suggests that in the interpretation of Homer his heroes were beginning to be turned into ethical types and figures. This was perhaps the effect of philosophy, and especially of Stoic philosophy, which was using Homer to point a moral. A passage in Seneca's treatise, *De Constantia Sapientis*, well illustrates this tendency.[2] He is arguing that the gods have given to his own age, in the person of Cato, a finer *exemplar* of the man of wisdom than they gave to an earlier age in the persons of Ulysses and Hercules, 'whom our Stoic philosophers have pronounced to be *sapientes* for their invincibility under all labours, their contempt of pleasure, their conquest of every terror'. The *sapiens* here is a term of art in Stoic philosophy, which signifies the true Stoic who stands at the antipodes to the foolish of this world (the *stulti*)—the man who cultivates the spark of divine fire in his nature which is an 'effluence flowing from the glory of the Almighty': the man who has the great virtue of 'apathy' in the face of all passion: the man who will face a voluntary death—an ἐξαγωγή or 'going out', as it was technically called—in any just case of need. If Seneca himself preferred Cato as the type of the *sapiens*, we learn from him that Ulysses served as a great *exemplar* to contemporary Stoics;

[1] *Epistles*, I, ii, *vv.* 17–31.   [2] Op. cit. II, § 2.

and in one of his own letters there is a passage which makes Ulysses—as he was probably often made in Stoic teaching and preaching—the peg of a little sermon on the true wisdom of life.[1] 'Do you ask', Seneca writes, 'where Ulysses wandered, instead of making sure that *we* never wander from the way? There is no time for hearing whether he was tossed to and fro between Italy and Sicily or beyond the bounds of the world we know:[2] there could not be any long wandering in limits so narrow [as those of physical space]. It is the tempests of the spirit which toss us to and fro daily; it is iniquity which drives us forward into all the troubles that befell Ulysses.' Ulysses, it is true, is not here an *exemplar*; and any moral he points is an involuntary moral—the moral that the wanderings of man's spirit matter far more than wanderings in space. But the Ulysses depicted is a 'type' Ulysses, rather than the actual Ulysses, the adroit and alert sea-rover; and it is the 'type' Ulysses which Latin antiquity bequeathed to Dante. Cicero, Horace, and Seneca, all gave him a picture of Ulysses as a pattern— the pattern of adventurous courage and of desire for knowledge of the 'greater things'. They all left the legacy of the *sapiens*, who was not as the *stultus*—of the *fortis*, who would bear up bravely even if the heavens fell.

The Middle Ages, by Dante's time, had added little to this legacy. Taught by Dares Phrygius, the medieval writers who embellished 'the matter of Troy' had associated Ulysses in a partnership with Diomed, and Dante follows that association in making the two the twin horns of the flame of fire which he sees in hell. Generally, Ulysses gains on the other Grecian heroes in the thought of the Middle Ages, and becomes the foremost figure. We can see the position he has acquired in the proverbial literature of the time from a Latin distich:

Turba muscarum fortis confunditur ursus:
Troiam non poterat devincere solus Ulixes.

---

[1] *Epistle* LXXXVIII, § 6.
[2] *Extra notum nobis orbem*—words which have their connection with Dante's words, 'esperienza...del mondo senza gente'.

There is strength in numbers: a swarm of flies may confound a bear; and even Ulysses could not conquer Troy by his sole strength.[1] Another example of the prominence he has gained may be found in the medieval legend of Troilus and Cressida—the richest of all the embroideries which were added to the story of Troy. The legend was already being embroidered in the course of the twelfth century; it grew and grew; and as it grew the figure of Ulysses was a conspicuous part of its texture. We can see the dimensions and character of his figure from Shakespeare's *Troilus and Cressida*. The conception of Ulysses which Shakespeare inherits from the Middle Ages is that of an absolute wisdom and an undeviating sanity of judgement. He stands above the coils of passion and the shifting currents of feeling with a cool detachment of view; but he can understand from within what he coolly surveys from above. It is he who is made to say:

> One touch of nature makes the whole world kin;

and he knows the hearts of men and women, as well as the 'greater things' of morals and policy. He acquires, it is true, something of a sixteenth-century touch: he has the foxy nature of Machiavelli's prince, and he knows

> The providence that's in a watchful state:

he preaches the beauty of 'degree', and of an ordered hierarchy in the commonwealth; he is the general master of policy, wisdom, prescience, and 'the still and mental parts'. This is not the Stoic 'type' Ulysses, tinctured and transfigured by Stoic philosophy into an example of Stoic virtue. Nor is it, again, the Ulysses of the Search, with a burning ardour for experience, and for following virtue and knowledge—the Ulysses imagined by Dante, who still trails some clouds of the Stoic tincture. Shakespeare's Ulysses is a medieval knight of the legend of Troy who has been modernised into a *politique*—but who yet retains a Greek touch of concern for 'the still and mental parts'. He is still, in some measure, himself;

[1] *Lateinische Sprichwörter und Sinnsprüche des Mittelalters*, edited by J. Werner (Heidelberg, 1912), p. 98. The proverb comes from a Basle manuscript, possibly of the fourteenth century.

but he has also suffered a change. He is part of the changing past—
a changing part of a past which itself is always changing. He is
a chameleon as well as a man. He becomes for each age the man
whom each age thinks into being ('There is nothing . . . but thinking
makes it so')—the adroit and alert sea-rover of the heroic age of
ancient Greece: the Stoic *sapiens* of the early Roman Empire, when
men of a republican temper were practising 'apathy' under the
frown of the tyrant and steeling themselves for a last 'going out':
the herald of the age of discovery, in the realm both of space and
the spirit, for the men of the time of Dante—or at any rate for
Dante himself: the sage and wily man of affairs, who has seen
many states and known their policies, for Shakespeare and the
men of Shakespeare's age.

III

'The herald of the age of discovery.' There is a prophetic touch—
unintended, but all the more notable for that—in Dante's story
of the last voyage of Ulysses. It was written at the beginning of
the fourteenth century. It tells of what happened at the end of the
fifteenth—the bursting of the bounds, the sailing round the Cape
of Storms, the finding of the Caribbean Sea; and, parallel with
this physical escape, the mental escape from the 'Schools' and the
schoolmen, and the free exploration of new seas of thought.

The beginning of discovery for Ulysses, as Dante tells the story,
is at the Pillars of Hercules:

> The marks that Hercules set far in view
> That none should dare beyond, or further learn.

It is here, in the Straits of Gibraltar, that Ulysses addresses his men,
and bids them go forward 'into the world without people', remembering the seed they spring from and the work for which they are
made—to follow virtue and knowledge. The Pillars of Hercules
were the old bounds of the Mediterranean world—the world's
barrier; the end of human endeavour; the ultimate verge; the
gates men may peep through, but cannot pass. This idea of the
ultimate verge recurs in the *Odes* of Pindar. 'Beyond the pillars

set up by Hercules, hero and god, to be witnesses of renown to the end of all voyaging, there lies a trackless sea.'[1] 'The waters that stretch away into the gloom from Cadiz are waters not to be crossed: turn the sails of thy ship back again toward the mainland of Europe.'[2] 'By the final reach of native manliness men have touched the Pillars of Hercules: follow virtue no longer, no further.'[3]

Dante knew nothing of Pindar's *Odes*. But he knew of the Pillars of Hercules, and he knew the classical tradition which made them the appointed bound. He had in his mind the old idea of the ultimate verge; and it may have been reinforced by his knowledge of the fate of the Genoese navigators, and possibly, too, by some knowledge of the Arab tradition that whirlpools always destroyed the adventurer who sailed into the waters of the Atlantic. But if he had the idea of fixed bounds, he had also the idea (which is its other side) of 'bursting the bounds'. Nor is it fanciful to believe that he shared this idea with other thinkers—or other dreamers—of the Middle Ages. It was hardly a scientific idea. Indeed, it may even be said to be an idea that depended on the absence of science; on the lack of accurate knowledge, ascertained by exact methods, about the extent of the world and the constitution of its elements. All things seemed possible when there was so little knowledge of the things which were actually possible. The alchemists of the Middle Ages may serve as an example; and even Roger Bacon himself believed in the philosopher's stone, which could transmute baser metals into gold. The adventurous soul might discover the material secrets of the universe by crucibles and suffumigations. Why should man not also discover a new and unpeopled world, sailing beyond the pillars, and penetrating the gloom that stretched away from Cadiz?

Unscientific, romantic, sometimes purely poetic but sometimes mixed with magic or even with charlatanry, the idea of 'bursting the bounds' persisted. It not only persisted: it eventually triumphed. There *was* an age of physical discovery beyond the Pillars of Her-

[1] *Nemean Odes*, III, 21-3.   [2] Ibid. IV, 69-70.
[3] *Isthmian Odes*, IV, 12-13.

cules. There *was* an age of mental discovery—which, it is true, was originally an age of rediscovery of the antique, but which passed, in the seventeenth century, into an age of discovery of new scientific truth. A great poet is always capable of great presentiments:

> And in such indexes, although small pricks
> To their subsequent volumes, there is seen
> The baby figure of the giant mass
> Of things to come at large.

Dante, like a poet, was visited by a presentiment. He took the figure of the great adventurer, always seeking new knowledge; and he made him the burster of the barriers—the prototype of the age of discovery and the herald of the spirit of the Renaissance.[1]

Ulysses, in the process, suffers a change. But then, as we have already had reason to notice, he had suffered change before, and he was to suffer it again. Not only does he suffer change: he also suffers the noble indignity of being made by Dante a type, an allegory, and a moral. That was a natural fate, in view of the general scheme and plan of the *Divina Commedia*. But that suffering, too, was a suffering which he had endured before. He had already become a type and an allegory for the Roman Stoics. It was little wonder that he became the same for a medieval poet. Allegory was a vital principle of medieval thought. It was the general method of the interpretation of the Bible. From the time of Origen and St Augustine, the idea had grown of the double, or triple, or even quadruple sense of the Scriptures; and St Thomas Aquinas, expressing this idea, had argued in his *Summa*[2] that besides the historical or literary sense of the text there were three

---

[1] Burckhardt, in Part IV, c. 2 of *Die Kultur der Renaissance in Italien*, speaking of a general Italian passion for the study and investigation of nature, notes that the *Divina Commedia* again and again attests the curiosity of Dante's own mind in the realm of natural philosophy. His similes show an exact observation of nature. He uses astronomy, and gives astronomical indications, almost with the precision of a navigator. He was drawn to a general study of cosmography: he wrote a Latin treatise, *De Aqua et Terra*. The voyage of Ulysses is an epitome of his own interests and his own hopes.

[2] *Summa Theologiae*, I, I, X.

other senses—the allegorical sense proper, in which the Old Testament is the 'type' of the New; the moral sense; and the anagogic sense in which a text typifies that which is in the glory to come. Indeed, the whole visible world was an allegory to medieval eyes, in just the same way as the Scriptures. Animals were allegories which suggested the virtues; and the volumes called 'bestiaries', or *bestiaria moralizata*, recorded the allegories. Precious stones were of the same order; and 'lapidaries' dealt with the virtues they shadowed. Men themselves became allegories; and the figures of the classical past, like the figures of the Bible, were drawn into service for the moral which they could be made to point or the anagogic interpretation which they could be made to serve. It was all the more natural that the Middle Ages should allegorise the figures of antiquity, as antiquity itself had already begun the process. The Stoic philosophers, who bequeathed so much to the Middle Ages, were already concerned with the allegorical interpretation of the Homeric poems—of the events they recorded and the persons they described—supposing that Homer was 'conveying through them, by means of allegory, knowledge and speculation as to nature and life'.[1]

Ulysses thus serves Dante (if we may use the terms of St Thomas) allegorically, morally, and anagogically. Allegorically and morally, he is a noble figure—an allegory of fortitude and wisdom; a moral type of venturesome courage, acting under the command of exploring and eager curiosity. Even anagogically, if we may speak

---

[1] T. B. Strong, *The Place of Scripture in the Church* (1917), p. 47. Dr Strong refers to the *Quaestiones Homericae* of Heraclides Ponticus, which proceeds on the principle πάντη ἠσέβησεν Ὅμηρος εἰ μηδὲν ἠλληγόρησε—'Homer was guilty of impiety throughout, if he wrote nothing allegorically.' Professor Chambers, in his *Thomas More*, pp. 78–9, deals with the medieval methods of allegorical interpretation, and gives some examples. Burckhardt, in *Die Kultur der Renaissance in Italien* (Part III, c. 4), notes that Dante had his own allegorical method, and that 'just as the earlier Middle Ages had put together type and antitype from the events and persons of the Old Testament and those of the New, so he generally combined a Christian and a pagan example of the same truth'. Accordingly, after the canto in which the pagan Ulysses comes, there follows a canto in which his Christian antitype, the Ghibeline Guido da Montrefeltro, tells how he too is 'set on flame of Hell' for having given fraudulent advice to Pope Boniface VIII.

from a purely human point of view, he may be said to 'typify that which is in the glory to come', and to show, as it were in a riddle, the achievement of a future age. But in a deeper sense of the word, and from a higher point of view, Ulysses is not a figure of *anagogē*, or of the leading or lifting up of the soul to a grasp of higher things. The story which Dante tells does not end with the bursting of the barriers. It has a further sweep; it ends with the fate of Ulysses the transgressor, and the doom of shipwreck and death which he suffered for his 'mad flight'. It is almost as if the poet, having turned his eyes to the future with a great presentiment, had resolutely averted them again, and turned back to the bounds of his age. The great speech of Ulysses to his men has stated, and stated nobly, the philosophy of the search for experience. But that is not the whole of philosophy, or even the greater half; and the end of the story redresses the balance and readjusts the perspective.

For five months Ulysses and his crew pursue their mad flight, making wings of their oars, and moving always to the left round the western coast of Africa, until they come in sight, under the stars of the Southern Pole, of the lofty Mountain in the Sea, dim in the distance, which is the Mountain of Purgatory standing at the antipodes to Jerusalem.[1] Then they find that what they have done is a thing forbidden to men; and 'as Another chose', who turned their first joy into mourning, they were caught by a storm, from off the strange land, which turned their ship round and round till it sank stern uppermost, and 'over us we heard the waters close'. For they had come, as Dante afterwards explains at the end of the first canto of the *Purgatorio*, 'to that desert shore which never yet saw man sail its waters who had experience afterwards of return'. It is not the pleasure of God that a living man should set foot in the realm of the dead. The uninhabited world—the *mondo senza gente*—which Ulysses had resolved to seek proves

---

[1] It would appear that Ulysses, after passing the Straits of Gibraltar, is conceived as sweeping in a great arc round the unknown coast of Africa, and moving back to the East, in the southern hemisphere, until he comes to the Mountain in the Sea exactly beneath the city of the Crucifixion.

itself, in the issue, to be the *mondo della morta gente*; the Search itself ends in death; and the Seeker, ignorant of grace, passes through death to the eternal fires of Hell. He had indeed felt an infinite ardour for experience of the world, and for knowledge of men's vices and virtues; he had cherished a deep sense of the duty of rational man to follow ἀρετή and ἐπιστήμη. But the ardour and the sense of duty had really been pagan things—the graceless merits of the unredeemed; and the man himself, in the works which he had actually done in the flesh, had used his tongue and abused the great human gift of rational speech for ends which were the opposite of God's intention—ends of fraud and deceit.[1] That is why he is punished, for all his merits, in the member in which he had offended. His tongue had been a fire and a world of iniquity: it had set on fire for him the wheel of birth, and it is accordingly set on fire by Hell.[2]

There is a tension, or even a dualism, in Dante's story of the end of Ulysses. There is a dualism between the idea of bursting the bounds and the conviction 'Thou hast appointed the bounds that he cannot pass'. There is a dualism between the ideal purpose proclaimed for the voyage—'Think on the seed ye spring from . . . follow virtue and knowledge unafraid'—and the actual course of the 'mad flight',[3] with its ending 'as Another chose'. Finally, and above all, there is a dualism between *fides* and *ratio*—on the one hand, the quiet of a contented faith in the known and inhabited world (ἡ οἰκουμένη) and the known and beaten track of the

---

[1] Cf. Aristotle, *Politics*, II, § 16: 'Man is furnished from birth with arms [such as speech] which are intended for the use of wisdom and virtue, but may be used for opposite ends.'

[2] James, iii. 6: 'The tongue is a fire: the world of iniquity among our members is the tongue, which defileth the whole body, and setteth on fire the wheel of nature [or birth—τὸν τροχὸν τῆς γενέσεως], and is set on fire by hell.' (ὁ τροχὸς τῆς γενέσεως is a notable phrase, rendered in the Vulgate as *rota nativitatis*. It may simply mean 'the circle of creation', or *orbis creaturae*; but it sets thought wondering and wandering eastward.)

[3] The phrase 'mad flight' (*folle volo*), used in the *Inferno*, recurs in the *Paradiso*, XXVII, 82–3, where Dante, looking downward from the Heaven of fixed stars, sees 'the mad track' (*il varco folle*) of Ulysses, away beyond Cadiz.

Christian system of knowledge: on the other, a philosophic passion, drawn from the antique past but looking to the undiscovered country of the future, which drives men in discontent to voyage alone through strange seas of thought 'into the world without people'. Dante himself knew the call both of *ratio* and of *fides*. He had heard the call of *ratio* from the *Ethics* and the *Politics* of Aristotle; and the first book of his *De Monarchia* bears evidence of what he had heard. The end of man, he there writes, *est actuare semper totam potentiam intellectus possibilis, per prius ad speculandum, et secundario propter hoc ad operandum per suam extensionem.*[1] The ideal purpose which Ulysses proclaims for his voyage is an Aristotelian purpose: indeed, it is almost couched in Aristotelian terms. Just as it is argued in the *De Monarchia* that the *vis ultima* of man does not consist in *esse apprehensivum, quia sic et participatur a brutis, sed esse apprehensivum per intellectum*, so it is said in the *Inferno*:

> Fatti non foste a viver come bruti,
> Ma per seguir virtute e conoscenza.

Thus Ulysses, in the course of his changes, is changed into a disciple of Aristotle; he becomes a figure of the Active Intellect (*Intellectus Agens*), which, using the 'apprehensions' of the Possible Intellect (or, in other words, the pictures framed in that reach of the mind which receives and digests the impressions of the senses), proceeds to speculation and thereby to the heights of action. All this is the call of *ratio*; and Dante, hearing that call, expressed it, and even proclaimed it, in the figure of Ulysses. But there is also the call of *fides*; and he also heard and also expressed that call. He expressed it in the *Inferno* in the fate of Ulysses—the shipwreck of *Intellectus Agens*; and he expressed it again, and still more clearly, in a passage of the *Purgatorio*.

Here Dante and Virgil are proceeding to that Mountain of Purgatory from which there once had arisen the storm that had shipwrecked Ulysses. Dante notices, with some alarm, that Virgil casts no shadow like that which his own body casts. Virgil explains: all things are possible to the Power of God, 'which doth not will

[1] *De Monarchia*, I, c. iv.

that the way of its working should be unveiled to us'. There is a world inscrutable to the Intellect:

> 'He is mad who hopes that reason in its sweep
> The infinite way can traverse back and forth
> Which the Three Persons in one substance keep.
> With the *quia*[1] stay content, children of earth!
> For if the whole before your eyes had lain,
> No need was there for Mary to give birth.
> Ye have seen desiring without fruit, in vain,
> Men such that their desire had been at rest,
> Which now is given them for eternal pain.
> Of Aristotle's and of Plato's quest
> I speak, and many more.' His head he sank
> Here, and no more said, and remained distrest.[2]

This is the end of the matter for Dante, as he too sinks his head. Ulysses, the Aristotelian figure of the Active Intellect, had a desire without fruit, and ending only in eternal pain, which would have been at rest if only he had known the grace of faith. That is the end of the Search—'of Aristotle's and of Plato's quest...and many more'.

But the idea of the voyage of Ulysses still persists in the mind, in the right of its own inner magic, and in spite of its ultimate doom. One forgets the shipwreck: one remembers the quest—the Western quest of Discovery—the mental quest in new seas of thought. Remembering the quest, one cannot but think of other records. Some of them are genuine and historical records of actual quests of Western Discovery, from Snorre Sturlason's record of the finding of 'Vinland the Good' by Leif Ericson, in the time of Olaf Trygvason,[3] to Hakluyt's record of the *Principall Navigations*,

---

[1] The *quia* is the simple fact 'that' ('hoti's business'), with no question of the *quare* or 'why and wherefore'.

[2] *Purgatorio*, III, 34–45. The translation is Laurence Binyon's.

[3] *Heimskringla*, The History of Olaf Trygvason, §§ 96–104. 'Vinland the Good', where the Norsemen found wild grapes growing near their landfall, is generally supposed to be North America, somewhere near the St Lawrence.

Voiages and Discoveries of the English Nation. Some, again, are stories and tales of imagination; and in these the Western quest of Discovery is blended with, or sublimated into, the mental quest in new seas of thought. Tennyson not only wrote *Ulysses*: he also wrote the *Voyage*; and here he told (in lines of which the last is an echo of one in Dante) how

> ...one fair Vision ever fled
> Down the waste waters day and night,
> And still we follow'd where she led
> In hope to gain upon her flight....
> And now we lost her, now she gleam'd
> Like Fancy made of golden air.
> Now nearer to the prow she seem'd
> Like Virtue firm, like Knowledge fair.

But it is perhaps in the *Paracelsus* of the young Robert Browning —a poem which he published, at the age of twenty-two, as long ago as the year 1835—that we may find an imagination which comes nearest to that of Dante. Here, too, the notion of quest rises to the spiritual plane. Browning uses the image of voyaging:

> Over the sea our galleys went
> With cleaving prows in order brave
> To a speeding wind and a bounding wave,
> A gallant armament;

but the image is an allegory of a spiritual thing.

> I go to prove my soul!
> I see my way as birds their trackless way.
> I shall arrive! what time, what circuit first,
> I ask not; but unless God send his hail
> Or blinding fireballs, sleet or stifling snow,
> In some time, his good time, I shall arrive.

It was in such a hope that Ulysses went. He did not arrive at the world for which he had hoped. But if the storm came upon him off the mountain, he knew at the last the pleasure of God and came to the judgement.

IV

THE CONNECTION OF THE RENAISSANCE
AND THE REFORMATION

I

'I believe that there *was* a Reformation. But I wonder whether the report of it has not been exaggerated; whether it meant so great a break with the past, and so absolute a departure from it, as some historians have depicted; and whether that past was itself so black, and so far from the way and the truth, as it has often been painted.

'I have heard of a Renaissance. But I should venture to doubt if there ever was one; or if there was, I should prefer to say that it was not one, but many.'

With some such words, in his younger days, when paradox had its charms, and there seemed to be point, as well as delight, in administering a preliminary shock to his hearers, the author of this essay used to begin a lecture on the sixteenth century. Perhaps it was something more than the charm of paradox which suggested the words. Perhaps it was also some hidden feeling for

> The fair sum of six thousand years'
> Traditions of civility.

But it would be folly, and paradox would be wearing cap and bells, if we were to deny the sense of rebirth which pervades the fifteenth and sixteenth centuries. It was a period of the three R's—or should one say of the three Re's?—the Classical Renaissance, which began in Italy, and spread into Germany and Western Europe: the Christian Reformation, which began in Wittenberg, Zürich and Geneva, pursued its peculiar course in England, and spread from Wittenberg and Geneva into Scandinavia, Scotland and Holland: the Reception of Roman Law, which began in Germany, was followed in Scotland by the recognition of 'the godly approved laws of Justinian the emperor', and even in England led to the foundation of Regius chairs of the Civil Law in the Universities of Oxford and Cambridge.[1] Nor was the period only an age of rebirth. It was also an age of discovery. Indeed it is possible to argue that discovery was the cardinal fact, and the true revolution, of the period. The historian of thought, directing his attention to movements of thought, is naturally concerned with what may be called the intellectual and spiritual recoveries—the recovery of the pure Greek tradition; the recovery of the pure doctrine of the Gospels. But thought itself may be profoundly stirred by the physical fact of discovery; and it is the part of wisdom to recognise that the intellectual and spiritual recoveries of the fifteenth and sixteenth centuries proceeded under the aegis, and were stirred by the revelations, of a continuous process of new discovery of the physical world.

Dante had linked the Western quest of Ulysses with a mental quest of new knowledge. Centuries later another thinker, at the very antipodes to Dante, connected discovery in the physical world with reformation in the moral. Jeremy Bentham, in the preface to his *Fragment on Government* of 1776, was stimulated by the discoveries recently made in the southern waters of the Pacific ('the most distant and recondite regions of the earth traversed and explored') to proclaim a dawning age of Enlightenment in which 'the grand principle' of utility should bring about a moral reformation 'correspondent to discovery...in the natural world'. It was natural enough that Bentham—who, 'like Archimedes of old', had cried 'Eureka!' when he first discovered the principle of utility in the course of his reading at Oxford—should connect that discovery, and the moral effects he expected from it, with the discoveries of Bougainville and Cook. But the thinkers of the sixteenth century—men of the type of Montaigne and Bacon—

[1] On Roman Law in Scotland and England, see Hatschek's *Englische Verfassungsgeschichte*, pp. 346-7. The influence of 'Byzantinism' in England, as he notes in a later passage (pp. 412-13), was chiefly seen in the realm of diplomacy, and in the habit of requiring a knowledge of Roman Law from envoys sent abroad and the members of the King's Council at home who dealt with foreign affairs.

could even more naturally, and with far more justice, proclaim a new age of renaissance of thought and reformation of life correspondent to their own great age of discovery. In 1486 the Portuguese Bartolomeo Diaz had rounded the Cape of Good Hope, which he called the Cape Tempestuous; and in 1498 Vasco da Gama, also from Portugal, had reached Calicut on the Malabar coast of India. In 1492 the Genoese Columbus (succeeding where the Genoese navigators of two centuries earlier had failed) reached the West Indies: in 1496 the Venetian Cabot (whose family originally came also from Genoa) sailed from Bristol to the coast of Labrador and Newfoundland:[1] in 1499 the Spaniard Pinzon—with Americo Vespucci on board to tell the tale and to give his name, by a curious accident, to a new continent—reached the coast of South America; and in the same year the Portuguese Cabral reached the same coast on a great circuit which took him eventually to the Cape of Good Hope and India. The sixteenth century thus dawned in the middle of great navigations; and as it took its course a whole *alter orbis*, or *mondo nuovo*, dawned with it on men's minds. The prophecy of Seneca had been accomplished,[2]

Venient annis saecula seris
Quibus Oceanus vincula rerum
Laxet, et ingens pateat tellus,

and Ocean had finally loosed her bounds to the general gaze. No wonder that Bacon was moved to plan a new scheme of knowledge,

---

[1] It is only just to render credit to the work done by the Italian genius in the matter of discovery. It is not only that Columbus and Cabot were Italians: there was a still earlier phase of attempts at discovery by Italian travellers and navigators, as early as the thirteenth century. Burckhardt remarks (*Die Kultur der Renaissance in Italien*, Part III, c. 1 *ad initium*): 'The true discoverer is not the man who happens to get somewhere first, but the man who has *sought* and then finds. It is he, and he only, who will stand in connection with the thoughts and the interests of his predecessors; and the account which he renders will be what it is in virtue of that fact. This is the reason why the Italians, though the priority of their arrival on this or that shore may be a matter of dispute, remain none the less the modern nation of discoverers *par excellence* for the whole period of the later Middle Ages.'

[2] Seneca, *Medea*, II, 374–8, quoted by Bacon in his essay on Prophecies.

or that he spoke of his scheme 'as a coasting voyage or *periegesis* of the New Intellectual World'.[1]

A letter written by a Renaissance scholar, Politian (Professor of Greek and Latin at the Academy of Florence till his death in 1494), is a vivid testimony to the interest which the new discoveries roused, even in their early stages, among the men of the New Learning. The letter was written before the voyage of Columbus, probably in the course of 1491: it was inspired entirely by the early Portuguese voyages down the coast of Africa and round the Cape of Good Hope; and it is addressed to John II (1481–95), King of Portugal and the two Algarves, and Lord of Guinea.[2] In it Politian offers to commemorate the great deeds of the Portuguese King and his people. 'What a scene of things hardly credible would be opened up to my view, if I were to commemorate voyages into unknown seas; the contemning of the Pillars of Hercules; a sundered world restored to itself; and barbarism, which we scarcely knew even by report, brought back to humanity. Then I could tell of new commodities, new profits, new comforts of life; accession to old knowledge, the corroboration of old things once hardly credible, and, with it, the end of our wonder at them.... You are recoverer as well as discoverer; you have not only discovered other countries, another sea, other worlds, and other constellations—you have brought them back from the eternal shades, and from ancient chaos, into the light of day.... Trustee and guardian of a second world (*mundi alterius sequester et janitor*)... you are uniquely worthy of honour from all who love the cult of the Muses.' Politian's pen is dipped in honey; but his words are a testimony of genuine feeling. He saw in the age of discovery a parallel to, and a part of, the age of the revival of learning. If scholars, by their discoveries, were restoring an old world of knowledge, navigators were also,

---

[1] Quoted by E. J. Payne, in the *Cambridge Modern History*, Vol. I, p. 65.

[2] The letter is mentioned by E. J. Payne, op. cit. p. 18. It comes at the beginning of Book X of Politian's *Epistulae*, and it is followed by an answer from John II, dated 23 October 1491. The 'two Algarves' were the southern part of modern Portugal (*Algarve dalem mar*) and the northern tip of Africa round Tangier (*Algarve daqem mar*).

by theirs, 'restoring the world to itself' and 'bringing it back' from the ancient shades of a long oblivion.

Politian wrote during the first raptures of discovery. Over a century later, as it came to its close, Bacon repeated the note which Dante had first sounded and Politian had sounded again in his letter to John II. For Bacon too—a Ulysses of later times—two quests are indissolubly connected. 'This great building of the world had never through-lights made in it, till the age of us and our fathers.... And this proficience in navigation and discoveries may plant also an expectation of the further proficience and augmentation of all sciences; because it may seem they are ordained by God to be coevals, that is, to meet in one age. For so the prophet Daniel, speaking of the latter times, foretelleth, *Plurimi pertransibunt, et multiplex erit scientia*, as if the openness and thorough passage of the world and the increase of knowledge were appointed to be in the same ages.'[1] The moral here drawn in the *Advancement of Learning* of 1605 is carried further in the *Novum Organum* of 1620. Bacon was fond of the parallel between the physical and the intellectual globe; and he had already spoken of himself, at the end of the *Advancement of Learning*, as having 'made as it were a small Globe of the Intellectual World'. The parallel is pressed home in a famous passage of the *Novum Organum*.[2] Arguing that we are the true ancients ('for the old age of the world is to be accounted the true antiquity') and that truth, being 'the daughter of time', might fairly be expected to be in our grasp, he pleads that we ought to match our knowledge of the intellectual world with our knowledge of the physical. 'Nor must it go for nothing that by the distant voyages and travels which have become frequent in our times, many things in nature have been laid open and discovered which may let in new light upon philosophy. And surely it would be disgraceful if, while the regions of the material globe—that is, of the earth, of the sea, and of the stars—have been

[1] *The Advancement of Learning*, Book II *ad initium* (repeated in the *De Augmentis Scientiarum*, II, x).

[2] Book I, c. LXXXIV. Later in the same book Bacon twice uses the analogy of Columbus for his own exploration of the intellectual globe—at the end of c. XCII and the beginning of c. CXIV.

in our times laid widely open and revealed, the intellectual globe should remain shut up within the narrow limits of old discoveries....' Bacon may here be like Politian in associating discovery with a new birth of learning. But he is totally unlike in his conception of the nature of learning. Not for him the return to the high road of antiquity. Rather 'the unbroken route through the woods of experience'. In Bacon the notion of discovery has triumphed over that of recovery: the New Learning has ceased to be the wisdom of the ancients, and has turned into modern science.

II

From the notion of discovery, however curiously it may have been intertwined with the notion of recovery, we must now return to the Renaissance and its search for the antique. Two doubts were hazarded in the beginning of this essay: whether there ever was a Renaissance, and whether, if there was such a thing, it would not be juster to say that it happened over and over again, and was many rather than one. The point of the first of these doubts is simple. It may well be contended that there never was a Renaissance in one sense—a sense in which the word has been too often and too indiscriminately used—the sense that about 1500, after the revelation of Greek to a dark and ignorant world, 'men opened their eyes and saw', apprehended a beauty not felt before, and were emancipated from the past. To hold such a view is, for one thing, a treason to the Middle Ages; a treason to Dante; a treason to the Italian painters of Sienna and Florence who were Dante's contemporaries; a treason to the earlier Troubadours and *trouvères* of France; a treason to the early *archipoeta* of the twelfth century, and to the author of the poem *Dum Diane vitrea* in the *Carmina Burana* of the thirteenth, who could already write Latin lyrical poetry of a wit and beauty which transcend the achievement of any of the Latin poets of the Renaissance.[1] For another thing such

---

[1] On the 'arch-poet' and his famous *Confession* see F. J. E. Raby, *Secular Latin Poetry in the Middle Ages*, Vol. II, pp. 180–90. On the *Carmina Burana* of

a view is in itself romantic and gaseous. It is based on a reading of shadowy meanings into a new and imported word which offered a large temptation to imaginative minds. The first instance of its use recorded in the *New English Dictionary* belongs to the year 1845; and Matthew Arnold spoke of it in *Culture and Anarchy*, twenty-four years later, as 'a foreign word to which I have ventured to give an English form'—the form 'Renascence'. No wonder it caught the fancy, as a word which was ἱερὸν καὶ σεμνὸν καὶ τερατῶδες. No wonder that it readily seduced many minds into a generous play of subjectivity.

If we reduce the word to an exacter sense, and take it to mean a rebirth of classical scholarship, with a more scholarly study of old texts and a discovery of new, we shall banish the first of our doubts, and confess that there was, *in that sense*, such a thing as a Renaissance. But having done that, we are brought face to face with our second doubt. Was this Renaissance, in this sense of the word, one or many? We have already seen that there is reason for thinking that it was many, and that it happened again and again.[1] It happened in the age of Charlemagne; it happened in the twelfth century, at Chartres and elsewhere; it happened again in the thirteenth century, with the recovery of the general body of Aristotle's treatises; it happened again in the Italy of the fifteenth and sixteenth centuries; and it was to happen once more—at any rate so far as Germany was concerned—in the age of Winckelmann. From this point of view it may be suggested, as indeed it has been already suggested,[2] that the notion of a continuous classical heritage is a safer and sounder notion than that of a Renaissance, or even of a series of Renaissances, and that it is better to think of the flowing stream, *in omne volubilis aevum*, than to think in terms of fountains which, long forgotten or hidden, are again revealed and unsealed

the monastery of Benediktbeuern see ibid. pp. 256–79. Jakob Burckhardt, in his *Die Kultur der Renaissance in Italien*, conjectures that it was an Italian poet who wrote some of the most moving of the *Carmina Burana*; but Dr Raby notes, p. 266, that the poems are 'French and German and, we may guess, English'.

[1] See above, p. 3.
[2] See above, p. 2.

in separate ages of revival. There have indeed been ages of revival, in which men were naturally impelled to say,

> juvat integros accedere fontes
> Atque haurire.

Even in antiquity itself Cicero could write, as he does in his *Academicae Quaestiones*:[1] *meos amicos...ad Graecos ire jubeo, ut... a fontibus potius hauriant quam rivulos consectentur.* But there is a wisdom, none the less, in 'following the little channels'—the channels of constant irrigation along which water is constantly flowing to quicken the vineyards and the olive gardens, and (if we may speak in a metaphor) to refresh all the works of man's cultivation and culture. The *rivuli* running through the ages are the essential and constant revival.[2]

Yet though we may emphasise continuity rather than revival, and though we may argue that, even in terms of revival, the Italian Renaissance of the fifteenth and sixteenth centuries was only one in a series, the fact remains—and it must be admitted—that the Italian Renaissance had a unique character, and exercised a unique influence. The reason is simple. The Italian Renaissance was not only a revealing of the Greek fountains: it was also, and at the same time, a revealing—partly to Italy itself, but even more to countries outside Italy—of an Italian way of life, congruous in many respects with the Greek way, which had gradually unfolded itself in the civic societies and the princely courts of Italy from the age of Dante onwards. Two things were united in one, and united because they were congruous. The 'changing past' of Greece had swung into congruity with the actual present of Italy;[3] and the Italian Renaissance derived its character from the inspiration of that

---

[1] I. 2. 8; cf. *De Oratore*, II. 27. 117.

[2] Dante knew the *rivuli*, descending from the green hills, and drawn into cool gentle channels:

> 'Li ruscelletti che dei verdi colli
> Del Casentin discendon giuso in Arno,
> Facendo i lor canali e freddi e molli.'
>
> (*Inferno*, xxx, 64-6)

[3] See above, pp. 21-4.

conjunction. Venice, Florence and Milan—Ferrara, Mantua and Urbino—had developed a *paideia* which answered the old *paideia* of Greece; and they had developed it on the same basis—the basis of the *polis*, or civic republic, intermixed with the *signoria* of the despot or *tyrannus*.[1] When Italy, therefore, offered the treasures of ancient Greece to Northern and Western Europe, she also offered them her own; and her own were similar treasures, achieved on a similar political basis, and spread over a similar range of art, literature, and a general style of life and culture. Her neighbours were naturally dazzled and stimulated by her double gift; and the Italian Renaissance, unique in itself through its double nature, was unique in its influence for just the same reason. This is a point which Burckhardt makes more than once in his great book on the culture of the Renaissance in Italy. 'We must insist upon it, as a main theme of this book, that it was not the revival of antiquity alone, but its intimate alliance with the genius of the Italian people present at its side, which conquered the world of the West.'[2]

We must thus confess, on a balanced view, that there is something to be said, after all, for a conception of the Renaissance which was perhaps too hastily dismissed at an earlier stage of the argument. There *is* a sense in which there was a Renaissance, and one

[1] Princely courts had played their part in the development of culture in ancient Greece, as they did in the development of culture in Italy about 1500. Philosophy had been studied at the court of Hermias the tyrant of Atarneus and at that of Dionysius II of Syracuse about 350 B.C. Philosophy—the same philosophy, the philosophy of Plato—was studied again at the court of Lorenzo de' Medici at Florence and at that of Dukes Federigo and Guidobaldo of Urbino.

[2] *Die Kultur der Renaissance in Italien*, Part III, c. I *ad initium*. The same point is made again at the beginning of c. IV of § IV: 'The age first developed individuality itself in its strongest form; and then it impelled individualism to an eager and extensive study of the individual in all his forms.... Between these two great processes we have had to set the influence of ancient literature, because the mode of conceiving and depicting the individual—and also human nature in general—was essentially coloured and determined by that medium. But the power of attaining the conception lay in the age and the people.' It will be noticed that in this latter passage the revival of antiquity becomes merely a medium for the expression of conceptions inherent in the Italians of the period. Here, it may be argued, Burckhardt pushes his point too far.

only: there is even a sense in which it may be said that this one Renaissance was a new revelation and a fresh apprehension of life. But this will only be true if we speak, not of 'the Renaissance' pure and simple, but of 'the Italian Renaissance'. We need the adjective as well as the noun; and adjective and noun are of equal importance. It was not only the revival of antiquity, and especially the revival (or, we may also say, the return in the course of its orbit) of the Greek past of the fifth and fourth centuries B.C., that mattered so much and stirred men so greatly. It was also the living and actual reality of the Italian present of the *quattrocento* and the *cinquecento*. It was, in a word, the two together, and the two together because the two were congruous with one another. On that basis, and within those limits, we may celebrate the revolution marked by the Italian Renaissance. It *was* a revolution in men's conception of values. It sacrificed something: all revolutions do: indeed, it sacrificed much, and much that mattered greatly. It was a secularist revolution; and it secularised the values of life. It made truth less of a divine revelation (if indeed it left any revelation at all), and more a fruit of human curiosity impelling human reason to discover new truths and to co-ordinate its discoveries. It made goodness less of an ascetic pilgrimage to another world, and more a matter of building a harmonious personality in the world of sight and touch. It made beauty no longer a snare, or, at its best, a handmaid of religion, but an absolute value, the very value of values, to be pursued for itself, and to be enjoyed for itself in a high felicity. Or rather—for all such sweeping generalities overshoot the mark—it went in these directions, but it did not go the whole way. The things which it had sacrificed were too good and too true to be lost. Revolution had to make its account with restoration and reconstruction. In the Reformation and the Counter-Reformation the account was made, and a reconciliation was achieved. Fortunately, there was an element in the Italian Renaissance which made reconciliation possible. That element was the element of pure and disinterested scholarship. It was the element of the pure 'revival of antiquity', disengaged from a worship of antique values which were pagan as well as antique.

It was possible to revive antiquity without reviving Pan. There were the Christian Scriptures, as well as the writings of Plato and Aristotle, which invited the study of scholars in their original text. There could be—and there was—a Christian as well as a Classical Renaissance, a Christian Renaissance as exact in its scholarship as the Classical, and equally resolved to approach and drink the fresh fountains of its origins. And if this Christian Renaissance was eventually to find its home in countries outside Italy, it was none the less an effect of the general stirring of the Italian Renaissance, and we may trace some of its earliest impulses in Florence. There is no great line of division between the Christian and the Classical Renaissance. They were intertwined as well as distinct.

It has just been said that the element of pure and disinterested scholarship was the saving grace of the Italian Renaissance, and made possible a reconciliation between the revolution which that Renaissance brought and the restoration which had also to come. If we consider this element of pure scholarship, we shall see that it moved in two channels. On its formal or pedagogic side, it expressed itself in schools. On its intellectual or spiritual side, it moved in the Universities.

In the schools of the Middle Ages the pupils had been made to learn and speak Latin, or to be whipped if they failed. Latin was still something of a living language, if it lived a low Latin sort of life. It was different from the Latin of Cicero: it had still some elements of growth—and therefore (it might be said) of corruption. The fight of the Renaissance was a fight for 'good and clean Latin' in the schools, with some instruction in Greek following eventually in the wake of Latin. This meant revolution in the curriculum— new and better text-books, particularly new and better grammars, and the study of classical authors of a different and purer style. A revolution in the curriculum meant also a revolution in the organisation of schools: new wine demanded new bottles; and a new type of school, which we have learned to call the grammar school, was a result of the Renaissance. The movement began in Italy; and it began at an early date. Vittorino da Feltre started a school at Mantua as early as 1425, in which he taught poetry, oratory and something of classical history and ancient philosophy, in the writings of the best Latin authors, to which he eventually added some of the classics of Greece; and as he combined some physical training, and some instruction in manners, with the intellectual discipline he sought to impart, so he also combined poor scholars, maintained at his own cost, with the sons of nobles who frequented his school. (The Renaissance was not an aristocratic movement, and one of its effects was to open a career to the talented poor.) In just the same way, and at the same time, Guarino da Verona conducted a school at Ferrara in which he associated a number of poor scholars, whom he partly or wholly maintained, with the son of the reigning prince and his companions. The Italian example spread, and Dean Colet's foundation of St Paul's School in 1512 is an English parallel. Its high master, William Lily, had studied Greek in Rhodes and at Rome; and he was the author of a Latin grammar which had long a considerable vogue. St Paul's was followed during the century by Christ's Hospital, Westminster, Merchant Taylors and Harrow: it was followed too by the grammar schools; and a new epoch of humanistic education was thus begun in England. With the rise of the Renaissance schools there also went the beginnings of a new science of pedagogy. Wimpheling in Germany published his *Adolescentia* in 1500— a work on 'the education of the adolescent' which is said to mark an era in the new science: the Spaniard Vives published at Antwerp in 1531 his *De Tradendis Disciplinis*; and in England Roger Ascham, of St John's College, Cambridge, wrote a treatise on education under the title of the 'Scholemaster' which was published two years after his death, in 1570.

In the Universities the path of the Renaissance was more difficult and devious, and it ultimately led the scholars who followed it to an unexpected goal. They began by attacking what, in their eyes, was the medieval obscurantism of the traditional Universities, and by seeking to let in the sweetness and light of good literature and good style: they ended—almost with a shiver and a start—on the brink of the Reformation. Resolved to 'set Dunce in Bocardo'— to imprison Duns Scotus and all his works—they found that they had helped to liberate a great genie of religious revival. But their original impulse was a simple impulse to challenge the vested interests and the old-established studies of the Universities of their day: to attack their clerical organisation, and to reform their scholastic curriculum.

In their organisation the Universities could be viewed as clerical corporations—closed professional bodies, which stood pharisaically aloof from the current of contemporary life and thought—exclusive guilds, which sought to reserve the 'mystery' of learning for their members. Acting upon this view, many of the scholars of the Renaissance preferred to be *laureati*—crowned with the laurel wreath, as Petrarch had been by the senator of Rome—rather than to bear the title of Master or Doctor of a University. Emperors, popes, princes, and academies, vied with one another in bestowing the laurel; but the Florentines made the honour posthumous, and accompanied it by an *éloge* of the dead.[1] Many scholars, however, had a natural desire to find places and positions and titles in Universities; to acquire chairs for themselves, and recognition for the New Learning which they professed, *intra muros academiae*. Not all grapes were sour; and to become a professor of eloquence or rhetoric in a University, or to be elected to a University chair of poetry, was a laudable ambition. But a further and higher reach of the ambition of Renaissance scholars was the foundation of new Academies—'extra-mural' societies of scholars existing in their own right, pursuing their own studies, and conferring their own distinctions. In Italy a number of these Academies arose during the latter half of the fifteenth century. The greatest was the Platonic Academy at Florence, already a home of philosophy in the days of Lorenzo de' Medici (1469–92), which attracted the Platonist Marsilio Ficino and the philosopher and theologian Pico della Mirandola (who came by way of Greek Neo-Platonism to a study of the Jewish Cabbala),[2] as well as Politian, the master of style,

---

[1] Burckhardt, op. cit., Part III, c. 4 *ad finem*.

[2] The Cabbala, or 'tradition', was a compilation of the Middle Ages, which mixed philosophy with theology, and both with a cult of the magic of numbers. Platonism, and even more Neo-Platonism, had already influenced its compilers;

and even the great Michelangelo himself—men whose studies and discussions, as we shall have reason to notice, had echoes and effects in Oxford and England during the sixteenth century. Next to the Florentine Academy and its philosophical studies, which were concentrated on the cult of Plato, we may commemorate the memory of the New Academy founded by the printer Aldus at Venice, which counted Erasmus and the Englishman Linacre (of All Souls College) among its honorary members, and helped to render the sovereign service of aiding by its advice the printing of a long series of Greek and Latin classics. The antiquarian Academy of Rome and the literary Academy of Naples were less conspicuous; but the Roman Academy regularly celebrated the memory of ancient Rome, and resuscitated and produced the Latin plays of Plautus.

The impact of the Renaissance scholars on the clerical organisation of the University of the time was not only a matter of rivalry —the rivalry of their laureateship with its degrees, or of their chairs of rhetoric and poetry with its old-established chairs, or even of their new academies with its ancient system and institutions. It was also, at any rate on occasion, a matter of deep and bitter controversy. The name of Reuchlin, a German scholar from Baden who had studied Greek and then turned from Greek to the study of Hebrew and the Cabbala, has attached itself to the bitterest of these struggles. The first of modern Hebraists, he was led to defend Hebrew books against a threat of suppression, and he was then indicted in an ecclesiastical court by the theologians of Cologne for venturing to defend them (1514). The theological faculties of Paris and Louvain rallied to the aid of the theologians of Cologne: the Renaissance scholars of Germany rallied to the side of Reuchlin. He was acquitted; and his acquittal was made

and it was easy for Pico, like his contemporary Reuchlin, to turn to it from a study of Neo-Platonism.

It is interesting to note that Pico, the Florentine nobleman and scholar who died untimely in 1494, at the age of thirty-one, engaged the thought and attention of More, who translated a Latin life of him into English as a New Year's offering to a nun, perhaps about 1505. More is said to have propounded Pico to himself as a pattern of life.

a triumph by the satires which the Renaissance scholars of Germany poured on the heads of their antagonists in the *Epistulae Obscurorum Virorum*. The result of the struggle was to vindicate freedom not only for Hebrew studies, but also for the study of Greek and that of the New Learning generally. Indeed, it was even more. The struggle had been fought on the confines between scholarship and theology; and it inevitably fostered the application of modern scholarship and its methods to Biblical criticism and theology. It was here that the Renaissance, in its ultimate trend, came to the brink of the Reformation. It was in this way too that it was led, by a simpler and more immediate logic, to challenge the scholastic curriculum current in the Universities.

In Italy itself the challenge did not go to any great length, or run into theological consequences. It was enough for Italian scholars to vindicate a place for their own Latin verses, continuing 'the sacred inspiration of Virgil', and to claim a right of way for the study of Greek texts. It was otherwise in Germany; and it was otherwise also in England. Here there gradually arose a movement which sought to substitute a new theology and a 'modern churchmanship' for the scholastic *corpus* of theology so nicely schematised by the rules of Aristotelian logic. We may trace this movement—a delicate growth which hardly touched the stormy history of the English Reformation, but settled itself quietly, none the less, on the soil of English thought—in the University of Oxford. Soon after 1450 Oxford began to be affected—here a little and there a little—by the Greek scholarship of Italy. William Grey of Balliol College, Bishop of Ely from 1454 to 1478, gave books from Italy to his old college. William Tilley of Selling (sometimes described as Prior Selling), a student of Canterbury College at Oxford and afterwards Prior of Christ Church, Canterbury—the friend of Politian and the patron of Linacre—acquired in the course of two visits to Italy (1464–7 and 1486) a rare collection of books which was doomed to be burned accidentally at Canterbury on the eve of the Dissolution. He had studied Greek at Bologna, and his collection included Greek manuscripts. Linacre had been his pupil in Greek at Canterbury, as well as his *protégé* at

Oxford; and, after becoming a Fellow of All Souls College, he continued his study of Greek in Italy from 1486 onwards. While he was there, he invited Grocyn, a Fellow of New College, Oxford, to join him: the two men studied together, and both became acquainted with Aldus, the printer. Grocyn on his return (about 1490) adorned his college with a collection (which it still cherishes)[1] of the earliest printed Greek and Latin classics—among them a copy of the Aldine Aristotle printed on vellum. Not only so, but he also lectured on Greek in Oxford.

It was in the Oxford of those days, during the last decade of the fifteenth century, with Greek books in some of the libraries and with Grocyn lecturing on Greek, that a seed began to grow. It would not have grown without Greek; but it grew without any great knowledge of Greek. Nor would it have grown without Oxford; but it was in London rather than Oxford that it was eventually destined to flourish. It was the seed of a new theology, or, as we may also call it, of the restoration of theology. It was a seed which John Colet planted, and which Erasmus watered. To understand how the seed came to germinate, we must turn to the lives of Colet and Erasmus—and incidentally to that of Sir Thomas More.

We have already spoken of the two friends Linacre and Grocyn, the one of All Souls and the other of New College; and we have already mentioned another Oxford scholar, William Lily of Magdalen College (the godson of Grocyn), who in the course of a pilgrimage to Jerusalem had stayed and learned Greek in Rhodes and at Rome, at about the same time when Linacre and Grocyn were in Italy together.[2] All these three had a tolerable knowledge of Greek. John Colet, the son of a Lord Mayor of London, who

---

[1] The writer would explain that he was once a Fellow of New College, and held the office of Librarian.

[2] In the matter of chronology it may be noted that Grocyn, born about 1446, was the oldest of the company of Oxford scholars. Linacre, born about 1460, came next. Colet and Lily, born in 1467 and 1468, were almost exact contemporaries. Erasmus was a year older than Colet: More, born in 1478, was the youngest, but he was already a student at Canterbury Hall, in Oxford, by 1492. It may be added that they were all—except More—in Orders.

had studied in Oxford at Magdalen College from 1483 onwards, never mastered Greek. But he had travelled in Italy between 1493 and 1496, and had studied the writings of the fathers and a little Greek; and he had imbibed in Italy, whether at Florence or elsewhere, the spirit and the zest of inquiry. From 1496 onwards, down to 1504, he lectured in Oxford on the Pauline Epistles; and his lectures on the Epistle to the Romans and the first Epistle to the Corinthians still survive. They mark a revolution in the interprétation of the New Testament. Deserting allegory and 'anagogy',[1] he sought to elicit the simple meaning of the actual text; he attempted what we may call a historical interpretation, and he cited Suetonius and other contemporary authors to elucidate the text of St Paul as he found it before him in the Vulgate. His own words deserve to be cited. Except for the parables, he said, 'all the rest has the sense that appears on the surface, nor is one thing said and another meant, but the very thing is meant which is said, and the sense is wholly literal'.[2] This was a revolution in the interpretation of the New Testament—and that on the crucial ground (on which Luther afterwards trod) of the interpretation of the Pauline Epistles. It was a revolution—differing essentially from that inaugurated by the Italian Renaissance, even if it had some of its roots in Italy—which was calculated to lead to the restoration of theology. It was a revolution with which Erasmus was brought into contact when he visited Oxford in 1499.

Erasmus, who was Colet's senior by a year or so, had been brought to England by a pupil whom he had just been teaching in Paris, William Blount, the fourth Baron Mountjoy. In London he met Thomas More, a young Oxford man of the age of twenty-one, who was now a law student at Lincoln's Inn, but occupied more with thoughts of religion and the study of Greek (William Lily and Grocyn, now both settled in London, were his teachers) than he was with the study of law. But it was his meeting with Colet, during a visit to Oxford, which influenced Erasmus most deeply, helping to determine the course of his life and, with it,

---

[1] See above, p. 68.
[2] Quoted in Professor Chambers's *Thomas More*, p. 80.

the trend of Renaissance scholarship. Colet and he talked together at Oxford, and Colet would have had him stay there to lecture, possibly on the Old Testament. Erasmus was not prepared to do so—it may be because he knew, in the depth of his mind, that he had not yet a sufficient grounding, and that he must first master Greek. But he saw and understood enough of Colet, and of what Colet was attempting, to be influenced permanently by what he saw. Colet, and the friends whom he inspired, were moving towards the recovery of an authentically interpreted Bible and a return to the teachings of the early Fathers. What would lie beyond that, they had not seen or calculated; and perhaps that is also true of Erasmus. What was already involved in it, and entailed by it, was something which Colet's circle had also failed to see, or, at any rate, seen imperfectly: but that is *not* true of Erasmus. He knew that a return to the teachings of the early Fathers meant the editing and the printing of good texts of their works. He knew that the recovery of an authentically interpreted Bible necessarily meant, for a start, the editing and the printing of as good a text as possible of the original Greek New Testament. Perhaps it was some faint inkling of this knowledge which made him decline the suggestion of Colet, that he should settle in Oxford by his side. In any case his subsequent life is sufficient testimony to his sense of the spade-work which had to be done before the restoration of theology could become an accomplished fact.

But it still remains true that the meeting of Erasmus with Colet helped to determine the course of his life and the trend of Renaissance scholarship. The friendship which grew from that meeting, one of his biographers has said, 'definitely decided the bent of Erasmus's many-sided mind'.[1] For the time being Erasmus left England, and he did not return for five years, nor indeed—for any length of stay—till his visit of 1511–14, when he lectured on Greek at Cambridge. Meanwhile, the Oxford circle had become a circle in London. More had always been there since he left Oxford (at the early age of fifteen) in 1493. Lily had settled there about 1500, and was instructing More in Greek and joining with him in trans-

[1] Huizinga, quoted by Professor Chambers, op. cit. p. 72.

lating poems from the Greek Anthology into Latin. Linacre of All Souls College, far more interested in using Greek for the promotion of science than for the restoration of theology, had also settled in London by the turn of the century, and was lecturing on the *Meteorologica* of Aristotle. Grocyn of New College had come to London, as vicar of a parish near the Guildhall, about 1499, and was lecturing at St Paul's on the Neo-Platonist *Celestial Hierarchies* of the so-called Dionysius the Areopagite, arguing—in defiance of the Middle Ages—that the author was *not* the Dionysius the Areopagite of the Acts of the Apostles. Above all, Colet himself came to London in 1504, as Dean of St Paul's, and inheriting his father's fortune in 1505 he already commanded the wealth which afterwards enabled him to found St Paul's School and to make his friend Lily its High Master. This Oxford circle settled in London—Colet, Grocyn, More, Lily, and Linacre; all of them (except More) in Orders; all of them (except Linacre) concerned for the restoration of theology; all of them (except Colet) eager students of Greek—was the background of the life of Erasmus during the first twenty years of the sixteenth century. Its influence lasted till the death of Colet and Grocyn in 1519. By that time More had already been caught into politics: Lily and Linacre died soon afterwards, the one in 1522 and the other in 1524; and the end had come.

But before it came, Erasmus had already achieved, or rather begun to achieve, that reconciliation between revolution and restoration—between the revolution of the Italian Renaissance and the restoration of the old faith—of which we have already spoken. He had seized on the element which, as we have also noticed, made that reconciliation possible—the element of a pure and disinterested scholarship; and he had used it to serve Colet's aim of the restoration of theology. Perfecting himself in Greek, as far as was possible in that age, he completed in Cambridge his collation of the Greek text of the New Testament, and published it at Basle in 1516. It was an imperfect text, but it was at once convenient and cheap;[1]

---

[1] Erasmus worked quickly in order to anticipate the appearance of the Greek text in Cardinal Ximenes's Complutensian Polyglot, which had already been

and it ran through Europe. It gave to men, as he wrote in his preface, 'the living image of that holy mind': it restored to them the *philosophia Christi*. Greek was the key which unlocked the door—'the key', as Professor Chambers has said, 'of the new religious teaching'; and with this key Erasmus had opened the door to which Colet's lectures at Oxford, nearly twenty years before, had already pointed—the door which opened to show what the New Testament really said and meant.[1] To the service thus rendered by his publication of the Greek text of the New Testament Erasmus added another. He made a new Latin translation; and he also wrote Latin paraphrases of all the books of the New Testament (except the Book of Revelation) in order to present their meaning to his contemporaries in the current language of their own day.

Besides his work on the New Testament Erasmus laboured also, and even more arduously, on the early Fathers. This was the other part of the restoration of theology—to recover the teachings of the early Fathers as well as the authentic text of the Bible. Accordingly he published editions of a number of the Latin Fathers, and made translations from the writings of some of the Greek. Among the Latin Fathers he edited the works of St Jerome, St Hilary, and St Augustine; among the Greeks he worked on Irenaeus, Origen,

---

printed by 1514 but, in the event, was not published (outside Spain) till 1522. He consulted few manuscripts; and his work had inevitable defects. But it *was* a Greek text of the New Testament, and one which all scholars could buy and read.

[1] Rabelais, in c. 54 of his *Gargantua*, records a verse of the inscription set upon the great gate of the Abbey of Theleme which may be used to indicate, in a parable, the nature of the work which Erasmus had done and the door which he had opened:

'Cy entrez, vous, qui le sainct Evangile	La parolle Saincte
En sens agile annoncez, quoy qu'on gronde:	Ia ne soit exteincte
Ceans aurez ung refuge et bastille	En ce lieu tressainct.
Contre l'hostile erreur, qui tant postille	Chascun en soit ceinct:
Par son faulx style empoissonner le munde.	Chascune ait enceinte
Entrez, qu'on fonde icy la foy profunde;	La parolle saincte.'
Puys, qu'on confonde, et par voix et par rolle,	
Les ennemys de la saincte parolle.	

and Chrysostom.[1] To understand the magnitude of the service which he rendered by his work on the early Fathers we must bear three things in mind. The first is that the manuscripts (and the early printed editions) of the writings of some of the Latin Fathers, such as St Jerome and St Hilary, were in a chaotic state—with corruptions, interpolations, and sometimes gaps. Erasmus might justly claim that he had found a jungle and cleared a track. The second thing is that the depth of the thought of the Greek Fathers, and especially of Origen, had been hitherto unrecognised, and almost, indeed, unknown. Erasmus might justly claim to have brought Origen into the light. The third thing—and the most important—is that the writings of the schoolmen of the Middle Ages had hitherto overlain the writings of the Fathers. Here Erasmus might fairly claim that he had attained, and made it possible for others to attain, a juster perspective. He made this claim in the prefatory letter to his edition of St Hilary, and he made it modestly. 'What would sacred learning be without the labours of Origen, Tertullian, Chrysostom, Jerome, Hilary and Augustine?...I do not hold that even the works of Thomas Aquinas or Scotus should be entirely set aside. They wrote for their age; and delivered to us much that they drew from the writings of the ancients and expounded most acutely....On the other hand, I cannot approve the churlishness of those who set so much store by authors of this class, that they think it necessary to protest against the providential revival of good literature.' A friend and contemporary of Erasmus made the claim more boldly. 'He saw that more than enough was made of scholastic theology, and that the ancient learning was set at nought....We begin, God be thanked, to see the fruit of his labours. Instead of Hales and Holcot, the pages of Cyprian, Augustine, Ambrose, and Jerome are studied by our divines in their due season.'[2]

[1] The edition of St Jerome appeared in 1516; that of St Hilary in 1522; that of St Augustine in 1529. The work of Erasmus on Origen was published in the last year of his life (1536).

[2] The two passages are quoted by Dr M. R. James in the *Cambridge Modern History*, Vol. I, pp. 607–8. The friend and contemporary of Erasmus was Beatus Rhenanus, a German humanist from Reinach, who edited his works after his

Such was the constructive service rendered by Erasmus to the restoration of theology; and such was the way in which, by a scholarly recovery of the great tradition of the past, he sought to promote the discovery of a true *philosophia Christi*. There was, it is true, another side to his nature, which made him a destructive critic as well as a constructive scholar. The master of a satiric wit, he was 'the Voltaire of the Renaissance', moved by a puckish spirit to laugh and lash at the follies, the superstitions, and the 'crass Judaism', which he detected in the Church of his day. It was not in vain that he was a student of the satirical Lucian; and we may even say that the Greek within him had something of a sceptical touch, tending to undermine the beliefs which another side of his mind was engaged in underpinning. But it was the constructive work which he did that won him the regard, the admiration, and even the idolatry of contemporary scholars. He was, in their view, 'a man by himself'; and Melanchthon addressed a poem *in Erasmum optimum maximum*. Here, expressed in his person, was an intellectual reformation, proceeding by the way of scholarship and peace to a new age of faith. Just as science and medicine were to be renewed by a return to the Greek, so too was theology. Just as the philosophy of Aristotle was to be purged from the accretions of the medieval Averroists by the recovery of his original text, so was the philosophy of Christ to be purged from scholastic accretions by the recovery of the Greek New Testament. It was all a matter of the mind and of its peaceable turning to the light; all a matter of the word, and beyond any need of the sword. As late as 1522 Erasmus could end his prefatory letter to his edition of St Hilary with the words: *Absit ubique rabiosa contentio, pacis et concordiae pestis; nec absint a studiis Gratiae, quas Musarum comites non temere finxit antiquitas.*[1] Was his prayer

death (1540–6). 'Hales' is Alexander of Hales, lecturer to the Franciscan order in Paris in the thirteenth century, who wrote a *Summa Theologiae*; 'Holcot' is Robert of Holcot, an Oxford Dominican and biblical commentator of the fourteenth century.

[1] The words 'rabiosa contentio' set one thinking. Erasmus—a Netherlands scholar, but adopted with acclaim in Germany as a 'German'—was beginning to feel the fire of German controversy. F. von Bezold, in his *Geschichte der*

(a prayer from the depth of a scholarly mind which, though it could be provocative, was naturally apprehensive and timorous) destined to be granted? And would 'dear Quiet' and the Graces attend the coming Reformation?

Certainly down to 1519 (the year, as has already been noted, of the passing of that London circle of friends from whom Erasmus had drawn so much—and also the crucial year of Luther's disputation with Eck at Leipzig, which set the scene for a new protagonist and a different plot) there seemed to be room for quiet and the Graces. It would almost seem as if before revolutions there was the autumn calm of a St Luke's summer. There was a charm of life in the years before the French Revolution; and Jeremy Bentham, in 1776, could celebrate, in the first words of the preface to his first book, 'an age in which knowledge is rapidly advancing towards perfection'. There was a similar charm, and a similar sense of advance, in the years before the Reformation. Erasmus himself, in 1517, was stirred by a sense of the dawn of a new era of peace—peace among states, and an end of the barbarity of war, with the Medici Pope Leo X as *auspex et dux*: peace in the Church, and a *renovatio fidei*, with the same auspices and under the same leadership. It was a dream. There were to be wars between states, bloodier than before: there were to be religious wars, and persecutions, in many of the states of Europe—fires at Smithfield, a Schmalkaldic War in Germany, wars of religion in France. No new theology would float quietly into harbour on a sea of peace and concord. No intellectual movement could bring to birth the great historic change of the Reformation,

> the bitter change
> Of fierce extremes, extremes by change more fierce.

There were great and turbulent forces which would take a hand; and they were forces with which Erasmus and his friends had

deutschen Reformation, remarks that 'the stormy nature of the enthusiasm' of his German admirers, and 'a pugnacity uncongenial with his own nature', may have made him uncomfortable even before 1522, and as early as 1517—the date of the Reuchlin controversy (p. 240). He also notes (p. 241) that Erasmus could not but feel 'the unruly bias of the *ingenium Germanicum*...'. His own genius shrank before *Sturm und Drang*.

hardly reckoned. There was the people, with its hatred of pastors who, in its view, fleeced instead of feeding the flock they ought to have tended. There was also 'the State', with its jealousy for a clerical organisation which, in its view, sought to rule by its side and to divide with it jurisdiction and income. When Luther came, he spoke to the people, and he remembered the State and its princes. Nor did he fear tumult: he rather courted it: the 'word' was to him a sword, and not an *eirenicon*. He therefore entered into war with the Papacy, believing that the Pope could not lead, and on the contrary was bound to oppose, a reform of the Church which went to the roots of the matter and enlisted people and prince on its side. These roots were finance and organisation as well as articles of belief—finance that both pinched the pocket of the people and contracted the purse of the prince: organisation that irked not only the prince, who felt its rivalry, but also the people, who felt and resented its control. To cut at these roots was war with the Pope, the centre of Church finances and the head of the Church's organisation. That war is the Reformation.

III

We naturally make our categories—'Discovery', 'Renaissance', 'Reformation', and the like; and the categories we make are not only natural, but also necessary, instruments for any understanding of the reality of history. We divide in order to conquer, and analyse in order to comprehend. But our categories and divisions are simply our own mental conceptions: they are abstractions, and not entities; and if they are tools for the understanding of reality, they are not reality itself. The reality of the historical process is an undivided and interpenetrated unity, in which Discovery runs into Renaissance, Renaissance into Reformation, and all three into one another. The age was all the three (indeed, more than all the three), and it was all the three in one. The Renaissance is not one thing, and the Reformation another: they are simply two conceptions which we apply to a single thing. Still less can we say that the Renaissance was one period and the Reformation another, or turn our conceptual distinctions into distinctions of time. The Renaissance did not stop, and the Reformation then begin. *Both* had been there already, long before the end of the fifteenth century; *both* continued to be there in the course of the sixteenth— and later still. The Renaissance survived in the scholarship of the Reformation; it survived in the philosophy of the Cambridge Platonists of the seventeenth century; it survived in North's Plutarch, and Chapman's Homer, and Hobbes's Thucydides, and much besides. We may pass from treating of the Renaissance (or rather of one of its phases) to treat of the Reformation; but the Reformation to which we turn still carries with it the Renaissance we leave. Scholars still continued to live and think, and to offer their homage and contribution to the general movement of thought. The web of the Reformation is shot through by the thread of scholarship.

But we may none the less take the conception of 'Reformation' as a separate basis of inquiry—recognising that it is but a conception, or a tool by which we divide and analyse reality with a view to its understanding; and while we do so we may go even further, and seek to divide and analyse the conception itself in its turn. From this point of view we may say, as indeed it has just been said, that there are two aspects of the Reformation: aspects which may, at any rate in thought (though less in the actual process of life), be distinguished from one another. The first is the political aspect, which concerns the relation of Church and State, or prince and papacy. The second is the social aspect, which touches the people at large, and is mainly concerned with the relations of clergy and laity and the limits of clerical control over ordinary human life. But here again the mental distinctions we draw are distinctions within a historic process which was an undivided unity. The actions of princes and the strivings of the people were intertwined; and if they sometimes went different ways, they went in the same direction and towards the same general goal.

1. The political aspect of the Reformation consists in the attempt of the State (which, in the language of the sixteenth century, means the governing prince, who is in himself *lo stato*)

to diminish or even abolish the papal claim to the exercise of a *condominium*. The issue thus raised, in the total range of its sweep (indirect as well as direct), touched life at many points. It touched jurisdiction, or the sphere of the rights of the clerical courts, with their centre and apex in Rome. It touched taxation, or the rights of the Papacy to draw revenues parallel with those of the prince; and here, by extension, it came to touch the general rights of the clergy, and especially the regular clergy of the monasteries, to draw the revenues of their large endowments. It touched education, or the rights of the clergy to control (in virtue of their *potestas docendi*) the teaching of schools and Universities. It touched the issue of patronage, or the right of the pope to determine (in virtue of his power of 'providing' for the Church) who should be collated to bishoprics and other similar clerical preferments.[1] In place of this system of *condominium* princes generally desired to establish their own *dominium*; and in the countries of the Reformation they carried their desire to the length of making themselves *summi episcopi*, or of assuming the title of *supremum caput* or, at the very least, 'supreme governor'. It was an old quarrel of two rival organisations, the kingship and the priesthood—a quarrel almost as old as time, and certainly as old as the Jewish State of the time of the Maccabees. In the Testament of the Twelve Patriarchs, which may be dated somewhere about 100 B.C., the patriarch Judah is made to say: 'And now, my children, I command you, love Levi, that ye may abide.... For to me the Lord gave the kingdom, and to him the priesthood, and He set the kingdom beneath the priesthood. To me He gave the things upon the earth; to him the things in the heaven. As the heaven is higher than the earth, so is the priesthood of God higher than the earthly kingdom.'[2] Innocent III

---

[1] '"Providere ecclesiae de episcopo", or "providere ad ecclesiam de persona", simply implies the act of promotion, but most frequently involves the superseding of the rights of all other patrons except the pope.' Stubbs, *Constitutional History of England*, Vol. III, p. 320, n. 1.

[2] The Testament of Judah, XXI, §§ 2–3. The Testament of Naphthali (v, § 4) has another phrase which may well remind us of Gregory VII: 'Levi became as a sun,...and Judah was bright as the moon.' This is the theory of the two lights in the firmament of the church militant.

might be speaking here. The Judahs of the sixteenth century—the kings and princes of England, Germany and Scandinavia—were to speak with a different voice.

What was it that led them to do so? To answer that question we must go back to the medieval Catholic Church, as it had established itself in the course of the two centuries from Gregory VII to Boniface VIII (1073–1303). Led by the Papacy, and basing itself on the triple foundation of a sacramental system (which gave it the keys of salvation), a system of canon law and church courts, and a system of scholastic theology, the Church was concerned to realise on earth the reign of *justitia* or righteousness—the general and comprehensive righteousness which St Paul had preached and St Augustine had sought to elucidate in the *De Civitate Dei*. The dictates of this righteousness which the Church sought to establish were to be found in the *lex divina* of the Scriptures, and more especially in the *lex evangelica* of the New Testament. But there was also another *justitia*, with its dictates expressed in another form of law and enforced by an organisation other than the Church. This other justice was that of the State; and the State, standing by the side of the Church, if on a lower level, was concerned to realise the reign of this other justice, and to do so in the things which belonged to its own proper sphere. What, then, was this other justice? Immediately, and in the first resort, it was a justice expressed in the positive law, or *lex humana*, which was based on the will of the people (for *lex est quod populus jubet atque constituit*); but ultimately, and in the last resort, it was a justice expressed in the *lex naturalis* which inspired and controlled every *lex humana*, and which was based on the reason of man seeking to discover the rules laid down by the reason of God for the guidance of human affairs. What, next, was the sphere of the things which properly belonged to the state, when it was seeking to realise the reign of a positive or human law which duly conformed to the law of nature? It was, in the theory of St Thomas Aquinas, a fourfold sphere. In economic matters, the state was concerned with providing security and satisfaction of the physical needs of life (*securitas et sufficientia vitae*): in legal matters, it had the duty of establishing a scheme of judical order: in moral matters, it was obliged to punish such acts as excited moral indignation in the minds of the majority, or menaced the very existence of society; and finally, in matters of religion, it was bound to provide, for those of its members who sought perfection, the opportunity of exercising, in peace and quiet, the faculty of contemplating the truth.

If this was the sphere of the state, a consequence inevitably followed about the sphere of the Church. That sphere would include the general guidance and control of moral matters, other than those specifically remitted to the state: it would include the general guidance and control of all matters of religion, where the state had only the ancillary function of 'providing opportunity'. But that is a general and abstract statement. What was involved in fact, when men came down to particulars? What was the specific sphere of the operation of the *justitia* which the medieval Church sought to realise in obedience to the *lex divina*? In seeking to answer the question we must not forget the organised system of means—the administrative staff, the legal apparatus of courts, and the financial resources—which the Church had at its disposal. We must also remember the large scope of the *potestas* conceived as inhering in the clergy by virtue of their orders—not only the *potestas ordinis* proper, in matters concerning the sacraments (and among them the sacrament of penance), but also the *potestas juris-dictionis* and the *potestas docendi*. When we take these things into account, we shall not be surprised if we find that a general state-ment of the Church's right of guidance and control which was formally confined to moral and religious matters issued in effect, and in practice, in the Church's exercise of a similar right in matters other than moral and religious. Economics and law may readily be held to involve moral and religious issues: indeed, they may actually involve them. You may make compartments; but it does not follow that your compartments will be water-tight. There is little that an organised church, resolved and equipped to act as the guardian of morals and religion, cannot draw under those two heads. St Thomas might remit to the State the economic sphere of the provision of security and satisfaction of the physical needs of life. But in actual practice the medieval Church was also concerned with economics: not only did she deal with the problem of relief of the poor, as a matter of the virtue of charity; she also dealt with the problem of interest and the problem of price-levels, because, in her view, they both involved moral issues. St Thomas, again, might remit to the state the duty of establishing a scheme of judicial order. But the medieval Church was also concerned with the establishment of such a scheme—partly, and indeed perhaps largely, because the state was as yet inadequate to its duty, but partly also because she felt that morals and religion must *always* and at all times carry the clerical *potestas* into the domain of law. On the civil side of law, she handled matters of marriage and wills, as things connected with her own sacraments; on the criminal side, she might seek, as she did in the eleventh century, to institute and enforce her own *pax Dei* among the bellicose feudatories; indeed, she might even seek, as she did in the thirteenth century, to act as the guardian and agent of a system of international law among warring states, pleading that kings who broke their treaties were guilty of the sin of perjury, and that the pope might properly take cognisance of the issue *ratione peccati*. That the Church should also be the guardian and agent of all education was a natural and inevitable claim. Here morals and religion clearly entered: the *potestas docendi* was peculiarly inherent in the virtue of orders; the *studium* was bound to be a clerical corporation. There was really, in the last resort, no limit to the sphere of the justice of *lex divina*; and the higher the aspirations of the leaders of the Church, the wider and wider became the extension of that sphere.

In the height of the Middle Ages the Church may be said to be claiming two universalities. The first is a universality in point of width and extension. The Church seeks to range over the whole of the area and all the classes of one universal society, and to bring that one society and its classes under the unitary direction of the Papacy. The second is a universality in point of depth and intensity. The Church seeks to penetrate down and down into all the issues —economic, legal, and educational—which can be brought under the comprehensive rubric of the justice of the *lex divina*. But both of these universalities began to be challenged increasingly in the last two centuries of the Middle Ages (1300–1500). The claim to universality in point of width and extension was confronted more and more by the fact, and the growing consolidation, of organisations called *regna*. The *regnum* was a territory or region—it cannot yet be called a nation, though it contained the germ of the nation and the national state of the future—which was the home of an *ecclesia* of its own, related indeed (and closely related) to the *una sancta ecclesia Catholica*, but yet calling itself *ecclesia Anglicana*, or *ecclesia Gallicana*, in just the same way as the *regnum* called itself *regnum Anglicum* or *regnum Gallicum*. What was to be the future of these kingdoms and their churches, and of their relations to one another? An answer to that question begins to appear in the theories of the Roman lawyers of the fourteenth century, of whom Bartolus of Sassoferrato was the greatest. Their theories are of crucial importance: they laid the foundations of views and opinions which were to become explicit, and even triumphant, in the sixteenth century. One of their theories, or rather conceptions, can only be noticed in passing. They conceived a society as primarily a state, and only secondarily a church. This was a conception natural to lawyers; but it showed a shifting of the balance of interest, which was to go still further in the sixteenth century. But there was another theory of the Roman lawyers which concerns our argument more closely, and leads directly to what we have called the political aspect of the Reformation. The lawyers might inherit the imperial tradition of a universal Rome, and they might be nominal imperialists; but they were beginning, in actual fact, to direct their attention to the *regna*, to admit their independence, to recognise their sovereignty, and to confess that they might be called empires. 'The King', they say, 'in his kingdom, is emperor of his kingdom'—*rex in regno suo est imperator regni sui*.[1]

[1] See C. N. Woolf, *Bartolus of Sassoferrato*, especially pp. 368–94. Bartolus himself, he notes, had only vindicated an independent sovereignty for the *civitas*, or Italian city-state, which he regarded as *sibi princeps*. But the doctrine which he applied to the *civitas* could be, and was, extended to the *regnum*; and Woolf notes (p. 380) that this extension may already have been achieved by Oldradus, one of the masters of Bartolus, and that it certainly appears in the writings of

The lawyers of our own Richard II may well have been thinking of this dictum, when they caused the king to be styled 'entire emperor of his realm'. In any case the dictum could be pressed to a serious consequence. If it could be said that the king in his kingdom was emperor of his kingdom, might it not also be said that there was also a person in the Church of the kingdom who was the pontiff of that Church? And might not this pontiff, if that were so, be the prince of the kingdom, who would thus become the *summus episcopus* as well as the *imperator*, and thus be supreme in all causes, 'as well...spiritual or ecclesiastical...as temporal'?

Such was the challenge which might be made to the universality of the Church in point of width and extension. Such, too, was the challenge which was actually made in the course of the Reformation. But the other universality—the universality in point of depth and intensity—might also come to be challenged. The Church could only penetrate and pervade all the issues of life as long as two conditions continued to be satisfied. The first was that the state should continue to remain inadequate to the performance of its primary duties—the duty of providing *securitas et sufficientia vitae* and that of furnishing an effective scheme of judicial order. The second was that the minds of men should continue to hang so much on the sacramental power of the Church, and on her right of giving and withholding access to her sacraments, that they were ready to accept a general enforcement of righteousness as something which was altogether a necessity of salvation. Both of these conditions were beginning to fade in the course of the fifteenth century. The modern state was beginning to appear, and was shouldering its duties. Princes were beginning to concern themselves with the relief of the poor: they were beginning to promote and control the provision of education. More important still, the attitude of the minds of men to the sacramental power—the general feeling of the people towards a system of works of righteousness enforced by a system of clerical sanctions in the confessional and

Baldus, one of his pupils. Woolf adds that 'in making the Regnum...an Empire within its own boundaries, the lawyers not only made possible the "Reception", but, in general, made possible the modern State'.

the church court—was also beginning to alter. A new conception of the working of inward faith and the operation of individual conscience was struggling to be born. Not only, therefore, was the political aspect of the Reformation, which concerned the relation of Church and State, already evident. The social aspect also, which touched the people at large, and concerned the relations of clergy and laity and the general limits of clerical control over human life, was already beginning to appear.

The argument has thus brought us, at the end of our summary view of the political aspect of the Reformation, face to face with its wider or social aspect—if we may use the word 'social' as a brief designation for that mixture of motives, partly spiritual and partly economic, which swayed the general feelings of society. But before we turn to this social aspect, a final word remains to be said about the political. What was the attitude of the Renaissance and its scholars to the political side of the Reformation? Briefly, it may be replied, their attitude was seldom favourable to the claims of the secular power. At the best they hung in doubt, or a state of suspension of judgement: more generally they turned to criticism, or even swung into opposition. It is true that the moderate and malleable Melanchthon, a kinsman of Reuchlin, who had lectured on Homer and studied the plays of Aristophanes, could induce himself to believe that the will of the prince had the force of an ordinance of God. But More, preferring the *sacerdotium* to the *regnum*, preferred also the death of a martyr to acquiescence in the Act of Supremacy and its principle of the supreme headship of the king over the Church in England; and even Erasmus, if he was cast in a more timorous mould, remained a free scholar who was courted by princes even more than he courted them or proclaimed their power. Generally the Renaissance scholars, who were mainly clergy themselves, believed in the *sacerdotium*, even while they disliked its abuses; and true to the nature of scholars they were Platonists rather than *étatistes*, following the *Republic* rather than the *Prince*, and devoted more to the ideal of a philosophic pedantocracy than to any form of autocracy. Campanella in a later age (1568–1639) was still faithful to the general Platonism of the Renaissance when, in his *Civitas Solis*, he enthroned the Sun, or 'the Metaphysician', and set under him the three magistracies of Power, Love, and Wisdom, with the magistracy of Wisdom charged to promote the cause of education, science, and culture.

2. In its social or popular aspect—as it touched the people at large, and was engaged in the general play of social life and movement—the Reformation was a revolt of the subject laity against a dominant clergy, not only enthroned in the pulpit as preachers, but also standing at the altar as mediators of the covenant and sitting in the confessional to judge.[1] The clergy thus bore in their keeping 'two massy keys...of metals twain'. The golden key of their power was the sacrament of the altar: the iron key was the sacrament (as it had come in process of time to be counted) of penance in the confessional. The iron key must first unlock the door of iron, before the golden key could open the door of gold; and by it there was thus given to the clergy a potent means of discipline, which might not only be penal and purificatory, but could also be extended to monetary consequences, if the practice were admitted of a monetary commutation of the purificatory penalties of penance. In the strict logic of the Church, the action of the priest in the confessional was sacramental, and not jurisdictional. He might indeed be sitting in the manner of a judge; but the confessional was not a court, and jurisdiction belonged to courts. The Church, however, had also its system of courts, local as well as central, with a range of appeal which ended in Rome; and these courts, in their dealings with marriage and wills, covered a province of life in which a multitude of men were included. Nor was this the whole of their province. The Church courts also dealt with heresy and sorcery: they dealt with the exaction of ecclesiastical dues such as tithes and mortuaries; and they claimed a province in the correction of sins which included not only sexual offences, but also the offences of usury, of perjury, and of defamation.

[1] Troeltsch in *Die Soziallehren der christlichen Kirchen*, pp. 218–19, enumerates as the three powers of the clergy: (1) the *Lehrgewalt*, (2) the *Sakramentalgewalt*, and (3) the *Jurisdiktionsgewalt*.

The popular revolt was a general revolt; but it was more of a revolt, at any rate immediately, against the sacramental and jurisdictional powers of the clergy than against their teaching and doctrine. What was at issue, in the first instance, was the sacrament of penance, with its system of obligatory satisfactions and *opera injuncta*, and its connected system of monetary consequences which may be generally designated under the name of indulgences: it was the range and the sweep of the courts of the Church, with their large cognisance of men's daily lives, their fees, and their protracted procedure; it was also the extent of clerical endowments, and the problems of the rents and the general management of the large estates of the clergy. Much of this is what we should naturally call economic; and it would be foolish to deny that the pinch of the purse was combined with a resentment against clerical discipline and the 'regiment of priests' in the causes and origins of the Reformation. But there was also present from the first—and indeed it was even older than the Reformation of the sixteenth century—a simple and struggling piety: the piety of the Lollard 'backwoodsmen' of the Chiltern Hills and the Forest of Dean; the piety of those who conned the books of devotion—the *Garden of the Soul*, or the *Twenty-four Golden Harps*—which were circulated by the Brethren of the Common Life in the Low Countries during the fifteenth century; the piety of family worship, in the villages of Northern Germany, feeding (as the Lollards also fed) on fragments of the Bible in the vernacular and on tracts and hymns. There was, in a word, a spiritual longing for an apprehended Christianity in the heart; and, mixed as men are, this motive was mixed with the pinch of the purse and the general fires of anticlerical resentment. The doctrine of Luther, like the doctrine of Calvin, had its roots in processes of thought and feeling which had long been germinating in the minds of ordinary men and women. Justification by faith is not a mere formula or gloss of theology which served to cover and colour an economic revolt. It may have had roots which spread downwards in the soil of economics; but its taproot descended into the mother earth of genuine religious experience. Just as the territorial organisation of Protestant churches in the sixteenth century' continued and extended a movement of secular authority which had already expressed itself (in the management of poor relief, for example, or in the promotion of education) during the latter half of the fifteenth, so the doctrine of justification by faith also continued, and also extended, a movement of simple piety which was already growing in quiet:

> Ut flos in saeptis secretus nascitur hortis.

Even the revolt against the organised discipline and the financial claims of the Church of the Middle Ages was based, by its very nature, on spiritual motives and religious sentiment. It is true that a visible organised church, seeking to realise the *lex evangelica* as a system of actual and practical justice (expressed in penitentiaries and canon law, and enforced in confessionals and church courts), was a great and imposing structure of what may be called 'objective faith'. Its effort was a gallant effort to make Christian ideals effective in all the ranges of life and for every rank and class. Much good was actually done: an ideal of Christian marriage was upheld; the virtue of charity was encouraged, and made a system as well as a virtue; a rude age was imbued with manners and virtue, and polished by the liberal arts. But there were two results, or two concomitants, of all this structure of objective faith; and both of these results were bound to produce a spiritual reaction.

In the first place a structure of objective faith involved a large element of bureaucracy. The system had to be administered; and just as the 'social service state' of the twentieth century necessarily demands a large staff of administrators, so the 'general service Church' of the later Middle Ages required a great staff which extended from the curialists of the papal court to the summoners in the parishes. This administrative staff, trained—at any rate in its upper ranges—in the canon law and the papal decretals, was juristic in its outlook. There had been a succession of great lawyer popes in the height of the Middle Ages, from Alexander III, through Innocent III, Gregory IX, and Innocent IV, to Boniface VIII; and the imprint of law and of legal conceptions and methods, which had always tended to give shape and form to the very theology of the Church in the West,[1] was naturally set on the growing staff which served this succession. But a juristic bureaucracy was not only juristic, and not only concerned, by its very nature, with the turning of the *justitia* of the Gospels into an expressed and enforced *jus*; it was also expensive. The array of courts—with their staff, their procedure, their documents, and their range of appeal—was a matter of constant cost. There ensued—and we may trace it from the thirteenth century onwards, if not earlier still—the epoch of the financier Church, skilled in levying and managing the monies it needed for its general service. There is no need to record the papal demands on the clergy for the payment of clerical tenths, or for the allocation of benefices which could be used to reward the administrative staff. In any case they fell on the clergy only; and we have also to remember that—at any rate in England—their actual benefit was often diverted to the king and his barons.[2] More important is the general system of fees (though even here we have to remember that the income which it derived from fees was the great source of the payment of such 'civil service' of the State too as existed in England down to the nineteenth century); for fees fell, like rain, on the laity as well as the clergy, and if an archbishop paid a fee for his *pallium*, or a beneficiary appointed by papal provision paid the firstfruits of his benefice to Rome, the laity were also involved in the fees arising from matrimonial and testamentary cases and from the general range of clerical jurisdiction. Many of

[1] This was the argument of Sir Henry Maine, in his *Ancient Law*. 'The nature of Sin and its transmission by inheritance—the debt owed by man and its vicarious satisfaction...these were the points which the West began to debate as ardently as ever the East had discussed the articles of its more special creed.... The difference between the two theological systems is accounted for by the fact that, in passing from the East to the West, theological speculation had passed from a climate of Greek metaphysics to a climate of Roman Law' (op. cit. p. 357).

[2] It has been noted that 'when papal taxation was at its height, more than 90 per cent of the proceeds [of clerical tenths] were granted by the Pope to the Crown' (Professor Powicke, in *European Civilization*, Vol. IV, p. 364). It should also be noted that the papal allocation of benefices, *jure provisionis*, was used for the benefit of king and barons as well as to remunerate continental clergy engaged in the papal service.

the fees of the laity might go to the local clergy: little might find its way to Rome by way of the transmission of cases to the papal Curia; but the Curia stood in general reserve, and the Curia was the general pivot of the financier Church. To the ordinary layman, as we may learn from popular literature, the 'somners and apparitors' of the Church made it wear the guise of a financial institution, which sold a compulsory benefit of *justitia* at a price which irked the buyer. Justification at the bar of a great organised system seemed too expensive (yet how could the system ever have worked if the workers had not received their hire?); and instead of the fulfilment of the command of Isaiah, *Omnes sitientes, venite ad aquas, et qui non habetis argentum properate, emite et comedite; venite, emite absque argento et absque ulla commutatione*, it seemed that 'silver and commutation' ruled a world in which buying and selling were the methods of justification. It was in this way that a system of objective faith fostered, by way of reaction, the recovery of a subjective faith which was already growing in quiet, but was forced to the rapid growth of a gourd by the heat of economic resentment.

Besides bureaucracy and the financial system which bureaucracy entailed, another result, or another concomitant, of a structure of objective faith was a formalism which turned faith into works and the spirit into a sequence of acts. If you seek to enforce a *lex evangelica*, precept upon precept, line upon line, in a code of enjoined performances—if, not content with the saying that 'God is a spirit, and they that worship him must worship him in spirit and in truth', you make Him a set of rules—you are led into a general theory and practice of the achievement of salvation by works; and you may fall into a general externality of forms and performances. (From this point of view we may say the Reformation was more than a '*reformation*'; it was a 'renaissance' of life itself.) At the best you will have a cult of sacraments, beginning in a cult of the great sacrament of the altar as a miraculous act which issues in a miraculous result, and proceeding from that to a cult of the sacrament of penance and of the due performance of the *poenitentia injuncta*. At the worst you will practise what

Erasmus called a 'crass Judaism', which ossifies the spirit of religion in the dead bones of observances, and makes forms and ceremonies its Alpha and Omega. Prayer becomes a recitation of formulas: there were even founded, in the fifteenth century, societies for mutual insurance in procuring the benefits of such recitation, each member contributing his quota and all members enjoying the gain.[1] Charity, too, becomes a series of acts for the accumulation of merit, practised for the benefit of the giver rather than in the interest of the receiver; and here, too, in the fifteenth century, we may trace a process of investment in charity which multiplied indigence, and made one contemporary say that in Germany there were fourteen beggars for every workman. When a system of indulgences was added, which introduced—or at any rate encouraged in the popular mind[2]—the idea that *commutatio* in money could dispense men even from formal prayers and formal works, the materialisation of religious sentiment grew to its height. If it was a dubious doctrine to hold that the performance of external acts and the observance of prescribed forms was a sufficient Christian life, it was a still more dubious doctrine to hold, or even to imply, that the Christian life was a commodity which could be bought and sold in the market by way of the changing of money. This was once more, and in a worse form, the financier Church; and once more it might seem that justification at the bar of an organised system of *justitia* was all too expensive. It is true that this growth of materialism in the Catholic Church of the West was purified and largely abolished by the Counter-Reformation; but it is also true that this purification and abolition depended largely on the previous work of the Protestant Reformation. In any case a general revolution against the formalism (and the attendant financialism) of the Church of the fifteenth century had long been

---

[1] F. von Bezold, in his *Geschichte der deutschen Reformation* (pp. 98–100), gives details. A layman could join a Cologne society by an annual contribution of 11,000 Paternosters and Avemarias. It is recorded of one man that, to make assurance sure, he joined thirty-five societies. Bezold remarks on the analogy of the Buddhist prayer-wheel.

[2] On the difficult and disputed subject of indulgences, see Dr T. M. Lindsay, in the *Cambridge Modern History*, Vol. II, pp. 121–8.

in preparation; and if it was a mixed revolution—partly a movement of mere thrift, and partly an insurgence of the pure spirit— it was only like other revolutions since the beginning of history. The movement of thrift will explain some parts of the Reformation: it will *not* explain its heights, or its exaltations, or its martyrdoms. The insurgence of a spirit of inward faith—the revival of direct religious experience in the hearts and minds of the common people, a revival parallel to the restoration of theology which Erasmus and his fellows sought to achieve among scholars, but following a course at once far loftier and far more stormy—will alone explain the altitudes (and equally the aberrations and the abasements) of the religious revolution of the sixteenth century. Men could sing O *altitudo*; but there were also times for lamenting *Adhaesit pavimento*. Yet the great hymns of the Reformation—for great hymns go with great periods of religious revival, and they did so in the early days of Franciscanism (and later of Wesleyanism) as well as in the early days of the Reformation—are a sufficient proof of its exaltations.

3. The religious revolution of the sixteenth century began in Lutheranism: it culminated in Calvinism. To Lutheranism God was a spirit: true justification came by faith which could knit the spirit of man to the spirit of God; and every man so knit enjoyed the priesthood of the believer and 'the liberty of the Christian man'. This was the positive side; but Lutheranism had also its negative side. Strong in its sense of the sovereign need, and the sovereign efficacy, of an apprehended faith living in the mind of the believer, it saw less need for the outward manifestation, in visible and tangible works, of the faith of each individual believer; and equally it saw less need for the outward manifestation, in a visible and organised Church, of the common faith of all gathered believers. There was an inherent subjectivity in Lutheranism; and this was to prove its great danger. Far from being unspiritual, or immersed in the play of materialism, it was only too spiritual; and that defect made it the sport and the victim of forces with which it had not reckoned sufficiently. Its doctrine of the sufficiency of faith for the individual believer might lead to the antinomianism—

the rejection of any notion of an obligatory *lex*—which St Paul had rebuked in the Church of Corinth, but which recurred among some of the Anabaptists. Its doctrine of the sufficiency of common faith as the bond of a society of believers, and its consequent failure to build any adequate system of religious community, produced a dependence on the secular authority which was to affect the future of Germany for centuries. If true believers saw little need for the effort of organisation, there were princes who were ready, and more than ready, to make the effort; and the Lutheran Church in each region slid into the position of a ghostly dependent on a godly prince who could act the part of *summus episcopus*—thus becoming (in the phrase of Hobbes) 'as it were a kingdom of fairies, in the dark'.

It was otherwise with the doctrine of the Reformed Churches proper, or Calvinism. If there was an inherent subjectivity in Lutheranism, it has justly been said that 'there was an objectivity in the Reformed ideal' of Calvinism.[1] That objectivity was two-fold; and it showed itself in both of the spheres in which Luther had fallen into subjectivity. In the first place Calvin never forgot the notion of an obligatory *lex evangelica*. He had been a student of law in his youth, at Orleans and at Bourges; and his study of Stoicism, in the writings of Seneca, had shown him the power and the value of a rule of moral conduct. It became for him the problem of problems to ensure that the conversion of men to the *vera religio* should also be a *conversio morum* which bore fruit in their words and deeds; and the institution of a holy discipline, enforced by the action of the Consistory, was his answer to the problem. In the second place, Calvin never forgot the need of a visible and organised Church. Here he was fortunate in the place of his work

---

[1] Dr Fairbairn, in the *Cambridge Modern History*, Vol. II, p. 348. The reader will naturally observe that this objectivity of Calvinism brings it back, in some sense, to what has been called, in the course of this essay, the medieval structure of objective faith, and that thus (if Milton's words may be altered) presbyter is priest writ again. There *was* a return in Calvinism. But it was a return on a different and higher level—a return to works which were self-enjoined by a stern sense of duty, and to a clergy which sprang from and served a free community of all the elect.

and the conjuncture of the times. The city of Geneva was a civic republic, newly liberated from an uneasy dependence on its bishop and the Duke of Savoy, and newly pledged to live according to the holy Evangelical law and the Word of God. Confronted by no territorial prince, Calvin could build on the firm foundation of an organised people which was at once a people and a congregation; and on that foundation he firmly built the visible body of an organised Church, with all its ministers forming a 'venerable company' which met in quarterly Synods, and with selected ministers joined to annually elected elders in the Consistory of discipline.[1] It was in this way that Calvinism achieved its twofold objectivity. And just as Lutheranism was led towards subjectivity by emphasis on a cardinal doctrine of justification by inward faith, so we may say that Calvinism was impelled towards objectivity by the tenacity of a cardinal conviction of election to grace by God's sovereign will and predestination. The elect had to prove themselves by their fruits—their manners and acts—alike to themselves and to others; and so knowing themselves, and known also to others, they became a visible body of order and organisation. It has, indeed, been suggested that the discipline which Calvin instituted, and the organisation which he built, are greater and more original than his theology, and that his theology of Predestination is only a sterner version of the doctrine of St Augustine.[2] But the ultimate rock of Calvinism—and it is indeed a stern and hard rock—is the rock of Predestination. It became, it is true, a rock of offence and a stumbling-stone to many. But the confessions which clung to it firmly—and this is true of free churches such as the Congregationalists, as well as of the Presbyterian churches generally—were the confessions which also retained

---

[1] Calvinism was thus a democracy—if it was also a democracy largely tempered by aristocracy. We may almost say that the city of Geneva gave to Calvin the principle of democracy; that he, in turn, gave the principle to the Calvinistic churches; and that they in turn (not only directly, but also indirectly, through the Congregationalists and the Baptists whom they influenced) gave the principle to the political communities of Holland, Scotland, Puritan England, and the Puritan colonies of New England.

[2] Dr Fairbairn, op. cit. p. 364.

their faith and maintained their organisation;[1] and to abandon it was also to abandon the discipline of life and the cohesion of order which it supported. The rock was firm as well as hard; and if it was rock it yielded water when it was smitten.

IV

Such were the issues of the religious revolution; and such were the ultimate consequences of the social or popular revolt against the medieval system of objective faith and all its accretions. The consequences were mixed, as the revolt itself was mixed: they blended economic factors with spiritual, and worldliness with otherworldliness. But when full allowance has been made for the debris and silt of the Reformation, the fact remains that its great main current was a current of clear living waters. It had come from the pure and intact fountains of the original Church; it had sprung from the Gospels, and been fed by the teachings of St Paul and St Augustine. The human mind cannot abnegate the greatest of all its inheritances; and in great ages there are great returns and great recoveries. The Reformation, like the Renaissance, but on a far higher plane, was a great return and recovery. From this point of view we may conceive it as being itself a renaissance—a renaissance of a religious tradition continuous through the ages, but flowing with a new volume, 'brimming and bright and large', through the sixteenth century and on beyond through the first half of the next.

The Renaissance itself, in its own specific and peculiar sense—the sense of 'New Learning' and the Revival of Scholarship—became absorbed, at any rate in part, in the substance and course of the Reformation. Here we must pause to distinguish two phases in the history of the relations between the Reformation and the

---

[1] Bernard Manning, *Essays in Orthodox Dissent*, pp. 191–3, argues that it was not a misfortune, but a blessing, for the English Congregationalists of the eighteenth century that in an age 'when the solvent acids of rationalism were so potent...a hard bitter rind of tough Calvinism covered their faith'. It is notable that while the Congregationalists clung to Calvinism, and preserved their integrity, the *English* Presbyterians of the eighteenth century, abandoning the theology of Calvinism, became in the main Unitarians.

Renaissance.[1] The first phase, which has already been treated, may be called that of preparation—but of preparation which ended in a halt, and even a recoil. Renaissance scholars, such as Erasmus, had already denounced, before the explosion of the popular revolt, the Judaism and the formalism, the finance and the fees, against which the revolt was directed. Renaissance scholars, and especially Erasmus, had already preached, and attempted to achieve, the restoration of Christian thought and of *vera religio* which the men of the Reformation desired and for which they laboured in anguish. But then there had come the halt, and even, with some, the recoil. Erasmus halted, repelled by a fastidious aversion from clamour, and by a scholar's dislike of the *rabiosa contentio* of furious disputants. Thomas More recoiled, feeling it wrong to offer even the show of violence to a majestical Church which rested on 'all the Councils made these thousand years'. So the first phase came to an end, with the execution of More in 1535 and the death of Erasmus in 1536.

But a second phase succeeded. In the year in which Erasmus died Calvin published the first edition of the *Christianae Religionis Institutio*, and settled in Geneva. The Reformation began to run clear through the filter-bed of Calvinism; and a sound Renaissance scholarship was an integral part of that filter-bed. Calvin himself was a humanist. He had studied at Paris, Orleans and Bourges; he had a sound Latin scholarship, and was the master of a good Latinity; and he had made some progress in Greek. The first work which he published was a commentary on Seneca's *De Clementia*, in which (it has been noted) he cites twenty-two Greek authors as well as fifty-five Latin; and his knowledge of ancient history is shown by a passage in the later edition of the *Institutio* where he

---

[1] In England the Reformation itself was a double process, which went on till the middle of the seventeenth century, or even later. There was an Anglican Reformation which, beginning with Cranmer, was still at work in the days of Andrewes and Laud. There was also a Puritan Reformation which, beginning in the reign of Elizabeth, rose to its height in the days of the Protectorate. The 'double Reformation' in England, producing both Anglicanism and Nonconformity, has a unique character which has deeply affected the general development of England, political as well as religious.

goes back to the history of classical antiquity (the ephorate in Sparta and the tribunate at Rome) to justify the doctrine that there might be a right and duty of resistance resident in 'magistrates constituted for the defence of the people to bridle the excessive cupidity and licence of kings'.[1] He had studied Roman Law, as well as ancient history: he was deeply steeped in the general classical tradition;[2] and he had the scholar's genius of interpretation. Under his influence, or of its own motion, Calvinism became the home of the second phase of the Renaissance—the phase which followed, as the first phase had preceded, the coming of the Reformation. It has been said that 'all the creative minds of the Reformed Churches were children of the Renaissance'.[3] We may count among them the humanist Theodore Beza, Calvin's successor, who gave to the University of Cambridge in 1581 the Codex Bezae, an early uncial manuscript in Latin and Greek containing the greater part of the Gospels and the Acts, and who, like Erasmus, edited a Greek New Testament and published a Latin translation of it. We may also count the Calvinist members of the French family of Estienne (the Stephenses), especially Robert the first, to whom we owe the *textus receptus* of the New Testament (which passed through the Elzevir Press of the seventeenth century down through the centuries to our own day), and to whom we also owe the division of the chapters of the whole Bible into verses —not to mention his *Latinae Linguae Thesaurus*, which in its edition of 1543 became the parent of the Latin dictionaries still used by scholars.[4] The succession of the Genevese scholars who belong to

[1] *Institutio*, Book IV, c. XX, § 31.

[2] It has been said of him that 'he built his system on the solid rock of Graeco-Roman antiquity'.

[3] Dr Fairbairn, *C.M.H.* Vol. II, p. 348. The *Academy* of Geneva may be called a university; the *College* of Geneva served as a school which prepared students for the Academy (cf. *infra*, p. 136, n. 1). The study of the classics— a passion with Calvin himself, who according to tradition read the works of Cicero once a year—was the basis of both.

[4] The son of Robert Estienne—Henri the second of that name—who published his books at Geneva (as Robert the first had done after his settlement in the city in 1551) is also worthy of remembrance in the history of scholarship. The edition of Plato which he published in 1578 (marked with the letters A TO E

the second phase of the Renaissance includes also Isaac Casaubon, who was born, studied Greek, and ultimately became professor of Greek, in Calvin's city, where he also married his second wife, the daughter of Henri Estienne (the second) the Genevese printer and publisher. Indeed, in the person of Casaubon, and in his marriage to Estienne's daughter, we may almost trace a microcosm of the scholarly activity of Geneva in the latter half of the sixteenth century—with its Academy training scholars and ministers in the general field of all learning, and its press pouring books (theological, classical, and general) into France and the whole of the Protestant West.

A classic and a theologian—editor of Athenaeus and Polybius and other Greek (and Latin) authors, and author himself of a treatise *De Libertate Ecclesiastica* and of *Exercitationes* in reply to the Catholic *Annales* of the Counter-Reformation scholar and cardinal Caesar Baronius—Casaubon[1] eventually, in the last years of his life (1610–14), became a prebendary of Canterbury and received a pension from King James I. Here the scholarship of Calvinism touches and blends with that of Anglicanism. In England too, as well as in Switzerland and Holland, we may speak of a second phase of the Renaissance, succeeding (as the first had preceded) the

down the side of each page) is still the source of the scholar's references to passages in the Platonic dialogues; and he published in 1572 a Greek *Thesaurus* which was even more exhaustive than the Latin *Thesaurus* of his father. A full account of the Stephenses is given in Vol. 1 of Mark Pattison's *Essays*, which also contains an essay on Joseph Scaliger and part of a life of that scholar.

Scaliger (Joseph de l'Escale, who claimed to belong to the Della Scala of Verona) must also be reckoned among the great scholars—and was perhaps indeed the greatest of all the scholars—of the second phase of the Renaissance. His troubled life was spent among the French Huguenots and, in its last phase (1593–1609), in the University of Leyden. He was the great glory of the Protestant scholarship of his time—a notable textual critic, a master of classical metres, and the first creator of a system of the chronology of antiquity. He spent two years at Geneva (1572–4) and taught in its Academy; but his Gascon temperament found the atmosphere of Geneva oppressive, and the pride of the descendant of Italian princes was offended by the narrow life of the *pédant* and the *caquetage de la chaire*.

[1] Mark Pattison's *Life of Casaubon* gives a full and fascinating account of his studies and wanderings.

coming of the Reformation. It was, indeed, less notable than the Calvinistic phase in Geneva. The scholarship of Anglican England, from the accession of Queen Elizabeth to the beginning of the Civil Wars, was mainly patristic or antiquarian, and ran little towards the study of the general classical tradition. But we may justly celebrate in its field the scholarship of Matthew Parker (of Corpus Christi College, Cambridge), who served sacred learning by his work on the Bishops' Bible, as he also served secular learning by his work on the early English chroniclers: we may celebrate the erudition and the judgement of Richard Hooker (of Corpus Christi College, Oxford), who based the ecclesiastical polity of Anglicanism on a broad and just foundation: we may celebrate the deep piety and the profound patristic scholarship of Lancelot Andrewes (of Pembroke College, Cambridge), of whom Isaac Casaubon wrote: 'Would that our Gallican theologians would imitate the bishop of Ely...they would reap a most plentiful reward for their moderation.' But we must also confess that Scaliger, who visited England in 1566, as Erasmus had visited it in earlier and brighter days, found little or nothing in England of what Erasmus had found; and nearly forty years later, in 1603, he warned Casaubon against 'the inhuman disposition' of the English. Yet Scaliger himself cherished a regard for some of the English scholars of his day: he had some correspondence with William Camden, the author of *Britannia*; and he had a deep admiration for John Rainolds (or Reynolds), the President of Corpus Christi College, Oxford, who lectured on Aristotle at Oxford and afterwards played a large part in the translation of the Prophets for the Authorised Version.

The Authorised Version of the Bible, achieved between 1607 and 1611 by the co-operation of some fifty scholars arranged in six different 'companies', is the greatest testimony to the grace of learning which resided in England during the second phase of the Renaissance. There were many translators and translations in England between 1568 and 1640—the age of North's Plutarch and Chapman's Homer—but this translation is incomparably the greatest, and the greatest on every count. The English Bible of

1611 is the ultimate consummation—at the long last, and after more than a century of perturbations—of the train of events which began when Erasmus met Colet at Oxford in 1499, and which moved further forward as he worked in Cambridge on the preparation of his Greek New Testament from 1513 onwards. The genius of Oxford and the genius of Cambridge—Rainolds from Oxford and Andrewes from Cambridge (to take two names only from among so many)—collaborated in the achievement; and their collaboration produced a national monument of literature as well as a work (at any rate for its day) of consummate scholarship. In Cambridge the spirit of the second Renaissance—the Renaissance which followed the Reformation—continued to flourish. The Cambridge Platonists have already been mentioned; but they must be mentioned here once more.[1] They had all been bred (except Henry More of Christ's) at Emmanuel College, Cambridge; they were all in Anglican Orders; and they gave to Anglicanism a philosophy which they largely drew (as Marsilio Ficino and Pico della Mirandola had drawn before them) from the treasures of Plato. Whichcote was the founder of the school: Henry More was its poet and mystic: Cudworth was perhaps its profoundest philosopher. Whichcote, according to Bishop Burnet, taught men 'to consider religion as a seed of a deiform nature'; and More and Cudworth carried his teaching into their speculations and their writings. They both knew the new physical philosophy of the seventeenth century, and they both corresponded with Descartes. Cudworth opposed the extension of Cartesianism to explain the action of living organisms, and in his *True Intellectual System of the Universe* he expounded the theory of a universal 'plastic nature' through which God controlled the movement of things. He also challenged the materialism of Hobbes, in his *Treatise concerning Eternal and Immutable Morality*; and here he vindicated, as Plato had done in challenging the Sophists, the claims of a morality founded on the nature of God and man. Tenison and Tillotson were his disciples; and we may justly say

[1] See above, p. 30; and on the Cambridge Platonists generally see Dr Inge, *The Platonic Tradition in English Religious Thought*, pp. 47–65.

of him, and of the members of his school, that in an age of mechanism and materialism they invoked the aid of Platonic thought to defend the spirit and faith of their Church.[1]

So the Reformation ran its course, fed from different watersheds, and drawing many tributary waters into its general stream. Princes of States made *their* contribution, in matters of finance and government. Peoples too played their part (and it was a great and dynamic part) in a surging revolt against the old order and a tentative movement—largely unconscious, but none the less deep and sincere—towards a new *via salutis*. But the scholars had also their part to play, and their own contribution to make; and they made it from first to last. They had been there as Heralds, in a bright and early dawn, which soon became overcast; and when the clouds had burst, and the rains had fallen, they were still there as Interpreters—thinking, explaining, and justifying. It was still their function to achieve that restoration of theology to which Colet and Erasmus had aspired. They had to think through, and to think together, the general movement which had stirred men's minds. They had to explain its significance in the light of the general tradition of Christian and classical thought. They had to guide the minds of men towards a future which should not be utterly divorced from the past—recovering for them the truth of the past, and gearing the trends of present movement into that abiding truth. This was the function, and the achievement, of the second phase of the Renaissance—particularly, perhaps, as it showed

[1] In the Catholic Church of the Counter-Reformation the influence of the Renaissance generally perished. The new scholasticism of the Dominicans and Jesuits made, however, some efforts to use the New Learning in order to defend and buttress the traditions and claims of Rome. We may cite the *Annales* of Baronius, and the work of the Vatican Library and its printing office under Sixtus V and his successors—work which issued in the publication of the Septuagint and of a revised text of the Vulgate, as well as in editions of the Fathers. But the Inquisition and the Index frowned on any further development of the free spirit of learning; and it is significant that Muretus, a French scholar who held a chair in the University of Rome from 1572 onwards, 'was forbidden to lecture on Plato's *Republic*, and with difficulty obtained leave to expound Tacitus' (Mark Pattison, *Essays*, Vol. I, p. 131).

itself in the scholars of Calvinism, but also as it showed itself in the scholars of the Church of England. There is, it is true, a latent wisdom in the mental movement of the mass which may transcend the conscious wisdom of scholars. 'The species is wise, and when time is given to it, as a species it almost always acts right.' But the scholar's function of interpretation is a necessary complement to the latent wisdom of any great movement of the general mind. He not only interprets the movement to itself: he also brings it into connection with the general system and capital of wisdom—the general inheritance of revelation and reason—of which he is, by his nature, the student and the custodian. Thus Calvin and the scholars of Calvinism linked the movement of the Reformed Churches first with the thought of St Paul and St Augustine, and then with the general thought of Graeco-Roman antiquity. Thus, again, the scholars of Anglicanism linked the movement of the English Reformation not only with the splendours of the Authorised Version and the learning and tradition of the Fathers, but also with the philosophy of Plato and the thought of ancient Greece. The restored theology of the Reformation was also a restoration and renaissance of true learning. The Renaissance did not end when the Reformation began. It only began again, and changed from the Herald to the Interpreter.

It was a stirring age, which wrote a great chapter in the history of man's traditions of civility. It began with the discovery of a new world and the simultaneous recovery of the old world of classical antiquity. It began when men were at once hearing the roll and thunder of Homer for the first time, and staring for the first time at the Pacific: when Greek scholarship was like a strong wine of delight, and men were filled with a heady sense of bursting all the known bounds of space. It moved on to wrestle with angels, and with problems of faith, grace, election, 'free will, foreknowledge absolute'. Carrying with it at once the spirit of discovery and that of recovery, it married the Reformation to which it had moved with the Renaissance from which it had come; and it did so by struggling to solve the problems of the present with the aid of the recovered wisdom of the past. In its course it reformed education as well as religious life. In its course it also produced a glorious flower of lyric and drama; a luxuriant crop of genial satire and meditative reflection (Rabelais and Cervantes, Montaigne and Bacon); the marvels of an architecture crossed with the antique, and the kindred marvels of schools of painting which similarly crossed medieval themes and motives with the ideas of classical humanism. Indeed the whole age was an age of cross-fertilisation. It was an age in which the whole of antiquity, acting freshly and in its first splendour, brought its contrast and its suggestion to act on, and to be acted on by, the whole of the present. For the recovered antiquity was not only classical antiquity; it was also Christian antiquity. It was St Paul and St Augustine, as well as Homer and Plato; it was the actual *philosophia Christiana*, and the actual Greek of the New Testament, as well as the actual philosophy of Plato and the actual Greek of the *editio princeps* of his Dialogues. The Renaissance and the Reformation, acting together and linked together, are both examples—or rather they are a single interconnected example— of that cross-fertilisation which is always the potent cause of new ideas and fresh aspirations.

If only we might pass, in our own age, through such a sweeping resurgence! But we have not that ignorance of the antique which made the ancient world a consuming fascination, and a transforming power, for the men of the sixteenth century. We know too much to be so much moved as the men of the Renaissance and the Reformation were. Their very defect was their strength. Because they knew so little of the past, they were deeply and utterly moved by its novelty. That was the source of their passion, and of the achievement to which it led; and that is why their age is, and must always remain, unique. A vivid, coloured age; an age of contrast and clash, but also an age—the greatest age—of crossing and cross-fertilisation; the age from which we are sprung, and to which we must always return to understand what we are.

V

THE EDUCATION OF THE ENGLISH GENTLEMAN IN THE SIXTEENTH CENTURY

I

There is a suggestive passage on the 'Idea of the Gentleman' in a work on England which was published in 1922 by Wilhelm Dibelius, Professor of English in the University of Berlin. Like many continental writers, but perhaps with a peculiar penetration and a touch of acid piquancy, he seizes on the idea of the gentleman as something specially English in all the course of its manifestation from the age of the medieval knight to the age of the public schoolboy of the reign of Queen Victoria. 'Among the things every Englishman is proud of', he remarks, 'is the fact that the idea of the gentleman is peculiar to England.' He proceeds to add that 'it *is* a fact';[1] and on the basis of this supposed fact he then proceeds, in turn, to a criticism of the idea. His criticisms have some justice; and in any case they are pardonable—if we take them, as they are intended, for criticisms of English national ideals —in a German scholar who was writing under the influence, and during the aftermath, of the defeat of Germany in the War of 1914–18. What is far more dubious, and indeed untenable, is the assumption of Dibelius that the idea of the gentleman is peculiar to England. It is a general European ideal. Its original fountain (as indeed Dibelius himself remarks, in an earlier passage of his argument) is to be found in the chivalry of the Middle Ages; and that chivalry, far from being peculiarly English, attained its zenith in France. Its more immediate source (as again Dibelius himself remarks in an earlier passage) is to be found in the Renaissance of the late fifteenth and the early sixteenth centuries; and the home of this Renaissance was Italy. It was Italy—or at any rate Italy primarily, and next to her Spain and France—which provided the English of the sixteenth century with their idea of the proper manners and

[1] *England*, by Wilhelm Dibelius, English translation (1930), p. 165.

training of a gentleman. The idea of the gentleman is a phase and a form of the development of European culture. The English were connected with that development; but they perhaps drew from Europe more than they gave. If they have kept what they drew with something of a continuous fidelity, and if they have cherished the lessons they learned for century on century, that is only a part of the general continuity of their national life. They have been faithful to their borrowings, as well as to their native products.

The theme of our argument here is the training of the gentleman, as it came to be conceived in England during the sixteenth century; the general process of his education; the virtues of body, mind and conduct to which that process was directed. But it is necessary first to study the sense which the word 'gentleman' had come to acquire by the sixteenth century. Who was the gentleman, and how was he to be defined? Even before the sixteenth century men were already clear that the word was a parti-coloured word which had gone, as it were, through successive strata of human experience and acquired a succession of associations. The first stratum was simple enough. Gentleman had originally meant the man of birth, good birth, gentle birth—the *generosus generosi filius.* The English gentleman, like the French *gentilhomme* and the Italian *gentiluomo,* has that original basis. But a second stratum soon came to be added; and the word 'gentleman' acquired the connotation not only of gentle birth or blood, but also of the spiritual qualities, both intellectual and moral, which befitted the gentle nature. This further connotation is already apparent in Chaucer by the end of the fourteenth century. In *The Romaunt of the Rose*[1] Love is made to say that it is not his 'entendement'

[1] Lines 2189–97 of Fragment 13 in Skeat's edition. Perhaps it may not be inapposite to add that, even before the time of Chaucer, the word 'gentleman' could already be extended, by that natural process of euphemism which is common to most languages, to denote the simple fact of a man. The Kentish *Ayenbite of Inwit* (quoted in the *New English Dictionary,* s.v. 'gentleman') speaks in 1340 of 'a rich gentleman y-robbed of thieves...'. But words go up, as they also come down. Chivalry starts from the Latin *caballus,* which to Horace meant an inferior riding horse or a pack-horse; and barons and baronage perhaps begin with the Latin *baro,* which to Cicero meant a simpleton, blockhead, or dunce.

To clepe no wight in no ages
Only gentle for his linages.
But whoso [that] is vertuous,
And in his port nought outrageous...
Though he be not gentil born...
...he is gentil, because he doth
As longeth to a gentilman.

In this passage Chaucer may even be said to have done more than add a second stratum. He has gone still further, and carried the word 'gentleman' forward into a third stage of meaning. Not content with holding that a gentleman must have his spiritual qualities as well as his gentle birth, he makes Love proclaim that gentle is who gentle doth *whether or no he be gentle born*. Gentleman means the qualities of 'gentilesse', even in the absence of gentle birth. This, of course, is a radical doctrine, which plunges its disciples into deep waters. Can a gentleman really be a gentleman if he is not gentle born? The question, as we shall see, agitated Tudor writers—among them Sir Thomas Elyot. It was, indeed, a troublesome question, in whichever way it was answered. If your answer were in the negative, you seemed to desert the side of the angels, and to sin with Lucifer. If your answer were in the affirmative, you might be held to be a rebel against the general idea of a graded and hierarchical society, with its 'degrees' hereditarily—and therefore naturally—fixed, which was commonly held by most Englishmen (and amongst them Shakespeare) long after Chaucer's time. But troublesome as the question might be, it was steadily there from the fourteenth century onwards. It had not only been raised by Chaucer: it had also been asked, in a rude form, by the rebels of 1381, and even earlier, and in a still ruder form, by the peasants of the French Jacquerie about 1356.[1]

[1] The couplet which John Ball took as the text of a sermon is famous:
'When Adam delved, and Eve span,
Who was then the gentleman?'
The peasants of the Jacquerie proclaimed the idea:
'Nus n'est vilains, s'il ne vilaine.
Se gentis hom mais n'engendroit...
Tout le monde vivrait en paix.'
(Quoted by P. Viollet, *Histoire des Institutions...de la France*, Vol. III, p. 204.)

In its literary form, as we find it in Chaucer, the question carries us naturally back, once more, to Italy and the early beginnings of the Italian Renaissance. In Italy a common urban life, peculiar to that country, had from an early date mixed the noble and the merchant, and even the artisan, in something of a common culture. In Italy, again, the Church, with its numerous episcopates, was freely open to all ranks. In Italy the *condottiere* might rise from any position to princely rank and station. In Italy, as we have already had reason to notice,[1] the sons of the poor could be educated, as they were by Vittorino da Feltre and Guarino, on a common footing with the sons of princes and nobles. Even before the Italian Renaissance Dante had already raised the question which Chaucer raised a century after his time. In the *De Monarchia*, referring to the dictum of Aristotle that 'nobility is inherited wealth and virtue', but omitting in his own conclusion any mention of wealth, he had laid it down *quod merito virtutis nobilitantur homines, virtutis scilicet propriae vel majorum*.[2] The sixteenth canto of the *Paradiso* opens with the words

O poca nostra nobiltà di sangue!

Above all, in the fourth *trattato* of the *Convito* (on which Chaucer may well have drawn), there is a long disquisition on true nobility, of which the pith may perhaps be found in two lines of the poem with which the *trattato* begins:

È Gentilezza dovunque è virtute,
Ma non virtute ov' ella.[3]

In Italy, therefore, and as early as the age of Dante (or perhaps even earlier still), the question of the nature of 'gentilesse' had already been raised, and the alternative had already been posed

---

[1] Supra, p. 85.

[2] *De Monarchia*, II, c. iii *ad initium*. The dictum of Aristotle comes from the *Politics*, IV, c. viii, § 9.

[3] The writer owes these references to Burckhardt's *Die Kultur der Renaissance in Italien*, V, 1. In a note appended by a later editor of Burckhardt's book, it is observed that the theme of nobility being due to virtue, and not to descent, was in Dante's age a commonplace of poetry and of disputations in schools of eloquence.

between *virtute* and *sangue*. But if the alternative had been posed, it remained for centuries swinging and oscillating in the balance. The writers of the sixteenth century are still vexed by the dilemma. Castiglione, for instance, in his first book of *Il Cortegiano*, makes the courtiers of Urbino take different sides in the matter. First Count Lewis of Canossa speaks. 'I will have this our courtier, therefore, to be a gentleman born and of a good house.... For nobleness of birth is (as it were) a clear lamp that showeth forth and bringeth into light works both good and bad, and inflameth and provoketh unto virtue as well with the fear of slander as also with the hope of praise.' Then the Lord Gaspar Pallavicini speaks. 'I say (in mine advise) that this nobleness of birth is not so necessary for the courtier.... I confirm your saying as touching the happiness of them that are born abounding in all goodness both of mind and body, but this is seen as well in the unnoble as in the noble of birth, for nature hath not these so subtle distinctions; yea,...we see many times in persons of most base degree most high gifts of nature.' Then the Count Lewis rejoins, appealing to common opinion. 'For as much as our intent is to fashion a courtier without any manner default or lack in him, and heaped with all praise, methink it a necessary matter to make him a gentleman [born], as well for many other respects as also for the common opinion, which by and by doth lean to nobleness.' There the matter is left: and it is left in much the same state by Ascham, in his *Schoolmaster*, published some half a century later in 1570. Ascham knew *Il Cortegiano*, in his friend Sir Thomas Hoby's translation which has just been quoted; and he refers to its 'trim teaching' in a paragraph of approbation. His own handling of the old dilemma is much in the manner of Castiglione. 'Nobility without virtue and wisdom is blood indeed, but blood, truly, without bones and sinews; and so of itself, without the other, very weak to bear the burden of weighty affairs. But nobility, governed by learning and wisdom, is indeed most like a fair ship, having wind and tide at will.... Therefore, ye great and noble men's children, if ye will have rightfully that praise and enjoy surely that place which your fathers have, and elders had, and left unto you, you must keep it as they gat it, and that is by the only way of virtue, wisdom and worthiness.'[1]

Here we may leave the literary debate, which had lasted for nearly three centuries, from the time of Dante to that of Ascham; and we may turn to the common sense and the legal wisdom of Sir Thomas Smith, reporting in his *De Republica Anglorum* (published after his death, in 1583) the actual manner and practice of his country in the matter of gentility. Following—but without acknowledgement[2]—Harrison's classification of 'the degrees of estates in the Commonwealth' (in his *Description of England*, which had just appeared in the first edition of Holinshed's *Chronicles*), Smith divides the parts and persons of the commonwealth into four sorts. The first is gentlemen; the second citizens and burgesses; the third yeomen; the fourth artificers and labourers. The first sort—the gentlemen of England—are in turn divided into two parts. The first part, or *nobilitas major*, runs down the scale from dukes to barons. In a word it includes all the members of the upper House of Parliament. The second part, or *nobilitas minor*, is a much larger body—so large, indeed, that it must be subdivided into a number of sections. There are three of these sections, in a descending series. The first is composed of knights, who have been duly dubbed and are entitled to be called Sir. The second consists of esquires, 'which', Smith says, 'we call commonly squires'; and the point about them is that they have coats of arms. The third section is that of gentlemen pure and simple, who, without being knights and without bearing coats of arms, 'be those whom their blood and race doth make noble and known', and whose mark is 'old riches or prowess remaining in one stock'.

Smith proceeds to discuss these gentlemen at some length. His definition has implied by its terms ('blood and race', and 'prowess

---

[1] Selden (quoted in the *New English Dictionary* under the word 'gentleman') repeats the theme of Ascham in his *Titles of Honour*. 'He that is...both descended from truly noble parentage, and withal following their steps or adding to their name, is the gentleman that may lawfully glory in his title.'

[2] The phrase is perhaps too strong. On the general question of the relation of Smith and Harrison, see Mr L. Alston's closely reasoned introduction to his edition of the *De Republica Anglorum* (1906).

remaining in one stock') that a proper gentleman must necessarily be a gentleman born. But very soon, within a page, he begins to alter the key of his music. 'As for gentlemen,' he reflects and says, 'they be made good cheap in England.' He means that anybody, whatever his birth, can become and be counted a gentleman in ordinary social usage. Gentle for Smith is (as already for Chaucer before him) he who gentle *does*, whatever he *is* by birth. The gentleman is made by his function in the commonwealth, and by his ability to perform it, rather than by his origin. 'Whosoever studieth the laws of the realm, who studieth in the universities, who professeth liberal sciences, and to be short, who can live idly and without manual labour and will bear the port charge and countenance of a gentleman, he...shall be called a gentleman.'

Having reached this point Smith raises the question, to which he devotes a chapter of its own, 'whether the manner of England in making gentlemen so easily is to be allowed'. He answers the question in the affirmative. 'No man hath hurt by it but he himself', since by taking the style of a gentleman a man simply incurs a greater obligation. Smith does not use the word 'obligation'; but that is the sense and core of his argument, and his idea of the greater obligation which gentlemen owe to the commonwealth is a notable idea. The obligation is various. There is a greater moral obligation: 'he must show a more manly courage ...higher stomach and bountifuller liberality than others.' There is a greater social obligation: 'he must keep about him idle servants, who shall do nothing but wait upon him.' There is a greater political obligation: 'he must and will (whatever it costeth) array himself and arm him according to the vocation which he pretendeth.' There is a greater intellectual obligation: 'he must show tokens of a better education.'

It is the last of these obligations which is here our immediate concern. But the educational obligation of the gentleman can hardly be divorced from the moral or—for that matter—from the political. It is the general way of life that is in question, as well as the method of training which fits men for that way of life. Our

general theme will therefore involve some breadth of consideration. It will lead us to survey the idea of the special obligation of
the gentleman (as that idea grew and flourished in England during
the sixteenth century), not only in the intellectual sphere, but also
in the sphere which may be generally called the moral: not only
in the way of education and training, but also in the way of
conduct and behaviour springing from, and corresponding to,
such education and training. We shall find, in the course of the
survey, that the sixteenth century evolved, largely under the
inspiration of the Italian Renaissance, and especially of its revival
of the study of Plato's *Republic* and Plato's *Symposium*, the idea
and ideal of what Professor Sir Walter Raleigh has called, in his
introduction to Hoby's translation of *Il Cortigiano*, 'the scholar
gentleman'. Indeed, we may find even more; for the idea and
ideal had a still larger scope than the term 'scholar-gentleman'
suggests. The scholar-gentleman was expected not only to be a
scholar and a gentleman, but also what Elyot calls a 'governor'.
In other words, he was regarded as bound to serve the commonwealth, under the prince, by doing some sort of political duty,
generally unpaid, in its behalf. That duty might be a duty in
the presence, either at the court or as a lord of the council;
more likely, in a rural country, with counties and hundreds
flung far and wide over its green and grassy spaces, it might be
a duty of serving locally on the commission of the peace, as a
magistrate entrusted with executing justice and maintaining truth
in days of turbulence and religious change. We might therefore
speak, in a triple term, of 'the scholar-governor-gentleman';
and indeed, unless we insert the word 'governor', we shall miss
something of the native and homespun quality of the Tudor
gentleman.

There are some four books in the rich literature of the sixteenth
century which may be said to deserve particular notice for the
light they throw on the ideal of the scholar-governor-gentleman.
The first is Sir Thomas Elyot's *Book of the Governor* (1531). The
second is Thomas Starkey's *Dialogue between Cardinal Pole and
Thomas Lupset*, on the nature of the 'very and true commonweal'

(written some time before his death in 1538, but not published till 1871). The third is Sir Thomas Hoby's translation of *Il Cortigiano* (1561). The last is Roger Ascham's *The Schoolmaster* (1570). Some account of their argument, and some reflections on its nature and implications, will serve to explain the ideal of their age.

II

There is one breach with the past, and one revolution in their general conception of education, which is common to all these writers. In the Middle Ages, as Professor Adamson noted in his *Short History of Education*, there were two separate types of education for two distinct and separate ways of life. There was the education of the clerk, in school and university, intended to produce the scholar: there was the education of the knight, conducted in the castle, and intended to produce the gentleman at arms. The revolution of the sixteenth century consists in the junction and interfusion of these two types. The Tudor gentleman is still something of the medieval knight, who had been taught courtesy, and the love of song and lyric, by the ladies of the castle in which he had been sent to reside during his early years, as he had later been taught martial exercises and the usages of war by the men. (Here, in this course of fourteen years, from the age of seven to that of twenty-one, with its break or change at the age of fourteen, is the far-off origin of our present system of 'preparatory' and 'public' schools; and here, in this early sending away of children, is also the origin of our traditional devotion to the ideal of the 'boarding' school. These methods of education, and the system of family and personal ethics which they imply or express, have a long and unbroken pedigree.) But the gentleman of the sixteenth century becomes also something of the clerk, not only versed in song and lyric, but also in literature generally (indeed he is often a poet himself, as *Tottel's Miscellany* of 1557 is already there to prove); versed, too, not only in literature, but also in some philosophy, both moral and aesthetic—some effort to comprehend the fundamental principles both of goodness and of beauty. Nor is this all. Being a governor (for the political development of the Tudor age had introduced the notion and practice of the gentleman serving the commonwealth in the capacity of magistrate) he will also know something of law; and his study of moral philosophy will thus be connected with some study of legal rules.

All this is expressed in Elyot's *Book of the Governor*[1]—the first book of importance on the theme of the gentleman which appeared in England in the sixteenth century. (Castiglione's book on the Courtier had indeed appeared, in the original Italian, three years earlier, and Elyot may have known something of it; but it did not appear in English, or acquire vogue in England, till Hoby's translation was published in 1561.) Elyot had mainly in mind, when he wrote of governors, those 'inferior governors' called magistrates, 'who shall be appointed and chosen by the sovereign governor'; but he suggests that they may well be termed governors pure and simple, without any qualification, since the supreme governor has a name of his own—the name of king or prince—by which he is sufficiently distinguished; and anyhow, he adds, in treating of their education in virtue and manners he will be treating of something which they have in common with princes, a saying which is not insignificant, suggesting as it does that the prince and the other or 'inferior' governors were after all of the same sort of metal. He is somewhat concerned, as Sir Thomas

[1] Sir Thomas Elyot (who died in 1546) had been in early life a clerk of assize on the Western Circuit and an Oxfordshire Justice of the Peace. He was afterwards clerk of the Privy Council; and after the appearance of his *Book of the Governor* he was made ambassador to Charles V. In his latter years he was Member of Parliament for the Borough of Cambridge. He had something of the scholarship of the Renaissance, and was a friend of More and Ascham. His *Book of the Governor* is said to be indebted to Petrizi's *De Regno et Regis Institutione*, published in 1518. It was a current book (seven editions had already appeared by the year 1580), and it was known to and used by Shakespeare. In addition to the *Book of the Governor* Elyot also published a number of translations or adaptations, including: (1) *The Doctrine of Princes* (1534), drawn from the oration addressed by the Greek orator Isocrates to the Cypriot prince Nicocles; (2) *The Education or bringing up of children, out of Plutarch* (c. 1535); and (3) some renderings of Platonic dialogues. He was also the compiler of a Latin-English dictionary.

Smith was afterwards to be, and as others had been in the past, with the question whether the governor should be of gentle birth. On the whole he thinks that he should be. 'Except excellent virtue and learning do enable a man of the base estate of the commonalty to be thought of all men worthy to be so much advanced, else should governors be chosen out of that estate of men which be called worshipful.' On the whole he is a hierarchist; a believer in permanent social grades, or hereditary 'degrees', in which men are naturally fixed, by a hierarchy of the human world which reflects the hierarchy of the universe.[1] Thus is the medieval doctrine of a system of estates, common to all Western Europe, but less deeply entrenched in England and Italy than in most other countries. (As early as 1385 Michael atte Pool, or de la Pole, the son of a merchant of Hull, had already been advanced to the dignity of Earl of Suffolk.) Elyot, however, is very English —and here he differs, as we shall see, from the doctrine of Castiglione's book of the Courtier (the difference of title is itself

---

[1] This hierarchical philosophy is set out in the first chapter of the first book of Elyot's work. It is set out in the same order of argument, and with the same images and illustrations, as Shakespeare afterwards used in the great speech on 'degree' which he puts into the mouth of Ulysses in Act I, Sc. iii, of *Troilus and Cressida*. (Elyot's was a well-known book, and Shakespeare naturally took it as the cue of his verse, in the same way that he took North's Plutarch in his *Antony and Cleopatra*.) Elyot, for example, having spoken of 'the discrepance of degrees, whereof proceedeth order', proceeds to argue, 'take away order from all things, what then would remain? Certes, nothing finally, except some man would imagine eftsoons "Chaos", which of some is expounded a confuse mixture.' Similarly Shakespeare, having spoken of the heavens themselves as observing degree in their order, and of communities as standing in place by degree, continues

> 'Take but degree away, untune that string,
> And, hark, what discord follows! Each thing meets
> In mere oppugnancy; the bounded waters
> Should lift their bosoms higher than the shores
> And make a sop of all this solid globe....
> This chaos, when degree is suffocate,
> Follows the choking' [of the commonweal]. (ll. 109–13, 125–6)

(The writer drew attention to Shakespeare's borrowing from Elyot, some years ago, in one of the weeklies; but he found that he had been anticipated by Mr E. E. Kellett, in his *Reconsiderations*, p. 43.)

significant)—in another assumption which he makes. This is the assumption that the gentleman whose training he intends to describe must serve the commonwealth; though he prefers to speak of the 'public weal', fearing, apparently, some suggestion of the vulgar mob and the common herd, in the other term. His gentleman is to be trained for duty and obligation—the duty and obligation of governorship and magistracy. That is English matter: matter of the public weal, which all are bound to serve in their station and degree; and it is a matter always present in the English writers of the sixteenth century.

The course of training which Elyot describes is largely based on the teaching of Plato; and indeed it is made to include a study of Plato's writings. He is mainly concerned with the crucial years from seventeen to twenty-three or twenty-four; but he assumes that at an earlier stage, during boyhood, the pupil has learned to read and love Homer and good poetry. For his later years Elyot advocates, *more Platonico*, that he should pay a particular attention to dancing, as having moral as well as physical and aesthetic value. He advocates, too, the study and practice both of music [1] and painting. Here the idea of beauty enters. But Elyot is even more concerned with the idea of goodness: goodness and public duty. In pursuit of that idea he proposes a course of study which is in the nature of a combination of the *Literae Humaniores* course at Oxford (not that that course existed till nearly three centuries after his time) with a course of 'reading for the Bar'. The first element appears in his advocacy of a study of philosophy, by which he means moral and political philosophy, in the classical authors, and especially in Plato; for 'above all other the works of Plato would be most studiously read', who 'for his wisdom and eloquence is named the god of philosophers'. The second element —the study of law, by which Elyot means the laws of England— should come, in his view, after the study of philosophy has been

[1] Professor Adamson notes, in his *Short History of Education* (p. 162), that at Westminster School the pupils had to go twice a week to the choir-master for instruction in music. 'The requirement', he adds, 'reminds us of the almost universal cultivation of music which was a feature of Elizabethan [or, perhaps better, Tudor] England.'

completed; and then the governor, at the end of his training, will not only be equipped with the knowledge of English law which he will need for his work, but will also be able to set that knowledge against the background, or on the foundations, of the moral principles of human conduct.[1] So the governor comes to his flower—versed in Homer and in good poetry: able to dance, make music, and paint; knowing the philosophy of the divine Plato and the sober rudiments of English law. He is a versatile figure—perhaps a poet himself (like Henry Howard, the earl of Surrey, or Sir Thomas Wyatt the elder, who were both contemporaries of Elyot, and both of whom figure conspicuously in the beginning of *Tottel's Miscellany*), as well as classic, philosopher, painter, musician and dancer: a gentleman indeed, and a 'true and very' governor.

[1] It is interesting to compare the general lines of Elyot's scheme of training with those of Johann Sturm's scheme of training for the gymnasium at Strasbourg, as they are sketched in his *De litterarum ludis recte aperiendis* of 1538. Sturm, a German scholar, and in his later life also a diplomat, was a friend of Ascham (who warmly commends in his *Schoolmaster* the *De Institutione Principis* which he 'wrote...to the Duke of Cleves'); and, interested himself in affairs as well as conversant with statesmen, he sought, like Elyot, to train a man of the type of the 'governor'. (The gymnasium at Strasbourg, which he directed for more than forty years, had many notable pupils; Calvin himself taught in it for a time; and Calvin's own Academy and College at Geneva owed much to the model of Strasbourg.)

Sturm's scheme of training, as proclaimed in the inaugural programme of the 'right method of founding schools' (which perhaps remained more of a programme than it ever became a fact), has many analogies with Elyot's scheme. Both Sturm and Elyot distinguish two periods of education; though Sturm would begin the second about the age of fourteen, and Elyot proposed to begin it about the age of seventeen. In Sturm's scheme the nine years of the first period, from the age of five to that of fourteen, are to be devoted to Latin and Greek authors and composition—apart from some study of arithmetic, geometry, astronomy and geography in the final year (which must have been sadly crowded); the second period, from the age of fourteen to that of nineteen, is to be given—much in the manner of Elyot—to Greek literature, philosophy (mainly as taught by Plato and Aristotle), and *one* of the higher faculties of law, theology, and medicine. (J. W. Adamson, *A Short History of Education*, p. 160.)

It should be added that Sturm's programme did not cramp music—as it cramped all other subjects outside the classics—into the last year of the first period. Music might go with the classics in *all* the years.

Thomas Starkey's *Dialogue between Cardinal Pole and Thomas Lupset* (Lecturer in Rhetoric at Oxford) is only concerned incidentally with the education of the gentleman. Its main theme is a greater question, which is the nature of 'the very and true civil life', or what he calls 'civility', and of the constitution and government of 'the very and true commonweal'. But Starkey is clear that the proper education of the gentleman is essential to good 'civility'; and in one vital matter he shows himself, when he proceeds to consider the proper lines and scheme of this education, more Platonic than even the Platonist Elyot. Elyot, in spite of his Platonism, would yet have had his governors trained by private tutors. This is a thing alien from Plato, who desired that his guardians should all receive a common education in a common academy. On the other hand, as we have to admit in justice to Elyot, it was a thing entirely congruous with the practice of his own age. It was still the custom, in his day, for the sons of the nobility and richer gentry to be educated by private tutors in the country-house of their father, though they might be educated there in company with the sons of their father's friends. The long subtitle which Ascham appends to his *Schoolmaster* is a proof of the continuance of this custom in the days of Queen Elizabeth. His book, he suggests, is a 'plain and perfect way of teaching children to understand, write, and speak in Latin tongue, but specially purposed for the private bringing up of youth in gentlemen and noblemen's houses'. The habit of sending the youth of the upper classes to some sort of public school belongs, in the main, to a later age, though it is to be noticed that there was an increase of wealthy pupils at Eton soon after the dissolution of the monasteries.[1]

Starkey departs from the custom of his time, and proposes that the sons of gentlemen should be given a common education in a common academy specially designed for their needs. He regards the existing 'universities, colleges, and common places' as intended

---

[1] J. W. Adamson, op. cit. p. 141. Professor Adamson notes, ibid. p. 180, that the life of Colonel Hutchinson, as told by his wife, is an admirable example of what private education could be at its best.

'to nourish the children of poor men in letters',[1] and as therefore belonging to a different class. Apart from that, and even if they were more generally open to the whole of the nation, he is clear that these 'universities, colleges, and common places' all labour under imperfections. 'Learning without virtue is pernicious and pestilent.... But this thing in studies and universities is neglected and despised, as it is in grammar schools. Wherefore there must be reformation for that—as in their manner of studies, which are confused, and by the reason of that we have few great learned men in our country.'[2] Not intended for gentlemen's sons, and imperfect in themselves, the existing 'common places' will not serve Starkey's turn; but they serve, at any rate, to suggest to his mind the need of some new 'common place' where the sons of gentlemen may get the virtue and the manner of studies which they need. Private instruction has proved itself a broken reed. At the best it is 'instruction in letters, without any respect of other exercise in other feats pertaining to nobility no less than learning and letters, as in all feats of chivalry'. At the worst, it is a matter of gentlemen's sons 'brought up in hunting and hawking, dicing and carding, eating and drinking, and, in conclusion, in all vain pleasure, pastime and vanity'. The day has come for a new common academy. 'We shall have, as it were, certain places appointed for the bringing up together of the nobility, to which I would the nobles should be compelled to set forward their children and heirs, that in a number together they might the better profit.... Here they should be instruct, not only in virtue and learning, but also in all feats of war pertaining to such as should be hereafter in time

---

[1] Starkey's *Dialogue* (published by the Early English Text Society, 1871), p. 187.

[2] Ibid. p. 203. Starkey was writing before 1538. But Thomas Lever, Fellow of St John's College, Cambridge (the great home of learning at that time), is no less critical in his three sermons of 1550, published in Arber's *English Reprints* in 1870 (see J. W. Adamson, op. cit. pp. 144–6). Ultimately, however, the English Reformation brought a reform of education as well as of religion—though in its course it also led to the misappropriation of educational endowments—and by the end of the reign of Elizabeth there had been: (1) some reform of the universities, (2) some reconstruction of grammar schools, and (3) the foundation of some new schools such as Christ's Hospital, Westminster, Rugby, and Harrow (supra, p. 85).

of war captains and governors of the common sort.... Of this
surely should spring the fountain of all civility and politic rule....'
It will be seen that Starkey, like Elyot, is anxious to train the
'governor'; and he is even willing 'to turn Westminster Abbey
and St Alban's and many other to this use...that, even like as
these monks and religious men there living together exercise a
certain monastical discipline and life, so the nobles, being brought up
together, should learn there the discipline of the common weal'.[1]

Starkey's plan is Platonic in intention, but it is a sketch, or an
outline, rather than a scheme. He leaves the curriculum of his
compulsory academies undefined. It will include moral discipline
and military instruction: it will also include some legal teaching,
for the pupils are 'plainly and fully to be instruct in the administration of justice both public and private'. But the essence of Starkey's
plan was not so much a new curriculum, though that was involved
in it, as a new institution. This institution was what came to be
known, in later days, by the name of 'Academy'; and Starkey
was one of the first—perhaps the very first—of its prophets. An
'Academy', as the term came to be used in the seventeenth century,
was a place for the instruction of gentlemen's sons in modern
subjects—modern languages, modern history, and modern geography—in order to fit them for the needs of their future vocation.
It left the classics to the Universities and grammar schools: it made
itself a 'real school', preparing its pupils to face the realities of
their future work. Starkey himself was still Platonically tinged,
and intent on virtue and learning: he was thinking of 'the groves
of Academe' rather than a modern Academy, and he could hardly
guess the nature of the chicken which would peck its way out of
his egg. Sir Humphrey Gilbert went further when he projected,
some forty years later, his scheme of 'Queen Elizabeth's Academy'.
The Academy was to be an institution in London, 'for education
of Her Majesty's wards[2] and others the youth of nobility and

---

[1] Starkey's plan is set out on pp. 187–8. His criticism of private instruction
comes on pp. 129, 186.
[2] Starkey had also been concerned about the education of wards, op. cit.
p. 186.

gentlemen'. The Universities would not serve: they studied 'only school learnings': the Academy was to study 'matters of action meet for present practice, both of peace and war'. Its pupils were to join at the age of twelve: they were to have a schoolmaster for Latin and Greek, and readers for logic and rhetoric; but more especially they were to have professors (much more highly remunerated) of political philosophy, applied mathematics, civil and common law, divinity and medicine.[1] There were also to be teachers of modern languages; teachers of horsemanship, fencing and dancing; a teacher of instrumental music, and a teacher of heraldry. Gilbert's project never matured, at any rate in England. It was in France, from the middle of the seventeenth century onwards, that Academies flourished and attracted pupils; and it might have been said of the England of the later Stuarts, as it had been said before of the England of the Middle Ages:

> Filii nobilium, dum sunt juniores,
> Mittuntur in Franciam fieri doctores.

Not till the nineteenth century, when old public schools were remodelled and a new crop of public schools arose (such as Wellington, Cheltenham, Clifton and Haileybury), were the ideas of Starkey and Gilbert translated into fact upon English soil. Then —in the inculcation of the virtues of *esprit de corps*; in the cultivation of organised games; in the introduction of modern studies and the institution of an 'army side'; in the general training of servants of the Crown on the civil as well as the military side—the old ideas came to fruition. The public schools of the Victorian age

---

[1] The professor of political philosophy was to deal with the civil and military organisation of states both ancient and modern. One of the professors of applied mathematics was to deal with military engineering and gunnery: the other was to teach cosmography and astronomy in their bearing on navigation. A full account of Gilbert's project is given in Adamson's *Short History of Education*, pp. 173–6. At about the same time that Gilbert planned his Academy, Johann Sturm was also proposing a military academy to prepare the youth of Europe for the long crusade against the Turks. It was to give instruction in arms and gymnastics, as well as in law, history, and other studies; and its pupils (who, as in Gilbert's scheme, were to join it at the age of twelve) were to prepare themselves by study and exercise for the practice of war. (Ibid. p. 166.)

were the late but abundant harvest of ideas which had already been sown in the sixteenth century. 'Fountains of civility and politic rule', they issued in a type of 'governor' who might have satisfied Elyot, and in a type of disciplined servant of 'the very and true commonweal' who might have comforted Starkey.

III

Castiglione's *Book of the Courtier* is an Italian book, and in the original Italian it is as old as 1528. But it became an English book in Sir Thomas Hoby's translation; and that translation first appeared in the third year of the reign of Queen Elizabeth. Several editions were published in the course of the reign; and we may almost say that Hoby's *Book of the Courtier* became the manual of the court of Elizabeth. Hoby himself was a man of some standing, who had been educated at St John's College, Cambridge, in the hey-day of its fame; had visited Strasbourg, and attended there the lectures of Johann Sturm; and had twice made the journey to Italy (1548–50 and 1554–5). His wife belonged to a remarkable family of sisters, trained by their father (the tutor of Edward VI) in the classics: the eldest sister was the wife of Lord Burghley: the second was the wife of Sir Nicholas Bacon and the mother of Francis Bacon. Any book published by Hoby would be likely to have some vogue; but the nature and style of Elizabeth's court— its learning and wit, its taste for letters, its pageants and progresses, its music and dances—was bound to give a particular vogue to the *Book of the Courtier*. It is easy to imagine Elizabeth herself engaged in its study, and musing perhaps over the lofty Platonic passages at the end of the fourth book, in which Master Peter Bembo (Latinist, cardinal, arbiter of letters, and associate, in his later days, of the Oratory of Divine Love) is made to speak of Beauty and Love, and the ascent of the soul through love to the vision and communion of heavenly beauty, and to speak so movingly that, at the end, 'the Lady Emilia...took him by the plait of his garment and plucking him a little said: Take heed, Master Peter, that these thoughts make not your soul also to forsake the body'.

Castiglione's book belongs to a *genre* which was common in the sixteenth century. You took some type or social figure; and you wrote a book about its proper qualities, and the proper method of producing and maintaining the qualities; and you were drawn in this way (as was natural in an age of changing values and new conceptions of the nature of culture) into some new theory of education. There is a whole literature of this didactic *genre* in the sixteenth century, which is parallel to what may be called the literature of 'characters' in the seventeenth century.[1] Machiavelli took the type or social figure of the Prince, and he wrote a book on the proper qualities of a 'new prince'. There is not much matter of education in *Il Principe*; but there are many other 'Mirrors of Education' for princes, or treatises (as they are often called) *de institutione principis*, during the course of the sixteenth century, which contain a good deal of such matter. Johann Sturm's *De Institutione Principis*, addressed to the Duke of Cleves, is warmly commended by his friend Roger Ascham: earlier still, in 1515, Erasmus had written his *Christiani Principis Institutio*; and the Spaniard Vives, in 1523, being asked by Catharine of Aragon to draw out a course of study for her daughter the Princess Mary, had composed and dedicated to the Queen a treatise *De Institutione Feminae Christianae*.[2] But princes and princesses were not the only social type which attracted the theorist and educational planner. There was also the governor, the courtier, the nobleman, the gentleman in general. One versatile writer at the end of the century, a jurist in the service of the Elector Palatine who went by the name of Hippolytus a Collibus, created a whole gallery of pictures of social types. In 1588 he published at Strasbourg the *Nobilis*; in 1593 the *Princeps*; in 1596 the *Consiliarius*; in 1600 the *Palatinus sive Aulicus*. Generally, however, the writers of the sixteenth century were content to paint a single portrait, and to offer not a 'great didactic' for all types but a didactic of some

---

[1] See Professor Nichol Smith's essay on 'The Character' in his *Characters of the Seventeenth Century*.

[2] Petrizi's *De Regno et Regis Institutione* is another example: see above, p. 133 n.

single type. Elyot took the governor or *Consiliarius*: Castiglione the courtier—*Palatinus sive Aulicus*: Ascham the schoolmaster or *Ludimagister*. But all these three, though each of them dealt with some particular side or aspect of culture and the transmission of culture—some particular side or aspect specially suitable to the special type of figure which they handled—were concerned, at bottom, with a common theme. They were concerned with the nature of culture or *paideia*: with the breeding which it entailed; with the influence which, once bred in the mind, it could exercise on character and conduct. Europe was seeking a culture, in that age of transition and mutation of values; and they sought to be guides in the search. It was the good fortune of Castiglione's *Cortigiano* that his conception of culture became the general European ideal (coloured, it is true, in each country by something of a national tincture) for that mixture of the clerk and the knight, the scholar and the gentleman, which was the general aim of the sixteenth century.[1]

In treating of the courtier Castiglione, who drew on his own experience at the ducal court of Urbino (especially under Duke Guidobaldo and his accomplished duchess Elisabetta Gonzaga, during the years 1504–8), was thinking in the first instance of the gentleman serving his prince personally and in the presence—not but what the gentlemen of the court were also to serve for matters

---

[1] It would be a fascinating study to examine comparatively the different national tinctures—the Italian, the Spanish, the French, the English, the German. The Spanish tincture might well deserve a special treatment in such a study. Here Antonio de Guevara would have to be mentioned, who published in 1529 *El Relox de Principes*, a didactic novel professing to be a life of Marcus Aurelius and a work of much vogue in the sixteenth century, translated into many languages. (It was translated into English, from a French version, by Lord Berners, in 1534, under the title of *The Golden Book of Marcus Aurelius*; and an enlarged edition of it was later translated by Sir Thomas North in 1558—more than twenty years before he published his translation of Plutarch's *Lives*—under the title of *The Dial of Princes*.) But perhaps *Don Quixote*—though it did not appear till 1605—would deserve the most special treatment. If any book made the idea of the gentleman a lovable idea, it was *Don Quixote*. France, one might say, contributed the writings of Rabelais (with their bright vision of the Abbey of Theleme) and the *Essays* of Montaigne: Germany, more didactic and heavy, the writings and the teaching of Johann Sturm.

of business in the council chamber and the field of war; but their special service was a service of leisure, and a cult of all the fine graces of leisure, in the social intercourse of the prince's salon. Castiglione's courtier is like, and yet unlike, Elyot's governor. Elyot's governor is a grave magistrate, and the sober background of the public weal is behind his goings and doings: Castiglione's courtier may indeed be a councillor of state, but he is also a man of wit and fashion, of gallantry and the arts. The circle of Elizabeth—Leicester, Raleigh, Sidney, Essex; perhaps particularly Raleigh—are after the pattern of Castiglione's courtier. In Leicester and Essex at any rate (though Sidney and Raleigh were of another mould, and even Essex played his part in the field of war at Cadiz and in Ireland) there is less sense of service to the commonwealth; and the actor who moves to the front of the stage is a man moved by the idea of cutting a dashing figure, dazzling the eye of the beholder, showing himself the pink of courtesy, loving with a grand passion, and expressing his love in a sonnet or in a sequence of sonnets. In a word it is personality—individual personality, growing to its own fine flower—which springs from the root of the doctrine of courtesy, as that doctrine was proclaimed in Hoby's translation of Castiglione's *Book of the Courtier*.

There is a new Italian[1] quality in this individual touch; and the quality shows itself in a variety of ways. It appears, first of all, in a passion for *virtù* (which is far from being our 'virtue', and is rather the attribute of the man who is a virtuoso in the art of life) —the *virtù* of shining like a star in the strength of a dazzling intellect backed by force of character. This was the *virtù* of which Machiavelli had written, engaged in a constant battle with *fortuna*: it was the *virtù* which he had detected in Cesare Borgia. The dazzling intellect might, or might not, be actually there: the force of character might be assumed as a mask, rather than worn

---

[1] Elizabeth herself had Italian tastes, and always conversed with Italians in their own language. Professor Pollard has noted that she was 'versed in Italian scholarship', and that 'in 1575 "nearly all" the privy councillors spoke Italian'. (*History of England, 1547–1603*, p. 179.)

as a natural grace or an actual power; but in any case there must be an appearance and exhibition of *virtù*. Castiglione's courtier must always excel, and always attempt to go some distance beyond all others,

αἰὲν ἀριστεύειν καὶ ὑπείροχον ἔμμεναι ἄλλων,

'using zeal and diligence', as the author says, 'to surpass others somewhat in everything'.

Another and cognate way ,in which an Italian quality of individualism affects the doctrine of courtesy and the portrait of the courtier appears in the cult of *sprezzatura*. *Sprezzatura* is an untranslatable word, which means a sort of high-souled and high-stepping magnanimity, with a careless fling of the cloak and an easy off-hand way: while you excel others, you must do it with effortless ease, as if you were doing nothing, 'employing in everything a certain disdain which conceals art'. One who was an undergraduate more than half a century ago in the University of Oxford cannot but remember, as a sort of modern parallel, a certain pose or mannerism which was current among some of the members of his college. They, too, used a certain disdain to conceal their art, seeking to excel all others in study without doing any work (or rather without any appearance of doing any work), and arming themselves with what was once happily described as 'the tranquil consciousness of effortless superiority'. But there is a closer, if far more ancient, parallel in the pages of Aristotle's *Ethics*. The high-souled man, or 'the Man of Pride', or (perhaps better) 'the Magnanimous Man', who appears in the third chapter of the fourth book of the *Ethics*, has more than a touch of *sprezzatura*. 'He thinks himself worthy of great things, being worthy of them'; 'to what end should he do disgraceful acts, he to whom nothing is great?' 'Not even towards honour does he bear himself as if it were a very great thing...hence he is thought to be disdainful.' 'He is the sort of man to confer benefits, but he is ashamed of receiving them.' 'Nor is he given to admiration; for nothing to him is great.' He has 'a slow step...a deep voice...; for the man who takes few things seriously is not likely to be hurried, nor the man who thinks nothing great to be excited'.[1]

How is the man of *virtù* and *sprezzatura* to be educated to his calling? He must be trained, of course, in arms and horsemanship; and here Castiglione speaks in the same terms as Thomas Starkey and Sir Humphrey Gilbert. For the rest, and to make himself an ornament in times of peace and leisure, when he serves in the presence and at court, he must be skilled in the classics; but he must also be 'well-languaged' in his mother tongue, all the more as it is 'tender and new, for all it hath been now used a long while' (a dictum which might be applied to English no less than to Italian, and which may serve to remind us that it became a court fashion in the reign of Elizabeth to be 'well-languaged' in the mother tongue after the manner of *Euphues*).[2] Besides the grace of a knowledge of the classics and of good language in the mother tongue, he must also be a musician and singer: he must be accomplished in the art of dancing ('in a manner of disguising', or masked): he must be skilled in tennis and vaulting: he must 'in no

---

[1] The passages are quoted from the translation of W. D. Ross in Vol. IX of the Oxford translation of the *Works of Aristotle*.

[2] It was, no doubt, the impact of the classical languages, now more widely diffused and more generally known by the writers of the age, which caused these searchings of heart about the mother tongue and the proper choice of words. Beginning perhaps in Italy, they spread to France, Spain, and England. Castiglione discusses at length the manner of the Tuscan tongue and the problem of new words, partly in his preliminary epistle (pp. 18–22 of the edition of Hoby's translation in *Tudor Translations*), and partly in his first book (pp. 70–8). A similar discussion had already begun in England, in Hoby's time, about the manner of the English tongue and the problem of admitting new words, as appears from the letter of Sir John Cheek prefixed to Hoby's translation (pp. 12–13 and Professor Sir Walter Raleigh's comments in his introduction, pp. xlii–xlvi); and the discussion continued into the days of John Lyly's *Euphues* (Part I, 1578, Part II, 1580) and of Shakespeare's *Love's Labour's Lost* (c. 1594). Spain produced—but not till the beginning of the seventeenth century—the *estilo culto* or 'Gongorism' of Luis de Góngora, with its pomp and its Latinisms. In France Rabelais is already satirising, by 1532 (in the sixth chapter of *Pantagruel*), the Limousin spruce-like scholar, 'who too affectedly did counterfeit the French language' with his concatenation of Latinisms; but the problem of the true nature of the French language was still vexed in the latter half of the sixteenth century and the days of the Pleiad (see Mark Pattison's essay on *The Stephenses* in Vol. I of his *Essays*).

wise leave out painting'; he must have a moderate knowledge of 'the game at chestes' (too great a proficiency at chess would not be seemly); and he should be well dressed, 'in all his garments handsome and cleanly', with 'a certain delight in modest preciseness', for 'the garment is withal no small argument of the fancy of him that weareth it'.

In these cursory and discursive remarks on the education of the courtier Castiglione is thinking and writing exclusively of men. But the life and intercourse of the court, as he describes it, includes the gentlewoman with the gentleman; and indeed the framework of his book, which is cast in the form of a dialogue, shows the Duchess governing the conversation of a salon, with the aid of the Lady Emilia (much in the manner which was long traditional in France); the members sitting in a circle together—'and in sitting they were divided a man and a woman, as long as there were women, for always the number of men was far the greater'. Generally it is Castiglione's aim 'to exalt the gentlewoman of the palace so much that she may be equal with the courtier'; and though he says little or nothing of the education of women (as it was afterwards practised in England in the days of Lady Jane Grey and the Princess Elizabeth, and of Hoby's wife and her sisters), he assumes an equal intercourse of the courtiers of both sexes and their sharing together a common culture. This was a useful lesson for England, and one of the graces of the court of Elizabeth. It was also the basis, for Castiglione himself, of the consummation of the doctrine of courtesy which comes at the end of the fourth and last book of *Il Cortigiano*. The end of all culture is an ideal love: an ideal love of the beautiful Beloved, which, beyond her, is a love of ideal Beauty itself and of God with whom that Beauty dwells. This is the end of the *Book of the Courtier*: an end well known, one may guess, to Edmund Spenser, and to Philip Sidney, and to Walter Raleigh.

> Under the arch of life, where birth and death,
> Terror and mystery, guard her shrine, I saw
> Beauty enthroned, and though her gaze struck awe
> I drew it in as simply as my breath.

It is here, and in the Platonism of Castiglione's final rhapsody, that we touch an influence on English thought and literature to which some reference has already been made,[1] but over which it is perhaps permissible to linger again for a moment. Platonism entered England, during the sixteenth century, by two main channels. The one was the channel of the *Republic* and its doctrine of the Idea of the Good. This was the moral and political channel; and its influence may be seen in the *Utopia* of Sir Thomas More, in Sir Thomas Elyot's plea for the government of understanding in his *Book of the Governor*, and in the argument of Thomas Starkey's *Dialogue* for the better education of nobles, the proper regulation of property, and the due direction of government to the benefit of 'the very and true commonweal'. The other channel is that of the *Symposium* and its doctrine of the Idea of the Beautiful. This was the aesthetic channel, but it also became the channel of a religious mysticism; and its influence may be traced in English poetry—in Spenser and Sidney, in the *Sonnets* of Shakespeare and the poems of Donne. But we must remember the commentators as well as the original (indeed, perhaps even more than the original) when we attempt to trace the influence of the *Symposium* in the England of Queen Elizabeth and James I. One of them was Marsilio Ficino, in his treatise 'On love or the Symposium of Plato'; another was Pico della Mirandola, who fused Platonism with Neo-Platonism in a commentary on a *Canzona de amore* by an Italian poet; a third was Castiglione himself, in the Platonically inspired speeches which he puts into the mouth of Bembo. Of all the commentators or glossators of the Platonic doctrine of beauty Castiglione, in Hoby's version, was the most readily accessible to English students and readers. It is little wonder that he is echoed in Spenser's hymns *Of Heavenly Love* and *Of Heavenly Beauty*, or that some refrains of his rhapsody may be traced in Sidney's *Astrophel and Stella*.[2]

[1] Supra, pp. 29, 30.
[2] The reader is referred to Professor Sir Walter Raleigh's Introduction to Hoby's translation, pp. lxx–lxxvii, for a full account of the matter.

IV

If the ultimate refinement of the idea of the gentleman in this Platonic doctrine of Beauty and Love may have influenced English literature, and even have added some faint foreign grace to the feelings and the behaviour of Elizabeth's courtiers, it can hardly be said to have touched the life of the ordinary English gentlemen of the sixteenth century. They had too home-keeping an affection; and their native idea of love was too much, at best, a matter of hum-drum Darby and Joan, and at worst of nicely calculated marriage settlements, for the higher reaches of Platonic love. Nor can the Italian *virtù*, or the Italian *sprezzatura*, be said to have entered deeply into the character of the Englishman. The drama, indeed, has a touch of these qualities: Marlowe and his contemporaries could paint the high-souled man; but the drama of Elizabeth and James I, when it shows this strain, is perhaps more a reflection of Italian models than a mirror of the native scene. On the other hand it may also be said that there has always been a touch of *sprezzatura*, whether native or imported, in that English idea of the gentleman which makes him essentially an 'amateur' —a flower of easy grace who is not as the professional, and who, whatever he does and however well he may do it, will always do it lightly. Alike in sports and in politics (which are perhaps connected, in this matter, by some channel of underground sympathy) the English have continued to cultivate, from the sixteenth century onwards, the ideal of the amateur and his easy unflurried grace of action. They cultivated it after it was dead in the countries of Western Europe in which it originally flourished. When the service of the state had been made a science elsewhere, Professor Pollard has remarked, Englishmen still preferred to consider it a task for intelligent amateurs.

Less than ten years after the appearance of Hoby's translation of *Il Cortigiano*, Roger Ascham's book of *The Schoolmaster* was post-humously published, in 1570. Ascham was a Yorkshireman who had been a student, and afterwards a fellow, of St John's College, Cambridge, between 1530 and 1545: 'a strong plain Englishman',

Dr Arber writes, 'with his love for all field-sports and cock-fighting, his warm generous heart, his tolerant spirit, his thorough scholarship, his beautiful penmanship'. He is a curious contrast to the polished Castiglione; and the first book of his *Schoolmaster* (which is largely a matter of his reminiscences and his personal likes and dislikes) is a curious and delightful book. Like a Yorkshire scholar, he blends a love of sports (riding, archery and the cock-pit) with a love of good and sober learning; and he has little liking for flounces and frills. He had addressed his *Toxophilus*, or 'School of Shooting', to all gentlemen and yeomen of England; and in his *Schoolmaster*, which is addressed more exclusively to the youth in gentlemen's and noblemen's houses, and intended primarily to be their school of 'writing and speaking in Latin tongue', he takes his cue from the sport, or the art, of riding. The wise riding-master gentles his pupils, and brings them to love and proficiency by his method: the wise schoolmaster should do the same; and instead of practising, as schoolmasters now do, the severity of a *plagosus Orbilius*, he should use a lenity of teaching. On the other hand, Ascham hastens to add, the parent has an opposite lesson to learn. *His* fault is 'clean contrary' to that of the schoolmaster. If the schoolmaster spoils the child by too much use of the rod, the parent spoils him by sparing the rod entirely. From seven to seventeen, when they are still left by their parents under some discipline, 'young gentlemen commonly be carefully enough brought up; but from seventeen to seven and twenty (the most dangerous time of all a man's life, and most slippery to stay in), they have commonly the rein of all license in their own hand'. Ascham blames fathers ('the wisest and also best men be found the fondest fathers in this behalf'); but he has also a word of reproof for mothers. 'The mother (of the household of our lady) had rather, yea, and will, too, have her son cunning and bold, in making him to live trimly when he is young, than by learning and travail to be able to serve his prince and his country both wisely in peace and stoutly in war, when he is old.'

Service to prince and country is thus what Ascham would have; and the method by which he would secure such service is expressed in the saying which he puts into the mouth of Lady Jane Grey, when he found her, 'the last time that ever I saw that noble and worthy lady...in her chamber, reading *Phaedon Platonis* in Greek'. He asked her how she came to find such pleasure in Plato. 'I will tell you, quoth she...one of the greatest benefits that ever God gave me is that he sent me so sharp and severe parents, and so gentle a schoolmaster.' Sharp and severe parents, working in co-operation with a gentle schoolmaster—that, in a word, is the method of Ascham for the education of the English gentleman in the English country-house. For the Court and its life, in spite of his praises of Queen Elizabeth (with whom he read Greek), Ascham has little use: he is English earth of the English earth; and though he commends Castiglione's book, 'so well translated into English by a worthy gentleman Sir Th. Hoby', he has ideas of his own, with something of a nipping north-country edge, which lie far closer to his heart. The gentle schoolmaster will first see to it that young gentlemen, from seven to seventeen, 'increase by reading the knowledge of tongues and learning'. (It is for this purpose that Ascham offers his own method of teaching Latin, set out in the second book of the *Schoolmaster*.) Then comes the turn of the parents, to see to it that the gentleman grown, from seventeen to seven-and-twenty, shall acquire the habit and discipline of his country—'to ride comely: to run fair at the tilt or ring: to play at all weapons: to shoot fair in bow [here the *Toxophilus* will serve] and surely in gun: to vault lustily, to run, to leap, to wrestle, to swim: to dance comely, to sing and play of instruments cunningly, to hawk, to hunt: to play at tennis, and all pastimes generally, which be joined with labour, used in open place, and on the daylight, combining·either some fit exercise for war or some pleasant pastime for peace'.

It is little wonder that with these ideas Ascham is critical of 'the fancy that many young gentlemen of England have to travel abroad, and namely to lead a long life in Italy'. The fancy offends his Protestant soul and his moral sense. 'This whole talk hath tended', he writes at the end of his first book, 'to the only advancement of truth in religion and honesty of living'; and he feels that the Italian journey tends to the advancement of neither. He quotes the Italian saying that 'an Englishman italianate is a devil incarnate'; he repudiates, with a frank disgust, 'the enchantments of Circe brought out of Italy to mar men's manners in England'. This is native and homespun thought; and it would hardly be agreeable to Elizabeth, who herself translated an Italian sermon and favoured Italian divines. It is true that Ascham confesses that he likes and loves the Italian tongue above all others—next the Greek and Latin. It is true that he pays his homage to *Il Cortigiano*, 'which book', he says, with a back-handed compliment, 'advisedly read and diligently followed but one year at home in England would do a young gentleman more good, I wis, than three years travel abroad spent in Italy'. But there is something in him which is averse from the Italy of his day. Perhaps he read with some reservation even the rhapsodies of Cardinal Bembo about Platonic love. Perhaps he preferred the grit of Yorkshire and the solid learning of St John's College to all the Italian polish which a year's reading of the *Cortigiano* could give. In any case he was not in tune with the Italianate fashion which he saw beginning in England. But then he was not in tune even with Malory's *Le morte Darthur*, 'the whole pleasure of which book standeth in two special points, in open manslaughter and bold bawdry'.

Ascham was himself robust, but donnish: cultured, and yet prejudiced: original to a degree, but also the admirer and imitator of his 'dearest friend…out of England', Johann Sturm of Strasbourg. The gentleman he sought to fashion had something of his own idiosyncrasy. There were two other writers of Elizabeth's reign who did something to fashion the gentleman, if they did so on different lines. One was a poet, Edmund Spenser, who would hardly have endorsed Ascham's verdict on *Le morte Darthur*. The *Faerie Queene* was intended to be the institution of a gentleman; it was meant, as Spenser says in his prefatory letter, 'to fashion a gentleman or noble person in virtuous and gentle discipline'. It was accordingly 'disposed into twelve books, fashioning xii moral virtues...as Aristotle hath devised'. Perhaps Spenser, the poet's poet, has made more poets than gentlemen; but at any rate he bequeathed to his country a good and gracious tradition of virtuous and gentle discipline. The other writer of Elizabeth's time who also wished to fashion a gentleman was Sir Thomas North. He had already translated and published, at the end of the reign of Mary Tudor, the Spaniard Guevara's *Dial of Princes*; but this didactic romance about the life of Marcus Aurelius could hardly compete with the charm and the grace of *Il Cortigiano*. There was more to be said for his version of Plutarch's lives of the noble Grecians and Romans, which he made from the French of Bishop Amyot (a translator general from the Greek, who also made a charming version of *Daphnis and Chloe*), and which was published in 1579. North's Plutarch rapidly became a book which took its place on the shelves of a gentleman's study along with Elyot's *Governor*, Hoby's version of *The Courtier*, Lambarde's *Eirenarcha* (the standard manual of the Justices of the Peace, which first appeared in 1581), and—it might be—Foxe's *Book of Martyrs*. Like Spenser in his prefatory epistle, North too explained in his preface that he was concerned to fashion a gentleman. If men will but read these lives, 'what service is there in war', he asks, 'what honour in peace, that they will not be ready to do for their worthy Queen?'[1]

[1] There is an interesting work of the eighteenth century, called *The British Plutarch*, which perhaps deserves to be mentioned. (The author owes his possession of a copy—in the new and revised edition of the year 1776—to the generosity of Mr Basil Blackwell.) It is an adaptation of Plutarch's idea, and contains 'the lives of the most eminent statesmen, patriots, divines, warriors, philosophers, poets and artists of Great Britain and Ireland from the accession of Henry VIII to the present time'. It is in six volumes, each containing some dozen or so lives. The object is edification and the creation of a type of character: 'by having before our eyes the *principles* of men of honour and probity, enforced by *example*, we shall be animated to fix upon some great model to be the rule of our conduct' (Introduction to the edition of 1776, p. vii). The work is 'ornamented with elegant frontispieces'. The frontispiece to the first volume represents 'VALOUR, WISDOM, and PIETY, conducting a British youth to the Temple of Fame'. It may be added that Cromwell was admitted into the British Plutarch, for the first time, in the edition of 1776. Perhaps his admission is one of the notable events of the year 1776—the year of the Declaration of Independence.

V

There are a number of different ways in which this essay might end. One way would be to describe, in some particular example— let us say Sir Philip Sidney—the actual pattern of a Tudor gentleman. Another way would be to seek to show how the general ideal of culture comprised in the general pattern of the gentleman —scholarship, courtesy, true love, and service to the commonwealth—became the inspiration of literature. (That would be a far larger theme than the theme, which has just been touched upon, of the inspiration derived by poets from the particular part or aspect of the ideal set out at the end of the *Book of the Courtier*.) Perhaps great literature always needs the inspiration of some general ideal of culture, some homogeneous and harmonious pattern of a four-square way of life. Without that pattern, poetic emotion and literary ardour may still be there (nature does not confine her gifts of grace and capacity to any particular epoch, and there is no evidence that they are scattered unevenly among the generations); but deprived of a channel or mould they may run zigzag and at will—as perhaps they do to-day, in much of our modern poetry. Certainly the ages in which there have been patterns of culture—the Periclean age in ancient Athens; the Augustan in ancient Rome; the Elizabethan age in Tudor England —have been great ages of literature.

But it is better to end on another note, and to face a doubt which cannot but gnaw at the back of the mind as one thinks of the gentleman. This ideal of the gentleman—where did it leave the common man, God's ordinary Englishman, and what mansion had it for him in its house? It is a difficult question to answer, though Sir Thomas Smith was feeling his way to some sort of solution. Generally, the Tudor age was bound in an old idea of established order and fixed degrees: an order established by nature; degrees fixed by a natural law of hereditary transmission. It is an idea as old as the book of Ecclesiasticus. It is true that the Jewish author, writing in the third century B.C., speaks of 'the scribe', where English writers of the sixteenth century A.D. speak of 'the gentleman'; but *mutato nomine* they tell the same tale. 'The wisdom of the scribe cometh by opportunity of leisure; and he that hath little business shall become wise. How shall he become wise that holdeth the plough...and whose discourse is of the stock of bulls?...So is every artificer and workmaster...so is the smith...so is the potter.... They will maintain the state of the world, and in the handywork of their craft is their prayer. *Not so he that hath applied his soul....He* will seek out the wisdom of all the ancients.... *He* will serve among great men, and appear before him that ruleth; *he* will travel through the land of strange nations.'

These words, written in Hebrew and then translated into Greek nearly two thousand years earlier, might almost serve to describe the Tudor gentleman—versed in 'the wisdom of all the ancients'; serving in the presence at the court, and 'appearing before him that ruleth'; travelling through the land of Italy. Indeed, they are almost echoed by one of the parties to a debate of the year 1541, which is reported in Strype's *Cranmer*. It was a notable debate, and indeed it has often been noted; but it deserves to be noted once more. A body of commissioners was dealing with the constitution of the grammar school at Canterbury. Some of them wanted to confine the school to the sons and younger brothers of the gentry. They argued that 'it was meet for the ploughman's son to go to the plough, and the artificer's son to apply the trade of his parent's vocation; and the gentlemen's children are meet to have the knowledge of government and rule in the commonwealth'. The argument met with a rejoinder. The rejoinder came from Thomas Cranmer; and like the argument which it rebutted it had precedents in its favour—precedents less ancient than the book of Ecclesiasticus, but at any rate as old as the days of Dante and Chaucer.[1]

Cranmer was a man who wavered: a sighing and sensitive reed, shaken by the wind. He said different things in different weathers, not only on this issue of class, but also on other issues which vexed men's minds and tried their souls in those troubled times—times

[1] Supra, pp. 125-28.

of which he might well have said (as Tom Paine said of his own in the first sentence of the first number of the *Crisis* in 1776): 'These are the times that try men's souls.' But one of the noblest things which he said, in any weather or at any time, was the rejoinder he made in 1541. 'I grant much of your meaning herein as needful in a commonwealth; but yet utterly to exclude the ploughman's son and the poor man's son from the benefit of learning...is as much to say as that Almighty God should not be at liberty to bestow His great gifts of grace upon any person... according to His most godly will and pleasure, Who giveth His gifts both of learning and other perfections in all sciences unto all kinds and states of people indifferently;...wherefore if the gentleman's son be apt to learning let him be admitted; if not apt, let the poor man's child, that is apt, enter his room.'[1] This is the doctrine of Dante and Chaucer; but it is that doctrine raised to a higher power because it is based more deeply on a foundation of religious faith. At the height at which he stands, Cranmer can see, and express, both sides of the issue in debate. He sees that a commonwealth needs a differentiation of social functions ('I grant much of your meaning herein as needful in a commonwealth'); and he emphasised that side afterwards when he challenged the rebels of 1549. But he also sees the other and greater side of the matter: that if God has made a world of degrees, like an ascending ladder, He has not fixed men irrevocably to the rung of their father's birth. He has not made a static and hierarchical world of hereditary rungs, to serve as a rigid mechanism: He has made a world in which things and men grow, by an evolutionary process, and He scatters the seeds 'of learning and other perfections' with a broad and prodigal hand, 'unto all kinds of states of people indifferently', in order that the world may grow, and grow abundantly, in all its parts—gentle and simple, rich and poor.[2]

[1] Strype's *Cranmer*, I. 127, quoted by A. E. Dobbs, *Education and Social Movements*, 1700–1850, pp. 83, 104.

[2] Tom Paine, in c. III of the second part of *The Rights of Man*, unconsciously repeats the argument of Cranmer in his own Radical terms. 'It is impossible to controul nature in her distribution of mental powers. She gives them as she pleases;...it would be as ridiculous to attempt to fix the hereditaryship of

It is perhaps a fancy—but who shall say that it is not a legitimate play of the fancy?—to think that the genius of Cranmer's words is enshrined in the catechism which comes at the beginning of the order of Confirmation in the First Prayer Book of Edward VI (1549): 'What is thy dutie towardes thy neighbour?...Not to covet nor desire other mennes goodes. But learne and laboure truely to geate my owne living, and to doe my duetie in that state of life: unto which it shal please God to cal me.' The crucial words are the last: they may almost be said to be the *one* word, 'shal'. Often misquoted, with 'shall' turned into 'hath' and 'please' into 'pleased', the words still stand in every version and every copy of the Book of Common Prayer. They imply a whole philosophy. Gentlemen not only 'be made good cheap in England': they are also made good cheap by God in the world He has made— a world in which any of us, wherever we are born, may be called by His will to a higher state, and prove that we are gentlemen.

Cranmer had much to do with the first Prayer Book of Edward VI, but it was not he who composed the Catechism or wrote these words. They have been generally attributed to Dr Nowell, a member of Brasenose College, Oxford, and a master of Westminster School from 1543 onwards; and it is certain that he wrote, in Latin, three catechisms—the Large, the Middle and the Small—of which the last is practically identical with the Catechism of the Prayer Book.[1] Others, however, have

human beauty as of wisdom;...there is always a sufficiency somewhere in the general mass of society for all purposes; but with respect to the parts of society it is continually changing its place.'

[1] The 'Small Catechism' was published *Latine et Graece* in 1574, and translated into English by Thomas Norton. Nowell himself was concerned in a famous case of constitutional law, in 1553, when it was decided that, being a member of Convocation, he was incapable of sitting in the House of Commons as member of parliament for a Cornish borough by which he had been elected. In spite of the testimony of Izaak Walton (who speaks of him as 'the good old man' who made 'that good, plain, unperplexed catechism printed in our good old service book'), it seems difficult to believe that Nowell was the author of the Catechism of 1549 or of the two 'Duties' which it contains. In 1549 he was only, as yet, a master at a school; and it was not till 1551 that he was made a

thought that the author was John Ponet or Poynet, a Fellow of Queens' College, Cambridge, who had become Cranmer's chaplain some time before 1547. This brings us nearer to Cranmer; but we are perhaps brought nearer still by another view, which assigns the authorship of the Catechism to Thomas Goodrich, like Cranmer a Fellow of Jesus College, Cambridge,[1] and Bishop of Ely from 1534 till his death in 1554. It is at any rate notable that, on the outside of the window of a gallery which he erected in the year 1550, there is cut in the stone the 'Dutie towards God' and the 'Dutie towards thy neighboure' in nearly the very same words as those of the Prayer Book of 1549; and it appears that Bishop Goodrich sat on the Committee which prepared the Prayer Book. But whoever the author of the words may have been, there they stand; and in any case they are a living index of the thoughts of the clergy of the Church of England about 'degrees' and ranks and stations in the middle of the sixteenth century.

There is also another and final index; and that is the simple index of fact. In 1552, as part of a scheme for the relief of the poor of London, which had already been set in train in the last days of Henry VIII, Christ's Hospital was founded, 'where the poor children are trained in the knowledge of God and some virtuous discipline'.[2] What was the training which these poor children, 'taken', as a contemporary remarks, 'from the dunghill', were given by the citizens of London 'in the house that was the late Grey Friars'? They not only learned the Catechism: they also received some training in the classics and produced their Grecians. Christ's Hospital stands as a monument to prove that 'men can rise on stepping stones' according to the gifts bestowed upon them and the call which they have received.

prebendary and received a license to preach. It seems more likely that Nowell's later writings on the Catechism (which first began in 1570 when he published the Large and the Middle Catechism) produced an *ex post facto* tradition that he was the author of the catechism of 1549.

[1] Goodrich took the degree of M.A. in 1514: Cranmer in 1515.

[2] Quoted in Adamson, op. cit. p. 147.

VI

OLIVER CROMWELL AND THE ENGLISH PEOPLE

I

Oliver Cromwell has no grave. His dead body, dug up by the Royalists after the King came back, at the beginning of 1661, was hung and beheaded, and then thrown into a pit.[1] As he has no grave, so, until recent times, he has had no memorial. It was not until 1845 that the first great book was dedicated to his memory; and then it was dedicated by a Scotsman, Thomas Carlyle, who collected and elucidated, in three volumes, his letters and speeches. It was not until 1899 that a statue was at last erected in his honour at Westminster, under the shadow of our Houses of Parliament. In general recognition, he is a late-comer into our national house of fame. But he has come at last, free from the shadows by which he was long obscured, and visible in his own true lineaments. To-day we can interrogate him freely.

'What is your substance, whereof are you made?'

What is his significance in English history? What is the cause for which he stands, and what are the elements of our national life which are embodied and incarnate in his memory?

He was born in the April of 1599, at the end of the reign of Queen Elizabeth, in the Eastern Counties of England, in a fen-land country which was the home of a deep and devout Protestantism. He had the genius of this country, and above all its religious temper, deep in his blood.[2] He was over forty-one when he first

---

[1] The pit was beneath the gallows at Tyburn, near Marble Arch. 'Where Connaught Square now stands, a yard or two beneath the street,...lies the dust of the great Protector.' C. H. Firth, *Life of Cromwell*, p. 452.

[2] Nobody who has lived in Cambridge can have failed to feel the peculiar genius of the Eastern Counties, with their far and pensive distances. In an agricultural age they must have been well populated, by a sober class of tolerably prosperous farmers, who were akin to the soil and the far-spread open sky. Here, in the sixteenth century, the Reformation struck its roots; and 'the fenland

appeared on the stage of public events, as member for the borough
of Cambridge, in the Long Parliament which met at the end of
1640. He died eighteen years later, in the September of 1658, a little
short of his sixtieth year. In these eighteen years he had wrestled,
in Parliament and outside, with grave religious and political
problems: he had made himself a great soldier, and ridden from
victory to victory in nine long years of war, from the middle of
1642 to the end of 1651; and finally, for the last five years of his
life, from 1653 to 1658, when he was already weary and spent, he
had carried on his shoulders the general burden of government,
as 'His Highness the Protector of the Commonwealth of England,
Scotland and Ireland'. He had served his generation simultaneously
in the political parliament, the military camp, and the religious
congregation. The last of the three had always been his true home.
From that home he went out to war and politics, and wherever
he went he carried its spirit with him. But military fame and
political power weighed with him as well as religious faith: he
was no pure saint, but a thunderer of war and a calculator of
political expediencies mixed with a seeker who sought for God.
In his various and comprehensive nature, which in the world of
action was what Shakespeare's was in the world of literature,
there were different and conflicting elements. His achievement is
as various as himself, and it leaves room for different and conflicting interpretations.

seminary' of Cambridge, drawing on the country round, became its particular
home. In the seventeenth century it was the district round Cambridge which
largely peopled New England; and it was the same district which was the
peculiar home of Independency, and the recruiting ground of the Ironsides.
Oliver Cromwell and Isaac Newton both represent, in their different ways, its
deep sense of the fundamental rules which govern nature and human life: they
both served, in their different capacities, in

'The army of unalterable law.'

Even to-day the Congregationalists and Baptists are stronger in Huntingdon
and Cambridge than in any other district of England. (Frank Tillyard, article
in the *Sociological Review* on 'The Distribution of the Free Churches in England',
January 1935.)

II

Shall we interpret him as the maker of the unity of the United Kingdom; the author of unification; the creator of one *Reich* or *Respublica*, which transcended and abolished local particularisms, and embraced all the British Isles? In a sense he was. The Lord Protector governed a single *Respublica*, in the Parliament of which representatives of England, Scotland and Ireland sat together for the first time. There was a single citizenship, a common constitution, a single system of trade, a common ordering of the basis of religious life, through all its borders. But this was not so much his own intention, as the aftermath and consequence of a civil war, in which all three countries had been engaged, and which, ending in the victory of one cause, necessarily ended in the enthroning of that cause over all the three countries. In any case—and this is the fundamental thing—the achievement did not last. It perished within two years of his death, when Charles II was restored to the throne in 1660. Scotland and Ireland went back to their old positions. If Scotland afterwards consented to a Union, in 1707, she consented to a voluntary and negotiated union, which owed nothing to the memory of Cromwell's experiment. If Ireland was afterwards, long afterwards, brought into a Union, in 1801, that union too was independent of his memory; and it has not lasted. What Cromwell did in Scotland and Ireland was written on wind and running water. The wind blew; the waters ran; and it went. Even the part of the Cromwellian settlement of Ireland which seemed most permanent—the planting of English landlords on more than half of the soil of Ireland—is gone. It began to go in 1870, when the principle of land purchase, or in other words of the substitution of peasant proprietorship in lieu of tenancy, was introduced in favour of Irish tenants: it finally went in the first decade of the twentieth century.

III

Another interpretation of Cromwell would make him the author of colonial expansion and imperial policy—the arch-founder, if not the first begetter, of the British Empire. In the days of a conscious passion for colonial expansion this was a natural interpretation. We always tend to interpret the past in the light of the prepossessions which we cherish in the present; and when we idealise colonial expansion as a sign of national vigour, a symbol of national prestige, and an expression of national responsibility towards undeveloped peoples and regions, we are apt to project our ideals into the past. There is a sense in which the interpretation of Cromwell's achievement in colonial and imperial terms is correct. His Admiral Blake pushed into the Mediterranean, partly in pursuit of fugitive Royalists who had taken to privateering, partly to police the seas against the Algerian pirates, and partly to make a display of English naval strength which might overawe Catholic powers inimical to the English Protestant Republic. This was the beginning of a policy of the acquisition of Mediterranean power which was afterwards steadily pursued. Again there was Cromwell's war with Spain, which virtually began at the end of 1654 and lasted for the rest of his life. This may be viewed as a challenge to the great colonial empire of Spain; and it certainly resulted in the conquest of Jamaica, in the West Indies, during the summer of 1655. Nor was this all. During his ascendancy a common Puritanism—a common basis of Free Church feeling—cemented more closely the colonies of New England to the government of Old England. Again a new Navigation Law of 1651 (not, it is true, due to Cromwell, and resulting in a Dutch War which ran counter both to his religious feelings and to his political sympathies) practically reserved the commerce of English colonies for English shipping. There even seems to have been a conscious theory of the necessity of the expansion of England. The words of Harrington, a political theorist of Cromwell's time, may be cited. 'You cannot plant an oak in a flower pot: she must have earth for her roots, and heaven for her branches.'

All this is well worth noting; and it all seems to lead naturally to the view that Cromwell, and Cromwell's England, were imperialists. But there are deep and cogent reasons against accepting such a simple and categorical explanation. Those reasons may be stated in one word—the word 'religion'. We must never forget that the England of the years in which Cromwell spent his active life—the England of the years 1620 to 1660—was an England in a great mood of religious exaltation. This exaltation was not a show or a cloak or an hypocrisy: it was the genuine spirit of the age. Moved by the influence of this spirit, the expansion of England was a religious expansion. This is apparent in two ways, different from one another, and yet complementary to one another. In the first place, the effective and permanent expansion of England—anterior to Cromwell, and beginning about 1620 in the form of Puritan emigration—was in no way due to political or 'geopolitical' reasons. It was not promoted by the State: it was undertaken from motives of religion in order to enable men to escape from the State and its policy of compulsory religious unity, and to find a religious haven or 'free port' for the unrestricted commerce of conscience. 'The expansion of England in the seventeenth century was an expansion of society and not of the State. Society expanded to escape from the pressure of the State.'[1] In the second place, and in the days when, under Cromwell, the State began to take a hand, the State itself—the Puritan State of the period of the Commonwealth—was predominantly moved by considerations of religion. We should be committing treason against the spirit of the age, and we should be guilty of false history, if we did not recognise the dominance of these considerations. When Cromwell embarked on war against Spain in 1655 (and it is by this war, and not the earlier Dutch War, which was *not* his, that we must judge

---

[1] George Unwin, *Studies in Economic History*, p. 341 (controverting Seeley's thesis in *The Expansion of England*). On Unwin's general view of Society and its relation to the State, see p. 459. He notes, in another passage (p. 28), that 'it is worthy of remark that, whilst the main feature of British history since the seventeenth century has been the remoulding of the State by a powerful Society, the main feature of German history in the same period has been the remoulding of Society by a powerful State'.

his motive), he was not acting on grounds of colonial expansion and imperial policy. The evidence may be found in his speech to Parliament, one of his longest, and the most curiously and deeply illuminated, of 17 September 1656. That speech has been cited by a German writer, Dr Carl Schmitt, in an essay on 'the conception of the political',[1] as a revealing illustration of the truth that the essence of 'the political' is the ability and the will to distinguish friend and foe, and highly to resolve on the negation of the foe. But the speech is not a speech in terms of 'the political', nor is it couched in the interest of the English State. It is a speech in terms of 'the religious', and it is couched in the interest of a common European Protestantism. The battle which Cromwell sees arrayed is not a battle of states, but a battle of faiths. It is true that he begins his speech by a frank confession of enmity: 'Why, truly, your great Enemy is the Spaniard.' But we begin to see into his mind as soon as he states the reasons and the ground of this enmity. The Spaniard is an enemy 'naturally, by that antipathy which is in him—and also providentially'. That word 'providentially', as Carlyle justly interprets it, means 'by special ordering of Providence'. It is the Providence of God which has put an enmity between the true religion and the religion which is not true, and therefore between the Englishman and the Spaniard. Nor is the true religion the cause or the interest of England only. 'All the honest interests; yea, all interests of the Protestants, in Germany, Denmark, Helvetia and the Cantons, and all the interests in Christendom, are the same as yours. If you succeed...and be

[1] Carl Schmitt, *Der Begriff des Politischen*, pp. 54–5. The author argues that political thought and instinct show themselves in the capacity of distinguishing friend and foe: the zenith of *die große Politik* is the moment in which the foe is recognized, concretely and clearly, as foe. Cromwell's speech of 1656 against Spain is cited as a particular evidence of this doctrine: 'Für die Neuzeit sehe ich den mächtigsten Ausbruch einer solchen Feindschaft—stärker als das gewiß nicht zu unterschätzende *écrasez l'infâme* des 18. Jahrhunderts, stärker als der Franzosenhaß des Freiherrn von Stein, stärker sogar als Lenins vernichtende Sätze gegen den Bourgeois und den Westlichen Kapitalismus—in Cromwells Kampf gegen das papistische Spanien.' Dr Schmitt proceeds to quote some sentences from the speech—sentences striking enough, in their isolation, but, in their general context, entirely removed from any idea of *die große Politik*.

convinced what is God's Interest, and prosecute it, you will find that you act for a very great many who are God's own.' It is therefore for 'God's Interest', and 'all the interests in Christendom', that Cromwell would have England stand. Not but what he feels (for it would be wrong to blink the truth or to deny some national prejudice) that England has some sort of special right or special duty to act. 'We are Englishmen: that is one good fact; and if God give a nation the property of valour and courage, it is honour and a mercy from Him.' But having made that confession, he adds at once, in his very next words: 'And much more than English! Because you all, I hope, are Christian Men, who know Jesus Christ, and know that Cause.'

Men's motives are always mixed. If religion shone in the forefront of Cromwell's mind, it would be folly to deny that mixed motives of Mars and Mammon—military and naval glory, territorial conquest and expansion, the profit of trade and commerce —were operative in the background. English Puritanism in general was something of a Midas, turning what it touched into gold, as well as an Antigone, resolved to obey at any cost the commandments of God. Oliver himself could say to his Council in 1654: 'Having 160 ships swimming...we think our best consideration had to keep us this reputation and improve it for some good, and not lay them up by the walls....This design would cost little more than laying by the ships, and that with hope of great profit.'[1] Again, if Cromwell could ejaculate, with a genuine passion, 'And much more than English!', he could also believe, as John Milton had said in his *Areopagitica* in 1644, that when 'God is decreeing to begin some great and new period in his Church...what does he then but reveal himself to his servants, and as his manner is first to his Englishmen?' There *was* a kind of Hebraic exclusive nationalism in the Puritans (after all, their minds were fed on the reading of the Old Testament); and though it had a religious basis, and could, in virtue of that basis, show a generous European side, it was apt to become, at the best an idealised, and

---

[1] Quoted from the *Clarke Papers*, Vol. III, p. 207, in G. M. Trevelyan's *England under the Stuarts*, pp. 322–3.

at the worst a commercialised patriotism. Professor Trevelyan has justly said that 'the Protector's mind could never logically separate this idealised patriotism from his Protestant and Free Church sympathies'.[1] Perhaps even we, three hundred years later, cannot make such a logical separation. The currents of this world are not always corrupted; but they are seldom, if ever, unmixed.

IV

When all is said, and when all allowances have been made, it remains impossible to explain the achievement of Cromwell in any simple political terms, whether of the unification of the United Kingdom, or of colonial expansion and imperial policy, or of both. The unification and the expansion were both incidental: they were both by-products, naturally enough thrown out, of great motions of the human mind and the stirring of great events which had other intentions and purposes. Those motions, and that stirring, had produced two Civil Wars, which lasted from the summer of 1642 to the autumn of 1651. In the course of these Civil Wars two things, both unprojected and unforeseen, had happened. In the first place all the three countries—England, Scotland and Ireland—had been involved. The end of the struggle necessarily entailed a new settlement of their relations; and that settlement, which was not originally in debate, but had been afterwards drawn into debate, was necessarily made, as has already been said, by the victor in the debate, and necessarily made on the basis of a unified system congruous with his own ecclesiastical and political ideas. It was an inevitable result; but it was as unintended as it was inevitable, and it proved to be as temporary as it was unintended. In the second place the Civil Wars, in the course of their long duration, had raised questions of foreign policy—questions of the relations of the British Isles to other Powers and the outer world. There had been threats of intervention during the wars; there was still the fear of intervention when they ended. Moreover, they had produced a military and a naval

[1] *England under the Stuarts*, p. 322.

force unparalleled before in our history, and unparalleled for long years afterwards—a drilled and disciplined army, which numbered 60,000 foot, horse and dragoons by the beginning of the Protectorate; and a navy vastly increased in strength and vastly improved in the quality of its officers and men. Fear was thus backed by force; and fear and force, guided by a religious crusading sentiment which was curiously mixed with an Hebraic nationalism (itself mixed, in its turn, with calculations of territorial conquest and commercial gain), issued in war with Spain. But this again was an aftermath and a by-product in the history of the Puritan Revolution and in the evolution of Oliver Cromwell. It was not an original part of the great struggle of his public life. It came at the end, in the winter of his years; and this is one of the cases in which we cannot judge by the end. We shall judge him better if we remember that at the end of the first Civil War, in the winter of 1646-7, he was seriously thinking of leaving England, with such soldiers as he could gather, to fight with the German Calvinists in the Thirty Years War.

V

This brings us back to the real core of Cromwell's achievement and his essential significance in the history of his country. He was the incarnation—perhaps the greatest we have had—of the genius of English Nonconformity, which is the peculiar and (it may even be said) the cardinal factor in the general development of English politics and English national life. He was the expression of the great Free Church movement which runs through our modern history, and therefore, fundamentally—because the two things are intimately and irrevocably interconnected—he was also the expression of what I would call the great Free State movement which also runs through our history. This is a deep and solemn thesis, which demands explanation; which needs qualification; but which, in the last resort and the general account, commands its own justification.

When Cromwell appeared on the scene, at the end of 1641, the current and dominant notion in England was the notion that a single political society was, and ought to be, a single religious society. It was a notion inherited from the Middle Ages, with the one difference that, while the Middle Ages had believed that a single *universal* political society involved a single universal religious society, seventeenth-century England believed that a single *national* political society involved a single national religious society. This was, in effect, a doctrine of religious territorialism. We may also call it a doctrine of the equivalence of *populus*, *respublica* and *ecclesia*; or, if we prefer the English terms used by Hooker, a doctrine of the equivalence of people, commonwealth and Church; or, if we use German terms, a doctrine of the equivalence of *Volk, Staat und Kirche*. Now in 1641 there were two schools of opinion which both accepted this doctrine, but none the less differed from one another. There were the Anglicans, who believed that all England should be a single Anglican Church, episcopally governed, and following a modified form of the old medieval ritual. There were the Presbyterians or Calvinists, who believed that all England should be a single Presbyterian Church, governed by presbyteries and synods of presbyteries, and following the new ritual of Geneva. These two schools, differing in spite of their common premise, not only differed on religious issues: they also differed in politics. The Anglicans, who found room for the King, in the system of episcopal government, as the supreme governor of the Church, were Royalists. The Presbyterians, who found room for a General Assembly, in the system of Presbyterian government, as the final authority of the Church, were Parliamentarians. But between them both, or over and above them both, there remained a *tertium quid*. This was the Independents; in other words, the members of the Free Churches; in other words again —to mention their two great main varieties—the Congregationalists and the Baptists. The essence of their position was that they denied what I have called the doctrine of equivalence, which was accepted both by the Anglicans and the Presbyterians. They did *not* believe that a single political society was, or ought to be, a single religious society. They did *not* profess the doctrine of religious territorialism. They were essentially and literally Nonconformists. They believed that any voluntary society of Christian men and women, in any area or neighbourhood in which they were gathered together, should be free to form their own congregation and to constitute their own Free Church.

This was a cardinal tenet which lay at the heart of Cromwell's thought, and vitally affected the development of England during his lifetime and for generations afterwards. It had large and general consequences. One of these consequences was the idea and practice of the limited State. According to this tenet, a political society had not the right to require and impose the pattern of a single religious society, corresponding to its own image, or to demand a uniform system of ecclesiastical government and religious ritual. Liberty of conscience and liberty of worship were fundamentals; and no human authority could defeat them or abridge them. This was a great and pregnant consequence; and it might, and ultimately did, widen out into further issues— the issue, for example, of free trade, or again that of free labour, to both of which something of a religious consecration came to be attached by virtue of the original and seminal idea of the Free Church.[1] So great, and so potent, was the genius of Independent Non-Conformity. But there was also another consequence of the cardinal tenet of the Free Church. This was the idea and practice of the democratic State, dependent on the principle of free association, and based on the deliberate thought of all its members, collected by due process of discussion and reduced, by that process, to the unity of a common sense. If the Independents did not desire a Church after the image of the State, they came to require a State after the image of the Church—that is to say, of

[1] The Liberal Party, the party of Free Trade, was also the party of Nonconformity in its hey-day; and 'the Nonconformist Conscience' (a term of derision, like the term 'Puritan' in its original usage, but a term of derision which turned to praise) attached a peculiar consecration to the doctrine of Free Trade. The Labour Party, which may be termed the party of Free Labour (devoted to the rights and the liberties of the trade unions), has drawn many of its leaders from the circles of the Free Churches; and the cause of the free churchman and that of the free 'tradesman' (in the sense in which the term is still used colloquially in Northern England) have obvious analogies and sympathies.

their own Free Church. Just as the religious congregation was to be freely constituted and governed, and to wait upon God until it discovered the common 'sense of the meeting' and thereby knew His way of righteousness, so the political association was also to be freely constituted and governed, and it too was to wait on the movement of the human spirit, going this way and that in discussion, until it too discovered a common sense and thereby knew the way of human justice and peace.

VI

These were ideas which seethed in the mind of Cromwell and the minds of his brother-Independents, and which they sought to realise in the hour of victory—in the years from 1653 to 1658, when both the Anglican Royalists, who stood for episcopacy and the divine right of the King, and the Presbyterian Parliamentarians, who stood for presbyteries and the sovereign right of a small and exclusive Parliament, had been defeated by the issue of the two Civil Wars. But that very phrase, 'the hour of victory', reveals a great paradox in the history of the Independents, which was also the paradox of Cromwell's life and achievement. In its very nature the cause of the Free Church is not victorious, and has no hour of victory; it is a protest and a challenge to an alien majority. It is the cause of a struggling minority—protesting, challenging, resisting. It is the cause of an Antigone, face to face with Creon and his edicts. When Antigone becomes Creon— when the resister himself is armed with the powers and resources of the State—there is an inherent paradox, or rather dualism, in his position. This dualism or paradox becomes all the more evident when we reflect that the strength of Cromwell, and of his Independent adherents, lay from first to last in the army. Cromwell began his effective career as a colonel of cavalry. He became, in 1645, Lieutenant-General of the whole army opposed to the King: he became, in 1650, its General. He was an army leader, carried by the army on its shoulders into control when the army became, at the end of the wars, the residuary victor in the struggle

—when the King had been executed, in January 1649, and when the small and exclusive Parliament, which stood for its privilege no less stiffly than the King for his prerogative, had been evicted in April 1653. It is true that the army was a remarkable and unparalleled army; and that in two ways. Largely under the influence of Cromwell, who when he first began to raise a troop of cavalry had insisted on having around him honest God-fearing men, it was an army penetrated through and through by the spirit of Independency—an army which assembled in meeting for prayer on the eve of any great issue, and would stop to sing a short Psalm even in the heat and passion of battle.[1] It was also an army penetrated by a democratic spirit—an army which held itself to be a great primary assembly of the people as well as a great congregation of the faithful. It had known, in its day, what we should nowadays call soviets of soldiers (they were then called Agitators or Agents of the regiments): it continued to know debates, projects of constitutions, discussions of Englishmen's rights and duties....But it was an army none the less. It gave its General a world of trouble. But he was its General; and he held it together as long as he lived.

This standing Free Church army (not all Free Church, for in its early days it had contained a number of pressed or conscripted soldiers, and in its later days it contained a number who followed the wars as an ordinary profession; but still predominantly Free Church) is a standing curiosity in our history, as its memory was a standing fear to later generations. Normally our Free Churches have stood away from the army: normally our army has stood in connection with the Crown and the Established Church, to which it then stood opposed. But these were revolutionary times; and this army was a revolutionary, and therefore abnormal, thing. It was a wedding of two different ideals—the ideal of the voluntary life in things temporal as well as spiritual: the ideal of the life

---

[1] During the battle of Dunbar, on the morning of 3 September 1650, 'the Lord-General made a halt, and sang the Hundred-and-seventeenth Psalm'. But he only halted till the horse could gather for the pursuit; and the Hundred-and-seventeenth Psalm is a psalm of two verses only.

which is schooled, regimented and drilled. The army in which these ideals were wedded believed in a free England, the home of free churchmanship and corresponding free citizenship; and yet it was constrained to hold England down by virtue of its very beliefs. After all it was a minority. In that it was true to the general genius of its cause, which in the general run of our history has been the cause of a struggling minority. But it was a minority which for the time being held the sword, and possessed might, majesty, dominion and power. It faced the majority boldly, but with a division in its heart, enforcing liberty, and yet disbelieving in force. The contradiction could not last; and it did not last. But there was nothing ignoble and nothing common or mean, in all the contradiction, and all the wrestlings and strivings, which vexed in their hour of victory the general body of Independents, the Independent army which was their core, and 'the great Independent', Oliver the Protector (not unfitly so called), who was summoned by a heavy and exacting destiny to reconcile the principles of the cause he led with the urgent needs of national healing and settling.

VII

The sole and ultimate responsibility of Cromwell, and the great period of his life by which his achievement and significance must ultimately be judged, belong to the five and a half years which lie between the eviction of Parliament in April 1653 and his death in September 1658.[1] True, he had been the dynamic and driving

---

[1] It is curious to reflect that the space of five and a half years was also the space given to Julius Caesar. Mommsen, in a famous passage of his *History of Rome* (Vol. IV, p. 557, in the English translation), remarks: 'Caesar ruled as King of Rome for five years and a half, not half as long as Alexander; in the intervals of seven great campaigns, which allowed him to stay not more than fifteen months altogether in the capital of his empire, he regulated the destinies of the world for the present and the future.... Thus he worked and created, as never any mortal did before or after him; and as a worker and creator he still, after wellnigh two thousand years, lives in the memory of the nations.' Cromwell's five years and a half were more pedestrian; and they were years uninterrupted by campaigns. But it would be curious to compare the fundamental significance of the five and a half years from 49 to 44 B.C. with that of the five and a half years from A.D. 1653 to 1658. Perhaps the balance would not tilt all on one side.

force for at least half a dozen years earlier, in every crisis of events. If any man won the war against the Royalists, it was he. If any man was responsible for the execution of the King, it was he. If any man left a mark upon Ireland—and a cruel mark at that—it was he. But the real test came when—the war won, the King dead, Ireland and Scotland reduced, and Parliament finally evicted —he and his army stood, at last, face to face with the final burden of decision. Fighting was over: the time for the short, sharp shrift of the sword was gone: the time had come for facing an opposition in peace, and by the methods of peace. The opposition was numerous—far more numerous than the government—and though it was various and divided, its different sections were gradually beginning to coalesce. On the extreme Right stood the Royalists and Anglicans: on the moderate Right (but still on the Right) there were some who were Presbyterian Parliamentarians, and some who were plain Parliamentarians, clinging to the notion of a traditional and historic constitution of which an historic Parliament was a necessary and essential ingredient. The Right in general, which carried with it the instincts of the country, was the side of civilianism in the face of military rule: it was the side of traditionalism; it was also, because that was part of the tradition, the side of religious uniformity. But there was also a Left, which went far beyond Cromwell and the main body of the Independents. There were political Levellers, or Radicals, who had a passion for the sovereignty of the people, manhood suffrage, the natural rights of man, and the whole of the full-fledged doctrine of revolutionary democracy which emerged in France in 1789. There were also the social Levellers—men who would be called to-day Communists, but who confined their communism, as was natural in an agrarian age, to an attack on property in land, and to the assertion that 'the Earth is the Lord's, not particular men's who claim a proper interest in it above others'. The social Levellers were few; but in raising the issue of private property, and in pressing it against the general and captains of the Independent army, they brought out a fact which must not be forgotten. Cromwell and the men with whom he worked were themselves, in many respects, innovators and radicals. But on the point of property they too were traditional and conservative. The doctrine of the Free Churches did not entail any social programme, or any new distribution of property.

In the face of this opposition Cromwell stood, first and foremost, as he had always stood, for religious liberty. He stood for the idea and practice of the limited State, which did not enforce religious uniformity, but was bound by the 'fundamental' of respecting Christian freedom of conscience and Christian freedom of worship. This meant an ensured and guaranteed toleration, obligatory on the State, and superior to the State, which thus became, under the compulsion of an overriding principle of religious liberty, the home of many forms of belief living in a common peace and interacting on one another in a mutual influence. But the toleration which was thus to proceed from the nature of a limited State was a toleration sadly and drastically limited in its own nature. Bound by the spirit of their own belief, which would only recognise as 'true religion' the Protestant form of religion, and only the more Protestant form of that form, Cromwell and his associates in the Free Churches could not tolerate Anglicanism, and far less Roman Catholicism. Both Prelacy and Popery lay beyond the pale. This was a large and sweeping exception to the principle of religious liberty—so large and so sweeping that it may seem, at any rate to our own age, to negate the principle. We have to remember that the initial range of the application of any principle is small, and will gradually grow with the benefit of time and the widening of men's minds. We have equally to remember that this principle, when it was enunciated, was a radical principle, and a flat contra-diction* of the current doctrine of the equivalence of people, commonwealth and church. The fundamental principle, in spite of the sad and drastic exceptions to its application, is that a man may freely hold his belief, and freely celebrate his worship, according to the motion of his spirit, and that no earthly authority may interfere with that motion. Cromwell, like Luther, had a firm hold of the idea of the liberty of the Christian man in the inner springs of his life; and that idea carried him even farther than Luther, because it lead him to deny, as Luther never did, the doctrine of religious territorialism—the doctrine of the equivalence of political and religious society. 'Truly, these things do respect the souls of men, and the spirits, which are the men. The mind is the man.'[1] He had stood for this idea in the first Civil War. 'For brethren, in things of the mind', he had written to Parliament in 1645, 'we look for no compulsion, but that of light and reason'. He had stood for it in the second Civil War. 'I desire from my heart', he wrote in 1648, 'I have prayed for,...union and right understanding between the godly people—Scots, English, Jews, Gentiles, Presbyterians, Anabaptists, and all.'[2] He stood for it still in the system he created in the days of his power and Protectorate. Religious funds and endowments were used for the common benefit of the Presbyterian clergy and of the Independent clergy of the Congregationalist and Baptist varieties. By the side of the clergy paid from these funds and endowments there also existed clergy, of whatever variety or denomination, supported by the free offerings of their own voluntary congregations. The Quakers were a notable example of such voluntary congregations; but the sects were numerous in these tumultuous times.

[1] The passage deserves quotation in full. 'The mind is the man. If that be kept pure, a man signifies somewhat; if not, I would very fain see what difference there is betwixt him and a beast. He hath only some activity to do some more mischief.' (Speech of 17 September 1656.) This is like Goethe:
'Er nennt's Vernunft, und braucht's allein
Nur tierischer als jedes Tier zu sein.'

[2] Quoted in C. H. Firth, *Life of Cromwell*, p. 205. The mention of the Jews deserves notice. Cromwell was personally favourable to the cause of the Jews, when they petitioned, in 1655, for freedom to reside for purposes of trade and to practise their religion. 'The fierce multitude of the Jews' had been ordered to leave England by Edward I in 1290; and there had been no Jews in England, except by stealth, for three and a half centuries. In the time of the Commonwealth the Jews were beginning to settle again in London; the petition of 1655 was a petition for the legal recognition of such settlement. The petition was referred to a committee of the Council; the committee co-opted two judges; the two judges gave it as their opinion that there was no law forbidding the settlement of Jews. Nothing was done by the committee; but the opinion of the judges opened the way for the quiet and unmolested return of the Jews to England. (S. R. Gardiner, *History of the Commonwealth and Protectorate*, Vol. II, p. 101; Vol. IV, pp. 11–15.)

Even the Anglicans sometimes met, illegally but by connivance, for public worship; and though even that was denied to the Roman Catholics, there was no other persecution of their belief, nor were they dragooned into attendance at alien forms of worship by fine and punishment, as had been the case under the previous law of England.

In this qualified form there was, under Cromwell, a brief summer of religious liberty—not improperly so called when we remember the period of compulsory religious uniformity which preceded it, and the similar period which followed it when King and Church and Parliament were restored in 1660. This summer had abiding fruits. Thanks to Cromwell, as one of his biographers has said, 'Nonconformity had time to take root and to grow so strong in England that the storm which followed the Restoration had no power to root it up'.[1] English Nonconformity, with its doctrine of the limited State, and its aspiration towards a religious liberty which might become also a liberty in other spheres, continued to be a salt ingredient of English life, which maintained its peculiar savour and produced some of its most vital characteristics.

VIII

Religious liberty is a great thing; but there is also political liberty. It was said above that there were two consequences involved in the cardinal tenet of Independency. One of them was the idea and practice of the limited State—the State limited by the principle of religious liberty: the other was the idea and practice of the democratic State—the State based on the principle of free association and free discussion. It is plain that Cromwell stood for religious liberty and the limited State: can it also be said that he stood for political liberty and the democratic State? We must frankly confess that in Cromwell's view, as his biographer has justly said, 'religious freedom was more important than political freedom'.[2] Religion stood in the forefront of his thought. But that is not to say that he had no passion for any liberty other than

---

[1] C. H. Firth, *Life of Cromwell*, p. 369. [2] Ibid. p. 483.

religious liberty. There is one of his speeches, brief but pregnant, of 3 April 1657, which lets us into his mind. He speaks of 'the two greatest concernments that God hath in the world. The one is that of religion, and of the just preservation of all the professors of it; to give them all due and just Liberty.' This he calls 'the more peculiar interest of God', or 'the Interest of Christians'. The other is 'the Civil Liberty and Interest of the Nation'. This is subordinate to 'the Interest of Christians'; 'yet it is the next best God hath given men in this world'. It is also congruous with it: 'if any think the Interest of Christians and the Interest of the Nation inconsistent, or two different things, I wish my soul may never enter into their secrets....And upon these two interests... I shall live and die....If I were asked, why I have engaged all along in the late war, I could give no answer that were not a wicked one if it did not comprehend these two ends.'

These are words—noble words—but what did he actually do? In the first place, he clung to the idea of the sovereignty of a written constitution—the constitution contained in the Instrument of Government, which had been produced, at the end of 1653, by the officers of the army. *Prima facie*, a constitution produced by the officers of an army, though it may be called an instrument of government, can hardly appear to be an instrument of political liberty. Moreover, in a country which had just emerged from a civil war originally waged in the name of the sovereign rights of Parliament, a constitution not produced by Parliament, and over-riding the rights of all subsequent parliaments, may well seem unconstitutional. These things are true enough; and Cromwell was to experience their truth in the course of his struggles with Parliament. But there are also other things which are true. The army which produced the constitution, through the agency of its officers, held itself to be a great primary assembly of the people; and by a section of the people, though only by a section, it *was* held to be such an assembly. But much more fundamental is the fact that the constitution, however produced, was a check and a limit, not only upon any parliament which subsequently assembled, but also upon Cromwell. It was a check and a limit which he voluntarily embraced and steadily upheld. It was indeed a check and limit which stood in lieu of the consent of the people, freely given and freely renewed. That could not be had, when the bulk of the nation stood in opposition, whether to the Right or Left. The written constitution was only a second best— a substitute for national consent. But at any rate it was something; and the idea struggling behind it, if not expressed in it—the idea of the sovereignty of a constitution made and accepted by the nation—was an idea in the true logic of genuine Independency.

In the second place, limited as he already was by a written constitution, Cromwell sought also to limit himself by the need of collaboration with Parliament. True, he had evicted a Parliament—the old Parliament of the Civil Wars—at the beginning of the period of his own immediate rule. But the Parliament which he evicted had become a narrow civilian oligarchy; and two months after its eviction, even before the Instrument of Government had been adopted, with its scheme of regular Parliaments, he summoned a new Parliament himself. After the adoption of the Instrument, two Parliaments sat; and one of them held two sessions. They were not freely constituted Parliaments: even so, they disagreed with Cromwell, and he with them; and they went their way. He was not a great parliamentarian; but neither was he an autocrat. After all, he had been a Member of Parliament himself, as the representative of Cambridge, from 1640 to 1653; and he never forgot this side of himself. He never deserted the forum entirely for the camp: he lived in both, and that was a great part of his greatness. He tried to live with Parliament, to work with Parliament, to reconcile an historic and traditional parliamentary system with the spirit of the Free Churches and the fact of a Free Church army. He did not succeed; but he did not desist from endeavour. He was at once inside and outside the main current of English history which makes for the sovereignty of Parliament —partly a soldier, and partly a civilian; partly a doctrinaire of the written constitution which aimed at setting religious liberty above the reach of Parliament, and partly a parliament man.

But there was always a deep trend of his nature which drew him to the side of liberty—civil and political as well as religious. He was a man of a natural vitality and vivacity—'of such a vivacity', says a contemporary, 'as another man is when he hath drunken a cup of wine too much'. He carried himself easily among his fellows: he had, says the same contemporary, 'familiar rustic carriage with his soldiers in sporting'.[1] He did not speak much, it was noted, but he had a gift for making others speak. These are only externals; but they are externals which suggest a free spirit, able and ready to move in free intercourse with others. The trend of his inward nature led him towards a deep feeling for the free motion of the free spirit. There was a sect of his time who were called 'Seekers', because they believed in the need of perpetual search for truth. He had a sympathy for them. 'To be a Seeker', he once wrote, 'is to be of the best sect next after a finder, and such an one shall every faithful humble Seeker be in the end.' This may remind us of a saying of Jesus, in a papyrus found in Egypt some forty years ago: 'Let not him that seeketh cease till he find, and when he findeth he shall wonder, and having wondered he shall reign, and having reigned he shall rest.'[2] Seeking; finding; wondering; reigning; resting—these words are, in a sense, an epitome of Cromwell's earthly course. But it is the word 'seeking' which is peculiarly characteristic. It suggests indeed one of his defects, to which I shall have to recur at the end—his habit of seeking and waiting for some visible 'evidence' from God, which made him an opportunist ready to identify the lead of events with the march of God's own providence. But it also suggests a great quality. He believed in the seeking mind. 'The mind is the man. If that be kept pure, a man signifies somewhat.' He believed that it was man's own business to keep the mind free. He held that it was 'an unjust and unwise jealousy to deprive a man of his natural liberty upon a supposition he may abuse it: when he *doth* abuse it, judge.' This implies, fundamentally, a grasp of the principle of

---

[1] The contemporary is Baxter, quoted in C. H. Firth's *Life of Cromwell*, p. 148. The man who noted Cromwell's gift for saying little, but making others talk, was Sir William Waller, quoted in Firth, ibid. p. 119.

[2] M. R. James, *The Apocryphal New Testament*, pp. 25-6.

what we may call *civil* liberty; and though there were civil liberties which, as we shall see, he restricted, the restrictions grew less as he himself gained a freer hand, towards the close of his Protectorate, and was less tied by the control of the officers of his army. In the same way—and this is a still more important matter—Cromwell's belief in the seeking mind led him to grasp the principle of *political* liberty. We must all seek together: we must all bring together the results of our seeking; and then we must discuss together the results which we have found. This is a conception which he had already attained by the autumn of 1647, after the end of the first Civil War, and which he expressed in the earnest debates on the future of England which were then being held in the victorious army. Not only is he clear that any plan for the future of England must be such that 'the spirits and temper of the nation are prepared to receive and go along with it'—a condition which, though he apprehended it, he failed himself in the event to satisfy—but he is also clear that any plan must be framed in the give and take of free discussion. This too was a condition which he failed in the event to satisfy. But it was none the less a condition which he had apprehended and never forgot. What a philosophic student of the debates of 1647 has written is fundamentally true. 'What Cromwell has learned from his experience of the small democracy of the Christian congregation, is the insight into the purposes of life which the common life and discussion of a democratic society can give.... This is his position—toleration and recognition of differences...combined with insistence that individual views shall submit to the criticism of open discussion.'[1]

---

[1] A. D. Lindsay, *Essentials of Democracy*, pp. 19, 36. Cromwell's stipulation of 1647, that 'the spirits and temper of the nation must be prepared to receive and go along with' any plan for the future of England, recurs again in his argument to the army in the midsummer of 1648. The Agitators of the regiments were pressing for a hammer-stroke of force. Cromwell pleaded for co-operation with the friendly elements in Parliament and an agreed solution. 'What we and they gain in a free way is better than twice so much in a forced way, and will be more truly ours and our posterity's.... That you have by force I look upon as nothing. I do not know that force is to be used except we cannot get what is for the good of the kingdom without it.' (Quoted in Firth, *Life of Cromwell*, p. 169.)

But he was doomed to find that discussion was too difficult an art to practise, for the simple reason that recognition and toleration of differences were not present. The conflicting views conflicted too much to submit to mutual criticism or to be reconciled by the process of discussion. There is a story that Cromwell, on the night of the execution of Charles I, came to look at the face of his dead king, and as he looked sighed out the words, 'Cruel Necessity'. Cruel Necessity was always upon him. He wrestles with this notion of Necessity sadly in his speech of 17 September 1656. There has been, he confesses, for some time a military rule of different parts of England by Major-Generals: there has been what he somewhat mildly terms 'a keeping of some in prison'; there have been other things—'which, we say, was Necessity'. He knows that this is a dangerous plea: 'I confess, if Necessity be pretended, that is so much the more sin', but he pleads it none the less, as 'a man of honest heart, engaged to God', who is lifted above pretension, and is only acting under dire and real compulsion. He pleads Necessity the more readily because the notion of it, as a thing sent and imposed by God, is mixed in his mind with another notion—the notion of Reformation, or, as he calls it, 'Reformation of Manners'. The people have sinned and gone astray: they must be recalled to God and the way of righteousness. Here the cause of Independency and the theory of the Free Church twists round, as it were, in the hands of its authors. It loses its edge of freedom: it begins to show a stern and sharp edge of compulsion, as of 'the sword of the Lord and of Gideon'. After all (we must always remember) the cause of Independency was also the cause of an army—a drilled and disciplined army, ready to impose drill and discipline on others as well as itself. This was the paradox or dualism always inherent in Independency and in the mind of 'the great Independent' who led its cause. On the one hand freedom, and no compulsion in things of the mind. On the other hand an Old Testament passion for reformation, like that of the Hebrew prophets...and behind this passion an army.

Two notions—the notion of Reformation, and the notion of Necessity—thus conspired against the notion of Civil and Political

Liberty. Necessity imposed arbitrary taxes, called 'decimations', on the property of Royalists. Necessity and Reformation combined instituted the system of the twelve Major-Generals, in twelve districts of England, who were charged both to repress political enemies and to suppress immorality. Civil liberty was restricted by the restriction of ale-houses and race-meetings. Political liberty was equally restricted by the same restrictions. Ale-houses and race-meetings were dangerous because the disaffected, and especially the Royalists, might meet there to discuss their grievances and to ventilate their criticisms. The political philosophy of Cromwell thus yielded to political exigency. He who had insisted, in the army debates of the autumn of 1647, 'that individual views shall submit to the criticism of open discussion', was within a decade stifling criticism and preventing open discussion. He did not suppress the central parliament; but there was a period—the period of these Major-Generals, who lasted from the autumn of 1655 to the spring of 1657—during which he suppressed the local discussion that sustains and underlies an effective central parliament. It was a period during which, on one occasion, he even 'swore roundly' at Magna Carta itself—the traditional palladium of English liberties, in the name of which Parliament had originally resisted Charles I. The best that can be said for Cromwell is that the period was transitory. It ended with the abolition of the Major-Generals in the spring of 1657. The last year and a half of Cromwell's life, from the spring of 1657 to the autumn of 1658, was a period of the decline of military power; of return to the civilian tradition of English life; of closer, if still imperfect, collaboration with Parliament; of less of the twin causes of Necessity and Reformation, and more of the cause of the Civil Liberty and 'Interest of the Nation'. We do not know what this period would have been if it had lasted. It did not last. Cromwell died.

IX

He was a man contrary in some respects to our English tradition. The written constitution which he upheld; the standing army which he led; the compulsory reformation of manners which, at one period, he sought—these are all alien from our permanent trend. But in one great thing, which is greater than all these, he was fundamentally true to the English genius—or rather to one side of that genius, which is not the whole, but is none the less an integral part and essential characteristic of the whole. He was, and is, beyond any other man, the expression of English Nonconformity, alike in its qualities and its defects: the reflection of its idea of the primacy of religious liberty, its idea of the limited State, its idea of the State based on free association and proceeding by free discussion. He was not, indeed, a true reflection in all that he did or all that he was. The time-mirror was too distorting: the limitations of his age, and the contingencies of contemporary events, made the reflection of religious liberty pale and thin, and that of political liberty dwarfed and stunted. But with all its imperfections the reflection stands, and will continue to stand, whenever we look at his face and lineaments.

Was he also characteristic of the English genius in another sense? A German writer on England, Professor Dibelius, has said that the mutations of our history have always the result 'of giving fuller scope for leadership'. 'Wherever the Englishman scents a leader, he always bows before him.'[1] Was Cromwell an example of our English passion for leadership? It would be hard to maintain that

---

[1] Wilhelm Dibelius, *England* (English translation), p. 495. 'Democratic forms', he adds, 'are merely so much stage scenery, behind which the few, or, it may be, a single individual, exercise almost unlimited command.' But Dibelius also remarks, a few pages later (p. 504), that 'the English achievement is, in the last analysis, not the individual achievement of single statesmen . . . but the collective achievement of the Anglo-Saxon race. England can live without great men . . . longer than any other country.' National traits have a way of inverting themselves suddenly, according to the demands of the context.

thesis.[1] Leadership, he deeply felt, came from God, showing itself in the 'evidences' He gave and the 'providences' He vouchsafed: it was simply his business to follow. The ordinary metaphor which he used of himself was the humble metaphor of a constable, keeping the peace, as it were, in the streets. 'His work was to keep several judgements in peace, because, like men falling out in the streets, they would run their heads one against another; he was as a constable to part them and keep them in peace.' This was a saying of the year 1655: it was repeated in a speech to Parliament of 13 April 1657: 'I could not tell what my business was, nor what I was in the place I stood in, save comparing myself to a good constable set to keep the peace of a parish.' The figure of Cromwell, as he saw it himself, is that of a homely English policeman— a policeman tired and weary, who 'would have lived under his woodside, to have kept a flock of sheep, rather than undertake such a government as this is.'[2] He did not regard himself as a leader; nor was he so regarded even by his own associates. Opposed by all who were not Independents, he was also compelled to wrestle with the Independents themselves; and the way which he eventually went, even to the very end, and even when he was more free from the political control of the army than he had ever been before, was the way which his officers pressed upon him rather than his own way. The history of the Commonwealth and Protectorate is not the history of Cromwell's leadership. There was always debate and discussion, tussle and compromise, even if it were confined to the limited circle of the Independents. The habit of the Independents was always a habit of congregationalism. Even the Independent army debated, because it was a congregation as well as an army. Cromwell was Cromwell, and he out-topped his contemporaries. But there were men of iron

[1] 'No theory of the divine right of an able man to govern the incapable multitude blinded his eyes to the fact that self-government was the inheritance and the right of Englishmen.' Firth, *Life of Cromwell*, p. 483.

[2] This passage merits a fuller quotation. 'I can say in the presence of God, in comparison of whom we are but poor creeping ants upon the earth, I would have lived under my woodside....' Quoted in Firth, *Life of Cromwell*, p. 440.

and deep speech by his side; and the action which he and they took was always collegiate action.

Common to most of these men, but peculiarly deep in Cromwell, was the conviction of Divine leadership. He, above all of them, was always seeking, by 'the dark lantern of the spirit', for evidences of the providential intentions and overrulings of God. To himself he was a man who was led—led by the hand—led through the wilderness. He was always waiting for the leader's hand. This stamped him, in the memory of many generations afterwards, as the consummate hypocrite. 'He lived a hypocrite and died a traitor', wrote one of our English poets a hundred years ago.[1] But his only hypocrisy, if it can be called such, was an over-readiness to throw the cloak of Divine intention and agency over his human acts. This was not a deception of others: it was a deception of himself, and a deception honestly practised. We must remember the mental world in which he lived—a world of pre-destined happenings, in which the moving finger of God was always writing the script. He always lived in that world: he always waited on the moving finger. The word 'waiting' recurs in his language; and this waiting and attendance on Providence—this expectation that God will provide, and this holding back for His time—slips readily into a sort of opportunism which is easily misinterpreted. 'I am one of those whose heart God hath drawn out to wait for some extraordinary dispensations.' 'Let us look into providences: surely they mean somewhat: they so hang together.' 'This hath been the way God hath dealt with us all along; to keep things from our eyes all along, so that we have seen nothing in all His dispensations long beforehand—which is also a witness, in some measure, to our integrity.' 'Sir, what can be said of these things?...It is the Lord only....Sir, you see the work is done by a Divine leading.'[2]

[1] The poet was Landor. Forster quoted his verdict as 'indisputably true' as late as 1839, in his *Statesmen of the Commonwealth* (Firth, *Life of Cromwell*, p. 476); and Forster was a Liberal in politics.
[2] These passages are drawn from various periods of Cromwell's life. The first belongs to the period of the political debates in the New Model Army in 1647 (Firth, *Life of Cromwell*, p. 180). The second comes from a letter to Colonel

It is a dangerous doctrine—this doctrine of a Divine leading. It consecrates; but it consecrates too indiscriminately. It was the source of Cromwell's strength; but it was also the source of his weakness. It enabled him to hide the exigencies and the calculations of politics behind a plea of the intentions of God. It enabled a man who loved mercy to practise sometimes a sad cruelty: it enabled a man who loved liberty to allege the necessity of oppression: it enabled a man who believed in open discussion to silence its play. If this was not hypocrisy, it was at any rate self-contradiction; and this self-contradiction was inherent in himself and in the cause which he championed. Perhaps it is also inherent in the English people—the English people at large, in its general historical career, and not merely the section of the English people for whom Cromwell stood, in the middle of the seventeenth century. If that be so, then Cromwell is typical indeed: he reflects not only English Nonconformity, but also the whole of England, in its mingled composition of strength and weakness, good and evil. It is hard for an Englishman to judge. We cannot see ourselves as others see us. Cromwell himself thought the English 'the best people in the world'. That, it must be confessed, sounds a very English saying. But he only thought them best if there was present in them, and when there was present in them, another people—'the people of God', a people ready to serve Him and follow Him faithfully.[1] He could believe, more readily than we can to-day, that such another people was actually present in the English people. We, at a later age, can only long, and pray, that it may be present.

Hammond, in whose hands Charles I then lay at Carisbrooke Castle, at the end of November 1648 (ibid. p. 213). The third comes from his speech to Parliament in July 1653 (ibid. p. 331). The last comes from a letter addressed from Ireland to the Speaker of the Parliament, in November 1649 (quoted in G. M. Trevelyan, *England under the Stuarts*, p. 327).

[1] This conception of the two peoples is admirably explained in Firth, *Life of Cromwell*, pp. 482-3.

X

There is one thing for which all Englishmen can admire Cromwell. When his thought ran clear, in its rare moments of distillation, he could write and speak English which moves the heart in the same way as Shakespeare's English. He often struggled in tortuous sentences and involved periods. But sometimes he speaks out like a man; and then his speech shows his stature. His last prayer, uttered a few days before he died, is unforgettable: 'I may, I will, come to Thee, for Thy People. . . . Lord, however Thou do dispose of me, continue and go on to do good for them. Give them consistency of judgement, one heart, and mutual love; and go on to deliver them, and with the work of reformation; and make the Name of Christ glorious in the world. . . . And pardon the folly of this short Prayer, even for Jesus Christ's sake. And give us a good night, if it be Thy pleasure. Amen.' Unforgettable words. So, too, are some other words, which may fitly conclude this account of his thoughts and achievements. 'Let us all be not careful what men will make of these actings. They, will they, nill they, shall fulfil the good pleasure of God, and we shall serve our generations. Our rest we expect elsewhere: that will be durable.'[1]

[1] These unforgettable words (quoted in Firth, ibid. p. 253) show clearly how Cromwell could make the English language become a trumpet. There is music too, if less magnificent, in an earlier passage that goes back to 1643: 'I had rather have a plain russet-coated captain that knows what he fights for and loves what he knows, than that which you call a gentleman, and is nothing else' (ibid. p. 92).

NOTE ON HEROES AND DICTATORS

Carlyle interpreted Cromwell as a hero. He was interpreting him in terms of the German Romanticism with which he was imbued— a Romanticism inspired by the idea of a pantheistic universe, which sees in the people an incarnation of God, and in the hero or leader the incarnation of the people. But has this Romanticism, when it is analysed, any real bearing on the historic interpretation of Cromwell? Does it represent, in any respect, the mind of Cromwell and his contemporaries?

Cromwell himself, as has already been said, never thought of himself as a leader or hero. He was simply a constable, keeping the peace in his little parish. Nor was he regarded as a hero or leader by his contemporaries, even when they stood at his side and belonged to his following. There was a time when John Lilburn, the Leveller, spoke of him as 'the most absolute single-hearted great man in England'. But Lilburn turned, and accused him of high treason; and there was no jury in England which would ever convict honest John for the contumacy of his free speech. No sweeping enthusiasm ever surrounded Cromwell: the gusts of opinion beat steadily on him during his life, as gusts of wind shook the house in which he lay dying during his last stormy days. In the divided and tumultuous England in which he lived he was a great and elemental force; but he was surrounded by other forces, and he was never an engulfing vortex. He was not a sole and accredited leader; and he led no sole accredited party. Parties, in any sense in which they are known to us, were still unknown in his days. There were only trends of opinion, mainly religious, but partly (and consequentially) political. A dominant trend of Independent opinion, expressed in the army of which he was General, carried Cromwell along—sometimes struggling, and always seeking for a general healing and settling—on the current of its tide. But there were also other trends and other tides; and in the swirling eddies in which they met he felt himself battered and buffeted, sighing to 'have lived under his woodside...rather than undertook such a government', or attempted so arduous a work of steering.

If there was something heroic in this, it was the ordinary workaday heroism of doing a job; preventing men from 'running their heads one against another'; keeping things going; getting the business of the country done. It was something in the ordinary tradition of England, before his time and afterwards: the Duke of Wellington, if he had lived in Cromwell's day, would not have done very differently, nor would Cromwell, if he had lived in the days of Wellington, have done very differently from the Duke. The heroic interpretation of Cromwell must condescend to an ordinary level of heroism: if he was *fortis Agamemnon*, others had been brave before, and others were also to be brave afterwards. But there remains, in the general quality and temper of those times—not in him only, but in the general body of the Puritan cause— a bravery and a heroism which cannot but seem exceptional. Was the English people, for once at any rate in its history, transfigured? Did it become a people of one heart—an incarnation, in its own view, of the purpose of God; brought into the harmony of the Divine order, with all its members serving God because they served the community ordained by God? If Cromwell himself was not a hero in the Romantic sense, was the people he governed an heroic people, for the time being, in that sense?

Cromwell, as we have seen, had a doctrine of the two peoples. One was 'the people of England'; the other was 'the people of God' in England—'a people that are to God as the apple of His eye'. By the people of God he meant the Puritans; and the Puritans were, in his view, the leaven that could stir the English people to be what he called 'the best people in the world'. This doctrine and this view demand close consideration. Here, if anywhere, the analogy between Cromwellian England and the Germany of Romanticism exists; and if it does not exist here, it is not a true and essential analogy.

The core of Cromwell's doctrine of the nature of the people is a religious core. It is belief in God, through Jesus Christ, which makes the people of God; and it is the people of God who make a whole people good, because they make it serve the purposes of God. There is nothing Romantic in this idea; and there is no conception of the people as an incarnation of God or a *chosen* race. Cromwell is thinking in terms of the *mind* ('truly, these things do respect the souls of men, and the spirits, which are the men'); and thinking in those terms he can welcome into the core and central leaven of the people all who are of the right mind—'Scots, English, Jews, Gentiles, Presbyterians, Anabaptists, and all'. It is true that Cromwell and his Puritan contemporaries cherished a sort of nationalism; but the community or nation for which they cherished this feeling was a community not of blood or race but of faith. The English nation for which they were passionate was a nation by adoption and grace, after the manner of the Old Testament—'a new Israel, a chosen people, directly covenanted with God'.[1] This may be called a religious nationalism. It is a form of nationalism in which the nation is not a religion, or the object of a cult, but, on the very contrary, religion and cult are the nation, and *they* constitute the foundation of its being. It is therefore a nationalism which runs easily and naturally into internationalism. There is nothing exclusive in the conception of 'a people of God' forming the core and leaven of a whole nation. The chosen people of one nation, and the whole of that nation through them, have a community and a fellowship with the chosen peoples of other nations, and with other nations through them. Cromwell himself and the Puritans generally were good internationalists. He could tell his Parliament himself that 'all the interests of the Protestants...all the interests in Christendom, are the same as yours'. Religion might constitute a chosen people; but it also constituted an international community of chosen peoples. It is true that this international community was itself exclusive. Cromwell could not transcend, on the premises from which he started, the idea of an international community limited to the Protestant world. Nor could he transcend, on the same premises, the idea of a martial and militant internationalism, engaged in a natural and providential enmity with the Roman Catholic world gathered under the leadership of Spain. But if his internationalism was exclusive, and even militant, his nationalism had never an exclusive quality. It was based too much on religion to exclude from its generous pale any man or body of men who professed that sovereign cause.

His nationalism was the less pronounced because, such as it was, it was always combined with a stern and rigorous sense of the direct and immediate responsibility of each individual to God. Deeper than the internationalism of the Puritan lay his individualism. He might serve

[1] These words were used by the writer in an essay on 'The Reformation and Nationality' which appeared in the *Modern Churchman* in 1932 (pp. 329–43). In that essay it was argued that there was an element of 'induced nationality' in the Reformation, derived from the study and imitation of the life of the Jewish nation, as recorded in the Old Testament. 'The example of the Jewish nation is a recurrent theme in the literature of the Reformation, and the Hebraism of the sixteenth century may almost be counted as a form of nationality—a form which reappeared in our English Commonwealth of the next century. Each of the Reformed peoples is encouraged to regard itself as a new Israel, a chosen people, directly covenanted with God.'

the chosen people, and through the chosen people he might serve the nation; but the service of which he always thought was the ultimate and lonely service which he owed directly to God. Community was not a word which bulked largely in his vocabulary; and he would never have said that service to the community was service to God Himself. Cromwell, essentially an Independent, and by the cast of his own mind an individual Seeker as well as an Independent, had no conception that even 'the people of God', though they might be of 'one heart and mutual love', were a uniform community, gathered in a single order or inspired by a corporate devotion. 'When I say the people of God, I mean the large comprehension of them *under the several forms of godliness* in this nation.'[1]

One of the observations which every visitor to England naturally and inevitably makes is an observation of the fact of national homogeneity, with a generally agreed basis of national life. Such homogeneity, and such an agreed basis, have to be won, and have been won, by an effort.

Tantae molis erat Romanam condere gentem.

But it was not in the days of Cromwell that homogeneity and an agreed basis were first, or finally, won in England. If any man 'imposed the yoke of peace' in England, it was Henry VIII rather than Cromwell; and it is Henry VIII rather than Cromwell who is the precedent and example for the dictatorial leader. If any Revolution ended by assuring to England an agreed basis of national life, it was the Whig Revolution of 1688, rather than the Puritan Revolution of the previous generation; and it is the Whig Revolution (with its prosaic sobriety, its compromises and its common sense), rather than the Puritan Revolution, which is the natural analogy and precedent for those who desire to achieve a permanent political settlement.

Cromwell had indeed a genuine passion for healing and settling; for unification: for an England settled within on the rock of religious liberty and reformation of manners, and great and glorious without because she was great and glorious within. But it was not given to him, or to those who thought with him, to achieve these things. Theirs was the triumphant but temporary explosion of a minority; and it passed. They left indeed a permanent legacy to England—the legacy of an ineradicable Nonconformity: the legacy of the Free Churches: the legacy

[1] Quoted in Firth, *Life of Cromwell*, pp. 482–3.

of a permanent idea of liberty, political as well as religious and civil, but pre-eminently and particularly the latter. But because they used force in the service of liberty (disbelieving in the force by which they acted, and yet acting by force in spite of their disbelief), they also left other legacies—the legacy of hatred of a standing army; the legacy of a rooted dislike of compulsory godliness; the legacy of contempt for the paradox of their cause, which could be, and was, interpreted as cant and hypocrisy. Yet their work was not unaccomplished. When they turned, as they did after 1660, from a victorious minority into a minority struggling for the just rights of minorities (toleration; liberty of worship; equality of access to education and civic rights), they came into their own, and they gave to England a great gift, essential and indispensable to her genuine tradition—the gift of the still small voice (after wind and earthquake and fire) of human liberty. The defeated Cromwells of hundreds of town and village chapels, scattered over England, carried on the heart of the cause of the victorious Cromwell, purged and purified; and the dust that lay in his unknown and unregarded grave still lived. So his actings fulfilled the good pleasure of God, and served their generations; and his rest was durable.

VII

PALEY AND HIS POLITICAL PHILOSOPHY

I

There is a sense in which William Paley, who was born in 1743, may be bracketed with Blackstone, his senior by twenty years, and again with Jeremy Bentham, his junior by five. It was the aim of all three to codify thought, and they all brought a cool and clear mind to the work. Blackstone codified the common law in an autumnal *vindemiatio*: Bentham, more like a nipping and eager spring, hurried gustily on to a new code based on the 'grand principle' of utility, and was still hurrying on at the work in his eighties, 'codifying away', as he said of himself, 'like any dragon'. Paley—half a Bentham and half a Blackstone—mixed the principle of utility with a native placidity in a code of moral and political ´philosophy which was partly critical, partly conservative, and wholly peculiar to himself. (Not that he codified only moral and political philosophy: he also produced, as we shall have reason to notice, a digest of the evidences of Christianity and a system or 'institutes' of natural theology.) United in a common aim of codification,[1] the three yet differed in the subjects they

---

[1] The period between 1765, when Blackstone's *Commentaries* began to appear, and 1802, when Paley's *Natural Theology* was published, may almost be called a period of the codification of English thought—parallel in its way (though very different in its scope and duration) to the period of the Code Napoléon. Besides Blackstone, Bentham, and Paley, there was also Adam Smith, who codified in 1776 the subject of political economy, and there was, too, Edward Gibbon, who—publishing in the same year as *The Wealth of Nations* the first volume of *The Decline and Fall of the Roman Empire*—began what may be called a 'code of history' which has endured to our own days. A brief chronological table will indicate the codes of the period:

1765–8   Blackstone's *Commentaries*.
1776   Adam Smith's *Wealth of Nations*.
1776–88 Gibbon's *Decline and Fall*.
1785   Paley's *Principles of Moral and Political Philosophy*.
1789   Bentham's *Principles of Morals and Legislation*.

handled and—even more—in their temper of mind and method of argument. They also differed in other ways. Blackstone and Bentham were both the sons of Londoners; Paley was the son of a Yorkshireman, and essentially a Yorkshireman himself. Blackstone and Bentham were both Oxford men, the one, like Dr Johnson, of Pembroke College (and afterwards All Souls), and the other of Queen's College: Paley was a Cambridge man, and the glory of Christ's College. Blackstone and Bentham were both lawyers—though Bentham was a barrister who only once had a brief, and even then advised the parties to compromise: Paley was a Cambridge tutor in Holy Orders who eventually became a parish clergyman, afterwards archdeacon and then chancellor of Carlisle, and finally sub-dean of Lincoln and rector of a parish in the diocese of Durham.

Paley was thus *tria juncta in uno*—a Yorkshireman, a Cambridge man, and a clergyman. We are fortunate in having a number of biographies which were published during the twenty years after his death in 1805. Perhaps the best, and certainly the most readable, is Meadley's *Memoirs of William Paley*, which was published in 1809. Meadley belonged to Sunderland, where Paley spent the last ten years of his life, from 1795 onwards, as rector of Bishop Wearmouth, a suburb on the north bank of the Wear about a mile from the sea. A banker's apprentice, and afterwards a businessman, Meadley had literary tastes: he founded the Sunderland subscription library, and he became a biographer of some note, who wrote lives of Algernon Sidney and others as well as a life of Paley. He was a dissenter and a follower of Charles James Fox; but living in Paley's parish he became his constant companion, and earned his sincere regard. The biography which he wrote of Paley is a work of research as well as of style; and while it is informed by Meadley's own principles, it is just and generous to its subject, without falling into adulation. The other

1794   Paley's *Evidences of Christianity*.
1802   Bentham's *Traités de Législation* (edited by Dumont), afterwards translated into English as *The Theory of Legislation*.
„   Paley's *Natural Theology*.

main biography was written by Paley's second son Edmund, a member of Queen's College, Oxford, who was afterwards vicar of the parish of Easingwold, near York; and it forms the first volume of a collected edition of his father's works which he published in 1825. Edmund Paley pays a compliment to the general accuracy of Meadley's *Memoirs*, and modestly states that he has only corrected some parts of the book, and confirmed or amplified others. His own life of his father is diffuse and somewhat dull; but it is as honest as the day, and it contains a good deal of valuable matter—family memories; a full account (which runs to some fifty pages) of the composition of the *Principles of Moral and Political Philosophy*; and, above all, a transcription, which comes in the course of this account, of some of the Cambridge lecture notes which were the basis of the *Principles*. Edmund Paley and Meadley together give a full and full-length picture of their subject; and the words of Horace may justly be applied to their joint labour—

Quo fit ut omnis
Votiva pateat veluti descripta tabella
Vita senis.

A Yorkshire tincture and colour clung to Paley all through his days. His father, of an old yeoman stock long settled in the parish of Giggleswick, in the limestone district of Craven, was for most of his life headmaster of Giggleswick Grammar School, where Paley himself received his early education; and his mother, 'a little, shrew-looking, keen-eyed woman, of remarkable strength of mind and spirits', was a native of the same parish. 'In a spot comparatively rude and rustic, like Giggleswick, in the free and familiar acquaintance with a people of strong mother-wit and Sabine simplicity, the peculiar genius of Paley was formed, void of art and abhorrent to all affectation.'[1] Such was the verdict of

---

[1] The words are those of 'Q.V.'—a resident in Cambridge who was himself a classical scholar—in a letter of the year 1808 which Meadley prints at the end of his *Memoirs*. The letter is valuable as giving the Cambridge impression and tradition of Paley four years after his death. 'At Cambridge, as you know,' the writer remarks at the beginning of his letter, 'Paley is one of our heroes.'

a contemporary. One who was born in a later age, on the other and perhaps brighter side of the Pennines, may perhaps be permitted to add that Yorkshiremen have two characteristics—a shrewd and sturdy common sense, and an admirable quality of thrift. Paley had both of these characteristics. He was a north countryman of the solid and sensible Yorkshire type; and his writings, from first to last, show the strength of his mother-wit. He had also the 'Sabine simplicity' of thrift and attention to money. This had been inculcated in him by his father, who from a legacy of £1500, and on an income which started at £80 and never rose beyond £200, accumulated a fortune of £7000—not to speak of the £2200 which his wife accumulated from her original fortune of £400.[1] There is a story, told by Paley himself to Meadley in his later years, which admirably illustrates both his own humour and his father's injunctions. They were riding together to Cambridge, in 1758, to secure his admission to a college, and he was following his father on a pony. 'I was never a good horseman, and...I fell off seven times.' (Paley's riding was indeed a marvel; and his equestrian exercises in the grounds of his rectory were a delight to the neighbourhood when he was sixty.)[2] 'My father, on hearing a thump, would turn his head half aside, and say, "Take care of thy money, lad."' He obeyed his father's injunctions. He practised, through all his life, 'economy on a plan'—not that he was ever, even for a moment, otherwise than genial and hospitable. One may reckon his income, during the last ten years of his life (1795–1805), from his rectory in the diocese of Durham, his subdeanery at Lincoln, his prebend at St Paul's, and a vicarage in Cumberland, at a minimum of £2200—not to speak of the

---

[1] The particulars are given in Edmund Paley's life of his father. It is curious, by the way, to note how carefully Meadley, too, sets down financial details, and lingers in his memoirs over the particulars and the values of Paley's various emoluments and the proceeds of his books.

[2] His son remarks, 'it was scarcely less painful to see his attitude on horseback than for him to use it', and he tells how his sober old horse, on hearing the cry of a pack of hounds, once 'undertook to carry him a-hunting, not at all for his pleasure'. Meadley tells how a wag of Sunderland once wrote on the door of the rectory grounds: 'Feats of horsemanship here every day, by an eminent performer.'

proceeds of his books. No wonder that, as his biographer notes, he 'was understood to have left a very competent fortune'. But it would be unjust, and singularly unjust, to charge him with penurious or miserly habits. If he was of yeoman stock, and kept a yeoman's habits—if he was an eighteenth-century clergyman, and practised the habits of his century in the matter of pluralities and non-residence—he never forgot the claims of justice and equity. At the end of his life he was busy with a scheme for imposing a tax upon non-residence, to be applied to the augmentation of small livings; and he even drafted it in the form of a parliamentary bill.

If a tincture of Yorkshire clung to Paley for the whole of his days, he was even more deeply imbued with the tincture and the general genius of the Cambridge of his day. He came to his father's old college, Christ's, as a sizar (his father had been one too) in 1759. It had been the college of John Milton in the seventeenth century: it was to be the college of Charles Darwin in the nineteenth; and to-day the portraits of all three—Milton, Paley and Darwin, each a notable and peculiar example of the genius of his century—hang in the hall of the college. Paley came to Christ's at the age of sixteen, an absent-minded north-country lad with a north-country accent he never lost, clumsy in gait and gesture, and somewhat uncouth in his countrified dress and his Sabine behaviour.[1] He followed the usual course of the day, which still demanded the keeping of a statutory number of 'acts and opponencies' (disputations in the old manner of the medieval schools) before the student could take the Senate House examination— an examination which was then, and long afterwards, almost exclusively mathematical, though it included some little sprinkling

---

[1] Generally slovenly, Paley sometimes burst into finery. 'He is said to have attracted general attention in the schools', his son narrates, 'by appearing with his hair full-dressed, a deep ruffled shirt, and new silk stockings.' This was the more striking, because when he grew warm in disputation with his adversary, 'he would stand with his head dropping upon one of his shoulders, and both his thumbs in his mouth: on striking out his answer with the animation of a εὕρηκα he would stretch his arms, rub his hands, and speak out his exultation in every feature'.

of ethics. He was no great reader (though there is a story that he was stirred to repentance and intense study at the beginning of his third year by a friend who came to his bedside at five o'clock in the morning and said, 'Paley, I have been thinking, what a d——d fool you are'); and his biographer suggests—what the course of his later life corroborates—that he was more indebted to observation and reflection than to books. The subjects of two of his 'acts' at the beginning of his last year are notable: the one was against capital punishment (to the end of his life he was always interested in law), and the other was *against*—but on a hint of the master of his college he readily inverted the thesis and made it *for*—the eternity of Hell torments. He distinguished himself in his disputations; he distinguished himself still more when in the Lent term of 1763 he came out senior wrangler in the Senate House Examination.[1] He had already begun to justify what his father had said of him when he went up to Cambridge: 'He'll turn out a great man;...he has by far the clearest head I ever met with in my life.'[2]

On going down he became a schoolmaster, on the recommendation of one of the tutors of his college, at an academy in Greenwich. Here he spent three years of his life (1763–6); and taking Holy Orders he added to his schoolmaster's duties those of an assistant curate, or, as he called it, 'a rat of rats'—the word 'rat' being, as his son says, his 'cant term' for curates. He was not so busy, however, but that he was able to take advantage of the neighbour-

[1] Paley must, of course, have been a good mathematician to come out first in an examination which was almost exclusively mathematical. But he had been trained by his father in the classics at Giggleswick: he taught Latin when he was a schoolmaster at Greenwich; and he won the Bachelor's prize for a Latin essay in 1756. He had also a general competence in Greek, sufficient, as a Cambridge classic afterwards remarked, to enable him to make acute and vigorous observations 'wherever in his *Horae Paulinae* any criticism on the Greek language is employed'. But, as the Cambridge classic also remarked, his study was always things more than words; and Meadley is probably right in suggesting that in mathematics, 'though he afterwards neglected them, might be laid the foundation of his future fame'. His sifting and probing mind had the cast of the Cambridge mathematician.

[2] A contemporary at Christ's said the same of him afterwards. 'It is difficult to say in what studies he most excelled...*so clear was his head*, and so retentive his memory.'

hood of London. He frequented the theatre at Drury Lane; but above all he frequented the Old Bailey and listened to criminal trials. This was a genuine passion. As a boy he had gone to the Assizes at Lancaster, and then come home and played at being a judge of his fellow schoolboys: a little later, just before entering Cambridge, he had attended the Assizes at York, listened to the trial of Eugene Aram, and watched him, as he said afterwards, 'get himself hanged by his own cleverness'. All through his life he cherished a lively interest in law. In his later Cumberland days he was intimate with the barristers on the northern circuit. In his last days at Sunderland he sat on the bench as a justice of the peace, and 'bore a good deal of sway at the weekly sessions', though he was blamed by some as hasty and irascible. If he had gone to the bar he might very well have become a great judge. The chapter on law in his *Principles of Moral and Political Philosophy* is one of the best; and his son says of him that 'he used to think himself formed for a lawyer, both from his fondness for...pointed investigation...and his cleverness in weighing evidence'.[1]

But his passion for attending the law courts, even when it was added to the duties of a schoolmaster and those of a curate, was not sufficient to engage the whole of Paley's mind during the three years he spent at Greenwich. In 1765 he wrote a Latin essay for the Bachelor's prize on the subject, *Utrum civitati pernicior sit Epicuri an Zenonis philosophia?* He took the side of Epicurus and championed the principle of happiness; and there is reason for thinking, as we shall see later, that the side he took and the success he won were something of a *clinamen* in the whole development of his future thought. (Prize essays, especially when they are successful, have a way of affecting men's future thoughts, and

[1] In an Assize sermon delivered at Durham in 1795 there is an eloquent and pointed account of the function and duties of a jury which might well have been delivered by a great judge (Meadley, op. cit. Appendix, pp. 117–18). But the finest tribute to Paley's legal gifts and judicious mind (which show themselves in all his writings) is that of Archbishop Whately, who, speaking of his *Horae Paulinae* in a lecture of 1859, remarks: 'I have often recommended the study of this work to *legal* students, not merely on account of its intrinsic value...but also as an admirable exercise in the art of sifting evidence.'

even their future careers; and it is interesting to notice that the career of Clarkson the emancipator began with the winning in 1785, twenty years after Paley's success, of the Bachelor's Prize for an essay on the lawfulness of slavery.)[1] At any rate Paley was successful: he won the first prize; and he dashed off a letter to a friend, without date or name, '*Io triumphe*: Chamberlayne [a Fellow of King's College and a notable classic] is second'. Winner of the first Bachelor's Prize in 1765, and already senior wrangler of his year in 1763, Paley was naturally called back to the service of his college. He became a Fellow of Christ's in the midsummer of 1766, and for the next ten years (1766–76) he resided and lectured in Cambridge.

They were years of hard work, during which he accumulated the ideas and the information which he used in the books of his later years. It was a period of seed-time, from which he reaped a large harvest afterwards; and one of his pupils, who attended his lectures and treasured the notes, believed 'that not a single idea has since been advanced in his writings which these manuscripts do not contain'. He must have been a stimulating lecturer, with his clear head and his awkward gestures, 'his language strong and perspicuous, though mixed sometimes with provincial but expressive words and phrases'. He had a happy habit of 'exciting the doubts and solicitude of his pupils', by beginning with an extreme and arresting statement of one side of a question, and then proceeding to a quiet and judicious examination of its truth; and several instances of this habit (notably in his treatment of property, which begins with the famous apologue of the pigeons) may be traced in his *Principles of Moral and Political Philosophy*. It was no wonder that the prestige of his college rose high during the ten

---

[1] 'Q.V.'—the Cambridge scholar already cited in a previous note—commends the Bachelor's prizes as 'calculated generally to improve the talents and direct the principles of ingenuous young men'. His theme is Paley's essay; but he also cites the essay of Clarkson in 1785, and refers with pride to the year 1792, when, in spite of the reaction against revolutionary France, 'the integrity of Cambridge umpires awarded the first prize to Tweddell's splendid and eloquent, but honest and bold, *Oratio pro aequa libertate*'. (Tweddell, who became a Fellow of Trinity College, died untimely at Athens in 1799.)

years of his residence. His knowledge, his humour, and the stories he told at his own expense, 'made him the life of the combination room'; but he was also the delight of undergraduates. 'Great as the distance confessedly is between an undergraduate of the lower orders and a tutor,' as Meadley pithily remarks, 'yet by tempering the dignity of his office with his wonted urbanity...he so far gained the confidence of his pupils that he was honoured and esteemed by all of them, by many loved and revered.'[1]

The subjects of his lectures were divinity and philosophy. In divinity he gave a course, every Sunday and Wednesday evening at eight o'clock, on the Greek New Testament; and this course was attended by all the undergraduates of his college. In philosophy it would appear that he gave two courses. One, intended for pupils in their first year, was a course on Locke's *Essay on the Human Understanding*.[2] Another course, intended for pupils in their second and third year, was a course of moral lectures; and this was the course which grew into the *Principles of Moral and Political Philosophy*. It is a matter of interest, and indeed of importance, to note the prescribed or recommended books which were then the basis of moral lectures at Cambridge. Dr Backhouse, Paley's predecessor as lecturer on ethics at Christ's, had used the *System of Moral Philosophy* of Francis Hutcheson (the

[1] It is perhaps worth adding, at the risk of bathos, another testimony of Meadley, that 'in addition to his engagements as a public tutor he had all along derived considerable emoluments from bestowing some hours daily on the instruction of private pupils'.

[2] This is the statement of Meadley, who adds that from Locke he proceeded regularly to Clarke *On the Attributes* (Samuel Clarke's Boyle lectures 'On the Being and Attributes of God', 1704–5) and to Butler's *Analogy*. Paley's son, however, states that he is not certain that his father lectured on Locke at all. 'Of his lectures on Locke I never heard, nor were they left among his papers with his other lectures.' On the other hand Meadley, who drew his information from Paley himself, is hardly likely to have been misinformed.

(It is curious to note that 'Clarke on the Attributes' seems still to be commemorated at Cambridge by the Seatonian Prize, founded in 1750 'for a poem on a subject conducive to the honour of the Supreme Being'. The will of the testator who founded the prize prescribes that 'the subject shall for the first year be one or other of the perfections or attributes of the Supreme Being, and so the succeeding years till that subject is exhausted'—when other subjects, such as Death and Judgement, may be set.)

Professor of Moral Philosophy at Glasgow) which had been published in 1753, and in which may already be found the famous definition of utility as the greatest happiness of the greatest number. Paley had probably attended Backhouse's lectures: he may possibly have been affected by them in his prize essay of 1765; and he would seem to have followed the practice of his predecessor in using Hutcheson's *System*, as he also followed the general Cambridge practice of his time in using the *Institutes of Natural Law* of Thomas Rutherforth (Regius Professor of Divinity at Cambridge and a Fellow of the Royal Society), which was published in 1754–6, and Abraham Tucker's *Light of Nature Pursued*, which was published in 1768 and afterwards.[1] We may count it a pity that he did not use Bishop Butler's *Sermons*, with their account of the moral sentiments, as one of his bases; and we may also count it a pity that he paid little if any regard to the *Ethics* of Aristotle. But we may none the less admire his lectures, as they were admired by his contemporaries, for what they were in themselves—for their pith, their balance, their apt illustrations, their flashes of humour, their shrewd common sense. They were a monument of the eighteenth century; and if they showed its defects, they also possessed its merits. It is no wonder that his pupils took copious notes, and that, as Meadley tells us, the notes were not only in the highest repute in his own, but eagerly sought after in other colleges.[2]

[1] Paley's son, who gives this information, speaks of Hutchinson, but this would appear to be a mistake, or a misprint, for Hutcheson. Abraham Tucker, a gentleman commoner of Merton College, Oxford, was a discursive would-be philosopher to whom Paley himself pays a special tribute in the preface to his *Principles of Moral and Political Philosophy*. Archbishop Whately thought that Paley was ill-advised in paying so much attention to Tucker's *Light of Nature*. 'It is a work like a gold-mine, containing many particles and some considerable masses of very precious metal, confusedly intermingled with much gravel and clay. I cannot think that Paley was happy in his choice of the portion which he selected. [It was from Tucker that he drew his argument against the existence of a moral faculty.] He would have found a much safer guide in the celebrated Bishop Butler.' (From a lecture on Paley's *Principles*, published in 1859.)

[2] Blackstone was lecturing at Oxford on the laws of England in the same decade, and the notes of his lectures were equally lent from hand to hand before they were published in the *Commentaries*. A full account is given by Paley's son,

Successful in his lectures—popular in his own college, and a welcome guest, for his wit and his conversation, in the rest of the University—Paley might easily have settled down to the comfortable life of a resident don for the rest of his life, and left no monument of himself but his lecture notes and his pupils. Fortunately for himself and posterity, he was called to a living and matrimony (two things which often arrived together in the lives of dons of that period) in the diocese of Carlisle. The call came to him in a way which was typical of the eighteenth century. His colleague and close friend at Christ's College (who made excursions with him during the long vacations in a single horse-chaise —Paley supplying the horse, as he afterwards also supplied the stories of their adventures) was John Law. John Law was the son of a remarkable man, a philosopher and a pluralist—Edmund Law, sometime Fellow of Christ's, afterwards Master of Peterhouse, Knightbridge Professor of Moral Philosophy, and also Bishop of Carlisle (all more or less simultaneously); the founder of a notable family, and the father of two bishops and a lord chief justice.[1] On becoming Bishop of Carlisle, in 1768, Edmund Law, 'after providing for his son', as Meadley notes, 'made Mr Paley the chief object of his patronage'. The son became a prebendary of Carlisle, and settled in the diocese in 1774: Paley left Cambridge in May 1776, was married in June to a Carlisle lady (whom he had met while visiting his friend in the long vacation of 1775), and settled down in the diocese for the next twenty years of his life (1776–95). He was folded in the seclusion and leisure of a country vicarage: he could ruminate his Cambridge lectures: a philosopher bishop was close at hand to stimulate him to production; and perhaps the incentive of a growing family, for which he had to provide, was an added spur to authorship.

in his life of his father (pp. 124–78), both of the lecture notes on moral philosophy and of their subsequent publication in 1785. The account includes a transcription (pp. 142–61) of part of Paley's own manuscript lecture-book.

[1] Paley had coached the son who became the Lord Chief Justice (and whose son, in turn, became the Governor-General of India and the first Earl of Ellenborough); and this—as well as a common interest in moral philosophy, and Paley's friendship with his other son—may have been a strong recommendation.

There is no need to follow the course of Paley's life, promotions, and movements, in the diocese of Carlisle. For a time he was resident at Appleby; but being made a prebendary of Carlisle in 1780, and afterwards archdeacon and chancellor, he became a resident in the city and the precincts of the Cathedral. He mixed, as his son records, in the society of Carlisle: it was there that he spent the longest continuous period of his life: it was there that he was long remembered with very kindly feelings; and it is there, in the chancel of the Cathedral, that he was ultimately laid to rest, with a monument to record his memory.[1] His public activities in Carlisle—his action in county politics, and his efforts to promote the movement for the abolition of the slave-trade—belong to a later stage of the argument and may be treated in connection with his politics and his political views. His literary activities were vigorous and notable. In less than ten years, between 1785 and 1794, he had published three remarkable books, any one of which was sufficient to establish his fame—a work on moral and political philosophy (1785); a work on the truth of the Scripture history of St Paul (1790); and a work on the general evidences of Christianity (1794). In that century, when an edition of a Greek play might lead to a bishopric, and an edition of the obscure *Cassandra* of the Alexandrine poet Lycophron to an archbishopric,[2] such works might be held to merit promotion. What was their effect on Paley's career?

There was a difference—not only in subject, but also, perhaps,

---

[1] There are two monuments to Paley in Carlisle Cathedral. (1) On the floor of the North Choir aisle there are three brasses in a row; the one in the centre is over his own grave (with the inscription: 'Here lie interred the remains of W. Paley, D.D.'); that on the right is over the grave of his first wife Jane, and that on the left is over the grave of his second wife Catharine. (2) On the East wall, behind the high altar, is a marble inscribed: 'William Paley, D.D., Archdeacon and Chancellor of this diocese', and below it another marble inscribed: 'To the memory of Jane—and Francis their son who died in his infancy—also Catharine widow of W. P.'

[2] John Potter, who edited Lycophron in 1697 and 1702, became archbishop of Canterbury in 1737. But he had also been Regius Professor of Divinity at Oxford (1707–15), and had published an edition of Clement of Alexandria in 1715.

in tone—between his work on moral philosophy, of the year 1785, and his two later works, of the years 1790 and 1794, which dealt with the theme of theology. His first work had a certain laicity; and it might be accused by some of a dangerous tone of liberalism, though it was also accused by others of a stolid vein of conservatism. There was only one offer of promotion which sprang from, or at any rate ensued on, the publication of the *Principles of Moral and Political Philosophy*. In 1789 Dr York, the Bishop of Ely, offered Paley the mastership of Jesus College, Cambridge. It is curious that he should have refused the offer. Acceptance would have brought him back to Cambridge, to an old and famous college of which Cranmer had been a fellow and Coleridge was shortly to become a sizar: it might have led on to fortune and the bishopric which his friends expected. Was Paley guilty of *un gran rifiuto*? At any rate he refused. He acknowledged the offer gratefully, five years later, in the dedication of his *Evidences* to the Bishop of Ely; but at the time he said *Nolo magistrare*. The motives which made him refuse are obscure. Perhaps he clung to his family life in Carlisle. Perhaps he preferred his modest emoluments in Cumberland (his son says that it was only during the latter part of his residence there that he cleared so much as an income of £500 from all his preferments) to a Cambridge post which, as Meadley notes, was 'more honourable than lucrative' Whatever his motives were, he remained in Cumberland.

But he was not to stay there to the end. If his first book might lead some to doubt his soundness, there could be no doubt about his two later books, and least of all about the *Evidences*. Here was a pillar of the Church; here too (as men began to discover from his expressions of political opinion, in pamphlets and otherwise, from 1792 onwards) was a good sound Englishman, who could be trusted to stand in the gate against the doctrines of Tom Paine, the activities of the new-fangled political societies, and all the flood of the French Revolution. His political opinions were perhaps subsidiary, though they may have counted for something: it was the *Evidences*, and their revelation of a pillar of the Church, which were final and conclusive. A shower of preferments began to fall soon after the publication of the *Evidences*, early in 1794; and this time there was no refusal. There were three of these preferments, offered by three different bishops. In August 1794, Dr Porteus, the Bishop of London, who had earlier been a Fellow of Christ's College in Paley's time, appointed him to a non-residential prebend in St Paul's Cathedral. Immediately afterwards the Bishop of Lincoln promoted him to the office of sub-dean in Lincoln Cathedral, where he was installed at the end of January 1795. A few months later, when he was in Cambridge, taking the degree of Doctor of Divinity, he received from the Bishop of Durham the offer of the valuable rectory of Bishop Wearmouth, a suburb of Sunderland. His cup was filled; and the tenor of his life was henceforth changed.

Hitherto, apart from his Cambridge days, Paley had belonged to the western side of Northern England—the district of Craven and the diocese of Carlisle. Henceforward, for the last ten years of his life (1795–1805), he belongs to the East, spending nine months of the year in his rectory in Sunderland and the three spring months in residence at Lincoln. (The non-residential prebend in St Paul's Cathedral did not affect his life.) Hitherto he had lived on a modest competence: henceforward his life was a life of opulence, ease, and comfort. The change was marked in still another way. His first wife had died in 1791: he was married again, and again to a Carlisle lady, at the end of 1795. The picture of his life in his last ten years, as it is sketched by his son and by Meadley, is a picture full of charm. He loved his spring residence in Lincoln: 'it was to him a great delight to see Lincoln, as he used to say, in all its glory, and to view its numerous gardens and orchards in full bloom and blossom.' He had other delights in Lincoln, especially the fortnightly meetings of the Literary Society, where 'after taking coffee, choosing books, and a little chit-chat, the evening was closed with a barrel of oysters and a rubber of whist, which Dr Paley highly enjoyed'. But it was the rectory at Bishop Wearmouth, with its park ('nearly a mile...of wall planted with fruit-trees'), and with 'such a house!...one of the best parsonages in England', which saw Paley most and delighted him best. Here he would take his equestrian exercise and exhibit his 'feats of horsemanship': here he would take his regular walks of musing and recollection—his youngest daughter following with a basket on her arm—'with the handle of his stick in his mouth, now moving in a short hurried step, now stopping at a butterfly, a flower, a snail: at one instant pausing to consider the subject of his next sermon, at the next carrying the whole weight and intent of his mind to the arranging some pots in his greenhouse'. But he had also a lively human interest, *nihil humani a se alienum putans*, and he moved freely and familiarly among his parishioners. 'At the end of the pier [his rectory was only a mile from the sea], on a stormy day, he would be found conversing with seafaring men upon their way of life;...so for ship-carpenters, rope-makers, sail-makers, coal-heavers, fishermen, he had also a train of inquiries.' One thing at which he delighted to look and which he liked to show to his friends was the celebrated iron bridge, with its span of 236 feet, which was built in 1796 and was one of the sights of the day, as indeed it was the boldest structure of its kind then to be seen in England. He watched its erection, carefully examining every pin and screw; and he used his observation of its structure—seen 'from a point below his garden, where from an opening of a deep and confined glen the spectator burst at once upon the expanse of an iron arch hanging as it were in the air above him'—to point a moral and adorn an argument, in his last book, on the natural evidences of design in the structure of the universe. It was indeed an historic bridge. The original design had come from the brain of Tom Paine—the author of *The Rights of Man* (a book which Paley had thrown into the fire when he found it in his house), and also the author of the *Age of Reason*. It is curious to think of William Paley contemplating, and contemplating with a deep admiration, one of the works of Tom Paine.[1]

[1] Paine, an amazingly versatile man (who studied engineering and yellow fever as well as politics and theology), was already constructing, in 1785, when he was still residing in America, a model of an iron bridge, of one arch, to be thrown over the River Schuylkill. He brought his model to Europe in 1787 in order to consult engineering authorities in France and England. (He tells us that he took the idea and construction of the arch from the figure of a spider's

From 1800 onwards, when he had attained the age of fifty-seven, Paley suffered from illness. He did not preach after the end of that year; but though he suffered from what was then called a 'violent nephralgic complaint', and was liable to recurrent attacks of pain, he persevered with a work on natural theology, which was published in 1802. It flowed naturally from a habit of observation (attested by his survey of the bridge and his readiness to glean not only from books but also from talks with all and sundry); and it accorded well with the general contentment of a mind which was satisfied with its own experience and prepared to project its own satisfaction into the world at large. (Walking one day with a friend, Professor Carlyle, at the mouth of the Solway Firth, he pondered for some time in silence, 'and at length, "Now see," says he to his friend, who expected a burst of some kind, "only

circular web.) Eventually he had his iron arch constructed by a firm at Rotherham, and it was then set up, and exhibited to visitors, on Paddington Green, in 1790, at a fee of one shilling each. But by the autumn of 1792, flying from a prosecution for seditious libel based on the second part of his *Rights of Man*, Paine disappeared to France, and became a member of the French Convention. 'The iron bridge, taken down at Paddington, and sold for other benefit than Paine's, was used in spanning the Wear with the arch of his invention.' (Moncure Conway's *Life of Thomas Paine*, c. XXIV *ad initium*.)

The phrase just quoted demands a brief commentary. Was the *material* of Paine's, iron bridge actually used in spanning the Wear, and did 'the arch of his invention' really furnish the *design* on which the bridge over the Wear was built in 1796? A controversy arose on these matters in Sunderland in 1859, when the bridge was being widened and largely reconstructed by Robert Stephenson. Some argued, and argued hotly, in favour of Paine: others were inclined to the claims of Rowland Burdon, a local member of parliament who had been largely responsible for the financing and erection of the bridge. A study of pamphlets and newspapers published in Sunderland in 1859 (for the opportunity of consulting which the writer owes his thanks to the Town Clerk of Sunderland) leads to the conclusion that (1) the material of Paine's iron bridge was actually used, and (2) Paine's model served as the original design, but was altered and improved by Burdon and the builder whom he employed, an ex-schoolmaster named Thomas Wilson—of whom, by the way, an engraved portrait survives with the amusing inscription, which shows that he too asserted his claims:

'I by myself, says little Tommy,
I am the man
Who built this bridge
And formed the wondrous span.'

look at the Goodness of God! How happy these shrimps are!'")
This was the last of his books, save for a volume of sermons
privately published for the benefit of his parishioners. He died in
May 1805, and in death he returned to the side of England to
which he essentially belonged. He was buried in Carlisle—the
place of his own abiding affection and the birthplace of both of his
wives. He left behind him not only his books, but also a sturdy
family. His eldest son, William Paley, was a barrister whose *Law
and Practice of Summary Conviction*, first published in 1814, attained
a ninth edition in 1926. His second son, Edmund, edited one of
the five editions of his father's works which appeared before the
accession of Queen Victoria; and the son of this second son,
F. A. Paley, was a classical scholar, whose texts and editions of the
Greek tragedians were still in current use at the end of the nineteenth century.[1] Not only in the first and second generation was
the ability of the family repeated. It appeared again, and appeared
in a woman, in the third generation. Mary Paley, Paley's great
granddaughter, was one of the first students of Newnham College,
and became its lecturer in economics. Married in 1877 to the
economist Alfred Marshall, she collaborated with him in his
Economics of Industry, and was his colleague and fellow-worker till
his death in 1924. Her portrait in the Marshall Library, a few
hundred yards away from that of her great-grandfather in the hall
of Christ's College, still testifies the debt of Cambridge to the
name and the abiding powers of the family of Paley.

II

Paley was a four-square man; and his fame rests squarely upon
four books. The first of these in time, and perhaps in order of
permanent importance, was the *Principles of Moral and Political
Philosophy* of the year 1785. Its genesis and argument will occupy

---

[1] F. A. Paley (1815–88) early became a member of the Roman Catholic
Church, which his grandfather might have regretted. But critics have remarked
that his introductions to the plays of Euripides were models of clearness; and
that might have satisfied not only his grandfather, but also his great-grandfather,
who admired clear-headedness.

us later; but two things may be said of it here. The first is that though it was the *primitiae* of his pen, and its author was unknown to publishers, it brought him a sum of £1000. *O sic si omnes* is the natural reflection of a writer on politics in a later age; but it is to be noted that his friend John Law, by this time an Irish bishop, had been busy with the publisher on his behalf, and had probably suggested what the fortunes of the book were likely to be—that it might be adopted in the University, and that it would then command a permanent sale. If he made any such suggestion, he was abundantly justified by the event. The senior tutor of Trinity College, acting as moderator in the University in 1786 and 1787, introduced the *Principles* as a standard book both in disputations (or 'acts and opponencies') and in the Senate House Examination: by 1799 it had become the staple—along with two books of Euclid and with simple and quadratic equations—of the examination for the ordinary or pass degree; and permeating Cambridge from top to bottom, 'it laid the foundations' (as Archbishop Whateley said, in the preface to his annotated edition of the first three books in 1859) 'of the Moral Principles of many hundreds—probably thousands—of Youths while under a course of training designed to qualify them for being afterwards the moral instructors of millions'. It had run through fifteen editions during its author's life, and through twenty-one by 1814; and 'analyses' prepared by coaches had begun to be printed and conned in Cambridge as early as 1794.[1] The other thing notable about the *Principles* is its

---

[1] An interesting essay might be written on the 'analyses', 'epitomes', and the like, of Paley's *Principles*, and still more of his *Evidences*. An 'analysis' of the *Principles* by C. V. le Grice had run into a seventh edition by 1820. An 'analysis by way of question and answer' appeared in 1824; and by 1842 there was an 'analysis with examination questions to each chapter and all the Senate-house papers'. Such is—or used to be—the fate of prescribed books. The fate of the *Evidences* (which descended to a lower and more comprehensive level, both of prescription and examination) was even sadder. 'Analyses' proliferated —all naturally printed in Cambridge, like the 'analyses' of the *Principles*—and an 'Analysis' of 1855 was furnished 'with rhymes for all authors quoted in the first eight chapters and an analysis with each chapter summarized in verse'. One may trace these poetic versions of Paley down to the end of the nineteenth century. But mnemonic poetry was an old device of Latin grammars.

galvanic effect on Jeremy Bentham, a young Oxford graduate and barrister who was five years junior to Paley. When it was published Bentham was absent in the south of Russia, where he was staying with his brother, Samuel Bentham, a naval architect and engineer who had been appointed by Prince Potemkin as superintendent of a shipbuilding yard. Here he heard from a correspondent that his 'grand principle' of utility—which Paley followed like most of his generation, but with a greater clarity than most—had been anticipated in print by a clergyman and an archdeacon. Bentham was stung into action. He had already printed, in 1780, his own *Principles of Morals and Legislation*, but his book, though printed, had not been published. Returning to England in the beginning of 1788, he ventured into publicity. (His first book— the *Fragment on Government*—had been anonymous; and he had all his life a way of writing, and writing interminably, without much regard to the existence of publishers or the benefits of publication.) His *Principles* thus appeared in the course of 1789; and Paley's *Principles* had in this way the unintended effect of provoking the publication of Bentham's.

The other three sides of Paley's square were all of a theological nature. Just as he used the moral lectures which he had given at Cambridge as the basis of his *Principles*, so he afterwards turned to the divinity lectures, which he had delivered to undergraduates on Sunday and Wednesday evenings, for the substance of his later theological works. (It has already been noted that Paley's life was to be a long harvesting of the seed he had already sown at Cambridge.) There is one exception. His *Horae Paulinae*, which was published in 1790, was largely an adventure (at any rate in the history of the author's own mind) into new and unexplored ground; and it has been generally counted the most original, if also the least successful, of all his works.[1] Intended to evince the

---

[1] But a faint pencil-note, in an old handwriting, in the copy of Meadley's *Memoirs* in the Cambridge University Library—a note appended to a passage in which Meadley speaks of the singular originality of Paley's design—runs, 'Biscoe preceded by 48 years—see his *Acts* 1742'. Biscoe, a dissenting minister, but afterwards a London rector and a chaplain to George II, had delivered in

truth of the Scripture history of St Paul by a comparison of his Epistles with one another and with the Acts, it was not only the fruit of a close study of the Epistles in the Greek (his son remarks that his Greek New Testament contained a great many more curious and critical notes in the epistolary part than were to be found in the Gospels); it was also the result, and a fine example, of judicial acumen in the weighing and sifting of evidence.[1] It was translated into German, with notes by one Dr Henke, in 1797; and it was being re-edited in England as recently as 1877. The *Evidences of Christianity*, published in 1792, depended much more than the *Horae Paulinae* on his old college lectures; but it departed more widely from their plan (if indeed, his son wonders, they ever had a discoverable plan) than the *Principles* had done, and it involved him in more research. Like the *Principles*, it ran with rapidity into new editions (there was a fifteenth edition within twenty years); and like the *Principles*, but even more, it became, as Paley prophesied to his publisher, 'a standard book... for the universities'. When Cambridge instituted a 'previous examination' in 1822, the *Evidences* was joined with one of the Gospels or the Acts, and with a prescribed part of a Greek and a Latin author, as the groundwork of the examination.

The third and last of Paley's theological works, and the completion of the square of his labours, was his *Natural Theology* published in 1802. This was begun and finished (in spite of illness) at Bishop Wearmouth: it was a new venture of Paley's mind under the influence of an east-coast air. The *Evidences* had been a defence of the truth of revelation, summarising all the arguments of eighteenth-century orthodoxy in a magisterial code, and drawing into a compendium the direct historical and the auxiliary testimonies provided by the records of the past. *Natural Theology* was complementary to the *Evidences*, in the sense that it was a compendium and summary of the evidences of religion which

1736–8 a course of Boyle lectures on 'the history of the Acts of the Holy Apostles, confirmed from other authors', which was published in 1742. Paley was perhaps acquainted with the work.

[1] Supra, p. 199n.

could be derived from the appearances of nature; but it was based more directly on Paley's own observation—as, for instance, of the iron bridge, 'or the backbone of a hare, or the pinion of a fowl', which he would take from the table to his study—though it was also based on promiscuous reading (he used the writings of Robert Boyle and John Ray and the researches of his contemporary Dr Priestley) and on correspondence with his friend and old colleague John Law, now Bishop of Elphin in Ireland. *Natural Theology*, like the *Principles* and the *Evidences*, was often reprinted, and had run through twenty editions in less than twenty years. It had the honour of appearing in an edition in four volumes (between 1831 and 1839), of which two contained dissertations on subjects of science connected with the work written by the Lord Chancellor and polymath Brougham.

All in all, the writings of Paley may be said to have made him the second Newton of Cambridge—*dimidiatus*, indeed, yet still an authority, in his own field of morals and divinity, only second to his great predecessor who reigned in the field of natural philosophy. But Paley had in his day an even wider diffusion. His books were conned, or at any rate they stood on the shelves, in country rectories and country houses.[1] They were quoted in Parliament: they were treasured by King George III himself. His argument for complete toleration of dissenters and their admission to full civil rights was used by Lord Grey (then Viscount Howick) in the House of Commons, as it was used there by others of his way of thinking; and Charles James Fox, when pressing the claims of the Irish Roman Catholics in 1805, cited the testimony of a writer, 'whose authority would have great weight not only in that House, but with all thinking men in the country—whose opinions no man who valued genius…learning…moderation could hear without deference and respect'. The feeling of George III for 'his Paley' is shown in a letter to Paley from a friend who was a canon

[1] The writer has two duodecimo volumes (one of the *Principles*, the other of the *Evidences*), bound in an old gilt calf, and inscribed in an elegant feminine handwriting with the name of the owner, and of the country house in which she lived, and the date 1823.

of Windsor, early in 1797. He reports a dialogue. 'Do you know', the king asks, 'who has taken my Paley out of my library?' 'No, sir,' the canon answers: '*I* have not.' 'Do you think Fisher has? ...It is bound in dark calf, and has blue letters on the back. I value the book highly, and would not be without it on any account.' A fortnight later, the king was still anxious about his missing Paley. (Was it a copy of the *Evidences*?) 'He thinks', the canon reports, 'he must have left it at Weymouth. He knows he took it with him in his pocket...he will send for another...and he is rather pleased...as he shall have one there to recur to as well as here, for he thinks it a very useful valuable publication.'[1]

How vividly the scene brings back to the mind the end of the eighteenth century! Paley himself was eighteenth century of the eighteenth century, alike in his life and his writings. He believed in an orderly and comfortable universe, finite and demonstrable, in which men could feel themselves easily at home. God could be justified to man's reason both from the evidences of history and the appearances of nature. He had made a good understandable world, like the bridge at Sunderland, or like a watch—a world intended for happiness and based on a design of utility. Like the world at large, the British constitution, as Paley depicted it in his *Principles*, was a good, understandable, demonstrable thing. Even the poor might be led by argument into felicity, in spite of any

[1] There is a curious passage in Hogg's *Life* of Shelley which shows how Paley's books penetrated into country-house libraries as well as to Windsor. Shelley's father, Sir Timothy, is speaking. '"There is certainly a God," he said; "there can be no doubt of the existence of a Deity; none whatsoever."...He felt in several pockets, and at last drew out a sheet of letter-paper and began to read. Bysshe, leaning forward, listened with profound attention. "I have heard this argument before", he said; and by and by, turning to me, he said again: "I have heard this argument before." "They are Paley's arguments", I said. "Yes," the reader observed, with much complacency, turning towards me, "you are right, sir," and he folded up the paper and put it into his pocket; "they are Palley's arguments; I copied them out of Palley's book this morning myself; but Palley had them originally from me; almost everything in Palley's book he had from me."... "Palley's arguments! Palley's books!" I said to my friend as we walked home. "Yes, my father will call him Palley; why does he call him so?" "I do not know, unless it be to rhyme Sally."' Hogg's *Life of Percy Bysshe Shelley*, ch. IX.

appearances of misery; and in 1792 he published a sermon (which he had preached two years before in a Cumberland village) under the title of *Reasons for Contentment, addressed to the Labouring Part of the British Public.* It is a world and climate of opinion which we of the middle of the twentieth century are bound to find strange and unfamiliar. It may even repel us; and we may speak in our haste of 'the doll's house'. But it would be wrong to condemn too hastily the picture which Paley drew of the world, or Paley himself. He had not the gnawing and splendid discontent of Bentham; but he was too clear-headed, and too much of a north-countryman, to live in any fool's paradise.

It is true that he took life easy, as the grass grows on the weirs. From a boy he had been a fisherman; and in his later days it was said that he would sit quietly by the banks of the Eden, content with a single nibble in the length of a whole summer day. On the other hand, he thought while he fished; and his friends could say that he composed his books under the pretence of angling. (A river-bank may be a safer asylum than a known and accessible study.) He had a great gusto for social pleasures—a barrel of oysters and rubber of whist—and it was said of him that no studious man ever entered more into the pleasures of society. But he was also a great conversationalist—humorous, well-informed, many-sided—and it may safely be said that he gave to society even more than he took. He was no great preacher: he was awkward in the pulpit, if he was also sincere; his sermons would finish abruptly, and though his son pleads that he stopped 'as soon as he had no more to say'—which is a thing as sensible as it seems to be rare—it may also be argued that he stopped because he had written no more and thought no further ahead. He is reported to have advised his pupils in his college lectures: 'If your situation requires a sermon every Sunday, make one and steal five.' This was a sally of Paleyan humour: his own practice was more moderate; and his son reports that the only stolen sermons amongst his collection were two from Hoadley, the latitudinarian author (and begetter of the Bangorian controversy) in the beginning of the reign of George I. Perhaps the son was generous to his father; and Leslie

Stephen doubted whether the rate of 'conveying' might not be put at a higher figure.

He was not original in his books. Indeed, he has been accused of plagiarism; but the accusation was unjust. For one thing the eighteenth century had less rigid ideas of literary property than those which we cherish (perhaps somewhat pedantically, with our mass of references) at the present day; Blackstone, for instance, in the introduction to his *Commentaries*, could lift some pages from Burlamaqui's *Principes du Droit National* without any acknowledgement.[1] But there is another and far more important point to be made on Paley's behalf; and it is a point which he makes himself. In the preface to his *Principles* (and what he says there may also be applied to his later works) he refers to authors 'whose thoughts, and sometimes, possibly, whose very expressions I have adopted'. He explains that he had kept no references; but he also proceeds to explain that his method had been to begin by drawing on his own stores and his own reflections, and then—but only then—to consult his readings for the further support or amplification of his views. His own conclusion deserves to be cited, and may justly claim to be accepted: 'I make no pretensions to perfect originality: I claim to be something more than a mere compiler.' He *was* something more than a mere compiler. He was, as has already been noted, one of the great codifiers of thought in an age of codification. He codified the thought of his time in the two fields of philosophy, moral and political, and of theology, revealed and natural. He was another Justinian, and a second Blackstone. A Justinian or Blackstone does not aim at originality: he is bound to borrow. Paley borrowed, like others of his stamp and cast of mind. The famous comparison of the world to a watch, from whose design and delicate adjustment you may argue to the existence of a maker—a comparison with which Carlyle made merry at Paley's expense—was a commonplace of the time.[2] But

---

[1] See the writer's *Essays on Government*, p. 136, and infra, p. 318.

[2] Lord Neaves, in a pamphlet containing a lecture on Paley delivered at Carlisle in 1883 (pp. 25-6), prints in parallel columns Paley's passage about the watch and the corresponding passage in Nieuwentyt's *The Existence of God*

at any rate Paley had a clear head. It was just what he needed for his task; and he became in virtue of it, as Leslie Stephen has said, 'an unrivalled expositor of plain arguments'—plain arguments, we may add, addressed to plain men by one of themselves. That was why he was able to bequeath, to a later and very different age, the best statement of the thought of the eighteenth century as it stood on the eve of the Revolution.

In himself he was far from being a cynic, and he was still further from being a self-interested and complacent conservative. There is indeed a touch of cynicism about many of his recorded sayings. But the fact was that he liked, like many of his fellow-countrymen (especially, perhaps, from Northern England), to make jests at his own expense; and the worst of such jests is that they may be taken literally by men of a more serious turn of mind. Paley was all the more liable to such a fate because it was almost impossible 'to tell what was joke and what was earnest' in his conversation, or to be sure whether a joke was meant or was entirely unintended. He was, even to himself, an incalculable Puck: a northern Robin Goodfellow. Stories of his sallies and his *faux pas* abound. Speaking of religious tests and the question of conscience involved in subscriptions, he said that 'he could not afford to have a conscience'. (*Prendendum est cum grano salis*: he *could* afford to sacrifice the chance of a bishopric rather than sacrifice the passage in his *Principles* on pigeons and private property.) Explaining his reasons for exchanging one living in Cumberland for another, he said that they were two or three: it was nearer to his house in Carlisle: it was fifty pounds a year more in value: 'and thirdly, I began to find my stock of sermons coming over again too fast.' Many of

---

demonstrated by the Wonders of Nature, a work published in 1715, and afterwards translated into English under the title of *The Religious Philosopher*. Paley may well have used the passage in Nieuwentyt's book; but if he did so, he was not unique.

It is curious to reflect that Thomas Carlyle and William Paley were both born in the eighteenth century. There is a whole world of difference between the mundane classical Paley and the transcendental romantic Carlyle. 'I don't pretend to understand the Universe,' Carlyle once remarked: 'it's a good deal bigger than I am.... People ought to be modester.'

the other stories about him (like the story of his falling seven times off his pony when he first rode up to Cambridge, and his father's remark on the occasion of each fall) are stories he told himself, and told at his own expense. He would have been elected instantly, and by acclamation, the president of a 'society for promoting indiscretion in conversation'—the sort of society for which one longs in the cautious precincts of a cathedral close or a resident University, where men are apt to 'talk delicately'. But he often hedged as discreetly in his books as he jumped recklessly in his talk. There is a compensation in men's minds; and the reckless talker is often also the cautious writer—just as the radical and adventurous thinker may also be the close student, and even the punctilious observer, of the rules of etiquette. Oxford and Cambridge colleges have produced examples of this mental law of compensation through all the centuries.

Paley had no enthusiasm; but to the eighteenth century, which identified enthusiasm with fanaticism, and counted it as a merit in a man, worthy of record on his tombstone, that 'he had no enthusiasm', this was a proof of sanity.[1] He was not ardent; but he had a genial good humour and a kindly heart; and generally cautious as he was in his writings, he could be incautious, and generously explosive, in dealing with the entrenched prejudices of property and preferment. In an age of careerism and place-hunting he steadily kept his own sturdy independence. He never indulged in time-serving, or 'rooted' (in his own expressive phrase) for the truffles of preferment. The angular and clumsy north-countryman, whose grotesque gestures and provincial accent excited an easy laughter, was not made of the stuff which succeeds by pleasing. It is true that he owed the first modest stages of his advancement in the Church to the patronage of the Laws; but his eventual success, which came late in his life, was due to his own solid merit and the merits of his writings. 'Preferment', he told the young clergy of Carlisle in an ordination sermon of 1781, 'should be pursued with moderate anxiety and by honour-

---

[1] Dr Johnson defined enthusiasm as 'a vain confidence of divine favour or communication'.

able means alone.'[1] He had a genial aversion from clerical cadging. He refused, while he was still a tutor in Cambridge, to be private tutor to the son of a great lawyer and judge, Lord Camden, though 'the situation . . . might have led, by honourable patronage, to the highest clerical dignity'. (We may remember that Adam Smith, already famous as the author of the *Theory of Moral Sentiments*, had resigned his Glasgow chair in 1763, only a few years before Paley's refusal, and become private tutor to Lord Townshend's two stepsons, the Duke of Buccleuch and his younger brother.) He jested at one of his colleagues in Christ's College, 'distinguished for his elegant and engaging manners . . . who has since attained no small eminence in the Church of England', and proposed that he should be appointed professor of 'rooting'.[2] Another jest became a legend—a distorted and apocryphal legend. In 1784 the young Mr Pitt, of Pembroke College, newly elevated to the office of prime minister at the age of twenty-four, attended service in St Mary's Church at Cambridge. A little before, in the general election of 1780, he had been rejected as a candidate by the University of Cambridge; now, he was greeted with adulation by many members of the University, who had changed their minds with the change of his fortunes. A story grew, and obtained some vogue, that at the service which Pitt attended in 1784 Paley had preached on the text: 'There is a lad here, which hath five barley loaves and two small fishes: but what are they among so many?' Apocryphal as it is (Paley was in Carlisle at the time, quietly finishing his *Principles of Moral and Political Philosophy*), the story has some foundation in fact. Riding one day with a friend near Carlisle, and talking about the bustle which Pitt's appearance would cause, Paley *had* said that if he had been there and asked to preach, he would have taken that passage for his text.

[1] The Appendix to Meadley's *Memoirs*, p. 82.
[2] A faint pencilled note in the copy of Meadley's *Memoirs* in the Cambridge University Library identifies the colleague as Porteus, who afterwards became Bishop of London and heaped coals of fire on Paley's head by being the first to offer him preferment after the publication of his *Evidences* in 1794.

But there is another story—a true story—which illustrates best of all the sturdy independence of Paley's mind. It has already been noticed[1] that it was his habit in lecturing, during his Cambridge days, to begin a theme with an arresting paradox, which he then proceeded to examine and qualify. (The worst of this admirable method is that the paradox will be remembered, and the qualification probably forgotten.) Following this method, he had started a discussion of the theme of private property, in the course of his lectures on ethics, with the paradox or apologue of the pigeons. The paradox, which eventually became Chapter 1 of Part 1 of Book III of the *Principles*, ran as follows in the lecture-notes, which only deviate slightly (in the position of a clause or some other purely verbal matter) from the printed text of 1785:[2] 'If you saw a flock of pigeons in a cornfield, instead of each picking where and what it liked, taking so much and no more than what it wanted— if, instead of this, you saw 99 of them gathering all they got into a heap, taking nothing for themselves but a little draff and refuse, keeping this heap for one, and that the weakest perhaps and worst of the whole flock; sitting round and looking on all the winter, while this one was eating and throwing it about and wasting it, and if one more hardy or hungry than the rest touched a grain of it, all the others instantly flew upon it and tore it to pieces—if you saw all this, you would see nothing more than what is every day practised and established among men. Among men you see the 99 toiling and scraping together a heap of superfluities and niceties for one, gathering nothing for themselves all the while but a little of the coarsest of it; and this one, too, oft-times the feeblest and worst of the whole set, a child, a woman, a madman, a fool; looking quietly on while they see the fruits of all their labour spent or spoiled, and if one of them take or touch the least of it, the others join all against him and hang him for the theft.'

[1] Supra, p. 200.
[2] The version contained in the lecture-notes is printed in the *Life* by Edmund Paley (pp. 139–40), who dates it about 1773 or 1774. The reader may be interested in comparing this version with the later text which he will find in any edition of the *Principles*. It is more natural and less polished in style than the later version.

One can imagine such a passage being a favourite with under-graduates, and coming through them to the ears of their tutors. One can understand how Paley's old colleague, John Law, when he was discussing with him the publication of the *Principles* in 1785, thought of the passage and its possible effects. 'Paley,' he said, 'that passage about the pigeons will not go down; it may prevent your being a bishop.' 'Well,' said Paley, 'bishop or no bishop, it shall stand.'[1] It stood, and it stands to this day. 'Pigeon Paley', as he was sometimes called, was never a bishop. But perhaps there were other reasons, besides the pigeons, for that. And perhaps one of the chief of them was that Paley himself had only 'a moderate anxiety' for a bishopric—if he had even that. It puzzled Meadley and Edmund Paley (who spends some pages on the problem) why he never became a bishop. We may guess that he was not himself seriously worried by the question.

III

Essentially an independent, and naturally of a judicious and even judicial frame of mind, Paley was interested in politics without being a partisan. His son, in the *Life* which he wrote of his father, is perhaps too anxious to disengage him from party. Writing about 1825 (the year in which the *Life* was published), in the period of Sidmouth and Liverpool, he describes his father as 'of every party, and friendly with men of all parties, but never exclusively attached to any'. It may be that this was essentially true; and it must be confessed that Meadley—a dissenter who combined a fervent admiration of Charles James Fox with a warm regard for Paley—frankly admits that 'his ideas were never biased by the creed of a party'. That was, no doubt, the impression left on Meadley's mind by his talks with Paley in his later days at Bishop Wearmouth. But there is often a succession of different strata in the formation of men's views; and it may be that the Paley of the early Cambridge days (1766–76), and even the Paley of the *Principles* (1785), cherished—however cautiously—views of

[1] The story rests on the authority of Paley's son, in the *Life*, p. 341.

a more liberal and partisan character than those of his later years, when the French Revolution had swept over men's minds and the name of Tom Paine was anathema. If there was such a change, it would not be surprising (many men changed in the decade between 1790 and 1800); and we may add that in Paley's case it would be likely to be less a change of ideas than of the balance and proportion of ideas. But it is important to consider whether there actually *was* any change—if only in order to understand the political theory of his book of 1785 *sub specie temporis sui*, and to avoid any danger of misinterpreting it in the reflected light of later years.

In the days when he was a Fellow and Lecturer of Christ's, we are told that he was 'held in very general esteem' by those of the liberal party. He was closely connected, as we have seen, with the family of the Laws, who belonged to the Whig side; and this connection was the cause of his first appearing in print, and appearing there as a defender of liberal principles. Soon after 1770 the question of subscription to the Thirty-Nine Articles was being seriously mooted; and in 1772 a clerical petition for relief, drawn up at the Feathers Tavern, was presented to the House of Commons. The cautious Paley refused to sign (it was on this occasion that he pleaded that 'he could not afford to have a conscience'); but when Edmund Law, the Master of Peterhouse, published a liberal pamphlet dealing with 'the propriety of subscription', and this pamphlet was attacked by the President of Corpus Christi College, Oxford, Paley sprang to the defence of Law and liberty, and in an anonymous pamphlet, by 'a friend of religious liberty', he answered the President's attack. He might refuse to sign a petition, but he was ready to publish his views. A dozen years later, in the chapter of his *Principles* which deals with religious establishments, he expressly states that subscription should be made as easy and simple as possible, and adapted from time to time to sentiments and circumstances.

There was another member of Peterhouse besides Edmund Law, the Master, with whom Paley was closely connected. This was John Jebb, who had been second wrangler in 1757, and was made a Fellow of Peterhouse in 1761, five years before Paley became a Fellow of Christ's.[1] Jebb was a remarkable and mercurial man, and he was the husband of a remarkable wife, who under the name of 'Priscilla' trounced in print the defenders of subscription to the articles, as she also trounced the opponents of her husband's scheme for a reform of the Cambridge examination system. Paley was a friend of Jebb and his wife, and frequented their company. He disappointed Jebb, who had hoped for his active support, when he refused to sign the clerical petition for relief from subscription; but he was one of his supporters in his plan for a new system of annual examinations (serving on the syndicate appointed by the University to consider the plan), and he may thus be counted—academically at any rate—among the reformers. Academic reformers, it is true, are sometimes political conservatives (just as political reformers, conversely, are often academic conservatives); and though Jebb himself was a thoroughgoing radical—political as well as academic, and religious into the bargain—there is no evidence that Paley's academic liberalism, which perhaps itself was never very strong, was married to the cause of political and parliamentary reform. If only one could have listened to the political discussion round the tea-table of the Jebbs, or at the Hyson Club (of which Jebb was one of the founders and Paley one

---

[1] Jebb's subsequent career deserves some commemoration. He resigned his fellowship upon his marriage, in 1764, and lived in Cambridge as a private tutor. He had a versatile and restless mind; he wrote on the *Principia* of Newton and lectured on the Greek New Testament—inclining to unitarianism in his lectures, but continuing to hold a rectory in Norfolk and livings in Suffolk till 1775. Resigning his preferments in 1775, he left Cambridge, where he and his wife had always been champions of reform, in September 1776, some three months after Paley's departure; and taking his degree of M.D. at St Andrew's (1777), he settled down to practise in London, becoming a Fellow of the Royal Society in 1779. It was during this period of his life that he made himself conspicuous as an advocate of parliamentary reform. He died in 1786; and three volumes of his theological, political and medical works were published in 1787. Paley had appeared before him, when he was acting as moderator in 1762, in the 'acts' opposing capital punishment and defending the eternity of the torments of Hell; and Paley often met him afterwards, from 1766 to 1776, both at his private house and in the sessions of a University Club to which they both belonged.

of the later members) which 'met to drink tea and pass the evening in rational discussion'! Had Jebb, with his lively mind (he started the study of Anglo-Saxon in his last illness), already invented, and did he propound to his Cambridge colleagues, the plan of a 'convention' for the reform of the constitution and the extension of the suffrage, which he afterwards launched in an address to the freeholders of Middlesex in 1779?[1] If he had, and if it was discussed in Cambridge, what did Paley say? The questions admit no answer.[2] All we can say is that many years later, when he published his *Principles* in 1785, Paley disappointed the reformers not only by his lukewarmness, as they thought it (but were they justified in so thinking?), in the matter of subscription to the Articles, but also by his 'apology for the incongruities of the British constitution' and his defence of the existing system of parliamentary representation.

But if Paley disappointed the Jebbs and their friends, it does not for an instant follow that he ceased to have liberal sympathies. They might sometimes be faintly felt: they might often be faintly expressed; but they were always there, and they were sometimes vigorous. We shall have reason to notice later, when we come to analyse the political philosophy of the *Principles*, that there was more—much more—than the chapter on pigeons and property which was calculated to offend the feelings of conservatives. But Paley's acts, in his Cumberland days, are even more eloquent than his writings. It is perhaps a little thing that in county politics he joined in a stand against the encroachments of the first Lord Lonsdale, and that he expressed himself unfavourably about the

---

[1] On Jebb's political activities see G. S. Veatch, *The Genesis of Parliamentary Reform*, p. 49.

[2] The nearest approach to an answer is supplied by a passage in a letter which Mrs Jebb wrote to Meadley, long afterwards, and which is reproduced in the *Memoirs*. After a party, at which Paley and other friends had been present, and Jebb, as usual, had spoken his own sentiments very freely, he remarked to his wife that 'he did not know what to make of Paley, for that he said nothing, upon which I observed that he had been very attentive, and gave it as my firm opinion that he would be very liberal. After a further acquaintance Mr Jebb told me that I was right, for that Paley, he now saw, from the course of his studies, was endeavouring to explore the truth for himself.'

'mushrooms' (or bogus forty-shilling freeholders) which sprang up under the fostering care of that expert electioneer. It is a much greater thing that he took an active part in promoting opposition to the slave-trade. He had already expressed himself against it in the *Principles* in 1785. In 1788 he wrote to the newly founded London Committee for the abolition of the slave-trade (perhaps the more readily because the cause was almost a Cambridge cause) to express his sympathy and offer his support. In 1789 he sent the committee an argument, which was circulated by it to the press, against the payment of compensation to slave-dealers and slave-holders in the event of abolition. Besides corresponding with Clarkson, he met him from time to time; and in 1792, after presiding at a public meeting in Carlisle to promote a petition to parliament in favour of abolition,[1] he urged on Clarkson a plan for establishing a colony (or colonies) of liberated negroes in Africa—a plan which the Sierra Leone Company had inaugurated in 1787, and began to realise in 1792, and which was carried still further by the constitution of the Liberian Republic afterwards. Whether—like many of the people of Cumberland (and of other counties)—he sought 'to break the neck' of the trade in slaves by abstaining entirely from West Indian sugar, we are not told. But he did what he could by other, and much more effective, means.

To him, as to other Englishmen, the French Revolution came as a shock, and as something in the nature of a moral catastrophe. But in the quiet precincts of a cathedral close, in the far North of England, it did not blow with the hurricane force which Burke felt in London; and the Yorkshire stuff of which Paley was made was less excitable than the Celtic genius of Burke. He bowed a little, but he was hardly bent. If Burke was moved to publish the *Reflections on the Revolution in France*, Paley was only moved—and that not till 1792—to publish a couple of pamphlets. There was talk, in that year, of the spread of corresponding societies (the London Corresponding Society had been founded early in the

---

[1] Meadley prints in his Appendix, pp. 139–52, a report of Paley's speech from the chair and of the resolutions passed, which resulted in the presentation of a petition later in the year.

year), and there was some circulation of Paine's *Rights of Man*, of which Paley 'found one or two copies...in his own family, and threw them into the fire'.[1] This was the cause of the publication of his two pamphlets; but neither of them was written for the occasion. The first was a sermon which he had preached in a Cumberland parish in 1790, and which he now took from a drawer and published (first in Carlisle, and afterwards in London) under the title of *Reasons for Contentment, addressed to the Labouring Part of the British Public*. The second was simply a reprint, with a brief introductory advertisement of two pages, of the chapter on the British Constitution in the *Principles* of 1785. The advertisement pleads, and pleads justly, that the principles of the chapter 'were not made for the times or the occasion, to serve any purpose or any party', but 'were committed to writing ten years ago'. Since that time, Paley adds, 'I have written nothing, and to speak the truth, have thought little, upon political questions; for, interesting as they may seem to be, or are,...there are other studies, in comparison with which even these are unimportant'. In a word, he was pressing on with the *Evidences of Christianity*, which he completed two years later.

This was the whole of Paley's counterblast to the principles of the French Revolution. By 1795 he was far more occupied in settling down to his new life in Bishop Wearmouth and at Lincoln than he was with the course of politics. If he spoke or acted at all in social and political matters, it was with balance and a cautious discretion. In an assize sermon which he preached at Durham, in the middle of 1795, and which was published in London, he argued that the possession of wealth meant the occupation of a public station and imposed an obligation of trust: that 'a great part of the public business of the country was [in England] discharged by the country itself', and therefore involved the

---

[1] In his later years, we learn from Meadley (*Memoirs*, pp. 109–10), Paley thought that the popular societies could not justly be charged with treason. Their real design was 'to render the influence of the people predominant, by making universal suffrage and annual elections the basis of a parliamentary reform'.

wealthier classes in a duty of public service; and that 'men of elevated stations are not placed above work'. This was the other side to the *Reasons for Contentment, addressed to the Labouring Part of the British Public*; and indeed a comparison of these two sermons is sufficient in itself to prove the essential balance of Paley's mind. In his life, as well as his sermons and writings, he continued, during his later years, to be open and hospitable to both sides. Like Burke, but with less of a fiery friendship, he consorted with French *émigrés*; and when some Catholic clergy from France were housed by the government in the barracks at Sunderland he sent them cart-loads of vegetables and talked with them in such Latin as he and they could muster. On the other hand he also showed himself impatient of insinuations against dissenters: he associated with some of the Methodists of Sunderland; and he made the dissenter Meadley his companion and his confidant. His son notes as a curious circumstance that of his more distinguished visitors at Bishop Wearmouth 'most...were well known to range themselves with the opposition'. He also notes that when a scheme of voluntary rationing was started by the more opulent and respectable, during the scarcity of 1799, with a view to helping the poor and labouring classes, Paley took the lead in shaping the scheme, and rigorously followed it himself in his household.

All in all there is little evidence for any real change in Paley's views after he left Cambridge in 1776, or after he published the *Principles* in 1785. He was a man of one piece, consistently liberal in his sympathies, but consistently cautious in their expression. Balance was a favourite idea of the eighteenth century: 'balance' is a favourite word in Paley's own vocabulary; and balance was characteristic of his system of ideas. 'It seemed', his son wrote of him, 'to be the turn of his mind to seek out and attain a balance in his opinions, on whatever subject his mind was employed.' In the same sense Meadley noted that his conclusions in matters of politics, 'whilst they will certainly displease the staunch advocates of regal prerogative, may even fail to satisfy the sanguine assertors of popular right'. His reading of the newspapers of the day ..ttested the balance of his mind. It was a passion with him: he confesses, in the *Principles*, that 'had I all the money, which I pay in taxes to government, at liberty to lay out upon amusements and diversions, I know not whether I could make choice of any in which I could find greater pleasure than what I receive from expecting, hearing, and relating public news; reading parliamentary debates and proceedings; canvassing the political arguments, projects, predictions, and intelligence which are conveyed, by various channels, to every corner of the kingdom'. But if his reading of the newspapers was a passion, it was a nicely calculated and regulated passion. 'He took in', Meadley notes, 'a daily London paper (the *Sun*) in the interest of successive administrations, and a weekly provincial one (the *Newcastle Chronicle*) attached to the Whig opposition, "to balance his opinions", as he used to say.'[1]

This balance of opinion, and this steady observance of the mean, show something of an Aristotelian quality. There is also a similar quality in the respect which Paley showed for the general body of received opinion. Mackintosh, the author of *Vindiciae Gallicae* (a famous reply to Burke's *Reflections on the Revolution in France*), observed that he employed his art 'to blend his own arguments with the body of received opinions'. The man who respects received opinion will be largely attached to things as they are; and Meadley noted of Paley that he was 'too much occupied with the practical difficulties of a change . . . to start any plans of reform, and he endeavoured rather to make the best of things in their present state'. A Cambridge correspondent of Meadley, who seems to have belonged to the liberal Wing, remarked in a letter written after Paley's death: 'I know there are persons who lament that intellectual powers like those of Paley were not more devoted

---

[1] Paley's son, perhaps too anxious to establish his father's political orthodoxy, suppresses the *Newcastle Chronicle*. Noting that his father 'was an eager devourer of a newspaper', he adds that 'one newspaper in a day . . . was quite sufficient for his politics; and as it is not unusual for us to form an opinion of a man's politics by inquiring what newspaper he reads, it may be well to mention that his was the *Sun*'. This is formally correct: the *Sun* was his one daily paper; but those who know the North will also know that the Northern weekly paper would lie close to Paley's heart.

...to the discovery of new truth, rather than to the establishment and recommendation of doctrines and principles already well known and believed.' The laments were natural, especially in view of his early promise; but those who uttered them perhaps failed to take sufficient account of the grain of his mind. With all his desire for balance, and even in spite of it, he was invincibly attracted to the side of received opinion and the *status quo*. His mind was powerful, but perhaps phlegmatic. It was acute enough to be drawn into occasional criticism—pithy and pungent criticism; but it recoiled on itself, in an instinct of self-preservation, at the prospect of controversy, or before the risk of trouble. A remark of his son is perhaps significant: 'he has been very frequently heard to say that he would never answer anything that appeared against him, for time would do that for him.' He was not prepared for the clash of argument: he retired into the comfort of silence, with 'a very strong dislike to the disturbance and disquietude of contending about anything'. He had in him, after all, something of the Epicureans whose side he espoused in his prize essay of 1765: he cultivated, like them, the quality of 'undisturbedness' (ἀταραξία).

IV

When we turn to the genesis of the philosophical ideas which Paley expresses in the *Principles of Moral and Political Philosophy*, it is natural to invoke once more the name and the philosophy of Epicurus. The essential principle of the book is the principle of happiness. The essential assumption is that God has intended the general happiness of mankind, and that acts are good or bad according as they promote or diminish such happiness. Utility is therefore the standard of action and the cause of obligation. If an act is useful in promoting happiness, it attains the standard of a right act; and we are therefore obliged to perform the act. This is Paley's version of what is generally called utilitarianism. How did he come by that version?

In answering that question we are bound to return to the prize essay of 1765, in which he had compared the philosophy of the

Epicureans with that of the Stoics, and decided in favour of the Epicureans. As we have seen, he may already have derived some inkling of the philosophy of the greatest happiness of the greatest number from the lectures of Dr Backhouse, which he attended in his undergraduate days; but it was the composition of the essay for the Bachelor's Prize which forced him to collect and express for himself his own ideas. The ideas which he expressed in the essay are fundamentally the ideas which he afterwards used in his lectures at Christ's College (between 1766 and 1776) and finally published in the *Principles* of 1785. There is thus a continuous line of thought which, beginning perhaps in the days of his attendance at the lectures of Dr Backhouse, runs through his own later lectures and ends in the doctrine of the *Principles*. An examination of the history of his famous definition of goodness may serve to show this continuity.

As it appears in the *Principles*, the definition runs in these terms: 'Virtue is the doing good to mankind, in obedience to the will of God, and for the sake of everlasting happiness.' Twenty years earlier, in the prize essay of 1765, he had already said something very similar. Dismissing, as he comes to the end, the teachings of the Stoics, and even of the Epicureans, as in themselves null and void, he turns to the Christian religion, and he seeks to argue that this religion reconciled and sublimated the teachings of both—the Stoic teaching or paradox that goodness is its own reward, and the Epicurean teaching that goodness has for its aim the pursuit and attainment of happiness. *Illuxit aliquando religio, cujus auctor est Deus, cujus materia veritas, cujus finis est felicitas. Religio aliquando illuxit, quae Stoae paradoxon in principiis vere Epicureis fundari voluit. Sufficit ad felicitatem virtus; virtutis tamen finis est felicitas.* This is explained in one of the English notes which he appended to his Latin Essay (he apologised for them, but they sadly displeased one of his judges): 'it was reserved for one greater than Zeno to exalt the dignity of virtue with its utility, and by superinducing a future state [and, with it, the goal of "everlasting happiness"] to support the paradox of the Stoic on Epicurean principles.' Here we may already trace, in embryo, the religious or supernatural sanction

which it was Paley's object to add to current ideas of utilitarianism
—ideas which were much the same as the ancient ideas of Epi-
cureanism. It would be foolish to read too much into the expressions of a young man of twenty-two, who was writing a prize
essay in a dead language; and Edmund Paley expresses a doubt
'whether any particular passages of the Essay may be produced as
indication of the bent of the writer's mind'. But it is not a question
of particular passages: it is rather a matter of the general argument;
and both in the essay itself and in the English notes with which it
is furnished the idea of utility is a recurrent idea. What is more
important, it is an idea which remains steadily recurrent in the
later expressions of his thought—as if, once accepted into his mind,
it had become a constant part of its furniture. The definition of
goodness, which connects it with its utility in the promotion of
happiness, is already to be found, word for word, in his Cambridge
lecture-notes on moral philosophy before 1776: it recurs *verbatim*
in a sermon delivered at Appleby in 1779; and so it progresses to
its final publication in the *Principles* of 1785. Paley was faithful to
his beginnings: the *Principles* agrees with the prize essay of 1765, as
the *Natural Theology* of 1802 agrees with the *Principles* of 1785.
His motto, it may almost be said, was *quod dixi, dixi*: when he had
said a thing, he had said it, and it remained with him for the
future.[1]

Such was the genesis of the philosophical ideas expressed in the
Principles. What were the causes which led to their publication,
and what was the temper of the times in which they were published? The immediate cause of the plan of publishing a book based

---

[1] Meadley, in the Appendix to his *Memoirs*, reprints some *Observations on the
Morality of the Gospels*, which Paley contributed in 1776 to a book written by
his patron Law, the Bishop of Carlisle. In one passage of these *Observations*
there is a remark that 'the Gospel maxims...are better than the *utile* or general
expediency of the modern, which few can estimate'. Basing himself on this
passage, Meadley suggests 'that his theory of morals was not altogether firmly
settled on the basis which supports it now'. But a single clause in a single
sentence is not sufficient to prove that he had changed or modified his views in
1776; and it may well be argued that Paley was only criticising a current
secular form of utilitarianism, while still remaining faithful to the religious
form which he had himself given to the idea.

on his Cambridge lectures was the urgency of his friend John Law (the eldest son of the Bishop of Carlisle) who, formerly his colleague as a tutor of Christ's College, was now again his colleague as a clergyman in the same diocese. Law pressed him to publish, 'knowing well enough', as his son puts it in his *Life* of his father, 'his prevailing taste for rubbing off the stiffness of school-learning and forming a reading-made-easy of an abstruse science'. Paley yielded easily to the pressure; and beginning the book soon after the outbreak of the War of American Independence (some time round about 1778) he brought it to an end and saw it published two years after the end of the war. It took him nearly seven years, though he had his lecture-notes before him; but he was busy with clerical duties and the care of a young and growing family. The temper of the times, and the course of the war, left some impression on the character of the book. His son observes that 'he fell in with times when uncourtly language became the fashion in politics'; and there are certainly passages in the *Principles* which seem to reflect the contemporary feeling against George III. But, as we shall see, these are only clouds in a sky which is generally clear; and indeed it was the critics of George III who were also the critics of Paley's *Principles*. If he fell in with the times, he also fell in—and that even more—with the general legacy of time and with 'things in their present state'. A general view of the argument of the *Principles*—and especially of its sixth and longest book, on 'the elements of Political Knowledge'—will suffice to make this clear.

V

1. The argument of the *Principles*, in the first two books (which bear the titles 'Preliminary Considerations' and 'Moral Obligation') is addressed to laying the foundations. Happiness is the end, or, as he had said in his prize essay, *finis est felicitas*. Therefore things are right or wrong, in morals and in politics, according as they are useful or the reverse—according, in other words, as they tend to promote or diminish happiness. 'Actions are to be estimated by

their tendency. Whatever is expedient is right. It is the utility of any moral rule alone, which constitutes the obligation of it.'

What is happiness? It exists when the amount or aggregate of pleasure exceeds that of pain: it is constituted of, or by, pleasure. Pleasures differ in nothing but in continuance and intensity; in the time for which they last and the depth to which they go. It follows that you are doing the things which belong to happiness—and which, as such, are useful, and being useful are also right—if you pursue and attain a surplus of continuous and intense pleasures. Such pleasures are those of social affection, which are both intense and continuous, and which are experienced, for instance, in the life of the family. (Paley, recently married, and watching his children with delight, could not but observe, 'I seem, for my own part, to see the benevolence of the Deity more clearly in the pleasures of very young children than in any thing in the world'.) Such pleasures, again, are those that come from exercising the faculties on some engaging end, which keeps them continually stretched and satisfied, for 'engagement is everything'; and they also arise from a prudent constitution of the habits—'to set the habits in such a manner that every change may be a change for the better', or, in the words of Paley's own favourite maxim, to 'learn to husband our pleasures'.[1]

So far, the tenets of Paley are much the same as those suggested by Bentham in the anonymous *Fragment on Government* (published in 1776, but probably unknown to Paley) and developed by him afterwards in the *Principles of Morals and Legislation* published in 1789. But Paley, being a clergyman, has something more to add; and the addition which he makes is the essence of his version of utilitarianism. Happiness is *the will of God*, and not merely the instinct of men. 'The world abounds with contrivances...directed

---

[1] In his emphasis on continuity of pleasure, and on a system of husbanding pleasures, Paley was remembering the Epicurean doctrine. Epicurus, disagreeing with the Cyrenaics and their doctrine of pleasure as the fine flower of the moment, bade men look 'to the happiness of the whole of life' (εἰς τὴν τοῦ ὅλου βίου μακαριότητα); and he counted the winning of friendship (or what Paley calls the social affections) as the greatest of the means which wisdom prepares for attaining this end.

to beneficial purposes', which make for happiness and prove God's will for the general happiness of mankind. (Here we may see, in advance, the argument of the *Natural Theology* of 1802.) It follows that 'the method of coming at the will of God, concerning any action, by the light of nature, is to inquire into the tendency of that action to promote or diminish the general happiness'. The introduction of the word 'general' here deserves notice. It is not my happiness alone that matters: it is my happiness as part of, and as a factor in, the *total* happiness. God intends the general happiness of all mankind; and I am obedient to His will only if I intend and pursue that general happiness. It is not clear how the original idea of a personal surplus of pleasure over pain can be reconciled with a development of ideas which may involve men in incurring, for the sake of the general happiness, a personal surplus of pain over pleasure. But that is a general difficulty of utilitarianism, which was afterwards to vex the spirit of Mill, but which failed to ruffle the placidity of Paley or even to enter his mind. He had leaped from hedonism to the general happiness by invoking the will of God; but he was unconscious of the leap.

By introducing the will of God to cover and glorify the general happiness, Paley added a consecration to current ideas of utilitarianism. He gave them a supernatural sanction. It was thus that he attained his definition of goodness: 'the doing good to mankind [by increasing its general happiness] in obedience to the will of God.' But that is not the whole of the definition. The final words are still to be added: 'and for the sake of everlasting happiness.' What is the effect of the addition? It is clear that the word 'everlasting' introduces a new phase of thought. Besides general happiness, in numerical extension, there must also be *durable* happiness, along the line of time: in a word, 'continuity' of pleasures must be protracted until it touches eternity. It is also clear that the addition of the word 'everlasting', like that of the word 'general', depends on the introduction of the supernatural sanction. It is the will of God which turns my individual in-this-life happiness into general everlasting happiness. But it is not equally clear that the introduction of the motive of everlasting happiness does not bring the argument back from the pursuit of the general happiness to an ultimate egoism. If the *causa causans* of action is my own everlasting happiness, I have hardly escaped from the prison of self into an ampler air. Paley's foundations have an engaging simplicity: but they have also a bewildering incoherence. Anything might be built upon them; but anything built upon them will have no stable foundation. The building itself may show good sense and shrewd observation. But, in spite of the title of Paley's book, it will not rest upon *principles*. Paley was not a metaphysician; and the discovery of principles was not his *métier*. There is a logical connection between Bentham's principles and the conclusions and structure of reform in which they are made to culminate. There is little connection—indeed, as we shall have occasion to notice, there is often a gulf of discrepancy —between Paley's principles and his conclusions.

2. Turning from his principles to the conclusions which he seeks to establish in matters of politics (his conclusions in matters of morals lie outside the scope of our inquiry), we may begin with his theory of rights, and consider how he applies that theory to the institutions of property and slavery.[1] Rights are generally conceived by Paley as powers of enjoyment by individuals which become rights, and cease to be only powers, when they conduce to the general happiness and are thus consistent with the will of God. What, in the light of this general conception, is to be said of the right of property? Paley begins his answer with the famous parable of the pigeons, which has already been quoted. Taken as it stands (especially if the reader comes to it fresh from reading the previous chapter, at the end of the second book, on the general rights of mankind—'the rights which belong to the species *collectively*'—of which the first is 'a right to the fruits or vegetable produce of the earth'), this parable may seem pure communism.

---

[1] His theory of rights comes at the end of Book II, under the head of 'Moral Obligation'. The treatment of property comes at the beginning of Part I of Book III, under the head of 'Relative Duties which are determinate'; that of slavery comes in the third chapter of Part II of Book III, under the head of 'Relative Duties which are indeterminate'.

But Paley, the master of arresting paradox, the lecturer who always loved to shock his hearers into attention by the art of thesis and antithesis (perhaps a relic or an effect of the method of disputation), has stated only one side of the question, and that only the *prima facie* side. He turns at once to the other. 'Hush,' he says in effect, 'all's right with property. God intended the earth to be used for the benefit of man: it cannot be properly or fully used unless it be divided in severalty: it cannot be so divided except by the law of the land.' The conclusion is that private property rests immediately on the law of the land,[1] and ultimately on the will of God for human happiness. *Lex terrae* is one with *voluntas Dei*: property, defended by both, is right—and being right it is also safe. Not, by the way, that Paley believes that *any* division of the soil made or enforced by the law of the land is necessarily useful or necessarily right. 'If there be any great inequality unconnected with this origin [that is to say with the proper and full use of the soil for the benefit of man], it ought to be corrected.' But he does not really face the question of the norm or standard of division which the law of the land ought to follow: he is generally inclined 'to make the best of things in their present state'; and his preliminary pigeons remain in a sort of unresolved antinomy with his final conclusions.

The argument, it will be noted, relates peculiarly, and almost exclusively, to land: Paley still thought in agrarian terms (as indeed was natural in a countryman); and the development of industry and industrial capital failed to engage his attention. But if he could justify property in land, he was dubious about property in persons, and he had qualms about the institution of slavery.[2]

---

[1] Paley mentions the view of Locke—that the right of property is based on the fact that a man has mixed his labour, and thereby himself, with the land which he cultivates—and he admits that it has some reason. But he argues that it is far from covering all cases; he also argues that the principle of need gives a better account of the first right of ownership than does the principle of labour —though the principle of need is also inadequate to cover all cases; and he reaches in this way his own final view that 'the real foundation of our right is THE LAW OF THE LAND'.

[2] See above, p. 225. A movement of humanitarianism was already stirring by 1785. Lord Mansfield's famous judgement in Somersett's case, which laid down

Slavery, he argues, is an odious institution, temporarily justifiable when a criminal is punished by it for his crime, or a captive in war for the delinquency of his nation, or a debtor for his debt; but it should end as soon as the crime is expiated, the national delinquency repaired, or the debt satisfied. The slave-trade, as distinct from slavery, cannot be justified at all: the slaves concerned are not criminals, debtors, or captives in war; the cruelty of their transportation is abominable; and the tyranny of the plantation system to which they are delivered for life, though defended by the tyrant's plea of necessity, is indefensible on any just count. Paley adds a notable reflection. 'The great revolution which seems preparing in the Western world may probably conduce (and who knows but that it is designed?) to accelerate the fall of this abominable tyranny; and when this contest and the passions which attend it are no more, there will succeed a season for reflecting whether a legislature which had so long lent its assistance to the support of an institution replete with human misery was fit to be trusted with an empire the most extensive that ever obtained in any age or quarter of the world.' These are the words which Paley uses in the text of the first edition. They are slightly altered and somewhat tempered in later editions. But as they stand, they throw a vivid light on his attitude to the War of American Independence and his views of the nature of the first British Empire, so closely connected with the practice of the slave-trade and the institution of plantation-slavery. They also show that the active sympathy with which he supported the committee for the abolition of the slave-trade, in 1788 and afterwards, was no sudden ebullition of feeling, but the result of long-cherished convictions.

3. From Paley's theory of rights it is natural to turn to his theory of government. He was the more concerned to establish a theory of government because he felt, as he says in the preface to the *Principles*, that political theory does, after all, exercise an influence on political action. Possibly, he notes, the influence of

that the law of England did not recognise slavery, and that the rights of slave-owners could not be enforced in English courts, had been given in 1771; and Clarkson wrote his prize essay against the slave-trade in 1785.

the theory of Rousseau was responsible for the troubles which had lately convulsed Geneva;[1] and 'throughout the political disputes that have within these few years taken place in Great Britain, in her sister-kingdom [Ireland], and in her foreign dependencies [the North American colonies], it was impossible not to observe... the prevalency of these ideas of civil authority which are displayed in the works of Mr Locke'. Of the theory of Rousseau, Paley has little or nothing to say in the course of his argument; but he is constantly concerned with the ideas expressed in the works of Locke. Whether or no he had ever lectured on Locke during the days of his tutorship at Christ's College, he was certainly familiar with his writings, and especially with the *Second Treatise on Civil Government*. It was his aim to answer Locke wherever, in his view, Locke seemed to require an answer (on the theory of property, for instance, or the theory of the *Social Contract*), and to substitute for his views an alternative view less likely to lead to political disputes. If political theories do influence political action—if, as Paley held, 'it is of *practical* importance to have the principles, from which the obligations of social union and the extent of civil obedience are derived, rightly explained and well understood'— it was his duty to provide a good theory and a sound statement of principles for his own age and generation.

This theory and statement are to be found in the sixth book of his *Principles*, which is entitled 'Elements of Political Knowledge', and is the longest and the best of all the six books of the work. He begins by asking why government *is* obeyed, and proceeds to ask why it *ought to be*. This is an inquiry on the one hand, and on

[1] Switzerland generally had been vexed, during the course of the eighteenth century, by class conflicts between an oligarchical patriciate and the mass of the citizens. In Geneva these conflicts were almost continuous during the century. There is another thing to be added. 'It was Geneva in particular from which the French, before they had yet emerged out of the sphere of theories, derived their examples of popular risings, of deliberative assemblies and imperious action on the part of private societies, and finally even a supply of agents versed in the art of insurrection.' (Professor Schollenberger, of Zürich, in the *Cambridge Modern History*, Vol. VI, p. 625.) If Rousseau, a citizen of Geneva, stimulated his own city, his city also stimulated France in turn, and served as a hearth of revolution.

the side of the subject, into the grounds of political obligation; it
is also an inquiry on the other, and on the side of government,
into the basis of political authority. In brief, it may be called an
inquiry into the duty of obedience and the right of sovereignty.
Why *is* government obeyed? Not for its power; and here
Paley employs once more his method of the arresting paradox.
'Could we view our own species from a distance,...there is
nothing in the human character which would more surprise us
than the almost universal subjugation of strength to weakness;
than to see many millions of robust men, in the complete use and
exercise of their personal faculties, waiting upon the will of a child,
a woman, a driveller, or a lunatic.'[1] The strength of government
is not its own strength: 'the physical strength resides in the
governed.' The reason why government is obeyed must therefore
be something other than strength; and that something other can
only be the opinion of the governed in favour of government—
an opinion which may be based on prejudice and a worship of
prescription, or on reason and a calculation of benefits, or on
self-interest and a fear of the consequences of disobedience. 'Civil
authority is founded in opinion.' This is as much as to say (as
T. H. Green did) that 'will, not force, is the basis of the state'. But
though Paley has grasped this idea, he has grasped it tender-
handed. If he had grasped it firmly, he would have argued that
the basis of government in public opinion involves a system of
popular government. As it is, he draws two contradictory conclusions from the idea that civil authority is founded in opinion.
One is that governments ought to treat general opinion with
deference. The other is that, in order to prevent any disturbance
of the basis of opinion, they ought 'to prevent great collections of
men of any separate party or religion, or of like occupation or
profession, or in any way connected by a participation of interest
or passion, from being assembled in the same vicinity'. Paley

---

[1] The last words of this passage on the paradox of government may remind
us of similar words in the paradox of property, where the owner is described as
'oft-times the feeblest and worst of the whole set, a child, a woman, a madman,
a fool'. Queen Elizabeth and Queen Victoria might have objected to the
collocation.

refers especially to the 'danger of an overgrown metropolis and of...great cities and crowded districts'. He was a countryman, and he may have had in mind the riots in London of 1780 and the mob which was led by Lord George Gordon (they alarmed Burke too, as we learn from his correspondence);[1] but in the general conclusion he draws he comes near to the teaching of Hobbes, that 'an infirmity of a commonwealth is the immoderate greatness of a town...as also the great number of corporations, which are as it were many lesser commonwealths in the body of a greater'.[2]

Why *ought* government to be obeyed? Not on the ground of contract, 'as has been usual with many political writers, at the head of whom we find the venerable name of Locke'. Paley condemns the notion of a social contract, first on the ground that the contract is not a historical *fact*, and secondly on the ground that if the *idea* of it is entertained 'as a fiction which furnishes a commodious explication of the mutual rights and duties of sovereigns and subjects', it is not even a good fiction.[3] The consequences to which the idea of a contract leads are too questionable: on the one hand it may buttress a government which is obsolete and useless, if such a government can plead that it has not violated the contract; on the other hand it may tend to dissolve, or at any rate cripple, a useful government, if its subjects can plead that it has violated any jot or tittle of the bond. There is only one case in which Paley will allow 'some imitation of a social compact'. This is the case of revolution; and here he cites the example of the

[1] See Burke's letters to his friends Champion and Shackleton (the first dated from 'what was London'), in his *Correspondence*, edited by Lord Fitzwilliam, Vol. II, pp. 350–5.

[2] In a later passage (Book VI, ch. IX) Paley remarks that 'great cities multiply crimes, by presenting easier opportunities and more incentives', and he suggests that 'these temptations and facilities can only be counteracted by adding to the number of capital punishments'—which Blackstone had estimated at 160, but which had increased since Blackstone wrote. It is perhaps hardly curious that Paley, who had opposed capital punishment in his undergraduate days (supra, p. 198), should advocate its extension in his middle age.

[3] It is interesting to compare Paley's criticism of the notion of contract in 1785 (which is partly drawn from Hume's critique in his essay of 1748 *Of the Original Contract*) with the criticism of Professor Buckland in 1945, in *Some Reflections on Jurisprudence*, pp. 63–6. There are some interesting parallels.

United States of North America (he would seem to be referring to the Articles of Confederation drafted by the Congress of 1777), where 'we saw the *people* assembled to elect deputies for the avowed purpose of framing the constitution of a new empire'. But generally he maintains that the real ground of political obligation—the real reason why government ought to be obeyed —is to be found in his own version of the principle of utility, and is, in a word, 'the will of God as collected from expediency'. We ought to obey our government because it promotes the will of God by promoting the general happiness of man. This is a combination of Sir Robert Filmer and Epicurus—a weaving of the woof of the *utile* (as Paley called it) with the warp of *jus divinum*.[1]

But if government ought to be obeyed for this reason, it may also be disobeyed—indeed, it ought to be disobeyed—for the very same reason. If government does not increase, but on the contrary diminishes, the general happiness, it loses its ground and forfeits its title; and resistance will be lawful, and will even be a duty, if the subjects, after weighing not only 'the grievance which is sustained or feared' but also 'the probable expense and event of the contest', decide that it is, on the balance, worth while. Here we find the same mathematical formula applied to the problem of resistance which Bentham had used, nine years before, in his *Fragment on Government*, when he argued that 'it is allowable to, if not incumbent on, every man...to enter into measures of resistance when, according to the best calculation he is able to make, *the probable mischiefs of resistance* (speaking with respect to the community in general) *appear less to him than the probable mischiefs of submission*'.[2] Paley applies the formula, in a notable passage of his argument, to the resistance of the North American Colonies after 1776. He premises that 'the interest of the whole

---

[1] At the same time it may fairly be said that there is some analogy between Paley's doctrine and the doctrine of Jefferson enunciated in the Declaration of Independence. When Jefferson appealed to 'the Laws of Nature and of Nature's God', and protested that all men were endowed by their Creator with the inalienable right to the pursuit of happiness, he was moving in a contemporary circle of thought in which Paley also moved.

[2] Op. cit. ch. IV, § XXI.

society is binding upon every part of it': in other words, he assumes that you are bound to think in terms of the whole of the British Empire, as it stood before 1776. 'Had I been an American,' he argues, 'I should have had to consider not only the happiness of America, but also the whole happiness of the empire...not indeed the happiness of every part...but whether what Great Britain would lose by the separation was likely to be compensated to the joint stock of happiness by the advantages which America would receive from it.' On this basis he concludes—cautiously, but still mathematically (we have to remember his Cambridge training in mathematics)—that if the colonies had been small, the balance might have gone against them: 'But when, by an increase of population, the interest of the provinces begins to bear a considerable proportion to the *entire* interest of the community, it is possible that they may suffer so much by their subjection, that not only theirs, but the whole happiness of the empire, may be obstructed by their union.'[1]

4. Paley would thus allow some liberty of resistance. But his general idea of liberty is somewhat limited. His main anxiety is for what may be called civil liberty, private liberty, liberty for a man to manage his own life so far as may be consistent with the general happiness of the community. From this point of view he is willing to accept, and he even ventures to suggest, 'a revision of many laws of this country; especially of the game-laws; of the poor-laws, so far as they lay restrictions on the poor themselves; of the laws against Papists and Dissenters'.[2] But if he has some concern for civil or private liberty, he has little anxiety for the enjoyment of political liberty, public liberty, the right of the citizen to have some share in the direction of the affairs of the

---

[1] Book VI, ch. III, *ad finem*.

[2] Blackstone, in his *Commentaries*, had also singled out for criticism the game-laws ('which have raised a little Nimrod in every manor') and the poor-laws; but he had gone further than Paley, and criticised generally the severity of English criminal law and the excessive frequency of capital punishment. Paley, in his chapter on Crimes and Punishments, discovers 'a just excuse for the multiplicity of capital offences', and, as has already been noted (p. 240, n. 2), he is even willing to suggest an addition to their number.

general community. This apathy, or 'undisturbedness', is some-what curious, and even contradictory. He has already argued that opinion is the reason why government is obeyed. He confesses, as has already been noticed, that his own greatest pleasure is 'hearing and relating public news; reading parliamentary debates and proceedings; canvassing...political arguments'. He liked to talk politics; but as he himself took no very active part in politics, and never professedly belonged to any political party, so he seems to expect his countrymen to be made in the image of himself, and to be content with doing what he was content to do himself. It does not matter to him, and it should not matter to them, how parliament is elected—provided that the persons elected are some-how sensible men, who will make sensible laws safeguarding civil liberty, and will also, in the process, provide the clash of parliamen-tary debates for the intelligent reader. It is the difficulty of this placid philosophy that Paley himself has already said that the persons elected on the present system make game-laws and poor-laws and recusancy laws which contravene civil liberty. It is a further difficulty that he himself lays it down that the people is freest which makes the best provision for the enacting of expedient and salutary laws. How can England be free when, on his own showing, it has not even made a tolerable provision?

But the full nature of Paley's views on liberty demands a further inquiry. They have not only to be studied in the abstract; they also have to be studied in the concrete, and in relation to actual forms of government. We must therefore inquire into Paley's view of the different forms of government. In particular, re-membering that he was writing for British readers, we must inquire into his view of the British constitution.

He classifies forms of government, in the usual eighteenth-century style inherited by Hamilton and Madison and expounded in the *Federalist*, into monarchies, aristocracies, and republics. He also adds to these three simple forms—and the addition is vitally important when we come to the British constitution—the mixed form of government 'composed by the combination of two or more of the simple forms'. He has some stirring things to say about the republic, which he also styles by the name of 'demo-cracy' or 'the democratic constitution'. He defines it as a form of government 'where the people at large, either collectively or by representation, constitute the legislature'. He holds that it has desirable qualities: he also holds that it is a form of government which is generally practicable, in large states as well as small. The desirable qualities which it possesses are twofold. On the one hand, and Paley puts this first, there is 'the exciting...and calling forth to the service of the commonwealth the faculties of its best citizens', or (in other words) 'the direction which it gives to the education, studies, and pursuits, of the superior orders of the community', by rousing and animating them to seek the reward of political dignity and importance. On the other hand, there are 'the satisfactions which the people in free governments derive from the knowledge and agitation of political subjects'. Thus desirable, a republic or democracy is also practicable: indeed, it may be argued to be practicable in any size of state. Here Paley runs counter to a general opinion 'that a republican form of government suits only with the affairs of a small state'. He acknowledges the force of the objection currently urged against a large republic; but he pleads that 'much of the objection seems to be done away by the contrivance of a large *federal* republic'. This was a plea which Rousseau also urged;[1] but Paley's plea has a peculiar interest because it is based on his observation of the development of the American Confederation, which preceded the final federal republic of 1787. The plea is modestly and tentatively urged. 'How far such a republic is capable of uniting the liberty of a small commonwealth with the safety of a powerful empire, or whether, amongst co-ordinate powers, jealousies would not be likely to arise, which, for want of a common superior, might proceed to fatal extremities, are questions upon which the records

[1] It is not only urged by Rousseau; it is also urged by Madison in the *Federalist* (xiv), where he argues that on the basis of federalism a large state may be a republic (though not a democracy, which—unlike Paley—he distinguishes from a republic, and by which he means the direct and primary government of the people), and that 'America can claim the merit of making the discovery the basis of a large and unmixed republic'.

of mankind do not authorise us to decide with tolerable certainty. The experiment is about to be tried in America upon a large scale.' This is a notable passage. It is true that Paley's description of a federal republic is based on a study of the Articles of Confederation of 1777, and that (writing as he was before 1785) he has no inkling of the true federal republic created in 1787. But it is to his credit that he studied the confederation of 1777–87, even if he miscalled it a federal republic, and that he foresaw its potentialities —and even the risk of 'fatal extremities' which was actually run in the American Civil War of the nineteenth century. Hamilton and Madison, when they wrote their articles for the *Federalist*, went far beyond Paley. But Paley already saw in a vision—darkly, indeed, and with some confusion between the federal principle and the principle of confederation—what they, with a more intimate experience, saw far more clearly and expounded more fully.

In his view of the British constitution (which is given in the seventh chapter of his sixth book, and which, as has already been noticed, was afterwards printed and sold as a pamphlet in 1792), Paley attains the height of his powers and writes a memorable page in the history of political theory.[1] He has already remarked, in the previous chapter on different forms of government, that 'a government receives its denomination from the form of the legislature, which form is likewise what we commonly mean by the *constitution* of a country'. When he comes to the British constitution, he is more specific. In words which are quoted by Dicey, and which anticipate much of the argument of his *Law of the Constitution*, Paley notes that the British constitution is simply that part of the ordinary law of the land which regulates the form of the legislature—a part which stands on the same footing as the

---

[1] It is now over forty years ago that the writer was advised by Professor Dicey, in a talk which he still remembers, to read and digest Paley's chapter on the British constitution. This was the beginning of an interest in Paley which has only increased with the passage of years. Book VI, ch. VII of Paley's *Principles* may well be compared with another famous chapter of another famous book— the sixth chapter, entitled 'de la constitution d'Angleterre', in Book XI of Montesquieu's *L'Esprit des lois*.

rest, and is equally alterable by the same process as the rest of the law. The British constitution being a mixed constitution, the law so regulates the form of the legislature that it is composed of King, Lords, and Commons as one tripartite body—'the monarchy residing in the king; the aristocracy in the House of Lords; and the republic being represented by the House of Commons'. This mixed legislature, like all other legislatures, has the sovereign or supreme power; and, as Paley has argued in the previous chapter, that power 'may be termed absolute, omnipotent, uncontrollable, arbitrary, despotic'—for 'as a series of appeals must be finite, there necessarily exists in every government a power from which the constitution has provided no appeal'. The mixed form of government may be mixed; but mixed as it is, it can do what it will.

This enunciation of a doctrine of sovereignty, garnished with such a wealth of adjectives, suggests (and may perhaps excuse) a digression. Why did Paley genuflect so low before the idea of sovereignty? The answer is that it was an idea which was in the bones of his age. Blackstone, twenty years before, had stated that 'there is and must be in all forms of government a supreme, irresistible, absolute, uncontrolled authority, in which...the rights of sovereignty reside'. Bentham, some ten years earlier, had indeed sought to criticise Blackstone; but even he had allowed that 'the supreme governor's authority, though not *infinite*, must unavoidably, I think, *unless where limited by express convention* [this, as he explains, respects the case where one State has, upon terms, submitted itself to the government of another], be allowed to be *indefinite*'.[1] What is called the Austinian doctrine of sovereignty is long anterior to Austin. It is the common doctrine of the latter half of the eighteenth century: it is not only the doctrine of Paley, Blackstone, and Bentham, but also the doctrine of Rousseau, whose *volonté générale* knows no limits. Burke indeed had some qualms. He too could speak of 'the unlimited and illimitable nature of supreme sovereignty'; but if he could enunciate he also dreaded legal theory. When it came to the actual exercise of sovereignty he had a large respect for prudence and conformity to

[1] *Fragment on Government*, ch. IV, § XXIII.

circumstances; above all he had a great regard for the general opinion of those who are to be governed. 'General opinion', he wrote, 'is the vehicle and organ of legislative omnipotence.'[1]

Paley, too, was willing to pay homage to 'general opinion' as well as to 'legislative omnipotence'. Was the homage equal, and did he succeed, when he sought to describe the British constitution, in reconciling *imperium* with *libertas* in his description? One naturally feels that a sovereignty so tremendous as that ascribed by him to the legislature should be broadly based on public opinion. Ought he not logically to cherish the same feeling himself, in view of what he has already said of opinion as the basis of obedience, and, more especially, in view of what he has also said about the desirable qualities of democracy? Ought he not, therefore, to allow that in the mixture and composition of the British tripartite sovereign body the part which is democracy or republic, and which is represented by the House of Commons, should be particularly strong, and particularly and evidently representative of opinion? He certainly makes some general admissions which seem to tend in this direction, and promise to open the doors to constitutional reform and the extension of the suffrage. He allows that 'that, after all, is most likely to be right and expedient, which appears to be so to the separate judgement and decision of a great majority of the nation'. He admits, again, in discussing the two ends of civil government essential to a good constitution—the end of 'the happiness of its subjects' and the end of 'its own preservation'—that the former is the greater, and yet 'there are many things in the English, as in every, constitution...to be vindicated and accounted for solely from their tendency to maintain the government in its present state and the parts of it in possession of the powers which the constitution has assigned them'—an admission on which it would seem to follow, both by implication and on his own principle of happiness, that such things might well be re-

---

[1] Burke's ideas on sovereignty are expressed in his speeches on the American question in 1774 and 1775, and in his Letter to the Sheriffs of Bristol of 1777. The quotation in the text comes from the Letter (Vol. II, p. 270, of the edition of Burke's *Works* in the World's Classics).

formed. But having made these admissions, he also makes a very English statement which modifies their effect. He suggests that the British constitution 'resembles one of these old mansions, which, instead of being built all at once, after a regular plan...has been reared in different ages, has been altered from time to time, and has been continually receiving additions and repairs suited to the taste, fortune, and conveniency of its successive proprietors'. It is possible to accept, and even to admire, this analogy: indeed, it is possible to draw from it the conclusion that mansions and constitutions, having been altered and repaired in the past, may well be altered and repaired in the present to suit modern taste and conveniency.[1] But that is not the conclusion which Paley draws. He proceeds to draw two different conclusions—one of them wholly true and admirable; the other very true, but trending, in the form in which it is stated by Paley, to disputable consequences.

The first of the conclusions drawn is that the theory of the British constitution, based largely upon its past, is different from the fact, as the fact stands in the present. You have, for instance, the theory of formidable royal prerogatives: you have the fact that in actual exercise these prerogatives have dwindled into mere ceremonies, and their place has been taken by 'a sure and commanding influence, of which the constitution, it seems, is totally ignorant, growing out of enormous patronage'. This is admirable; and it shows that Paley, as Dicey has noted, saw far more clearly than Blackstone into the true nature of the constitution as it stood in the early years of George III.[2] The other conclusion is also

---

[1] Dicey, in his *Law and Opinion in England* (pp. 135–6), quotes Paley's analogy and adds, 'the revered mansion was not only antiquated, but in many respects so unsuited to the requirements of the times, that it was to its numerous inhabitants a cause not only of discomfort but even of misery'.

[2] *Law of the Constitution*, p. 9, n. But Blackstone, writing as a lawyer, was bound to state the legal theory: Paley, interested as he was in the law, was more free to look at the facts. It should also be added that, even if he wrote as a lawyer, Blackstone could look at the facts; and in his chapter on the King's Revenue (*Commentaries*, Book I, ch. VIII), he shows himself aware of the influence which Paley notes, and of the 'adventitious power' and 'persuasive energy gained by the Crown through the great increase of its patronage.

striking, and in its measure profound. It is that, in a growing constitution, the adoption of projects of reform may lead to un-intended and uncalculated consequences. 'Political innovations commonly produce many effects beside those that are intended. The direct consequence is often the least important. Incidental, remote, and unthought-of evils or advantages, frequently exceed the good that is designed or the mischief that is foreseen.' This is very true and just; but is the consequence which Paley appears to draw—that you had better leave things alone—equally true and just? Unintended consequences may defeat expectations, or fall far short of them; but they may also transcend them and go beyond them, and 'a man may go out to find his father's asses and find a kingdom'. Is the one possibility to be always regarded, and the other to be forgotten? We never know the ultimate results of our actions. But if that were made a ground of inaction, we should never act at all.

5. Here we may leave generalities and begin to 'condescend upon the particulars' of Paley's age and the schemes of its reformers. The reformers—among them Paley's old friend, John Jebb of Peterhouse—were arguing that owing to an out-of-date system of constituencies, and an antiquated and restricted suffrage, the House of Commons was not representative of opinion; that in consequence the influence of the Crown, exerted through its control of patronage, could be and was exerted to manipulate this unrepresentative body; and that only a measure of parliamentary reform could enthrone opinion in its proper seat and restore the liberty and happiness of the people. What was Paley's attitude to their argument? It was almost entirely negative.

Dealing first with the House of Lords, he makes short shrift of the claims of opinion when it runs counter to the views of that House. He had previously installed opinion as the basis of civil authority; he now finds that 'when we observe what is urged as public opinion to be in truth the opinion only, or perhaps the feigned profession, of a few crafty leaders', swelled by numbers who join in the cry without judgement or understanding, 'we may conceive occasions to arise in which the commonwealth may be saved by the reluctance of the nobility to adopt the caprices or yield to the vehemence of the common people'. He then turns from the Lords to the House of Commons. Here he begins, in his usual manner, by an arresting paradox—adding what may be called 'the paradox of representation' to the paradox of property and the paradox of government which he had previously stated. 'There is nothing in the British constitution so remarkable as the irregularity of the popular representation'; it is 'a flagrant incongruity'. He states the facts trenchantly—200 members of the House of Commons elected by 7,000 votes; a voter sometimes possessing the ten-thousandth part of a single representative, and sometimes enjoying the right of appointing two himself; half of the House obtaining seats by election, and the other half by purchase or the nomination of great land-owners. But just as he had found an answer to the anomaly of property, so he has also an answer to the anomaly of representation. If a House so irregularly representative is actually composed of 'men the most likely by their qualifications to know and to promote the public interest' (which is a *petitio principii* hidden in a conditional clause), 'it signifies little who return them' (which is a withdrawal of any homage previously done to opinion); but even so (here opinion returns, discrowned but triumphant) 'the representatives are so connected with the mass of the community by a society of interests and passions that the will of the people, when it is determined permanent and general, almost always at length prevails'.

Finally, coming to the Crown, Paley proceeds to defend its influence. He is willing, indeed, to accept some measure of economical reform which will reduce the patronage of the Crown; but he argues generally that patronage creates an attachment and influence sufficient to counteract 'the restless arrogating spirit' of popular assemblies, and thus forms a barrier, in Walt Whitman's similar phrase, 'against the never-ending audacity of elected persons'. He even adds—with that frank assumption of the dominance of interested motives in politics which may also be found in Adam Smith—that the reason why the colonial assemblies of North America had proved so recalcitrant was that the king and government of Great Britain had no patronage in the colonies. 'To this cause, excited perhaps by some unseasonable provocations, we may attribute, as to their true and proper original, (we will not say the misfortunes, but) the changes that have taken place in the British Empire.' This passage seems sadly to contradict the view of the American Revolution which Paley had expressed in an earlier chapter when he was dealing with the problem of resistance.[1] It is also a passage which is sad in itself. It inevitably suggests the reflection that the sort of temper which Paley displays was the real cause which made change inevitable. Would a reformed parliament have shown the temper which Paley and the parliament of 1774–80 showed? One can only answer that within seven years of the passing of the Reform Bill of 1832 the Durham Report had been issued, and a reformed parliament had shown that it was resolved to learn the lessons of the past and to behave to Canada as its predecessor had failed to behave to the earlier colonies of North America.

But it would be an error, and a grave injustice, to judge the philosophy of Paley's *Principles* in a temper of severity. To us he may appear conservative, and even retrograde. To the reformers of his own age—but only to them—his opposition to parliamentary reform and his defence of the influence of the Crown seemed 'certainly liable to great objection'. But that was not the general view of his contemporaries. They noticed 'the boldness of his general reasoning' (which is certainly bolder than his treatment of particular problems, and often discrepant from it); and the governing circles of the day saw no reason to think of him as an ally. Meadley remarked that it had been frequently suggested that 'the promotion of Mr Paley was impeded by the freedom of his manner in the story of the pigeons;...by his judicious limita-

---

[1] Supra, pp. 241–2. But in justice to Paley it should be noted that there was some substance in his argument. An American historian has recently remarked that 'England's failure to create a civil list in the colonies weakened the colonial governors in their struggles with the assemblies. Without the patronage made possible by a civil list, the governors were deprived of one of the strongest weapons of the executive authority.' (John C. Miller, *Origins of the American Revolution*, (1945), p. 32.)

tion of the duty of civil obedience [or, in other words, his treatment of the problem of resistance];...by his just and striking remark that the divine right of kings is like the divine right of constables;[1] and still more by his enlightened views of religious establishments and toleration'. We may doubt whether Paley's political philosophy affected his promotion adversely; and in any case we have still to examine his views on religious establishments and toleration. But Meadley's catalogue of the liberal elements in his philosophy is sufficient to prove that, for his age, he belonged, if not to the Left, at any rate to the Left Centre.

A writer of a later age, which possesses more than a century and a half of added experience, may add some further reflections which go to defend the general integrity and sanity of Paley's view of politics. He was caught in the idea of the mixed constitution, and committed to a belief in the necessary equality and balance of its three parts; he had to make room for the king and the House of Lords, and therefore to give to the House of Commons no more than its proper third of power. The balance of the constitution, which produces an equilibrium of the parts and the stability of the whole, was a conception common to Paley with most of the thinkers of his age (Burke himself included), and it formed an inevitable part of the common stock of their minds. To Paley it meant two things. It meant, in the first place, a balance of *power*, by which one part of the constitution served as a counterpoise to another; with the king's negative (not actually exercised since the time of Anne, but still a potential force, as George III more than once showed) checking the power of the two Houses to frame laws, and, vice versa, with the king's power over the military forces countervailed by the power of parliament to pass annually the Mutiny Act required for their discipline. It meant, in the second place, a balance of *interest*, by which each part had not only power, but also a motive to use power, and was nerved by an interest of

[1] The remark, which comes at the end of chapter IV of Book VI, is not original. It is borrowed from the beginning of Hume's essay 'Of the original Contract', where Hume remarks that 'a constable, no less than a king, acts by a divine commission'.

its own to defend its rights and to assert the limits of the rights of the other parts. Such an interlocked constitution, calculated on the model of a cantilever bridge, was necessarily static. It did not lend itself to schemes of reform. The balance would be disturbed if you altered the nice adjustment. It is less remarkable that Paley, with his eyes inevitably clouded by the idea of balance, was unable to see the coming of parliamentary reform, than that he was able to see the emergence of the cabinet system. Blackstone had not seen it: at any rate he had never mentioned it in his *Commentaries*. Paley was more far-sighted, or at least more frank. Perhaps he was helped to be frank by a happy, if erroneous, idea that the cabinet was a part of the general system of balance. (Actually the cabinet system is the end of checks and balances;[1] it means the enthronement of the legislature, and ultimately of the House of Commons.) The king, he argues, has the choice of ministers; but his choice is controlled by his obligation to choose as his ministers men 'who are found capable of managing the affairs of his government with the two houses of parliament'.

Not only was Paley caught in the idea of the mixed constitution: he was also caught, inevitably caught, in the general system of contemporary ideas and contemporary sentiment. To us there appears to be a gulf between his general principles and his particular conclusions; but the more one studies history, and seeks to penetrate into the spirit of past ages, the more one realises that the particular conclusions drawn from the same set of general principles vary from age to age. Paley stated, and stated well, the general democratic argument; but his particular conclusions were a defence of rotten boroughs and an apology for royal influence. This seems to us contradictory. But before we pass that judgement, we must make ourselves at home in the eighteenth century, when lords *were* lords and bishops bishops, and all who mattered were gentlemen. It was a deferential age, with a large respect for

---

[1] On the other hand it may be argued that checks and balances still survive, if in a new form, under the cabinet system, in the sense that the cabinet *in esse* is always confronted and criticised, and may on occasion even be checked, by a cabinet *in posse* composed of the Leader of the Opposition and his colleagues.

'the superior orders'—a phrase which recurs in the *Principles*.[1] The eighteenth century, with all its charm and its classicism, was more set in a hierarchy of classes than previous centuries. The sixteenth century could produce a Cranmer who believed in a free career for capacities.[2] The seventeenth century knew a Colonel Rainborough who thought that 'the poorest he has a life to live as the richest he'. The eighteenth century had to wait till its close for Tom Paine's *Rights of Man*. Paley, who was eighteenth century of the eighteenth century, was embedded firmly in its ideas. The notion that universal suffrage, or even any extension of the existing suffrage, logically resulted from the general principle of the sovereignty of public opinion, was a notion inconceivable to a sound thinker so embedded.[3]

6. Such, on a general view, is Paley's philosophy of the State. We now come, in conclusion, to his philosophy of the Church—or, more exactly, to his philosophy of the relations of Church and State. This is expounded in a pithy chapter which bears the title 'of religious establishment and of toleration'. The chapter begins with the proposition that 'a religious establishment is no part of Christianity; it is only the means of inculcating it'. This is explained to mean that no form of church-government was instituted by the Founder of Christianity, and that church-government is therefore a human institution, which, as such, is founded in, and must be judged and regulated by, its utility. But Paley does not pause to

[1] The writer remembers hearing Mr Justice Holmes, of the American Supreme Court, say in 1929 (he was then a man of eighty-eight): 'When I lunched with John Stuart Mill in the House of Commons, about 1866, he struck me as the one man of the English middle classes who did not labour under a conscious sense of inferiority.' If deference was the habit about 1866 (we may remember that Bagehot was still theorising about deference in his book of 1867 on the English Constitution), it was much more likely to be the habit eighty years earlier, when Paley published his *Principles*.·

[2] *Supra*, p. 156.

[3] Paley, in a footnote to the chapter on the British constitution, argues that if the right of representation is natural, 'no doubt it must be equal; and the right, we may add, of one sex as well as of the other'. He appears to regard this as a *reductio ad absurdum*. 'Every plan of representation that we have heard of begins by excluding the votes of women, thus cutting off, at a single stroke, one half of the public from a right which is asserted to be inherent in all.'

inquire whether the form of government of a church, even if it be a human institution, may not best be instituted independently of the State, and set up by the Church itself, acting as a spiritual society which possesses spiritual autonomy in matters of doctrine, worship, government, and discipline. He seems to identify—at any rate he does not distinguish—church-government and church-establishment; and leaping, as it were, from the one to the other he proceeds to argue in favour of a 'religious establishment'—an 'established church' or 'national religion', as he also terms it—which is instituted by the State. On this basis he advances three consequential propositions. The first is that 'a class of men should be set apart by *public authority* to the study and teaching of religion'. The second is that the maintenance of this class should come 'from revenues assigned by *authority of law*'. The third is that in the appointment of the members of this class a test or subscription, which will logically be imposed by *the same authority*, should be required from those who receive such appointment. 'The very notion of a national religion includes that of a test.'

A thinker to-day may be puzzled by Paley's unexplained leap from the notion of church-government to that of church-establishment. It would hardly have puzzled his contemporaries. They were still thinking (as we may see from the speeches and writings of Burke)[1] in the terms of Hooker's philosophy. They believed that a nation or people was an organised state which was also, and simultaneously, an established church; that all who belonged to the national state belonged also to the national church, which was thus co-extensive in membership with the national state; and, finally, that the government of the national state must also be the guide and governor of the national church. It was set down in the *Laws of Ecclesiastical Polity* that 'in...a Christian state or kingdom one and the self-same people are the church and the common-wealth', or, in other words, that a people is at once, and co-extensively, an *ecclesia* and a *respublica*; it was also set down that 'it is expedient that their sovereign in causes civil have also in

---

[1] See the writer's *Essays on Government*, pp. 211, 227-30.

ecclesiastical affairs a supreme power'.[1] Paley accepted this philosophy as part of the atmosphere of his times: he was writing half a century before the dawn of the Oxford Movement and the emergence of a new philosophy of the spiritual autonomy of the Church. His contemporaries had no quarrel with his general view of religious establishment: the one quarrel which any of them had was on the particular point of subscriptions or tests for the established clergy. The liberals with whom he had once consorted in Cambridge thought that his attitude to what they regarded as the abuse of subscription was, if anything, more objectionable than his attitude to the abuses of an unreformed parliament: they felt that he was not only illiberal, but also inconsistent with his past self. Yet he is easy, and even generous, in the requirement which he actually makes. The logic of his argument for establishment committed him to some form of subscription for clergy belonging to the establishment; but the temper of his mind suggested—and this is the proposal which he actually makes—that 'tests and subscriptions...ought to be made as simple and easy as possible', and 'should be adapted, from time to time, to the varying sentiments and circumstances of the church in which they are received'.

It is in his remarks on what he calls 'oeconomical questions'— and especially on the question, 'whether a parity amongst the clergy, or a distinction of orders in the ministry, be more conducive to the general ends of the institution'—that Paley may seem most open to the criticism of a later age. He lived in an epoch of disparity amongst the clergy which ranged from great and rich bishoprics, some of them endowed with princely revenues, to the position of poor and struggling curates (he had been one himself) whose income, from an earlier average of £30–40 a year, was slowly rising, in his own day, to an average of £70.[2] He

---

[1] This latter passage comes in Book VIII, ch. III, § 6—that is to say in one of the later books which are not certainly Hooker's own work.

[2] The figures of the income of curates are taken from Professor Sykes's *Church and State in England in the XVIIIth Century*, pp. 206–8. *The Black Book* of the period of the Reform Bill (in the edition of 1832, pp. 24–6) cites the case

accepted and was ready to justify the system of the epoch. 'The system', he writes, 'corresponds with the gradations of rank in civil life, and provides for the edification of each rank by stationing in each an order of clergy of their own class and quality'; moreover, 'the same fund produces more effect', in stimulating able men to take orders and encouraging the industry of those who have already done so, 'when distributed into prizes of different value than when divided into equal shares'. This is all that is said in the *Principles*; but it is sufficient to show that sense of deference to the established hierarchy of classes, and that recognition of interested motives, which marked Paley's age. The same sense, and the same recognition, are equally evident in a sermon on 'a distinction of orders in the church', preached in 1782, which drew down on Paley's head the animadversions of the poet Cowper.[1] Something similar may also be traced in an earlier sermon of 1781—an admonitory sermon to the young clergy, preached at a general ordination—in which advice is offered to curates on 'oeconomical questions'. The first virtue suggested is frugality, or 'oeconomy upon a plan adjusted to circumstances and expectations'. Another is retirement: 'half the faults of young clergymen originate in an impatience of solitude: to learn *to live alone* comprises in one sentence the most important advice.'[2] Solitude for the lower clergy—but for the higher the more pleasing duty 'to provide friends and companions for the superior as well as for the middle orders of the community'—this was the gist of the matter.

It is in dealing with the problem of toleration, rather than in his

of Dr Sparke, the Bishop of Ely, ascribing to him an income of £27,742 from his see and its dependencies, and adding that his two sons and his son-in-law had each an average income of some £4000 a year from the preferments which they owed to his patronage.

[1] Cowper had read a favourable report of the sermon in a monthly review, and he wrote to his friend Unwin to express his own unfavourable opinion. He objected especially to Paley's idea of prizes: 'the prize held out in the Scripture is of a very different kind.' The report of the sermon, and Cowper's animadversions, are printed in the Appendix to Meadley's *Memoirs*, pp. 85–93.

[2] This sermon is also printed in the Appendix to Meadley's *Memoirs*, pp. 78–84.

treatment of the problems of religious establishment, that Paley is at his best. Here he shows a liberality which was in advance of his age; and here, for once, his particular conclusions have the same breadth as his general principles. He begins, indeed, by stating a proposition which may seem to cast a shadow on the argument he intends to advance. Addressing himself to the question whether the civil magistrate has a right to interfere in matters of religion, he propounds the view that, on his own principle of general happiness, that right must be recognised. The civil magistrate is limited only by considerations of general utility; and he may therefore interfere—indeed, it may even be said that he *ought* to interfere—whenever his action, *in its general tendency*, may be said to be conducive to the common interest. There is no sphere of exemption. 'There is nothing in the nature of religion, as such, which exempts it from the authority of the legislator when the safety or welfare of the community requires his interposition. . . . Religious liberty is, like civil liberty, not an immunity from restraint, but the being restrained by no law but what in a greater degree conduces to the public welfare.'

This may seem an unpromising beginning. And yet we should all confess (even though some of us might cherish a higher conception of the claims of spiritual autonomy than Paley is willing to allow) that the civil authority cannot be precluded from acting in matters of religion. We might refuse to ground its action, as Paley does, on the principle of general utility, which has a dangerous latitude of application; we might prefer to base it on the needs of public security and the maintenance of law and order; but we should still admit that there are matters of religion in which the civil authority is entitled and even bound to act. The real question is that of the degree to which it can act, and of the temper in which it should act. On this question the views of Paley are as wise as they are liberal. In the first place he allows the right of religious resistance, just as he has previously allowed the right of civil resistance.[1] In the second place, when he comes to examine the degree and sort of interference which may be

---

[1] Supra, pp. 241-2.

conducive to the general happiness, he draws attention to the saving words of his formula that an act of interference is justified when (and only when) it is conducive to the common interest *in its general tendency*. From these saving words he deduces two maxims. The first is 'that any form of Christianity is better than no religion at all'; and it is in the strength of this maxim that he advances the argument that the civil authority may choose and establish a form of religion—provided that the magistrate, in so doing, should 'consult the faith of the nation rather than his own'. The second maxim is 'that of different systems of faith that is best which is the truest'; and it is in the strength of this maxim that he argues the case for toleration.

The argument which he advances is simply an expansion of the maxim; but it is none the less a notable expansion. All regulations concerning religion should, according to the maxim, be principally adapted to the advancement of truth. But 'truth results from discussion'. Discussion should therefore be free; and free discussion means toleration. 'In religion, as in other subjects, truth, *if left to itself*, will almost always obtain the ascendency.' This is well said: it suggests, in advance, the argument which J. S. Mill was to use in his *Essay on Liberty*, published nearly seventy-five years later; it recalls the argument which Oliver Cromwell had used, over a century earlier, in the Army debates recorded in the Clarke papers; it suggests, in a word, the sturdy English feeling (which has been the mother of parliamentary government as well as of toleration) that truth can be trusted to come from discussion and the free clash of minds engaged in debate.[1] It is this feeling which inspires Paley's great and principal

---

[1] 'Complete liberty [for others] of contradicting and disproving our opinion is the very condition which justifies us in assuming its truth for purposes of action.' (Mill's *Essay on Liberty*, ch. II.) Cromwell's argument, in the Putney debates of the Army, may be found in Woodhouse's *Puritanism and Liberty*, pp. 31–2, 84, 101–2, and 103–7. It is an argument for 'the liberty of a free deliberation'; for 'liberty of speech to come to a right understanding of things'; for recognition of the fact that 'God is not the author of contradictions', and, with it, of the principle that the way to reconcile contradictory interpretations of His truth is for each to admit that he may be mistaken and on that basis to

argument for toleration; and if he adds 'some auxiliary considerations'—as that 'the confining of the subject to the religion of the state is a needless violation of natural liberty', and that 'persecution ... vitiates the public morals by driving men to prevarication'— these are only the outworks of his main defence.

But toleration is of two kinds—partial and complete. Partial toleration was what had hitherto been practised in England since the Toleration Act of 1689; and it had consisted in allowing dissenters an unmolested freedom of worship, but also in excluding them from offices in the State. Complete toleration adds to freedom of worship the admission of dissenters, without distinction, to all the civil privileges of other citizens: it removes any civil disability imposed on the ground of religion. Complete toleration was not conceded finally in England before the passing of the Universities Test Act in 1871;[1] but Paley, in 1785, is already an advocate of such toleration. For him, with the one exception of refusal to bear arms, there is no tenet in any of the Christian sects which incapacitates its followers for the service of the State. 'I perceive no reason why men of different religious persuasions may not sit upon the same bench, deliberate in the same council, or fight in the same ranks, as well as men of various or opposite opinions upon any controverted topic of natural philosophy, history or ethics.' He is tender to Catholics as well as to Protestant dissenters; the one ground he allows for proscribing them is the *political* ground of their connection with Jacobitism; and any restrictions imposed on that ground 'ought not to continue one day longer than some visible danger renders them necessary to the preservation of public tranquillity'.

accept the rule, Let the rest judge. 'If in those things we do speak, and pretend to speak from God, there be mistakes of fact—if there be a mistake in the thing or in the reason of the thing—truly I think it is free for me to show both the one and other, if I can. Nay, I think it is my duty to do it.' (Op. cit. p. 101.)

[1] The repeal of the Test and Corporation Acts in 1828, and the passage of the Catholic Emancipation Act in 1829, had removed religious restrictions on admission to the service of the Crown, municipal office, and membership of parliament. But the removal of religious restrictions on membership of, or office in, the old Universities was not achieved until 1871; and even then some relics of the old restrictions still remained.

All in all, Paley's philosophy of Church and State is, in his own words, 'a comprehensive national religion, guarded by a few articles of peace and conformity, together with a legal provision for the clergy of that religion; with a complete toleration of all dissenters from the established church, without any other limitation or exception than what arises from the conjunction of dangerous political dispositions with certain religious tenets'. This is not an ungenerous philosophy. Indeed, Paley is even willing to consider a plan 'for the legal maintenance of a clergy...without the preference of one sect of Christians to others'—a plan, in other words, for the religious establishment not of one national form of religion, but of a number of forms. The plan, he explains, 'is said to be attempted or designed in some of the new states of North America'. He treats it with some sympathy, as 'undoubtedly the best which has been proposed upon this principle'; but he also sees and describes its difficulties. None the less, when he comes to deal with the issue of toleration (he had described the plan earlier under the head of religious establishment), he recurs to the idea of concurrent establishment. 'If there exist amongst the different sects of the country such a parity of numbers, interest and power as to render the preference of one sect to the rest...a matter of hazardous success, some plan similar to that which is meditated in North America,...though encumbered with great difficulties, may perhaps suit better with this divided state of public opinion than any constitution of a national church whatever.' Not only, therefore, is he willing to leave all sects uncontrolled by recusancy laws, and completely tolerated in their religious profession; he is even willing to think—tentatively, it is true, and dubiously—of different sects being equally aided and supported by public authority.[1] When we reflect on these views, we cannot but come to the conclusion that, immersed as he was in his age, Paley could yet rise above it. Steeped in the feelings of the eighteenth century, and living by its

---

[1] Some analogy to this idea may be traced in the policy of the Netherlands, which has made allowances from its budget to a number of different churches— mainly to the Dutch Reformed Church and other Protestant Churches, but also to the Roman Catholic Church, and, in a less measure, to the Jansenists and the Jews.

current standards, he could yet write with a judgement and insight which still command our respect. A sturdy Yorkshireman and a good Cambridge scholar, he has also an essential English quality, alike in his merits and his defects.[1] He was not of the stature of Milton and Darwin; but there are good reasons—not only of college piety, but also of a wider scope—why his portrait should still continue to hang in its place by the side of theirs in the hall of Christ's College.

Note. Apart from the chapter on law, or, as Paley entitles it, 'Of the administration of justice', which has already been incidentally mentioned as one of the best in the *Principles*, there are two others which deserve notice, though they lie outside the scope of this essay. One of them is the chapter on principles of political economy, which is entitled 'Of population and provision, and of agriculture and commerce as subservient thereto': the other is that on international relations, or, as Paley styles it, 'Of war and military establishments'. The former may still be read with profit by the student of economics; its principle of the value of a large population for increasing the general happiness of a nation—a principle shortly to be challenged by another clergyman, Malthus—is one to which economic thought would seem to be returning to-day, after a long period of deviation. The other chapter, brief as it is, contains some pregnant remarks on a vexed theme of the philosophical theory of the state—the theme of the relation between public and private morality; and its discussion both of the justifying causes and the proper conduct of war gives further evidence, if any were needed, of Paley's shrewd understanding and general balance of judgement.

[1] Dr Hutcheson Stirling, the author of *The Secret of Hegel* and a life-long student of philosophy, noted that 'all the Germans omit any mention of Paley, one of the most masculine and truly English of thinkers and writers'.

VIII

NATURAL LAW AND THE AMERICAN REVOLUTION

I

On the eve of the American Revolution the thirteen colonies on the Atlantic seaboard had a population of about two and a half millions, or nearly a third of the population of Great Britain. In environment, and in the unconscious but incalculable effects of environment on mind and temper, the colonial population was very different from the British. Set among the boundless spaces and infinite resources of a great continent, and engaged in a pioneering life, it had developed a limber and loose-knit society of self-reliant rural freeholders, which stood in marked contrast with the increasingly industrialised and urbanised society of Great Britain. In racial composition, too, as well as in environment and its effects, the colonial population was already beginning to show a distinctive character. By 1736 (so it has been calculated) 'fully two-fifths of America's white population was of other than English extraction'.[1] The effects of new strains of race and blood, as well as those of a new environment, were already issuing in a different nation. They were also issuing, by a natural consequence, in a different stock of political ideas.

It is easy to fall into a mistaken idea of the extent of the contact, and the amount of community of ideas, between the two sides of the Atlantic in the middle of the eighteenth century. One remembers the lively intercourse, and the constant coming and going, of the first half of the seventeenth century: one forgets that things had become very different afterwards. In the reign of Charles I the University of Cambridge had produced some remarkable men who had emigrated to New England. Massachusetts had received as many as four who all became famous in its

[1] C. H. Van Tyne, *The Causes of the War of Independence*, p. 345.

annals—John Winthrop, of Trinity College, its first Governor; John Cotton, also of Trinity (and afterwards a Fellow of Emmanuel), its great divine; John Harvard, of Emmanuel, the principal founder of Harvard College; and Nathaniel Ward, also of Emmanuel, the chief compiler of the Massachusetts 'Body of Liberties' of 1641. Connecticut had received Thomas Hooker, of Emmanuel, to whom it owed its democratic religious system of congregationalism and the equally democratic political system of its 'Fundamental Orders' of 1639: Rhode Island had received Roger Williams, of Pembroke, who was not only a theologian and the apostle of toleration, but also a political philosopher and a forerunner of Locke. There were no similar exports in the reign of George II. There was still, indeed, emigration to America; but the stream was of a different character, little likely to carry ideas or to maintain intellectual contact. Nor was there any reverse stream (at any rate in volume) of colonists returning to Britain, for education or visits, and refreshing themselves in the stimulus of British thought and ideas. The contact of minds had been stopped or blocked; and neither in the way of export from Britain, nor in that of colonial return and refreshment, was there any great commerce of ideas.

British emigration to the colonies, in the course of the eighteenth century, was mainly a movement of transported felons and indentured servants, or, as an American historian has said, 'broken men, bond servants, "gaol birds", the lees and settlings of the old world'.[1] Many thousands, perhaps some hundreds of thousands, came in 'this nondescript host' from Great Britain; but these British emigrants were not the only newcomers. There were also the Scotch-Irish from Ulster, of whom 4000 came in the one year 1718, and nearly 200,000 had eventually come within the next sixty years. These were men of a vigorous type, who became backwoodsmen and pioneers on the frontier western fringes of the colonies. Less rugged and independent, but also settled on the

[1] V. L. Parrington, *The Colonial Mind* 1620–1800, pp. 133–6, where a full account is given, especially of the methods used for securing indentured servants.

western fringes—mainly of the middle colonies and especially of Pennsylvania—were the Germans imported from the Rhine valley by speculative immigration agencies. This change in the character of the new immigrants, and even in their stock, was bound to affect the descendants of the original immigrants of the seventeenth century. The newcomers imported no elements of culture, and no set of ideas, which would keep the old colonial strain in touch with the British development of the eighteenth century. A cleavage of culture, of religious temper, and of social and political ideas, was the inevitable result.

On one side of the Atlantic Britain had now settled down under the rule of a landed aristocracy and the system of the Anglican Church; on the other the American colonists were living (at any rate in New England) as 'townships' of independent landowners and as 'congregations' of Independents attached to their local chapel. On the one side, again, Britain had developed, since the Revolution of 1688, the idea and practice of parliamentary sovereignty, and had vested government in a parliament which carried, or supposed itself to carry, the person of the British people, and accordingly acted, or claimed to act, with a plenary and general power. On the other side the American colonists, thrown on themselves by the inevitable pressure of colonial conditions, and compelled to think and act for themselves, were naturally wedded to the idea and practice of their own direct and immediate sovereignty, believing that government was properly vested in the people itself, and should either be exercised directly by the people, in the immediacy of its own town-meetings, or, if it were delegated to representatives, should be delegated only to representatives who were locally chosen, locally resident, and locally inspired in their action. In this sense, and from this point of view, America may be said to have kept the English democratic ideas—the ideas of popular right; the ideas of the Puritan Revolution and the Puritan New Model Army—which had been current in England about the middle of the seventeenth century; and she may be said to have done so while England herself was moving away from those ideas (whether we regard the movement as going forward or backward) to the different idea of a sovereign parliament representing the people *pleno jure* and exercising accordingly—as Blackstone and Bentham, Burke and Paley, alike believed—an unlimited and illimitable authority. True, the American ideas of popular right were at first peculiar to the colonies of New England, and were hardly shared by the middle colonies such as New York and Pennsylvania, or the Southern colonies which stretched from Maryland to South Carolina. But during the eighteenth century a movement of internal emigration was carrying the stock and the ideas of New England into the other colonies. There was plenty of inter-colonial movement, especially from New England to the South-West; and while old England had ceased to pour its new ideas across the Atlantic, New England was beginning to pour *its* ideas across its borders. This was a process involuntarily fostered by the British government itself, when, early in the eighteenth century, it instituted a colonial post office. Not only were commercial contacts encouraged by the post office: cultural and political connections were also aided; newspapers circulated, learned societies corresponded, and eventually, when troubles began, 'committees of correspondence' communicated with one another by means of the British Post Office. The smithy of ideas in Boston could send its sparks flying far and wide.

There was thus little circulation of ideas from Britain across the Atlantic, even if there was a growing circulation of ideas among the colonies themselves. Nor, as we have noticed, was there any great movement of return on the part of the colonists, which would bring them back to Britain for a season *antiquam exquirere matrem*. There was, indeed, a certain amount of temporary migration to England for educational and professional purposes. Though the colonies possessed their own Universities,[1] the three greatest

---

[1] Harvard College was founded in 1636; the College of William and Mary, at Williamsburg in Virginia, received its charter in 1693; Yale College is as old as 1718, and its first beginnings as early as 1701; Princeton received its first charter in 1746; and King's College in New York, which in 1784 became Columbia College (and subsequently Columbia University), received its letters patent in 1754.

of them—Harvard, Yale, and Princeton—were all under the control of dissenters; and Yale in particular was regarded by Episcopalians as 'a college remarkable for...its republican principles...and its utter aversion to Bishops and all Earthly Kings'.[1] From the middle and southern colonies, which were largely Episcopalian, young men were therefore sent in some numbers, during the eighteenth century, to Oxford and to Cambridge. The names of ninety-eight (forty-two at Oxford and fifty-six at Cambridge) have been traced in the period before the Revolution; more than half came from Virginia and South Carolina, but as many as seventeen came from Massachusetts.[2] Besides the stream which trickled to Oxford and Cambridge there was also another stream which flowed to the Inns of Court. Not till 1779 was there any law school in the colonies; and as many as 181 colonists (including some forty who had already been students at Oxford or Cambridge before they joined) were admitted to the Inns of Court before 1776. They, too, came in the main from the middle and southern colonies, and especially from South Carolina and Virginia.[3] Among them were men of some note in the history of the American Revolution—Daniel Dulany, for example, the author of *Considerations on the Propriety of imposing Taxes in the British Colonies*, who had been at Eton and Clare before he joined the Middle Temple; and John Dickinson, the author of *Farmer's Letters* and a leader of the Whigs of Philadelphia, who had also read law in the Middle Temple. But the most famous of the American lawyers, and those who exercised the greatest influence, had been trained in law offices in the colonies, and had never joined the Inns of Court or gone through a formal course of legal education. Joseph Galloway of Philadelphia, the author of the

---

[1] Quoted in J. C. Miller, *Origins of the American Revolution*, p. 142.

[2] Willard Connely, in *The American Oxonian*, January and April 1942. It may be added that some of the ninety-eight had been educated at English public schools before going to the University; thus Daniel Dulany of Maryland (a pamphleteer of the revolutionary period whose argument commended itself to Chatham) had been at Eton before he joined Clare College in 1733. His son also became a member of Clare College in 1760.

[3] C. H. Van Tyne, *England and America*, p. 93.

Plan of Union of 1774, was a product of Philadelphia. James Wilson—one of the greatest of American lawyers, a maker of the Constitution of 1787, and the first professor of law in the Law School instituted by the University of Pennsylvania in 1790—had indeed been a student in the University of St Andrew's before he emigrated to the colonies; but he had learned his law, and served his apprenticeship to his profession, in the law office of John Dickinson. Even in Virginia Patrick Henry was a home-trained lawyer (trained with rapidity and largely trained by himself); and in Massachusetts and the other New England colonies there were very few who had ever made the voyage to the Inns of Court. James Otis, the author of *Rights of the British Colonies*, and John Adams, the second President of the United States, had both been trained in Boston. When it came to the great debate between Britain and America, the lawyers who mainly conducted it on the American side were home-trained lawyers. The British-trained lawyers in the colonies hardly counted in the struggle. It follows that though the British and the American lawyers, on the two opposite sides, were debating in common terms of the common law of England, they were debating in different tempers and with different lines of approach. Even in the common field of law there was a good deal which was different. We can hardly wonder that in other fields—commerce, religion, political ideas—there was an even larger difference.

II

It will serve to illustrate this difference, and to show the emergence of a separate stock of legal and political ideas in the American colonies, if we turn our attention more particularly to the New England colonies, and especially to the city of Boston.[1] The population of New England, at the time of the Revolution, was about 650,000, or one-quarter of the whole population of the colonies. Of this 650,000 half were resident in Massachusetts, the

[1] A special and thorough study of New England ideas and principles may be found in A. C. McLaughlin's *Foundations of American Constitutionalism* (1932), which traces their development from the seventeenth century onwards.

core of New England; and the sanctum of this core—the brain of Massachusetts, which radiated its messages, by pamphlets, newspapers, and correspondence, through the whole of the colony and far beyond—was the city of Boston. It was indeed a small city, with a population which did not exceed some 16,000. Only some 500 or so of these 16,000 were regular voters in the town meeting, at any rate in the days immediately before the Revolution; and even this inner nucleus of 500 tended to be managed by a 'caucus club', or inner ring, which settled matters in advance by consultation with the merchants' club of wealthy traders. But the coming of revolution excited and swelled the town-meeting; and in any case a little leaven will leaven a large lump. It was so in Boston. Leavened itself by its leading and fermenting spirits, Boston leavened all Massachusetts: Massachusetts in turn affected the whole of New England: New England in turn, already beginning to send emigrants from its 'rocky pastures' into more fertile fields, influenced the rest of the colonies. Nor was Boston ignorant of itself or unconscious of its power. Self-consciousness, often passing into the introspection of a Henry Adams or a Henry James, is an old characteristic of Boston, perhaps inherited from the stern self-examination of its Puritan forefathers. A writer remarked, about 1774, that Bostonians believed that 'God has made Boston for itself, and all the rest of the world for Boston'.

Boston to-day is a great American city, with majestic motor-cars sliding swiftly and silently through its streets, except when they are inextricably blocked. But the past is still living in Boston. To have lived for a time in an old house on Beacon Street, looking across the grass of the common; to have walked up the slope of the common to the State-house, on the site of which the old colonial assembly used to meet, or to the King's Chapel, where the governor regularly attended service, or to the 'old south meeting-house', where the townsfolk met for politics as well as for prayer; to have crossed the River Charles into Cambridge (the other Cambridge, with its *alter Tiphys* and its *altera Argo*), and to have walked in the Yard of Harvard College, where scholars have thought and taught since 1636—all this is to be carried back swiftly and silently into the past. The past into which you are carried is a period of some dozen or more years, from the time of the speech of James Otis challenging writs of assistance, in 1761, to the battle of 1775 on the hill (Breed's Hill or Bunker Hill) which commands the harbour and city of Boston. The memories of those years still live in the city, and the city still lives on their memories. They were turbulent years—turbulent mentally and, after the 'tea-party' of 1773, turbulent physically. The town-meeting began to be crowded: a radical and popular wave of opinion came like a bore or an eagre into the channel hitherto occupied by the few—the few whose title had once rested on grace and election, but had latterly come to repose on money and merchandise. The caucus club altered its character: it 'took in a large number of mechanics', and a mechanic was now generally chosen to be its president. Mobs paraded the streets; if you disagreed with their views, you were liable to be tarred and feathered: nonconformist Boston had a passion for conformity. Samuel Adams was now in his glory— a Harvard graduate, and the manager of a malting business; a believer in natural rights, and (even more) a manager of com- mittees and caucuses and a manipulator of popular assemblies and passions; an enthusiast firmly convinced that liberty—liberty as conceived by Boston—was the ordained purpose of God, and that he was its instrument. John Adams, too, might be seen abroad, or his lamp might be seen burning late in his study; a lawyer and a kinsman of Samuel; anxious, angular, subtle, honest, tenacious till death of his founded opinions in the face of all obloquy; a man from whose loins, as from the root of Jesse, there sprang successive generations of inherited ability to carry on the tradition of the family and the service of the commonwealth. There were others, too, besides the two Adams kinsmen; there was the passionate Otis, another notable lawyer, a 'fiery and feverous man', whose mind at last went awry (but not until he had done great service in the cause of his city and colony), and who died at last from a stroke of lightning; there was Oxenbridge Thacher, who appeared in court along with Otis, and was a member of the same law club as he and John Adams; there was John Hancock, a merchant who could run a cargo, but who was also the owner of the works of Milton and Beccaria, a correspondent of our English John Wilkes (as were also Otis and Adams), and the man whose name appeared first in the signatures to the Declaration of Independence. It is hardly surprising that the contemporary English view of Boston was critical and even acid. It was regarded as a 'mobbish' city: 'obstinate, undutiful and ungovernable from the very beginning'; 'the centre of American politics, and the source of all the controversy'; 'a noisy turbulent place, inhabited by people of coarse insolent manners,...playing at politics, and aping the ways of serious citizens'.[1]

It is true that Boston was not the only hearth of revolution, or the only circle in which political ideas were ventilated. There was also Philadelphia, the greatest city of that time in North America, with a population of 40,000, with printing presses and newspapers, and with a notable ferment of ideas perhaps aided by the mixed character of its Quaker and German strains. Benjamin Franklin came from it; Tom Paine came to it, thanks to his introduction; sober lawyers and thinkers—such as John Dickinson, James Wilson, and Joseph Galloway—moved in its streets. But Boston was senior and superior to the other towns of the colonies. Behind it stood the history of a century and a half of anxious religious life, sometimes all too anxious, and even, upon occasion, sadly and bitterly intolerant. Beside it, in the neighbouring Cambridge, stood an old University college, with an equal length of history. In its chapels there was a notable succession of preachers (such as Cotton Mather and Dr Mayhew), who were teachers as well as preachers; in its law-courts and law-offices there was an equally notable body of lawyers, locally trained in their own tradition, and pursuing in their club or *sodalitas* not only the study of law but also high inquiries into the problems of political theory. It was a chief home of the printing-press; it was the special home of the spoken word and the use of the public platform. Its human material was still, in the main, homogeneous English stuff; and in

---

[1] See J. C. Miller, op. cit. pp. 153, 252–3; C. H. Van Tyne, *The Causes of the War of Independence*, p. 327.

this it differed from Philadelphia, as it also differed from New York. Its thought was hard thought: thought as hard as an act; thought which tended to translate itself rapidly into the hammer-stroke of the act. What was the substance of its thought, and what were the circles in which it was formed?

There were two main circles. The first was that of the clergy: the second was that of the lawyers. The clergy of Boston, and of Massachusetts generally, were Calvinists or Presbyterians in doctrine, but congregationalists or separatists in the matter of organisation. Both of these factors contributed to make them the exponents of political radicalism.[1] From the theological doctrine of Calvinism they drew the principle of the supremacy of God's Law to all earthly kings and governments; from the congregational organisation of the church of each township, with its separate church covenant and its freely associated company of 'gathered' adherents, they drew ideas of autonomy, and of autarky or self-sufficiency, which were bound to enure to political consequences. Burke—the agent in London of the colony of New York, and versed in the temper and feelings of the colonists—noting the general fact of 'an averseness in the dissenting churches from all that looks like absolute government' remarked on the peculiar strength of this sentiment in America. 'The religion most prevalent in our northern colonies is a refinement on the principle of resistance: it is the dissidence of dissent, and the protestantism of the Protestant religion.'[2] Under this 'dissidence of dissent' the preacher was a great and solemn figure: the instructor of his flock, and of all his people, in politics as well as religion. The philosophy

[1] V. L. Parrington's work on *The Colonial Mind* (especially Book 1, entitled 'Liberalism and Puritanism') gives a full but not altogether sympathetic account of the Puritan heritage and its development in New England. The third chapter in C. H. Van Tyne's *England and America* explains the religious position at the time of the Revolution; and the chapter on 'the American Mind' in John C. Miller's *Origins of the American Revolution* (pp. 136–44) has a section on the same theme.

[2] In the same sense, but more emphatically, a British visitor to Boston wrote (in 1768, three years after the speech on conciliation with America in which Burke had used his famous words), 'The Bostonians are presbyterians; they are all of republican principles.'

of the preacher was a philosophy that the Bible was the fundamental law of all life—and therefore a 'higher law' set above all states and their doings; that earthly authorities were subordinate to God's Word, and to His people interpreting His Word by their conscience; and that the clergy, both as God's ministers and as the appointed voice of the people, were bound, in the spirit of Elijah, to warn mere earthly authorities, and to prescribe the limits which they must observe.

The people treated the preachers in the light of this conception. As early as 1681 the people of Massachusetts, confronted by a demand from the government of Charles II that their representatives should appear at Westminster, before the Court of King's Bench, to defend the rights which the colony claimed under a charter of incorporation granted by the Crown in 1629, consulted their ministers. The ministers advised them 'to abide by what rights and privileges the Lord our God in His merciful providence hath bestowed'; and rebutting the argument that the people had forfeited the rights conveyed to them under the charter, they announced that 'though according to some corrupt and unrighteous laws they might have done so, yet according to the laws of righteousness and equity they had not done so'.[1] Here already— almost a century before the American Revolution, and more than a century before the American Constitution of 1787 which ultimately issued in the final authority of the Federal Supreme Court—we find something in the nature of a clerical 'supreme court' in Boston, similarly interpreting and enforcing the conclusive power of a sovereign document. But the sovereign document which the ministers interpret is more than a constitution: it is the document of God's Word, bestowing inalienable rights and privileges under its irrefragable 'laws of righteousness and equity'.

The ministers not only acted as judicial interpreters of the Bible. They had also at their fingers' ends the English democratic ideas of the seventeenth century, as those ideas were expounded by Milton, Sidney, and Locke; and being teachers as well as preachers, they

[1] C. H. Van Tyne, *The Causes of the War of Independence*, p. 34.

used those ideas in the pulpit to instruct their congregations. Their sermons, especially those which were delivered during the period of elections, were largely sermons on political science; and these sermons, from the middle of the eighteenth century onwards, were often printed as pamphlets by resolution of the provincial assembly. A famous sermon so printed was that delivered at Boston by Dr Jonathan Mayhew in 1750. It was entitled *A Discourse concerning Unlimited Submission*, and it was preached on the anniversary of the execution of Charles I. The argument was that God himself was 'limited by law; not indeed, by acts of parliament, but by the eternal laws of truth, wisdom, and equity, and the everlasting tables of right reason'. This is partly an echo of the past, and of the doctrine enunciated by the Boston ministers in 1681, but it is also a prophecy of the future; and John Adams said afterwards: 'If you wish to investigate the principles and feelings which produced the Revolution, study Dr Mayhew's sermon on passive obedience and non-resistance.' Not only were new sermons thus printed: old sermons of the past were also rescued from oblivion and reprinted. One was a sermon of a Massachusetts minister of the year 1687, which bore the title *Democracy is Christ's Government*, and which was reprinted just before the Revolution; but still more notable was the republication, in 1772, of two tracts or treatises which had been published in 1710 and 1717 by John Wise, the minister of Ipswich in Massachusetts, who had drawn an argument for the principles of congregationalism from the theory of natural rights expounded in Pufendorf's *De Jure Naturae et Gentium*, and had concluded that 'a democracy in church or state is a very honourable and regular government according to the dictates of right reason'.[1]

---

[1] Quoted in V. L. Parrington, *The Colonial Mind*, p. 122. Professor Parrington gives a full account of Wise and his democratic political philosophy (pp. 118–25). That philosophy is notable, alike for its basis in the law of nature and for its own substance. When Wise wrote that 'the end of all good government is to cultivate humanity, and promote the happiness of all and the good of every man in his rights, his life, liberty, estate, honour', he was stating, and stating admirably, the ideas which Jefferson afterwards restated in the first two paragraphs of the Declaration of Independence. His theory of the double contract

Here, it may not be irrelevant to remark (even at the risk of digression), we may trace a common and natural expedient of revolutionary epochs. To encourage themselves when they are leaving the way of prescription for that of revolution, men take to themselves the comfort of revolutionary precedents: in a word, they rescue and reprint the revolutionary literature of the past. Ulrich von Hutten, in the early days of the German Reformation, had rescued and printed anti-papal literature which had first appeared during the Investiture Contest of the eleventh century. Thomas Cromwell, in the early days of the English Reformation (1535), had helped a printer to produce an English version of the antipapal *Defensor Pacis*, written by Marsilio of Padua two centuries earlier. During the English Civil War, in 1648, the Huguenot *Vindiciae contra Tyrannos* (first published in 1579) appeared in an English version, which is said to have been due to the suggestion of a member of the Long Parliament. During the struggle between Whigs and Tories, in the reign of Charles II, the Whigs exhumed and published the precedents of the opposition to Richard II to support their cause. In the eighteenth century itself the English 'republican Whig' Thomas Hollis (who presented books to Harvard College as well as to other seats of learning) was reprinting and adorning with emblems of liberty the writings of Locke, Sidney, and other authors whom he had adopted as champions of his cause. The men of Massachusetts had good precedents when they reprinted the sermons of bygone ministers and the tracts of John Wise.

Thus the pulpit and the printed sermon or tract, whether old or new, were disseminating a set and system of political ideas—ideas

---

is also notable—first the contract of society, by which 'they...interchangeably each man covenant to join in one lasting society'; and then the contract of government, 'whereby those on whom sovereignty is conferred engage to take care of the common peace and welfare, and the subjects on the other hand to yield their faithful obedience' (quoted in A. C. McLaughlin, *Foundations of American Constitutionalism*, pp. 71–2). This theory goes beyond that of Locke, who had stopped at the contract of society, and contented himself with a theory of government as resting on trust (and *not* on contract): it shows a thoroughgoing application of the covenant principle of congregationalism.

18-2

of the only sovereignty of the Bible; of the indefeasibility of God's law and the rights which that law bestowed; of the right (or rather the duty) of offering resistance, on the ground of such law and such rights, to any mere human government by which they might be infringed; of the congruity of political democracy with the religious democracy of God's Church. It was in this set or system of ideas that Samuel Adams grew; and from it he imbibed the spirit which made him the great agitator of his time, who so shook the trees that, as far as any one man could, he brought down the Revolution. The subject of his thesis in 1743 for Harvard College—still largely under the control of the ministers, and still mainly a place for the training of ministers— was 'Whether it be lawful to resist the Supreme Magistrate, if the Commonwealth cannot otherwise be preserved'; and like Dr May-hew seven years afterwards he answered 'Yes'. More than twenty years later, in 1765, he was arguing, at the time of the Stamp Act Congress, that the rights of the colonists 'are founded in the law of God and nature and are the common rights of mankind', and that 'no law of society can, consistent with the law of God and nature, divest the inhabitants of this province of those rights'.[1] A little later still, in a Boston town-meeting held at the end of 1772, he was still arguing, in the same sense, that the British policy 'restraining us from erecting slitting mills for manufacturing our iron, the natural produce of this country, is an infringement of that right with which God and nature have invested us'.[2] Samuel Adams was always true to the philosophy of his instructors.

From the circle of the clergy and their pupils[3] we may now turn

[1] Quoted in J. Truslow Adams, *Revolutionary New England*, p. 332.

[2] Quoted in S. E. Morison, *Sources and Documents illustrating the American Revolution*, p. 94.

[3] The account here given of the clergy and their influence has been limited to Massachusetts. It is at first sight puzzling that the other main centre of revolutionary ideas should have been episcopalian and aristocratic Virginia. But the Virginian planters had always been ready to stand for their rights (an aristocracy can be as conscious of its rights as any democracy); and in 1774 they were deeply exasperated by the provisions of the Quebec Act, which in their view denied them the prospect of extending their plantations into the western regions on their frontier. The Virginian clergy, an established clergy dependent on the

to the other circle—that of the lawyers. The lawyers in the colonies generally were a numerous and powerful body. Burke, in his speech on Conciliation with America, noted that 'in no country perhaps in the world is the law so general a study'; he remarked on the number of lawyers sitting in the Continental Congress of 1774; he recounted the great sale of Blackstone's *Commentaries*, recently published in England between 1765 and 1769, and re-published in Philadelphia in 1771. To mention the names of the chief lawyers in the colonies, during the period between the passage of the Stamp Act and the signing of the Declaration of Independence (1764–76), would be to mention the names of nearly all the chief actors in the events of the period; for the events of these twelve years were dominated by the lawyers. Here we are only concerned with the lawyers of Boston and Massachusetts —men such as James Otis, Oxenbridge Thacher, and John Adams. The notable thing about them is that like the preachers, but even more than the preachers, they were deeply concerned with the essential problems of political science. They were lawyers of ability, who enjoyed good practices; but they pursued the study of political science as well as the study and practice of law. This was partly due to the nature of some of the law-books they studied —Pufendorf's *De Jure Naturae et Gentium* (1672); Burlamaqui's *Principes du Droit Naturel* (1747); Vattel's *Le Droit des Gens ou Principes de la Loi Naturelle* (1758). All these writers—but perhaps especially Vattel, in the first section of his book, which is entitled *De la nation considérée en elle-même*, and which deals with the natural system of the internal government of states—were dealing largely with matters of political philosophy, rather than with

planters for their tithes of tobacco, largely followed the lead of the aristocracy. It has been calculated that of one hundred episcopalian clergymen, in Virginia, almost a half were on the revolutionary side, and only thirteen were openly loyalist (C. H. Van Tyne's *England and America*, pp. 77–8). Much the same was true of South Carolina. The position was different in the middle and northern colonies, where episcopalians were generally loyalists, 'while Dissenters, especially Presbyterians and Congregationalists, were assumed to be patriots' (ibid. p. 76); and it may be noted that, in the colonies at large, 80 per cent of the revolutionary leaders were Dissenters, and over 75 per cent of the chief loyalists were Episcopalians.

matters of law: they were treating, like philosophers, of a system of ideal rights under a code of ideal law; they were not dealing, as lawyers generally do, with a system of actual rights under a code of actual law. Even Blackstone himself, in the preliminary introduction to his *Commentaries* (the argument of the *Commentaries* themselves is very different), allowed himself to be led by his reading of Pufendorf and Burlamaqui—and specially of the latter —into the enunciation of a political philosophy which quarrelled sadly with his own later exposition of the actual law of the British constitution.[1] It is little wonder that Otis and John Adams should have followed a way which Blackstone himself had already trod.

But there was also another reason, besides their study of the writers of the school of natural law, which impelled the Boston lawyers to turn to political science. This was the circumstances of their times. 'These are the times that try men's souls', Paine afterwards wrote, at the end of 1776, in the first sentence of the first number of the *American Crisis*; but the trial had already begun by 1764. In an obscure time of troubles, when the light-houses of the ordinary law gave little light, the lawyers were compelled to look to the general beacon-lights of the philosophy of the State for guidance in steering a course. They had heard the sermons of the preachers; but they also discussed the principles of politics among themselves and in their own circle. There was a lawyers' club or *sodalitas* in Boston, from 1760 onwards, to which John Adams, Otis, and Thacher all belonged. It read and discussed the lawyers of the common law, Coke and Blackstone; it read and discussed the lawyers of the school of natural law, Grotius, Burlamaqui and Vattel; it also read and discussed Locke's *Treatises on Civil Government* and even Rousseau's *Du Contrat Social*, which had just been published in 1762. This law club, as an American professor has said, was 'really a political science club'.[2] Indeed, there was a general lively interest, which was not confined to the lawyers, in the whole subject and literature of political science. John Adams noted that in 1765 'the principles, the objects and trends of

---

[1] See the writer's *Essays on Government*, pp. 136–8.
[2] C. H. Van Tyne, *The Causes of the War of Independence*, p. 337.

government became the topics of discussion in all companies and at the firesides of private families'. The record of the libraries and the reading of some of the prominent Bostonians is notable. Hooker, Hobbes, and Locke; Harrington (whose *Oceana* was particularly studied) and Algernon Sidney; Montesquieu and Rousseau—-these names recur. It is not surprising that John Adams should have studied them all—and Grotius, Selden, and Pufendorf into the bargain. But Samuel Adams too had read many of them, and he had also read Vattel (which is perhaps, as we shall have reason to notice later, a matter of some significance in its bearing on his development); Dr Samuel Cooper, a Boston clergyman, had read and could quote Burlamaqui; and whether the merchant John Hancock had read his Milton or his Beccaria, at any rate he owned their works. It is little wonder that, with all this reading, we should find echoes of the political philosophers in the American State documents of the period, or that Vattel, for instance, should be quoted in a memorial addressed by Massachusetts to its agent in Great Britain about 1765.[1]

It has been noted by more than one American historian that the study and the quotation of the classics of political science during the period of the American Revolution was something more than an academic parade of learning. Men studied and quoted Milton, Sidney, and Locke, not because they were scholars (though some of them certainly were), but because they felt as Milton, Sidney, and Locke had felt, and because they were speaking an ancestral language which was still their own natural tongue. 'Writers of seventeenth-century England were known and used by the Americans in their protests against king and parliament; but the

---

[1] C. H. Van Tyne, op. cit. p. 344, n. 1, quotes a table showing the degree of frequency with which political writers were quoted in America before 1776. Locke leads with twenty-two quotations, and Hume follows close with twenty; Montesquieu has ten; Grotius and Harrington each have eight; Sidney has six; and Hooker, Pufendorf and Vattel each have four. But it is not only a matter of specific quotations. The echoes and adaptations perhaps matter even more; and we find the arguments of Vattel thus echoed and adapted in the resolutions of a town-meeting at Concord, in 1776, which demanded the summoning of a constitutional convention to frame a constitution on first principles. (S. E. Morison, *Sources and Documents*, p. 177.)

point is that the New Englanders in their own history had kept these principles in their primitive and compelling simplicity.'[1] 'Locke did not need to convince the colonists, because they were already'convinced; and they were already convinced because they had long been living under governments which did, in a rough and ready way, conform to the kind of government for which Locke furnished a reasoned foundation.'[2] For once, a political theory was concrete in the actual fact of life and daily experience; and it is this conjunction of theory and experience which is the essence of the American Revolution. Lord Acton remarked on the conjunction, thus adding the testimony of an English to that of American historians. Lecturing on the influence of America on the course of the French Revolution, he noted that what America supplied was 'the system of an international extra-territorial universal Whig, far transcending the English model by its simplicity and rigour: it surpassed in force all the speculation of Paris and Geneva, for it had undergone the test of experiment'.[3]

Stimulated by a native experience which enabled them to realise, with a vivid feeling denied to contemporary Englishmen, the doctrines of the English writers of the seventeenth century, the American lawyers became writers as well as readers; they produced pamphlets, memorials, declarations, and eventually constitutions, which had a masculine vigour of thought and expression. This is true not only of the Boston lawyers, but also of the lawyers of Philadelphia and other cities. It has been said of the thirty years before the French Revolution of 1789 that they form 'a period of French history when the significant events were books, not acts'. It may be equally said of the dozen years before the Declaration of Independence in 1776 that they mark a period of American history when the significant events were books which were also acts. The books, it is true, were pamphlets, or sometimes series of articles, rather than fully fledged books; but they were pamphlets and articles of an incisive logic and a persuasive force. In Boston three

[1] A. C. McLaughlin, *Foundations of American Constitutionalism*, p. 68.
[2] Carl Becker, *The Declaration of Independence*, pp. 72–3.
[3] *Lectures on the French Revolution*, p. 20.

of the lawyers—Otis, Thacher, and John Adams—were also pamphleteers and authors. Otis published in 1764 his *Rights of the British Colonies Asserted and Proved*; Thacher, another member of the *sodalitas*, published in the same year his *Sentiments of a British American*; John Adams, writing as *Novanglus*, and using arguments which anticipate the Imperial Conference of 1926, combated in a series of articles the conceptions of empire which were advanced by the loyalist judge Daniel Leonard.[1] In Philadelphia there were three other lawyers who, like the Boston three, were also pamphleteers and authors. John Dickinson published in 1767-8 his *Farmer's Letters* (or 'Letters from a Farmer of Pennsylvania to the Inhabitants of the British Colonies'); James Wilson, Dickinson's pupil, published in 1774 his *Considerations on the Nature and Extent of the Legislative Authority of Parliament*, a work of close legal argument and far-reaching legal conclusions; and Joseph Galloway, speaker of the lower house of Pennsylvania, not only produced the Plan of Union among the colonies in 1774, but also published a *Candid Examination of the Mutual Claims of Great Britain and her Colonies* in the same year. Nor were these the only authors of Philadelphia. There was also the voluminous Benjamin Franklin; and there was the greatest of all pamphleteers in the English language, Tom Paine, the stay-maker and 'jockey of Norfolk', who had come to Philadelphia with an introduction from Franklin (then in England) in 1775, and by the beginning of 1776 had electrified America with his *Common Sense* and given the signal for independence.

Further to the South, in Maryland, there was Daniel Dulany, at first a great opponent of the Stamp Act but afterwards a loyalist, who published at Annapolis in 1765 his *Considerations on the Propriety of Imposing Taxes*. Still further to the South, in Virginia,

---

[1] In 1768 John Adams had already published a *Dissertation on the Canon and Feudal Law* (it appeared originally in the *Boston Gazette*, and was afterwards published in London), in which he had argued that British liberties were 'original rights, conditions of original contract, coequal with prerogative and coequal with government', and that 'many of our rights are inherent... established as preliminaries even before a parliament existed' (R. G. Adams, *Political Ideas of the American Revolution*, pp. 166-8).

there was Thomas Jefferson, a home-trained lawyer who had proceeded from the College of William and Mary to the office of the leader of the Virginian Bar. He published in 1774 a *Summary View of the Rights of British America* (containing the resolutions which he had drafted as instructions for the delegates of Virginia to the continental congress) in a pamphlet which was widely circulated in America and ran through a number of editions in an English reprint. It was this *Summary View*, and the draft resolutions which it contained, which led to his drafting the Declaration of Independence, and served as the basis of its recital of the injuries and aggressions of George III. Less known to fame, but reckoned by Jefferson as the author of 'the first pamphlet on the nature of the connection with Great Britain which had any pretension to accuracy of view', was Richard Bland, who published at Williamsburg in 1766 *An Enquiry into the Rights of the British Colonies*, and anticipated the argument of John Adams by contending that Virginia was an equal partner with Britain in the empire. Another Virginian lawyer of far greater fame, Patrick Henry, was not an author; but he was an orator and agitator whose speeches—especially a speech introducing the Virginia Resolves on the Stamp Act, and a later speech introducing the resolutions of 1775 for arming the Virginia militia—were long remembered and constantly recited. In a sense he is the Virginian parallel to Samuel Adams in Massachusetts. Adams, however, was not a lawyer, as Henry was (though he had received some legal training); but he was an agitator of far greater acumen than the ebullient Henry, and he was also a busy journalist who wrote, with an indefatigable pen, a multitude of political articles. He too, on any estimate, deserves a place and a station among the American writers who conducted the legal and constitutional argument of the Revolution.

III

It has already been noted that there was a divergence between the American lawyers, especially those who were home-trained, and the lawyers of Great Britain in the temper and line of approach from which they conducted the argument.[1] But here it is necessary to make a distinction. We must distinguish between two separate spheres—the legal sphere in the narrower sense of the word, or the sphere of private law, which is concerned with the rights and duties of persons in private or civil life; and the constitutional sphere, or the sphere of public law, which is concerned with the mutual rights and duties of the government and the citizen in public or political life. It is true that the nature of English law makes such a distinction difficult for Englishmen; for under it, as Paley noted and Dicey repeated,[2] the law of the constitution is simply a part of the ordinary law of the land, on the same footing as the rest, and equally alterable, by the same process, with the rest. But it is none the less necessary to make the distinction in treating of the argument between Great Britain and the American colonists; and indeed it is a distinction which the American lawyers not only imply, but also increasingly press, in the course of the argument. We may therefore assume the distinction, and proceed to trace its consequences. In the sphere of private law American and British lawyers were agreed. They understood the same thing, and they did the same sort of thing; and English legal decisions have always continued to be cited as precedents and authorities in the judgements of American courts. In the sphere of public law they were far from being agreed, and they argued at cross-purposes. The reason was simple. 'The political evolution of America', as Dr Lawrence Lowell has noted,[3] 'branched off from that of England early in the eighteenth century...thereafter the changes in the British constitution found no echo on the other side of the Atlantic, largely, no doubt, because taking the form of custom, not of statute, they were not readily observed.' This is a fact of crucial importance. The American lawyers knew the English constitution and English constitutional law down to the time of the death of Queen Anne. They did not know it after that date. It had altered, and was still being altered—not by statutes which they could read and understand, but by changes of con-

---

[1] Supra, p. 268.   [2] Supra, p. 245.
[3] *Government of England*, Vol. II, p. 472.

stitutional convention which were not recorded in statutes, were not described by Blackstone, and were little, if at all, understood in America. The enthroning of parliament as the great organ of a system of parliamentary government which had inherited the royal supremacy in the Church and the royal control of plantations; which was feeling its way to a cabinet system; which, unrepresentative as it was in structure, was becoming in spirit more and more sensitive to the opinion of 'the Public'; which, with all its imperfections, was making for the greater liberty of the subject, both civil and religious—all this was inevitably hidden. The American lawyers still thought, in the main, in seventeenth-century terms. Those terms were far from being ignoble. There was much in the seventeenth century—a reaching for first principles; a searching for fundamentals—which transcended the more complacent development of the spirit of the eighteenth century. But to argue in seventeenth-century terms with men who were arguing in terms of the eighteenth made debate exceedingly difficult. 'Lord Coke', as he was called by the colonists, when they appealed to his doctrine of the sovereignty of the common law over all the powers of government, could hardly be reconciled with Lord Mansfield; and though Camden (as we shall have reason to notice later) could agree in 1776 with the dictum of Hobart, in a case of 1614, that 'an Act of Parliament made against natural equity is void in itself', he was a solitary figure in England, however much his view might be acclaimed across the Atlantic.[1] The seventeenth century on one side of the ocean fought in the dark, and fought at cross-purposes, with the eighteenth century on the other.

There were three different grounds which were successively taken by the American lawyers in challenging the action of the British Parliament from 1764 (the year of the Stamp Act) to 1776. The first was the ground of the actual constitutions of the colonies

---

[1] Camden, arguing against the Declaration Act of 1766 in the House of Lords, said 'the legislative has no right to make this law...you cannot enact anything against divine law'. (On Camden's view see R. G. Adams, *Political Ideas of the American Revolution*, pp. 127–31.)

themselves, as expressed in their charters or other documents. This may be termed the ground of colonial constitutional law. The second was the ground of the actual constitution of Great Britain and the British Empire, which was not similarly expressed, but might be discovered (at any rate in part) from statutes and judicial decisions. This may be termed the ground of British constitutional law; but it was a less definite ground than the first, because the British constitution tended to become, for the American interpreter, not what it actually was, but what he thought it should properly be. The third ground was the ground of ideal or natural law, and of the ideal or natural rights proper to any and every constitution which conformed to natural law. This may be termed the ground of natural constitutional law—in other words of a constitutional law which was neither colonial nor British, but as wide as the realm of nature, whatever that realm might be. It may also be termed, in Lord Acton's phrase, the ground of 'the international extra-territorial universal Whig', sempiternal as well as universal, and claiming validity *semper et ubique* for the principles of his creed. These are the three grounds stated at the end of the preamble to the Declaration and Resolves of the first continental congress, in the autumn of 1774. 'The inhabitants of the English colonies in North America, by the immutable laws of nature, the principles of the English constitution, and the several charters or compacts [of the several colonies], have the following rights.' The order in which the grounds are here stated is the reverse of the order of time in which they had actually been used during the ten years since 1764. This was natural enough: the immutable laws of nature had come to the front by 1774, and were accordingly stated first. But in order to follow the course of the debate, and to understand the progressive development of ideas, we must begin with the colonial 'charters or compacts', and end with 'the immutable laws of nature'.

1. Some of the colonies had given themselves the constitutions by which they lived. Connecticut, for example, had framed in 1639 its own 'Fundamental Orders', which have been described

as the first written constitution known to history;[1] and Rhode Island, though it received a charter in 1663, had originally governed itself by its own conception of democracy. Generally, however, the constitution of a colony depended upon a charter granted by the British Crown. It is true that it also depended (as the historian must always remember, though the colonies tended to forget) on the 'commissions' and the 'royal instructions' issued by the Crown to colonial governors on their appointment. But the attention of the colonies which were possessed of charters was particularly fastened upon them; and the New England colonies, in particular, were strongly attached to their charters.[2] Massachusetts, indeed, had lost her original charter of 1629, in spite of appeals to the 'laws of righteousness and equity' urged by her clergy in its defence when it was challenged in the English courts; and she had been eventually forced, in 1691, to accept a new charter from William and Mary—a charter far better (because far more liberal) than the old charter defended and demanded by the ministers and their followers. But time soon sweetened what had originally been a bitter pill; and by 1770 the compulsory charter detested by their forefathers had become a palladium of liberty both to Samuel and to John Adams. They developed the theory that the charter of 1691 was a finally sovereign body of constitutional law (in the same sense in which the American Constitution of 1787 is finally sovereign to-day), overriding, as such, the acts of any legislature, even the British, which were incompatible with its terms. Samuel Adams contended that the charter of 1691 (the liberal provisions of which 'had in fact...been forced upon the

[1] On the Fundamental Orders see J. Truslow Adams, *The Founding of New England*, p. 192. It is worthy of notice that in Connecticut (and also in Rhode Island) the people chose their own governors, as they had made their own constitutions. In other colonies the governor was appointed by the Crown. (C. H. Van Tyne, *The Causes of the War of Independence*, p. 35, n. 1.)

[2] According to J. C. Miller (*Origins of the American Revolution*, p. 128), 'most of the colonies did not have them'. But they existed in Pennsylvania and Maryland, as well as in Massachusetts and some of the other Northern colonies; and while some of the colonial leaders deprecated attachment to charters, as tending to develop particularism among the different colonies, the argument drawn from charter rights was an argument generally used.

Massachusetts leaders, fighting against them to the last ditch')[1] was a 'contract' to which the people of Massachusetts on the one side, and King William and Queen Mary on the other, were the two consenting parties; and John Adams also, arguing as *Novanglus* in 1775 that allegiance was due to the British Crown 'by our own charter and province laws', contended that 'we, as well as the people of England, made an original express contract with King William'. If the charter could thus be imaginatively stretched and extended into a contract, it followed in logic that it could not be altered without the consent of both of the parties. Samuel Adams went even further, and added an additional refinement. He argued that the charter of Massachusetts had established a balance of power among the several branches of the legislative—the representative house, the council, and the governor—and that any alteration of the balance was an alteration of the constitution, as settled by the charter, being destructive of the 'equilibrium without which we cannot continue a free state'.

Such attempts to make charters fundamental, whether on the ground of the contract supposed to be involved in their nature, or on that of the balance of power supposed to be contained in their terms, were inevitably destined to shipwreck. For one thing the separate charters of a number of separate colonies could hardly provide any common basis of resistance. Nor had all the colonies charters; nor, again, were the charters, where they existed, in agreement with one another.[2] But there was another and graver difficulty which beset all attempts to make charters the legal ground of challenge to the action of the British Parliament. The charters, in their original inception, had been legal instruments of incorporation granted to 'companies' (such as the Virginia and the Massachusetts Companies) which were of the nature of business companies. The colonies had indeed grown to greater dimensions, and their charters had also grown with them. But

---

[1] J. Truslow Adams, op. cit. p. 447.
[2] 'The Pennsylvania charter expressly recognised taxation by Parliament—the charter of Maryland, on the other hand, denied the right of Parliament to tax Maryland directly.' (J. C. Miller, op. cit. p. 128.)

colonial charters, as legal instruments issued by the English Crown for the purpose of vesting bodies of persons with legal rights, remained legally cognisable in the English courts, which could inquire into their validity and into the validity of acts undertaken on the ground of the rights they conferred. Nor was that all. Charters were also legally variable by the King in Parliament, as the final legal authority in the system of English law. Legally, therefore, the argument might be used—as it was used by Blackstone and pressed by Lord Mansfield—that colonies acting under charters were *pro tanto* corporations, acting as such within the limits of their charter rights, and liable to the rule of *ultra vires* if they exceeded those limits; and the further argument could also be used that, over and above the restriction of the rule of *ultra vires*, the chartered colonies were also restricted by the right of the sovereign grantor to vary the terms of the grant. Such arguments might have been answered, or at any rate met, by a line of argument which has been recently followed by some English thinkers, and even some lawyers, in dealing with the rights of societies such as trade unions and free churches. It might have been contended (as the late Lord Haldane contended in arguing for the Free Church of Scotland in 1904) that a living society grows and extends its purposes, and should not be cramped in its growth either by a rule of *ultra vires* or by any restrictive assertion of the final sovereignty of the state. This, in effect, was what Burke contended when he pleaded that the colonies had *grown* to the dignity of great nations and should be recognised as such, and that the sovereignty of the English Parliament (although it existed and had been recently declared in 1766) should not be pressed in restriction. But this was *not* the contention of Massachusetts, or of the other colonies which took their stand on the ground of charters. Their contention was the opposite.

The chartered colonies did not argue for growth: they argued for the restrictive force of their 'charters or compacts',[1] even

---

[1] The alternative term 'compact', used in the preamble to the Declaration and Resolves of 1774 (perhaps on the suggestion of Samuel Adams), is not really an alternative. It is an addition; and an addition which, legally, is in-

against the grantor. It was they who were pressing the idea of *ultra vires*, in the mistaken notion that it served the purpose of defending their rights, instead of advancing the opposite idea of growth which was far more calculated to advance their cause. Some of the American writers, it is true, took a different line. James Otis protested against any analogy between a colony and 'a corporation of button-makers'. Daniel Dulany pleaded that it was 'as absurd and insensible to call a colony a common corporation, because not an independent kingdom,...as it would be to call Lake Erie a duck-puddle, because not the Atlantic Ocean'. Both Otis and Dulany imply the idea of growth, though they do not enunciate it clearly. But the Adams cousins, John and Samuel, who took the ground of unalterable contract, both stood at the opposite end. It may be added that they also stood at the wrong end, not only because there was no contract in question—there was merely and simply the grant of a charter—but also because the king's grant of a charter was not, and could not be, unalterable, but admitted of variation by the action of the king in Parliament. The colonies could not fruitfully stand on the ground of their charters. They could not fruitfully stickle for the peculiar rights which they enjoyed as chartered colonists under the terms of charters. That was a broken reed. They had to go further and to take a wider scope. They had to stand for the common rights which they, along with all other English freemen, possessed by virtue of 'the principles of the English constitution'. That was what they next attempted to do, and that was the second ground which they took.

defensible. The charters had never been compacts made between two equal parties. On the other hand the idea of compact had long been deep in the American mind, especially in New England: had there not been a Mayflower Compact, as early as 1620, to 'covenant and combine...together into a civil body politic', and was not the 'covenant' of the congregation the basis of each of the New England churches? It was natural for New Englanders to see compact in a sphere of affairs where there was no compact—that is to say, in their colonial governments, and in the relation of those governments to England—as well as in their churches, where there actually was a compact. (See A. C. McLaughlin, *Foundations of American Constitutionalism*, pp. 3-30.)

2. Before we turn to the American interpretation of 'the principles of the English constitution', some words must be said about one way in which those principles had actually operated in the American colonies before the Revolution. It was an old principle of English law that there was a fundamental distinction between colonies 'by settlement' and colonies 'by conquest or cession'. In the latter the Crown could legislate freely, by Orders in Council or otherwise, and could establish a form of constitution at will. In the former settlers were regarded as carrying with them the English laws in being at the time of the settlement, and as enjoying all their benefits; and in them any form of constitution created by the Crown must contain a representative body possessing powers of taxation.[1] The colonies of North America, whether they were formally regarded as colonies 'by settlement' or as colonies 'by conquest or cession', were treated in effect as if they were colonies by settlement:[2] they enjoyed the benefits of English law and the right to a representative body possessing powers of taxation. In these colonies (as also in those which were planted in the West Indian islands) the Crown established elective assemblies (they still exist, and have existed continuously for more than three centuries, in the Bahamas, Barbados, and Bermuda); and the elective assemblies of the colonies grew steadily from strength to strength. In Virginia, for example, it had already been stated, in the original charter, that the colonists were to enjoy all liberties, franchises, and immunities, 'as if they had been abiding

[1] The distinction is noted by Blackstone (*Commentaries*, Vol. I, p. 107) and explained in Sir Anton Bertram's *The Colonial Service*, pp. 158 seqq.

[2] Blackstone (loc. cit.) states that 'our American plantations are principally of this latter sort' (i.e. colonies by conquest or cession). James II took the view that Virginia and the New England colonies were got by conquest (Van Tyne, *The Causes of the War of Independence*, p. 25); and there was a general tendency towards the establishment of 'royal provinces' (i.e. provinces treated as colonies by conquest or cession) at the end of the seventeenth century. (In 1685 there had been only two royal provinces; by 1763 there were as many as eight.) But though this might legally enable the Crown to legislate freely by Orders in Council or otherwise, and even to establish a constitution at will, it did not actually affect the existence and action of colonial assemblies—except for a brief period under James II (1686-9), when colonial assemblies were abolished and the single rule of an appointed governor and council established.

and born within this our realm of England'; and as early as 1619 the governor had convened an elected House of Burgesses, consisting of two delegates from each settlement. Massachusetts, indeed, began as a theocratic oligarchy, managed by the governor of the Massachusetts Company and his twelve assistants. By 1634 it had swung to the opposite extreme: *all* the members of the Company, assembled in general court, had succeeded in becoming a primary legislature. Soon, however, this primary legislature was dethroned by a representative body: new settlements arose at a distance, and demanded the right to send 'deputies'; yielding to the demand, Massachusetts followed the example of Virginia. The attendance of 'deputies' from each new settlement, as the spreading colonists roamed further afield, became a general practice, not only in Massachusetts, but also in the other colonies.[1] The practice grew, as it were, from the soil, and sprang from the spirit of the dwellers on the soil of each new settlement; but it was also encouraged by the English government, and it would hardly have grown without that encouragement. It was the general policy of the English government (perhaps with the idea of encouraging emigration) to promote the formation of elected assemblies; and this policy was corroborated by a definite ruling of the English solicitor-general, in 1724, that a colony of British subjects could not be taxed except by a representative body which they had themselves elected or by the British Parliament.

Growing in this way partly from the soil, but partly also under English encouragement and by virtue of a principle of English law and an English legal ruling, the colonial assemblies acquired such power that it may justly be said, as it has been said by an American historian, that 'the most notable political development in the empire during the eighteenth century was the extension of the powers of the provincial assemblies at the expense of the royal

---

[1] This admission of every new settlement as a constituency, and this view of the representative as a 'deputy' (who must be resident in his constituency and express its views), soon differentiated the colonial assemblies from the English parliament, with its haphazard system of constituencies and the claims of its members (mostly not resident in their constituencies) to express their own views at their own discretion.

authority'.[1] Indeed, the English government had prepared a rod to scourge itself; or, more exactly, it had pursued two contradictory policies, which inevitably conflicted with one another. On the one hand, it had extended to the colonies—whether they were colonies by settlement or colonies by conquest or cession; whether it did so by charters or other grants, or by simple recognition of a *fait accompli*—the rights of freemen under English law, and especially the right to a colonial assembly possessing powers of taxation. On the other hand it had also extended to the colonies —wherever it could (and that was almost everywhere)—the system of the royal governor with his 'commission' and 'royal instructions'. The two things inevitably quarrelled; and indeed there was a constant quarrel, from the beginning of the eighteenth century, between each colonial assembly and the resident British governor. 'The most notable political development' was perhaps less the extension of the powers of the provincial assemblies, considered in themselves; it was, even more, the growth of a struggle between their growing power and that of the governor. It was an easy step from the conduct of a struggle with the British governor to the beginning of a struggle with the British government. That was the step which was taken in 1764, and which led to the Declaration of Independence twelve years later.[2]

Against this background we may now consider the challenge offered by American lawyers to British claims on the ground of the British constitution, as they interpreted its nature. There were

[1] J. C. Miller, *Origins of the American Revolution*, pp. 31–2.

[2] Could the ultimate struggle have been avoided? There was perhaps one possible way—that the British government should have recognised the growing strength of the colonial assemblies by making the royal governor and his council finally responsible to the assembly, and thus adding the grant of responsible government to the previous grant of a representative system. This, as we can now see after the event, was the logical way; and it was the way actually followed in Canada after the Durham Report of 1839. But among all the suggestions actually made for finding a way of solution (there were various proposals, for instance, on both sides of the Atlantic, for a new imperial parliament containing colonial representatives) this was one which never emerged. Responsible government was too recent a growth in England itself, and the cabinet system was too immature, for the men of 1764–76 to see their full implications, or to dream of their application to the problem of imperial relations.

two possible ways of approaching the theory of the British constitution. It might be approached from *below*, by way of a consideration of the rights of the subject. It might be approached from *above*, by way of a consideration of the sovereignty of parliament. We may begin by considering the first of these ways.

(*a*) Blackstone, in the first book of his *Commentaries*, and under the general head of 'Rights of Persons', had asserted three 'primary rights' of all Englishmen—security of life, liberty of movement, and property; and he had then gone on to assert five further 'auxiliary rights', which served as barriers to protect and maintain the primary rights—the constitution and powers of parliament, the limitation of the King's prerogative, the right of applying to the courts for redress, the right to petition the King or either house of parliament, and the right of having arms for defence 'as a public allowance, under due restrictions, of the natural right of resistance'. There were thus eight rights—three of them primary and five auxiliary—which the colonists could argue that they carried with them as Englishmen across the Atlantic. At any rate this could certainly be argued in the colonies 'by settlement'; and it did not really matter that some of the colonies were formally regarded as colonies by conquest or cession, for all the colonies were much of a muchness and were treated as such (for instance in the matter of colonial assemblies) by the British Government. Had not the legal adviser to the Board of Trade and Plantations said, in 1720, that let an Englishman go where he would in lands claimed by England, he carried as much of law and liberty with him as the nature of things would bear?[1] In any case the colonists claimed for themselves all the rights of the subject which could be enjoyed under the English constitution. They claimed the right of property; and from that they went on to claim the right to be free from having their property taken, in the form of a levy of

---

[1] Quoted in C. H. Van Tyne, *The Causes of the War of Independence*, p. 23, n. 3. The words 'as the nature of things would bear' are perhaps a restriction. Blackstone states—speaking of colonies by settlement—that 'such colonists carry with them only so much of the English law as is applicable to their own situation and the condition of an infant colony'. (*Commentaries*, Vol. I, p. 107.)

taxes, except with their own consent. But was their claim in regard to taxation a claim to a right which existed under the British constitution? The answer to that question was not easy. The Virginia assembly certainly resolved, in 1765, that 'the taxation of people by themselves, or by persons chosen by themselves to represent them,...is...the distinguishing characteristic of British freedom, without which the ancient constitution cannot exist'; and the Stamp Act Congress, which contained representatives from a majority of the colonies, similarly voted, a little later in the same year, that it was 'the undoubted birth-right of Englishmen that no taxes be imposed on them but with their consent given personally or by their representatives'. But there were two difficulties which confronted this contention.

In the first place it was not a 'characteristic of British freedom' or an 'undoubted birth-right of Englishmen' that taxation involved the consent of every tax-payer given personally or through his elected representative. In England itself many tax-payers paid taxes who had not joined, and could not join, in the election of a representative. Manchester and Birmingham were not constituencies at all; and in the constituencies which actually existed it was not all Englishmen—indeed, it was only a fraction of Englishmen—who voted. The colonists were claiming as Englishmen, and under the English constitution, a right which was not enjoyed by many Englishmen in England. Their claim to a right of personal consent to taxation as a right enjoyed under the English constitution was an untenable claim—at any rate if the English constitution were interpreted to mean that constitution *as it existed in England*. But might not another interpretation be possible? Could not the English constitution be interpreted to mean the constitution *as it existed in America*, and not as it existed in England? In other words could it not be argued that while in England the primary right of property and the auxiliary right to enjoy the benefit of parliament were *not* added together to produce the result that property could only be taken from a tax-payer by representatives whom he had helped to elect, in America the two rights *were* added together to produce that result? Such an argument, if it is analysed, will be seen to depend on the assumption that in America, and for America, the colonial assembly, with its more equal system of constituencies and its broader franchise, must be regarded as taking the place of the English parliament, with its haphazard system of constituencies and its narrower franchise. But the whole argument (and particularly the assumption on which it depends) presents us with a second difficulty, or rather congeries of difficulties. How could there be two interpretations of the English constitution at the same time? How could it be proved, on any interpretation of the English constitution which professed to be couched in terms of law, that the colonial assembly took the place of the English parliament in America, and thereby extruded that parliament from America? And even if that could be proved, did it not result from the proof that the ground of challenge was being shifted—and shifted *back*—from the terms of English constitutional law to those of colonial constitutional law? That only meant argument in a circle, which landed you back at the point at which your argument had already shown itself weak.

We may thus conclude that, upon a theory of the English constitution which begins from a consideration of the rights of the subject under that constitution, the colonists failed to make their case good. They might plead that they were claiming as Englishmen: in reality they were claiming as men who were accustomed, and felt that they had somehow a right, to something more than Englishmen had—to a more equal system of constituencies; to a broader franchise; to a different conception of the function of representatives, which made them 'deputies'; to a firmer grip and a larger control of their own private property. They could not base the claim which they made to the enjoyment of rights on colonial constitutional law; that, as we have previously seen, had shown itself an inadequate ground. Equally, as we have just seen, they could not base it on English constitutional law; that too, when it was tested and tried, had shown itself similarly inadequate. They were therefore driven, in the event, to base their claim to the enjoyment of rights on *natural* constitutional law. The rights of Englishmen under English law were an inadequate defence; there remained a recourse to the rights of man under the law of nature—the rights of 'the international extra-territorial universal Whig' under a law as ubiquitous as himself. The 'order of democracy', to which Dulany claims that the right of the subject not to be taxed without his consent essentially belongs, was not the order of the English constitution. The fundamental right of property, on which John Dickinson relies in the *Farmer's Letters* ('we cannot be free without being secure in our property, and we cannot be secure in our property if without our consent others may as by right take it away'), was not so fundamental in the system of the English constitution that you could resist parliamentary taxes to which you had not consented either personally or by your representatives. To find a firm defence for the 'order of democracy' and the fundamental right of property (for property as well as democracy, and perhaps even more than democracy, was always an issue during the years between 1764 and 1776, and indeed in the later years of the making of the American constitution), you must go to nature.

(*b*) We may now leave the theory of the English constitution which begins from a consideration of the rights of the subject, and turn to the theory which begins from a consideration of the sovereignty of parliament. We have already seen that the colonial view of the rights of the subject implies in advance the notion that the sovereignty of the English parliament is limited—limited by the right of property belonging to the colonists, and limited therefore by their right of paying only such taxes, in diminution of that right, as either they themselves, or their own elected representatives, had explicitly consented to pay. We shall have occasion to notice presently that this notion of the limited nature of the sovereignty of parliament was one which the colonists held even more generally, and applied to other matters besides the matter of taxes. But before we examine their notion, it is important to understand the idea and practice of parliamentary sovereignty on the English side, and to understand it in the form which it had assumed in the eighteenth century. During the course of that century—indeed the development may already be traced from the Restoration of 1660, and still more from the Revolution of 1688—there had been a great development of the power of 'the sovereign legislative' at Westminster. That development of power had been twofold. It had been partly internal; and here there had been an increase of the *content* of parliamentary power, achieved at the expense of the Crown. It had been partly external; and here there had been an increase of the *extent* of parliamentary power, achieved by the assertion of its overseas scope and its general control.

Internally, and in the content of its power, the parliament at Westminster had taken over from the Crown the control of the Church, which had ceased in practice to be a matter of royal governance and had become instead a matter of parliamentary regulation; and *pari passu* it had begun to take over the control of 'plantations' or colonies, which it sought to withdraw from the sphere of the Crown and to transfer to that of the legislature.[1] These were the natural and inevitable results of the Revolution of 1688, which had, in effect, enthroned the Houses of Parliament. Externally too, and in the extent of its power, the parliament at Westminster had been equally affected by the results of the

[1] Incidentally it may be noticed here that the movement of parliament towards the control of the American plantations, at the expense of the Crown, introduced an inevitable complication into the relations between the American colonists and Great Britain. It made those relations a matter of what may be called a triangular duel. There was something of a struggle between Crown and parliament about the colonies, at the same time that there was also a struggle between Crown and parliament acting together (for both were equally involved in a cause which was common to both) and the recalcitrant people of the colonies. In other words, the tension between the colonial assemblies and the British government was complicated by another tension *within* the British government, a tension between the executive side and the legislative side of that government. It is this triangular duel which helps to explain the growth of the power of colonial assemblies in the eighteenth century; 'with the Crown and parliament at cross-purposes, the colonial legislatives were able to enlarge their powers' (J. C. Miller, *Origins of the American Revolution*, p. 33). The paradox thus emerges that the colonial assemblies and the British parliament were both growing in power simultaneously (with the prospect of an ultimate collision); and indeed the further paradox emerges that the colonial assemblies were growing in power *because* the British parliament was also growing in power.

Revolution of 1688. By the Act of Union of 1707 it had ceased to be merely an English parliament, and had become instead a British parliament, competent to legislate for Scotland as well as for England. A few years later, in 1719, it passed a declaratory Act affirming its right to legislate for Ireland over the head of the Irish parliament at Dublin. By 1766—when, at the moment of repealing the Stamp Act of 1764, and to counterbalance that repeal, it passed another declaratory act, affirming its right both to tax and legislate, 'in all cases whatsoever', in the American colonies—the Parliament at Westminster was clear in its own mind that it was an imperial parliament, competent to legislate for all the territories in the allegiance of the Crown. Growing alike in content and extent, and supported in its growth by British liberal opinion, which regarded it as the organ of liberty and the brake on the power of the Crown, the Parliament at Westminster had moved—it is true by a natural evolution, but none the less it *had* moved—to a new and more majestic position, and to a new and more majestic conception of the dignity of its position.

The colonists, as we have already noticed,[1] had not moved equally, or at the same pace. They were still in the state of mind, so far as politics were concerned, of the seventeenth century. There was an open breach in the community of ideas between the two sides of the Atlantic; and the colonists were accordingly led, first to challenge the content of parliamentary power, then to challenge the extent of parliamentary power, and finally to challenge both. They were all the more led to offer the challenge because they too, after all, had moved; because they too, after all, were not altogether in the state of mind of the seventeenth century. To speak more exactly, they *were* in that state of mind in regard to the powers of the British parliament; but they were *not* in that state of mind—indeed, they were in a very different state of mind—in regard to the powers of their own colonial assemblies. Assisted and encouraged by the growth of their population, they had developed and increased the powers of their assemblies in a steady process of growth; and they had done so

[1] Supra, pp. 265, 283.

particularly in the same period of the eighteenth century in which the British parliament itself was developing its own power. They had waged a crusade—long, sometimes bitter, and always unrelenting—against the colonial governors who came to them from London: they had sought to regulate and pare their salaries; they had pitted their own representative character (and, where they could, their charters) against the commissions and instructions of their governors and all the ways of their governors. They were easily impelled to extend the scope of the struggle. If the British parliament entered the lists against them, the crusade and the challenge of the colonial assemblies would now be directed against the sovereignty of parliament itself.

Soon after the accession of George III the British parliament began to enter the lists. It was led, almost accidentally,[1] to assert, by the Stamp Act of 1764, a sovereign right to tax; and beginning on that slippery slope it was drawn on to assert the theory of a general sovereignty (by the Declaratory Act of 1766) and to

---

[1] It is often said that the Seven Years War precipitated the American War of Independence, by freeing the American colonists from the fear of the French in Canada which had hitherto kept them in restraint. But the effects of the Seven Years War were also felt more directly, and that in at least two ways. In the first place Pitt—a great war-minister, ready to go to any length in order to secure the greatest possible co-operation in the conduct of war (as other war-ministers have also been in later ages)—had promised after 1758 to reimburse the colonists for their military expenditure in the war; and by fulfilling the promise he had left Great Britain so burdened with debt (while the colonies, in comparison, were relatively debt-free), that his successors in office were driven to attempt to tax the colonies on the plea of equality of sacrifice. In the second place the colonists had taken advantage of the emergency of the Seven Years War to press their claims against the colonial governors to new and further lengths; and the governors had again and again been driven to yield to their demands, and had thus increased their growing power to a point at which it invited some pruning and correction. (J. C. Miller, *Origins of the American Revolution*, p. 38 and pp. 35-6.)

If war may be regarded as an accident, it can thus be said that it was 'almost accidentally' that the British parliament was led, in both of these ways, to attempt to assert its sovereignty—partly in order to secure some equality of sacrifice, and partly in order to readjust a disturbed political balance. The moral that emerges is that victory has its defeats. The price of victory in the Seven Years War was concessions that set in motion a train of events which ultimately ended in the surrender of Yorktown. Men and nations pay for what they buy.

attempt to turn that theory into practice. The answer of the colonists to this assertion and this attempt differs at two different periods. In the first and longer period, which extends from 1766 to 1774, they go upon the assumptions: (1) that the colonies are indeed contained as subordinate parts in a whole, which forms a single empire, and as so contained are generally subject to an imperial legislature, but (2) that they are exempt from the control of that legislature in respect of financial laws imposed and enforced for the sake of revenue, and in that respect are immune from the scope and content of the sovereignty of parliament. During the second period—a brief period of little more than a year (1774-5) —they go upon the assumptions: (1) that the colonies are not subordinate parts of a single empire (inasmuch as they are states or autonomous communities in themselves), and are not therefore subject to the legislature at Westminster, which is *not* an imperial legislature and has no extent of sovereignty which carries it across the Atlantic, but (2) that they are still in the allegiance of the English Crown, or rather of the English king acting as their personal king, and acting as such by virtue of a 'personal union' which makes him king simultaneously of two or more separate States.

In the first of these periods (1764-74) the challenge of the colonists is only addressed, as yet, to the scope and content of the powers involved in the sovereignty of parliament. It is only a question of 'How much', and not a question of 'Whether or no'; a question of how much sovereignty parliament may be recognised as possessing, and not a question of whether or no there is any sovereignty at all which extends across the Atlantic. Admitting, or at any rate not denying, that parliament reaches across the seas, the colonists argue, none the less, that the content of its power is limited, and does not include the power of imposing taxes in America, other than those which may be imposed incidentally (in the form of indirect taxes) by virtue of its separate and acknowledged power of regulating the trade of the empire as a whole. Their argument, as we have already seen, was generally based on the plea of 'the rights of the subject'—the rights of the English subject, wherever he might be—under the rules of the English constitution. The rights of the subject were in this way pitted against the sovereignty of parliament; indeed, they were enthroned above it, and made a limit upon it. But the argument, as we have also seen, was an invalid argument; the alleged right of the English subject—not to be taxed without his consent given personally or by his representative—was *not* a right, even in England itself. Nor was this all. There was a further and greater difficulty. Even if it had been a right, it would have been a right which, like all other rights, was subject to the ultimate cognisance and regulation of parliament. It would not have been enthroned as a limit above the sovereignty of parliament; on the contrary, that sovereignty would necessarily have been above it, and therefore a limit upon it. At any rate that was the logic of English constitutional law, if you argued in terms of that law as it stood at the time of your argument. You might indeed seek to escape that logic; but you could only do so by leaving the ground of English constitutional law, and taking your stand on the ground of the law of nature. This was what James Otis was already attempting to do—though with some hesitation and some self-contradiction—as early as 1764; and his attempt demands some examination, all the more as it shows that even during the first period of struggle colonial thinkers were already beginning to take the ground of natural law.

Otis assumes, in his pamphlet of 1764, that parliament has an 'uncontrollable power', or, as he also calls it, a 'supreme, sovereign power'; and herein he is on common ground with the general English thought of the time. But he adds to this assumption two propositions of a different character. One of them is that parliament should be reconstituted on a new imperial basis, with a just and proportionate representation of the colonies.[1] But this first

---

[1] The idea of a new imperial parliament was at one time entertained, but afterwards abandoned, by Franklin; it was also an idea which appealed to Joseph Galloway, though he actually proposed in his 'plan of union', as a second best, a purely American Congress or 'grand council' of all the colonies. Parallel to these three American advocates of the idea (Otis, Franklin and Galloway) there were also three advocates in Great Britain—Thomas Crowley, a Quaker merchant, who proposed in 1766 the election of 'the first parliament

proposition (which he afterwards recanted) was less important than the second. In his second proposition, which is hardly consistent with his assumption of the supreme, sovereign, and uncontrollable power of parliament, Otis advances the view that an act of parliament against any of God's natural laws, which are immutably true, would be contrary to truth, equity, and justice, and consequently void; and he proceeds to the conclusion that it has been—and still, by implication, should be—the function of the judges to declare the nullity of any such act. This is a notable proposition; and it looks both backward and forward. It looks backward, in the sense that the idea of the limitation of the sovereignty of parliament by 'natural laws which are immutably true' is an idea based on the dictum of an English judge of the seventeenth century, Hobart, who had declared in 1614 that an act of parliament against natural equity is void in itself, 'for *jura naturae sunt immutabilia*, and they are *leges legum*'. (On the other hand this dictum of Hobart stands solitary and unparalleled, except for the statement of a similar view by Camden in the House of Lords in 1766; and though Otis affirms the contrary, it seems never to have been applied by any English court.[1]) The proposition of Otis also looks forward, in the sense that the idea of judicial disallowance of legislative acts which are contrary to a higher and overriding law is a herald and forerunner of the power which the federal Supreme Court eventually came to assume after 1787. (On the other hand there is a great difference between judicial disallowance based on a hypothetical law of nature and judicial disallowance based, like that of the Supreme Court, on the actual

of the British Empire'; Francis Maseres, a lawyer of one of the Inns of Court, who published in 1776 a pamphlet on the expediency of admitting American representatives to the House of Commons; and Adam Smith, who in the same year advocated the idea in his chapter on colonies (Book IV, ch. VII) in the *Wealth of Nations*. But the idea had no vogue in England; and it also fell on stony ground in America, where the colonists naturally said: 'We are not interested; we should be outvoted in such a parliament; and besides, if we entertained the idea, we should be sacrificing what we prefer—our own right to tax ourselves by our own assemblies in our own way.'

[1] See Keir and Lawson, *Cases in Constitutional Law*, p. 2. For the statement of Camden in 1766 see above, p. 284.

and known provisions of a written constitution.) But while the proposition of Otis thus looks both backward and forward, it is in itself, and as it stands at the time and date of its enunciation, a proposition which goes outside the sphere of English constitutional law. Otis is really escaping—though he tries to hide his escape from himself, and seeks to argue that he is still moving within the ambit of English courts and the orbit of English judges—into the uncharted world of the general law of nature. It is significant that he quotes from Vattel's *Principes de la Loi Naturelle* in the course of his argument. When he writes that 'there can be no prescription old enough to supersede the law of nature and the grant of God Almighty, who has "given all men a right to be free"', he has really abandoned the logic of English constitutional law for the revolutionary logic of a higher and diviner law.

Already, therefore, in the first period (the period from 1764 to 1774), there were explosive ideas at work, and that in spite of the fact that this period was one of general acceptance of the idea of a single empire and general belief in a single imperial parliament, limited indeed in the content of its powers, but otherwise competent for the whole empire. New ideas emerged, and a new challenge was offered to the sovereignty of parliament, in the second and briefer period which began in 1774 and ended in 1775. After the 'Boston Tea-party', at the end of 1773, and the passing of a number of coercive acts in retaliation by the British parliament, a new situation arose. The Stamp Act of 1764 had raised the one question of taxation. The 'Coercive Acts' raised the whole question of the general legislative sovereignty of parliament. In a word, the old issue of 'How much'—the issue of the exact content of the powers possessed by the British parliament in virtue of its sovereignty—was dropped; and the new question emerged whether the British parliament had any sovereignty at all, and whether any of its powers extended across the Atlantic. The answer given by John Adams of Boston and James Wilson of Philadelphia was an answer in the negative. Parliament, they now argue, possesses no content of power in the colonies, of any sort or kind; and the reason why it possesses no power is the simple fact that the *extent* of its power is limited—limited in the sense that it cannot cross the ocean. The sovereignty of parliament stops short, and ceases altogether, when in touches the American seaboard. The American colonies are sovereign states and autonomous communities. They are ready to recognise the king of Great Britain as also their king, and to pay him allegiance: they are not willing to recognise the British parliament as their parliament, or to pay it any obedience. The king is common, the personal king; but he alone is common. 'There are fourteen parliaments in the empire, one at Westminster, thirteen more in the several capitals of the thirteen colonies.'[1]

This, again, is an argument which looks both backward and forward. It looks backward, in the sense that it marks a reversion from the closer, if still imperfect, imperial system of the eighteenth century to the loose and inchoate relations of the first half of the seventeenth century, when the colonies were still in the process of foundation and the English parliament, still engaged in a struggle with the Crown, was too busy at home to take much thought for affairs overseas. From this point of view it may be contended that the colonists were appealing to history; attempting to go back in time to the period before the Revolution of 1688, which had established parliamentary supremacy; seeking to revert to an old and sole dependence on the Crown, as the one 'Head of the Empire'. But their argument, if it looked backward, and had a historic tinge, may also be said to look forward, and to be a shadow cast before by the coming events of a later age. From this point of view it may be contended that they were anticipating the results of the Imperial Conference of 1926 and the Statute of Westminster of 1931: they were moving towards the view that they were 'autonomous communities...equal in status, in no way subordinate...though united by a common allegiance to the Crown'.[2]

But both as history and as prophecy the colonial argument of this second period (1774–5) was a difficult argument. Historically,

---

[1] C. H. Van Tyne, *England and America*, p. 104.
[2] R. G. Adams, in his *Political Ideas of the American Revolution*, writes in the main from this point of view.

it was more than difficult: it was highly dubious. In the first place, the king to whom alone the colonists now sought to confine their allegiance was a new type of king—not the historic and actual king of the seventeenth century, but a new revolutionary king who was merely a symbol of allegiance, and nothing more than a symbol. The last thing which the colonists desired was a Stuart king who was armed with prerogative. In the second place, and in regard to parliament, it was not the case that the parliament of the seventeenth century (or, for that matter, the parliaments of earlier centuries also) had ever refrained from acting outside the 'realm' of England, or that the parliaments of 1688 and afterwards had been usurpers and encroachers when they proceeded so to act. This was the argument advanced at the time by the colonists, and it has been repeated by a contemporary American historian;[1] but the evidence is clear that even if parliament had legislated less frequently before 1688 for territories beyond the realm than it did after 1688, it had always had the right so to do, and *had* done so from time to time. Prophetically, there is more to be said for the colonial argument. It was an anticipation of the ideas and the practice which were to establish themselves in a later age—an age removed by a century and a half from that of the colonists. We may well regret that the anticipation was removed by so great a span of time from its eventual accomplishment. But we must

---

[1] Professor C. H. McIlwaine, in a work entitled *The American Revolution* (1924), argues that the English parliament, under English constitutional law, could not bind Englishmen beyond the realm; that the Long Parliament usurped this power by an act of 19 May 1649; that the parliaments of 1688 and afterwards adopted and continued the usurpation; and that colonial resistance from 1764 onwards was a just and constitutional resistance to this parliamentary usurpation. His argument is met and answered by another American historian, Professor R. L. Schuyler, in his *Parliament and the British Empire* (1929). He shows that from 1300 onwards the English parliament had legislated for territories or dominions beyond the realm; and he gives a number of instances of such legislation, especially for the Tudor period. King and parliament were never separate; and the king-in-parliament had the same width of extension as the king. The colonial argument of 1774–5 (which separated parliament from the king and denied its competence outside the realm) was thus a revolution, and not the restoration which it professed to be and which Professor McIlwaine attempts to prove that it was.

also recognise that an anticipation of a far-off future is by its nature of little weight, and can exercise little influence, in the logic of the present. To live in the logic of the present, during the years 1774-5, was to live under a king-in-parliament who was sovereign not only for the realm but also for the dominions beyond the realm. You might try to escape from that system either into the past or into the future, appealing either to history or prophecy. You might go back to the seventeenth century, when king and parliament seemed to be separate, and you might say that you would make it your standard. But whether or no your interpretation of the seventeenth century was accurate, you were actually living in the eighteenth century and under the conditions of the eighteenth century. Again, you might go forward into the twentieth century —if you could see the shadow of coming events. But again, you were living in the eighteenth century, under its actual conditions of a king-in-parliament competent both for the realm and for the dominions beyond the realm. Escape from the present had to be made *in* the present. Under the conditions of the present, any escape which was made *in* the present must be a total escape from the whole British constitution. The conditions of the present were a king-in-parliament ubiquitously competent. You could not have the pseudo-antiquarian or the prophetic figure of the 'king-outside-parliament'. If you ejected parliament, you ejected also the king. If you left the British constitution in part, you also left it *in toto*. You went simply and altogether outside the constitution— not into its past; not into its future; but simply outside it—and you faced the fact of revolution.

This was what was eventually done in 1776. The ideas of the second period had proved more explosive than those of the first; and the doctrine of John Adams and James Wilson had ended in total secession. They had begun by rejecting parliament: the Declaration of Independence completed their work by rejecting the king. The whole stress of the Declaration was laid on the king's iniquities. It had to be. The king was the last link left by the development of the colonial argument; and in cutting the last link left, it was necessary to enlarge, and even to concentrate, on the imperfections of the last link. But the imperfections of George III were only a negative ground; and in any momentous crisis of destiny men and communities will always seek a positive justification. What was the positive justification for going outside the English constitution? It could not be anything in the constitution. It could only be something outside it. It could only be 'the Laws of Nature and of Nature's God'—these, and the 'unalienable rights', proceeding from those laws, to 'life, liberty, and the pursuit of happiness'.

3. The Declaration of Independence enunciates finally and authentically the radical idea which had long been stirring in the American mind. However much the colonists had sought to base themselves on actual law and actual rights—whether they alleged their own charters or compacts, or the legal rights of all English subjects, or the legal limits of the sovereignty of parliament (either in content or in extent) under the English constitution—they had all along been ultimately driven from each of the grounds they alleged to the final ground of natural law and their natural rights; and they had always mixed an appeal to that law and those rights with the arguments which they attempted to draw from actual law and actual rights. Fundamentally, the appeal they made to natural law and natural rights was an appeal to their own ideas of what ought to be law and what ought to be rights—no matter what law might actually be or what rights actually were. Jefferson once said of Patrick Henry, who refused to trust in charters, that he 'drew all natural rights from a purer source—the feelings of his own heart'.[1] The feelings of their own hearts about what ought to be were the inspiration of the colonists generally. Any revolution—and the American Revolution *was* a revolution—must base itself on those feelings. There can be no revolution—no attempt to substitute what ought to be for what is—on any other basis. The colonists had found that the actual rights belonging to them as colonists under their charters were not enough. They had found that the actual rights belonging to them as Englishmen under the English constitution were not enough. They therefore claimed the

[1] Quoted in J. C. Miller, *Origins of the American Revolution*, p. 128.

ideal rights belonging to them as men under the common law of mankind and the natural law of God. They claimed that a people was entitled to live as it felt in its heart—when the feelings of its heart were lifted to the universal plane of nature—that it ought to live and *must* live. A people which makes that claim, and makes it resolutely, is likely to have its way. But to make that claim is to go outside the orbit of actual law.

The first continental congress, in 1774, was still seeking, as it were, to run three horses abreast—the several charters or compacts; the principles of the English constitution; the immutable laws of nature. It began accordingly by referring to the immunities and privileges granted to the colonies by royal charters, or secured by their several codes of provincial laws. Then it referred to Blackstone's list of the three primary rights of all Englishmen; and it also invoked (by implication, and by citing clauses and borrowing phrases from the English Bill of Rights) his further list of the five 'auxiliary rights' belonging to all English subjects. But the essence of its Declaration and Resolves is the ultimate and final reference to the immutable laws of nature; and when the congress recited a number of acts of parliament as 'infringements and violations of the rights of the colonists', it was putting its trust in the leading horse of natural law. This is much the same as to say that it was putting its trust in Samuel Adams. He was one of the delegates to the Congress, and one of the most active delegates. He had brought with him from Boston ideas of the law of nature which he was resolved to press. We may almost say that it was he who entered natural law for the running.

In appealing to the immutable laws of nature the colonists were not merely appealing to the feelings of their own hearts or their own ideas of what ought to be. They were indeed doing that; but they were also doing something more. They were expressing a set of ideas current in the continental law-books of the school of Natural Law (the books of Pufendorf, Burlamaqui and Vattel), which their own lawyers had read, and upon which their lawyers drew. Nor was it only in such law books that this set of ideas could be found. It could also be found in Locke, who not only knew

Hooker's theory of the principles of natural law, but was also acquainted with the speculations of some of the continental jurists who belonged to the school of natural law.[1] (He had lived for a time in Holland, and he knew the thought of the continent.) What is more curious, and even paradoxical, is that this set of ideas might also be found in the pages of the sober Blackstone, who had incorporated the ideas of Pufendorf and Burlamaqui (but more especially of Burlamaqui) in the general introduction to his *Commentaries*. (It is true that he contradicted them afterwards, and contradicted them flatly, in the *Commentaries* themselves; but it was easy to read and absorb and quote the earlier *dicta* of Blackstone without noticing, or perhaps even reading, the later course of his argument.)[2] The sword of Blackstone was two-edged. It could cut in favour of colonial claims as well as of British rights.

It has already been noticed that the colonists had also another source, over and above all the law-books whether continental or English, for the set of ideas about natural law and the natural rights of man which they were seeking to express. They had also—at any rate in New England, and especially in Massachusetts, if not in Virginia and the South—the minister, the pulpit, and the sermon. The theological appeal to the laws of righteousness and equity, and to the everlasting tables of right reason, was a consecration of the legal appeal to the laws and tables of nature. Samuel Adams felt the force, and availed himself of the strength, of this consecration; he could speak, and speak with conviction, of 'our rights... to enjoy that liberty wherewith Christ has made us free'. But in the colonies generally—in Pennsylvania, for example, and perhaps still more in Virginia—it was the *legal* appeal to the laws and tables

---

[1] Professor Becker, in his work on *The Declaration of Independence*, remarks: 'The lineage is direct: Jefferson copied Locke and Locke quoted Hooker.' But Locke had read and used other writers as well as Hooker.

[2] An example may be cited. Professor Van Tyne (*The Causes of the War of Independence*, p. 237) asks: 'What did Christopher Gadsden [a planter of South Carolina, who had been to school in England] mean by allusion to those "latent though inherent rights of society, which no climate, no time, no constitution, no contract, can ever destroy or diminish"?' The answer is simple. Gadsden was merely quoting Blackstone—except that he transposed the opening words, which in Blackstone's text are 'inherent (though latent)'.

of nature, and to the statement of those laws and tables to be found in law-books, which mainly and mostly gave shape and form, definition and expression, to the surging feelings of the heart. 'Natural law was the first line of defence of colonial liberty.'[1] The note of natural law, if it is not dominant until 1776, is constant from the beginning of the period of the Revolution. In 1762 Massachusetts already pleads 'the natural rights of the colonists—the same with those of all other British subjects, and indeed of all mankind'. In 1764 James Otis is already quoting Vattel's book, published six years before, *Principes de la Loi Naturelle*. In 1765 Christopher Gadsden is already urging the colonists to 'stand upon the broad common ground of those natural rights which we all know and feel as men and as descendants of Englishmen'. Samuel Adams, from first to last, was eloquent of nature and nature's rights. Jefferson achieved the final and classical expression of the American idea of natural law; but he said himself that all the authority of that expression was derived from 'the harmonizing sentiments of the day, whether expressed in conversation, in letters, printed essays, or the elementary books of public right'. He was the Justinian of his day, who codified prevalent sentiments; but

> Justinian's Pandects only make precise
> What simply sparkled in men's eyes before...
> Waited the speech they called.

There were two ways in which the theory of natural law affected American thought and action. The first way was that of destruction. It served as a charge of powder which blasted the connection with Great Britain and cleared the way for the Declaration of Independence. The second way was that of construction. It served as a foundation for the building of new constitutions in the independent colonies from 1776 onwards, and for the addition to those constitutions (or rather to some of them) of an entrance-hall or façade called a declaration of rights. The idea of nature can be

---

[1] J. C. Miller, *Origins of the American Revolution*, p. 126. He also notes that 'what Americans particularly relished in John Locke was his emphasis upon natural law'.

revolutionary; but it can also promote and support evolution. It worked in both ways in the American colonies. First it made revolution; and then, when that was done, it fostered evolution. In order to understand its accomplishment, we must pause to consider its principles and to examine its potentialities.

IV

We may begin by noting (for it is a fact of crucial importance) that the English thinkers and lawyers of the eighteenth century have little regard for natural law and natural rights. Indeed, it may be said that natural law is generally repugnant to the genius of English legal thought, generally busied with a 'common law' which, however common, is still peculiar, and anyhow is sufficiently actual, sufficiently practical, sufficiently definite, to suit the English temper. To Burke any speech of natural law and natural rights is metaphysics, and not politics. To Blackstone—though he is inconsistent, writing in one way when he theorises on the nature of laws in general, and in another when he comments on the laws of England—the law of nature is not a concern of English courts, and may therefore be treated, for their purposes, as non-existent. To Bentham, when he wrote the *Fragment on Government* in 1776, the law of nature was 'nothing but a phrase': its natural tendency was 'to impel a man, by the force of conscience, to rise up in arms against any law whatever that he happens not to like'; and a far better clue—indeed 'the only clue to guide a man through these straits'—was the principle of utility.

The general view of the English thinkers of the period may be resumed in two propositions. In the first place, law is a body of rules which is recognised and enforced in courts of law; and it is simply that body of rules. Since the courts of law recognise and enforce both the judge-made law of tradition and the statute law enacted by parliament, law is these two things, and only these two things. Since, again, the judge-made law of tradition may be regarded as an *opus perfectum* (so, at any rate, Blackstone seems to think), and since law now grows only or mainly by the addition of the statutes enacted by parliament—since, in a word, it is parliament only which now gives new rules to the judges, either by amending the law of the past, both judge-made and parliament-made, or by enacting fresh law *de novo*—parliament must be acknowledged as 'the sovereign legislative', maker and author supreme of all law, an uncontrollable authority acting by its own motion, 'as essential to the body politic' (so a member of parliament declared) 'as the Deity to religion'. Such is the gist and sweep of the first of the two propositions. The second proposition is similar, and may be said to be consequential. It is a proposition affirming that constitutional law is not in any way different in kind from the rest of the law, but is merely a part of the general law. It is simply that part of the general law which, as Paley says, 'regulates the form of the legislative'. Being part of the general law, it is subject, like all other law, to the control of the sovereign legislature—which thus regulates itself and determines its own form. You cannot therefore distinguish between constitutional law and ordinary law, or say that the one is made and amended by one process and the other by another. In origin, and in kind, the two are simply identical; and they are under the same control. You cannot say that a law is unconstitutional; if it *is* a law—that is to say, if it is made by parliament—it is necessarily constitutional. In a word, the legal is also the constitutional: 'the terms *constitutional* and *unconstitutional*', as Paley writes, 'mean the legal and illegal.'

In the light of these two propositions we may now turn to natural law, and note how it differs from English law in regard to both. The origin of the idea of natural law may be ascribed to an old and indefeasible movement of the human mind (we may trace it already in the *Antigone* of Sophocles) which impels it towards the notion of an eternal and immutable justice; a justice which human authority expresses, or ought to express—but does not make; a justice which human authority may fail to express—and must pay the penalty for failing to express by the diminution, or even the forfeiture, of its power to command. This justice is conceived as being the higher or ultimate law, proceeding from the nature of the universe—from the Being of God and the reason of man. It follows that law—in the sense of the law of the last resort—is somehow above law-making. It follows that law-makers, after all, are somehow under and subject to law.

The movement of the mind of man towards these conceptions and their consequences is already apparent in the *Ethics* and the *Rhetoric* of Aristotle.[1] But it was among the Stoic thinkers of the Hellenistic age that the movement first attained a large and general expression; and that expression, as has already been noticed in an earlier essay,[2] became a tradition of human civility which runs continuously from the Stoic teachers of the Porch to the American Revolution of 1776 and the French Revolution of 1789. Allied to theology for many centuries—adopted by the Catholic Church, and forming part of the general teaching of the schoolmen and the canonists—the theory of Natural Law had become in the sixteenth century, and continued to remain during the seventeenth and the eighteenth, an independent and rationalist system, professed and expounded by the philosophers of the secular school of natural law. Hooker, indeed, may still be said to belong to the medieval tradition; but the general theory of the seventeenth century, as we find it in Grotius, Pufendorf, and Locke (and also in Hobbes and Spinoza), is a modern and secular theory. Most of the continental writers of the secular school of natural law composed their treatises in Latin; and this, as it diminished their influence in the contemporary world of general readers, has also served to obscure the importance of their ideas in the judgement of posterity. But Grotius and Pufendorf could both be read in a French translation;[3] and during the eighteenth century Swiss writers on natural law—Burlamaqui and Vattel—were publishing their works in French.

---

[1] On the idea of 'natural justice' in the *Ethics* see the writer's translation of the *Politics*, pp. 365–6, and on the idea of 'natural law' in the *Rhetoric* see pp. 369 and 372.

[2] *Supra*, pp. 10–11.

[3] The Huguenot Barbeyrac had translated and annotated Grotius's *De jure belli et pacis*; and he had done the same for two of the works of Pufendorf—his *De jure naturae et gentium* (1672), and his *De officio hominis et civis secundum legem naturalem* (1673).

It is perhaps the language of these Swiss writers rather than their originality (the work of Vattel, for instance, was largely based on the *Institutiones juris naturae et gentium* of the Halle professor Christian Wolff) which explains their vogue. But it would be unjust to withhold the meed of recognition which is due to the eighteenth-century writers of Switzerland who dealt with law and politics. They include Rousseau (himself not untouched in his theory by the influence of speculation on natural law), as well as Burlamaqui: they include de Lolme, the author of a work, famous in its day, on *La Constitution d'Angleterre*, as well as Vattel. Switzerland gave much to the world—and not least a clear statement of the theory of natural law—in the days when revolution was simmering in America and in France.[1]

There were two conceptions which Americans could draw, and were actually beginning to draw in the years before 1776, from their reading of the Swiss and other writers who dealt with the theme of natural law. Both of these conceptions were very different in character from the two propositions in which we have sought to resume the views of the English thinkers of the period. According to the first conception, law is more than a body of rules recognised and enforced in courts of law. There are two laws, and not one only. There is natural law, the law of reason, the law which ought to be; there is positive law, the law of tradition, the law which actually is. The former may be called a juristic (or even a philosophic) concept: the latter is the law of actual practice and daily enforcement. Yet the former is regarded, none the less, as in some way overswaying the latter; and a positive law which runs counter to the higher law of nature is conceived as a law which lacks the sanction of inner authority. This conception has its attractions. There is something dazzling about the idea of a law which comes from the very nature of man, 'as he comes from the

---

[1] See above, p. 238, n. 1. Burlamaqui, de Lolme, and Rousseau all belonged to Geneva. Vattel came from Neuchatel. All their books were recent and current at the time of the American Revolution. Burlamaqui's *Principes du droit naturel* was the oldest, and had appeared in 1747. Vattel's *Principes* appeared in 1758; Rousseau's *Du Contrat Social* in 1762; de Lolme's book on the English Constitution in 1771.

hand of his Maker'; a law out of time, and eternal; a law out of space, and ubiquitous. But it is also a difficult conception. Who knows exactly what natural law is? Who enforces it regularly in cases of conflict between its prescriptions (at the best indeterminate) and the definite rules of positive law? The answer of the jurists of the school of natural law has an uncertain sound. Positive law, they felt, should properly be other than it was. But while it was what it was—while there were courts behind it who knew and could state what it was, and a sovereign behind the courts who was ready and able to enforce their findings—had it not better be obeyed?

The second conception which could be drawn from the writings of continental jurists of the school of natural law offered less difficulty; and, indeed, it was destined to have a long and lasting influence in American history. According to this conception a distinction has to be drawn between 'fundamental law', which regulates the constitution, and the ordinary or civil law of the land. This distinction is clearly drawn in the first book of Vattel's treatise, in a passage well known to Samuel Adams and the members of the Boston *sodalitas*.[1] The nation itself establishes the constitution, and is thereby the author and maker of fundamental law: the legislative has only the power *d'abroger les anciennes Loix Civiles et les Loix Politiques non-fondamentales, et d'en faire de nouvelles.* So far as the legislative is concerned, the fundamental laws should be sacred, because they stand above it; and they should equally be stable, because they stand outside it and are 'excepted from its commission'. *C'est de la Constitution que ces Législateurs tiennent leur pouvoir; comment pourroient-ils la changer, sans détruire le fondement de leur Autorité?*[2]

If we put together these two conceptions—that of the distinction between natural and positive law, and that of the distinction

---

[1] Book I, ch. III, § 34.

[2] This is a passage quoted by Otis in his *Rights of the British Colonies* in 1764 (see Van Tyne, *The Causes of the War of Independence*, pp. 230-1). It has already been noted (supra, p. 279) that Vattel was quoted in a memorial addressed by Massachusetts to its agent in Great Britain in 1765, and that his opinions were echoed in a Concord town-meeting of 1776.

between fundamental and ordinary or civil law—we shall see that they impose a double limit on the legislature. It is limited by fundamental law, in the sense that it cannot, of itself, vary or add to that law: it is limited also by natural law, in the sense that, even when acting in its own sphere of ordinary or civil law, it cannot, or should not, run counter to the principles of natural law. We may add that the two limits—that of fundamental law and that of natural law—may be easily equated, or even identified. In other words, it is possible to argue that fundamental law, or the law of the constitution, is simply a form or expression of natural law. Such an argument may be defended in two ways, or on two grounds. In the first place, you may plead that when a nation makes its constitution it is acting according to the natural law which authorises any society of free men freely to determine the permanent basis and form of their social life. In the second place you may plead that, in addition to acting by natural law in the *process* of creating a constitution, a nation may also incorporate natural law in the *product* which it creates. It will do so if it adds to its constitution a declaration of the rights of man—the rights belonging to man by virtue of the law of nature: and it will do so even more clearly if (as the people of Pennsylvania, for example, did in 1776) it declares the declaration 'to be a part of the constitution never to be violated on any pretence whatever'.

This equation or identification of fundamental law, or the law of the constitution, with the law of nature was something which, as we shall see presently, had a peculiar appeal to American thought and a particular influence in American history. But before we turn to that theme we shall do well to pause for a moment, and to notice that even in English thought the idea of a superior natural law, and that of a 'sacred' and 'stable' fundamental law of the constitution, had both been once entertained. We may, if we wish, pit the two propositions which resume the views of the English thinkers of the eighteenth century against the very different conceptions which could be drawn from the views of Vattel and the other writers of the school of natural law. But, having done so, we are bound to add that conceptions similar to those of Vattel

316

and the other writers on natural law can clearly be traced in the English thought of the seventeenth century. This is a fact which may serve to explain their ready adoption by the American colonists. If they had been merely the conceptions of continental jurists, they might have been less welcome. When they could be traced in the *dicta* of the English lawyers and the English constitutional documents of the seventeenth century, they could claim a native pedigree.

We may begin with the idea of the overriding supremacy of the law of nature as against actual or positive law. That was an idea which, as we have already had reason to notice,[1] Hobart had expressed in the case of *Day* v. *Savadge* (1614), when he had said that 'even an Act of Parliament made against natural equity...is void in itself; for *jura naturae sunt immutabilia*, and they are *leges legum*'. The doctrine, it is true, was never applied by any court: it remained, as it were, suspended in the air. But it was remembered and quoted by colonial lawyers over a century and a half after it had been enunciated; and they could argue that it had been confirmed by Locke ('the law of nature stands as an eternal rule to all men, legislators and others'), and was being corroborated in their own time by Lord Camden, when he argued in Parliament in 1766 that 'you cannot enact anything against divine law', and appealed on behalf of the Americans to 'the natural law of mankind and the immutable laws of justice'.[2] The other idea—that of a

---

[1] Supra, p. 302.

[2] Supra, p. 284. The American lawyers, it may be added, used another and parallel, but different, doctrine, which they also found in English law-books of the seventeenth century. This was a doctrine, not that there was an overriding *natural* law, common to 'all peoples that on earth do dwell', but that there was an overriding *native* law, peculiar to the people that dwells in England (and in the English dominions), such that an 'Act of Parliament...against Magna Carta and the natural rights of Englishmen...is therefore...null and void'. It was a doctrine which the American lawyers drew from the *dicta* of 'Lord Coke', who had sought to assert the unalterable sovereignty of one part of English law (the part which dealt with the elementary liberties enshrined in Magna Carta and the main rules of the common law) over all the rest, and to make it the final arbiter in the disputes between king and parliament. This is a peculiar view, which may be traced even before Coke (medieval parliaments had sometimes sought to make Magna Carta an unalterable fundamental), but which died with

sacred and stable 'fundamental law' of the constitution—had a less respectable pedigree. You could not here quote law reports, backed by the authority of Locke and the eloquence of Lord Camden. You could only quote (if you thought it politic, and there is no evidence that the American lawyers did) the example of the Instrument of Government of 1653. That was hardly a respectable authority: it belonged to a period of interregnum, which was a blank in the statute book. But Americans could remember—even if they did not say—that the Instrument contained fundamental provisions which were above parliament, were outside parliament, were therefore not alterable by parliament, and indeed were not alterable at all or by any sort of method.

Even in the eighteenth century the ghost of the idea of natural law continues occasionally to haunt English thought. ('The undying spirit of that law', Gierke once wrote, 'can never be extinguished: if it is denied entry into the body of positive law, it flutters about the room like a ghost.') It was a ghost which visited Blackstone. Borrowing, in the introduction to his *Commentaries*, from the Swiss Burlamaqui, without understanding the explosive nature of the borrowed material (or even acknowledging that it was borrowed), he postulates a 'law of nature, coeval with mankind...superior in obligation', and such that 'no human laws are of any validity if contrary to this'. But having admitted the ghost in one section of his introduction, he banishes it in another. When he comes to the point, and asks himself what the judges are to do if parliament enacts an unreasonable law, he denies them at once any power to reject it; for 'that were to set the judicial power

Coke. It is something separate from the idea of the overriding supremacy of the law of nature, though it has some analogy to that idea.

At the same time it is to be noted that Coke himself, in his earlier life, had paid homage to the law of nature. In Calvin's case (1608) he had argued that the allegiance of the subject to the sovereign was due by the law of nature; that this law of nature was part of the laws of England; that the law of nature was before any judicial or municipal law in the world; and that the law of nature was immutable and could not be changed. True, he was arguing for the natural duty of allegiance. But his argument might be used for other purposes. John Adams of Boston knew, and used, his argument. (McLaughlin, op. cit. p. 130, n. 1.)

above that of the legislature, which would be subversive of all government'. In the same sort of way, and in a similar sphere, we find Bentham toying with the idea of a fundamental law of the constitution which may limit the legislature. He calls it (the argument comes in the anonymous *Fragment on Government* of 1776) by the name of an 'express convention'. But he confines his idea of an express convention limiting the legislature to the one case of federal unions, where (and where only) he conceives that the act of union—the constitutional document expressing the terms of union—may limit the future action of the legislative body. This is an anticipation of the American constitution of 1787 (and a notable anticipation), rather than a reflection which casts light backwards on the case of the American colonists before 1776. Even within the limited range of his 'express convention' Bentham was still very cautious about admitting the notion of an unalterable fundamental. Having made a concession, he draws back at once. 'God forbid', he writes, 'that the limit itself should not be alterable in the future by some process, if the march of history and the need of reform demand.' He would limit the legislature by a fundamental document in one case, and one case only; but even in that case he would not limit the march of history and the need of reform by unalterabilities. He had an English fear of the mirage of fixed and unalterable verities, which has sometimes led churches to tie their hands by unalterable confessions and institutions, as it has also led states to mortgage their future by unalterable declarations and constitutions—both forgetting (as he would have said) 'the march of history'; both forgetting that the one thing fixed and unalterable is change.

We may thus allow that English thought—particularly in the seventeenth century, but also, in some measure, in the eighteenth—could occasionally pay homage to the law of nature and to the idea of fundamental law; and we may therefore admit that the American lawyers of the period of the Revolution could appeal to English thought as well as to that of the European jurists who belonged to the school of natural law. But it is important to notice, if we are to understand the eventual breach between

England and America and the separate development of American thought, that the general run of English ideas was away from, and not towards, the 'natural' and the 'fundamental'. The English thinkers, practical and even pragmatical, preferred to emphasise the positive character and the parliamentary basis of law. They remained generally faithful to the two propositions in which we have sought to resume the essence of their ideas:[1] (1) The only law was that of the courts: parliament only could give law to the courts; and when parliament had given it, that law was law, and could not be criticised or checked by any supposed law of nature. Americans who quoted the law of nature must be 'in an original state of true Indian innocence';[2] they were embracing the dangerous doctrine that 'the obedience of the subject is not due to the laws and legislature of the realm farther than he, in his private judgment, shall think it conformable to the ideas he has formed of a free constitution...'.[3] Not that the English thinkers of the eighteenth century were in favour of passive obedience, or believed that a law must always and in any case be accepted. On the contrary they recognised and championed the right of civic resistance. Blackstone, for instance, allows resistance, as an 'exertion of the inherent (though latent) powers of society', if necessity and the safety of the whole should require a recourse to that last extremity; and Bentham and Paley, as we have already noticed,[4] are equally ready to allow resistance, in the name of the sovereign principle of utility, if an act of government tends to diminish the general happiness of the community. It is not the right of resistance which English thinkers deny. What they deny is that, when you resist the law, you can plead that you are standing on the ground of law—the ground of a supposed law of nature. What they assert is that, when you resist the law, you are going outside the law—as, in a given contingency, they are willing to

[1] Supra, pp. 311–12.
[2] Quoted from an English newspaper article of 1775, in J. C. Miller's *Origins of the American Revolution*, p. 156.
[3] The protest of the House of Lords, in 1766, against the repeal of the Stamp Act, quoted by Van Tyne, *The Causes of the War of Independence*, pp. 224–5.
[4] Supra, p. 241.

allow that you may. (2) Just as, in the English view, there was no such thing as a natural law which could be pitted against the positive law, so there was also no such thing as a fundamental law which was separate from, and superior to, the rest of the law. There was no law of the constitution which stood above and outside the law made by the legislature and recognised by the courts. You could not appeal to the law of the constitution, any more than you could appeal to the law of nature, as the ground for disobeying a law. The law of the constitution was simply one part of the law, on the same footing as the rest; and it was nothing more.

V

The attitude of the colonists was inevitably very different. It is true that they too were Englishmen, and as such by their nature legally-minded. On the other hand, they were determined to resist, and to vindicate what, in their view, were their rights. But they also wanted to resist by proper process of law, and they wished to be sure that their rights *were* rights—legal rights—rights based and entrenched in law. There was a necessary dualism in the position which they had to adopt and the case which they had to defend. One side of their nature drove them to bid defiance to law; another side impelled them, and impelled them no less strongly, to invoke the comfort of law. In the dualism of their position they naturally caught at the idea of a corresponding dualism of law. Englishmen at home might be unitarians, seeing all law as one, and as one *in gremio parliamenti*; the Englishman across the seas was different, and he could readily turn into a dualist, finding a second and higher law *in gremio suo*, and opposing it to the lower law of parliament or any other human authority. Not that this was really a 'turning', or a sudden conversion from previous darkness into the new light of nature and nature's law. It was an old conviction of the Puritans that there was a law of God which stood above the laws of men—'eternal laws of truth, wisdom and equity', as Mayhew had said in his sermon of 1750, 'and the everlasting tables of right reason, that cannot be repealed or thrown down and broken'. When Samuel Adams and James Otis became the modern disciples of Vattel, they were also recovering and renewing an old inheritance of their own soil.

In the first phase of its operation, down to the Declaration of Independence adopted by the continental congress on 4 July 1776, the law of nature, with its corollary of fundamental law, was a weapon of resistance, an instrument of revolution, a destructive force which abrogated the connection between the American colonies and Britain. The colonists defied law, parliament-made law, in the name of law—the law 'natural' and the law 'fundamental', both conceived as standing above parliament, and either regarded as being connected or even identical with the other.[1] Engaged in resistance, and using the 'inherent (though latent) powers of society' which Blackstone himself had allowed, they based their use of those powers on the inherent though latent law of nature, and boldly opposed what they thought ought to be to what actually was. 'Whenever men become sufficiently dissatisfied with what is, with the existing regime of positive law and custom, they will be found reaching out beyond it for the rational basis of what they conceive ought to be. This is what the Americans did in their controversy with Great Britain; and this rational basis they found in that underlying preconception which shaped the thought of their age—the idea of natural law and natural right.'[2]

The ground thus taken broadened the issue, and broadened it in two ways. In the first place, the adoption of natural law as the ground of struggle produced a general war of ideas, and a great debate of rival theories, which engaged the attention of a listening world. Lord Acton laid emphasis on this result, in his lectures on the French Revolution. Quoting the words which Daniel Webster had applied to the action of the American colonies ('they went to war against a preamble: they fought seven years against a declaration'), he noted that 'the contest was plainly a contest of principles, and was conducted entirely on principles by both sides'.[3] A

---

[1] Supra, p. 316.
[2] C. Becker, *The Declaration of Independence*, p. 134.
[3] Lord Acton, *Lectures on the French Revolution*, p. 25.

contest of principles (nowadays called 'a conflict of ideologies') has its dangerous side. It leads to the statement of logical extremities: it carries issues out of the haze which is the natural climate of compromise. But it has also its finer side; and this became clear in the course of the struggle. The particular was lifted to the level of the universal; rights were vindicated for their own sake, and not on the ground of consequence; they were claimed as common liberties, and not as peculiar franchises. The colonists felt that they were defending a common cause—the cause of Corsica and Paoli (whom France had expelled in 1769); the cause of Poland, which had undergone the first partition in 1772; the cause of Sweden, which had suffered a *coup d'état* in the same year.[1] They could thus transform, and by transforming diffuse, the old principles of Locke and the Whigs; and henceforth 'the uprooted Whig, detached from his parchments and precedents, his leading families and historic conditions, exhibited new qualities'.[2]

This broadening of the struggle into a war of ideas, or contest of principles, thus naturally led to a second broadening. A contest based upon principles for which universality is claimed is bound to be also a contest of universal effect and influence. The uprooted and generalised Whig was necessarily also a world-Whig. The enunciation of the law of nature and its system of natural rights was a spark which travelled everywhere. Emerson wrote of the farmers of Concord, sniping at the British in 1775, that they

> ...fired the shot heard round the world.

It was not so much 'the embattled farmers' whose guns were so universally heard: it was rather the thinkers and lawyers, gathered in the continental congress in 1776, whose words—only words, but words can matter far more than guns—were universally broadcast. The movement of revolution which was destined to traverse Europe began first in Philadelphia, in that year 1776. We

---

[1] J. C. Miller, *Origins of the American Revolution*, p. 331. The sad thing was that the vindicators of liberty were also the men who denied it to the loyalists among themselves, and imposed a compulsory conformity by every form of pressure.

[2] Lord Acton, op. cit. p. 26.

who live in Europe too readily see the year 1789 as the year in which it was said: 'Behold, I will make all things new.' A wider view will show us that the year of change was the year 1776. There had indeed been ideas of change in Europe—particularly in France, and above all in Paris—even before 1776. But 'the spark that changed thought into action', as Acton said, 'was supplied by the Declaration of American Independence'. 'It surpassed in force', he added, in a passage already quoted, 'all the speculation of Paris and Geneva, for it had undergone the test of experiment, and its triumph was the most memorable thing that had been seen by men.'[1]

The appeal to natural law which inspired the Declaration, and served as the destructive force which 'broke the bonds' of Britain, was an appeal originally indigenous to Boston and proceeding from the temper of the clergy and the lawyers of Massachusetts. Otis had already made the appeal at the time of the Stamp Act, in 1764, pleading that government 'has an everlasting foundation in the unchangeable will of God, the author of nature, whose laws never vary', and concluding that 'an Act of Parliament...against any of his natural laws...would be contrary to eternal truth, equity, and justice, and consequently void'.[2] Samuel Adams had echoed the appeal, ingeminating 'the immutable laws of nature', and inducing the Massachusetts assembly and the town-meetings of Boston and Concord to repeat his ingemination. An indefatigable apostle, he induced the Boston committee of correspondence, in 1774, to proclaim, 'We are entitled to life, liberty and the means of sustenance by the grace of Heaven' (words which are almost echoed in Jefferson's phrase, in the Declaration, that 'men are endowed by their Creator with certain inalienable rights', among them 'life, liberty, and the pursuit of happiness'); and carrying his gospel to Philadelphia, in the same year, he had

---

[1] Lord Acton, op. cit. p. 20.

[2] *Rights of the British Colonies* (in S. E. Morison's *Documents of the American Revolution*, pp. 5, 7; see also above, p. 302.) The treatises of John Wise, republished in 1772, may also be counted among the forerunners of the Declaration (supra, p. 274 and n.).

helped to insert an appeal to 'the immutable laws of nature' in the Declaration and Resolves of the first Continental Congress.[1] Moving from Boston to Philadelphia, the appeal to the law of nature travelled further still, and came to Virginia. Here it entered the mind, and found its final and classical expression from the pen, of Thomas Jefferson. Using the authority of what he called 'the harmonising sentiments of the day', and adding to them the fruits of his own wide reading in the radical political theory of seventeenth-century England and eighteenth-century France, he became the draftsman of natural-law principles not only for his own countrymen, but also, through them, for the world. The inscription on his tombstone, which records him as 'author of the Declaration of American Independence and the statute of Virginia for religious freedom' (and also 'father of the University of Virginia') was an inscription of his own choice; and it is as just as it is simple. But he was an 'author', as indeed he himself admitted,[2] only in the sense in which codifiers are authors. He only made precise what was already waiting speech; or rather, he only said finally what others were already saying. The first clause of the Virginia Bill of Rights, drafted by George Mason, contains the essence of the preamble to the Declaration of Independence; and the Virginia Bill of Rights bears a date which is three weeks prior to that of the Declaration.[3]

The Declaration of Independence made natural law the basis of resistance and the ground of secession. But it not only contained an appeal to the final principles of natural law: it also contained, or at any rate implied, a theory of the British Empire—a theory of what it should be (or rather a theory of what it should have been, and was not) which is designed to explain why it had to be left and why a secession had become inevitable. There is in it, as

---

[1] Supra, p. 308.   [2] Supra, p. 310.

[3] The first clause of the Virginia Bill of Rights has, however, its differences. Reciting 'that all men are by nature equally free and independent, and have certain inherent rights', it recites those rights as consisting in 'the enjoyment of life and liberty, with the means of acquiring and possessing property, and pursuing and obtaining happiness and safety'. Jefferson's recital, which omits property, is confined to the seven words 'life, liberty, and the pursuit of happiness'.

an American historian has said,[1] 'a close union of the natural-rights philosophy of government with a conception of the empire as a confederation of free peoples submitting themselves to the same king by a voluntary compact freely entered into, and terminable, in the case of any member, at the will of the people concerned'. It is true, as the same writer adds, that while 'the natural-rights philosophy, although clearly formulated, is not argued but... taken for granted, the theory of British-colonial relations is not even formulated', but only implied in the long statement of grievances against the British king. But there is such a theory of the British Empire, as that empire should be, in the background of the Declaration; and the theory is not only combined, but also connected, with the natural-rights philosophy. It is by virtue of natural law, and in consequence of the inherent 'right of the people to alter or to abolish' any form of government destructive of the ends of society and the natural rights of its members, that Jefferson assumes a conception of empire as properly a society of 'autonomous communities...freely associated as members'. Here, in its theory of empire as well as in its philosophy of natural rights, the Declaration opens a door to vistas of the future. If the natural-rights philosophy is a prelude to the French Revolution and the movement of European liberalism, the theory of empire is a harbinger of the conception of the British Commonwealth defined by the Balfour Committee of the Imperial Conference of 1926 and enshrined in the Statute of Westminster of 1931.[2]

We have spoken of the first phase of the idea of natural law, down to the Declaration of Independence, as showing its destructive force as an instrument of revolution. Even in that phase, however, as the course of the argument has shown, the idea was also constructive. It not only broke the bonds of the ancient British connection: it also universalised the old and parochial

[1] Becker, *Declaration of Independence*, p. 130.
[2] The writer would here refer to his *Ideas and Ideals of the British Empire*, pp. 94–103, and to R. G. Adams' *Political Ideas of the American Revolution*, which seeks to bring those ideas into connection with the movement of opinion in the British Commonwealth during and after the War of 1914–18.

philosophy of Whiggism, making it an 'international extra-territorial' power, and it also pointed ahead to a new conception, and a new definition of empire. In the second phase of its operation, which is already beginning in 1776 with the foundation of new constitutions in each of the separate states, the idea becomes entirely positive and wholly constructive.

We may distinguish two different periods of positive and constructive work in the stage of American development which stretches from 1776 onwards. The first stage was that of the making of new state constitutions for each of the seceding colonies. The idea of natural law had nerved them to the act of secession; but it had its dangerous side, and it began to show that side. What, after all, is natural law; how do you know it, what is the basis of its interpretation, and by what sanctions are you to enforce it? As for knowing it, there is no fixed code; there is only a theory diffused in a number of different law books. As for its interpretation, and equally for its enforcement, this will tend to be a matter for each and every person—or, at the best, for each and every group of persons who can somehow manage to agree with one another. But this makes the law of nature what I, or we, may like; and that leads to a chaos of liberty. Such a chaos was what the House of Lords had already feared, in 1776, when it protested against the dangerous doctrine that the obedience of the subject went no further than he, in his private judgement, should think conformable to his own ideas.[1] It is what a South Carolina delegate to the continental congress described in a letter of 1776: 'the inhabitants of every colony consider themselves at liberty to do as they please upon almost every occasion.'[2] The law of nature left abundant room for constructive work. Indeed, it made such work imperative. But it was ready in company with its ally—the notion of a 'fundamental' law, expressed in a sacred and stable constitution—to inspire the work. The work was done between 1776 and 1780, when eleven of the new states gave themselves new constitutions, and seven of the eleven added to those con-

---

[1] Supra, p. 320.
[2] Quoted by H. E. Egerton, *The American Revolution*, p. 124.

stitutions a declaration of human rights. The old colonies, now new states, thus acquired a fixed and accepted rule of life which regulated the liberty of their inhabitants and conciliated it with a known system of law and a declared body of rights. The problem of the relation of the individual inhabitant and the state in which he lived was thus settled; and for the old individual and subjective interpretation of what was 'natural' or 'fundamental' there was substituted the common and objective standard of a promulgated constitution and a solemn declaration of rights. This was a great achievement. The honour of the American Revolution consists less in battles and martial triumphs than in the creative effort—conducted in the midst of war—of building constitutions and declaring systems of rights.[1]

In the second period of positive work an even greater problem emerged than that of the relation of the individual inhabitant to the state in which he lived. This was the problem of the relation of the individual state to the general confederation embracing all the states. The confederation had also to acquire a fixed and accepted rule of life which regulated the liberty of the member-states and conciliated it with a known system of binding federal law. Here too each state had considered itself at liberty to do as it pleased upon almost every occasion—to give or withhold men and money; to accept or reject a policy for the conduct of trade and finance. Here too a common objective standard had to be substituted for the individual and subjective interpretation which each state tended to put on the old 'articles of confederation' which had been drafted in 1777. This was done in 1787, by the creation of a new and binding federal constitution. That constitution had a double effect. It not only provided a fixed rule for the relations of individual states to the central federation. It also helped to confirm the rule already fixed in each state for the relations between itself and its individual inhabitants, and it did so

---

[1] See A. C. McLaughlin, *Foundations of American Constitutionalism*, p. 87; cf. also p. 93: 'we do not as a rule grasp the fact that this [the setting up of state governments and the drafting of state constitutions] is what gave distinction to the Revolution.'

by putting a central federal force at its back. The constitution of 1787 thus served as a double cement.

There is a difference between these two periods—that of the making of the state constitutions from 1776 to 1780, and that of the making of the federal constitution in 1787. During the first period the idea of a sovereign natural law—and, to a less extent,[1] of a fundamental and overriding law of the constitution, standing apart from ordinary law—was still an active idea. In the second period the idea of a sovereign natural law has faded; but the idea of a fundamental and overriding law of the constitution (which is now connected with the federal constitution) is still persistent, and indeed particularly active. We have already seen that the idea of natural law and that of fundamental law are ideas which may be connected. We shall have to show, in the sequel, how they can be, and were, divided. Meanwhile, it is to be noted that the fading of the idea of natural law, in the years after 1780, was natural and even inevitable. When the colonies were resisting Britain, they had to plead natural law as the ground and the justification of their resistance. When they had left the British Empire, and become independent states, they had still to plead it in the process of building for themselves new systems of politics—all the more as it was still fresh in their minds and still ringing in their ears. When they were fully embarked on their own independent life, in 1783 and afterwards, they had to think in practical terms of what may be called a business problem—the problem of finding a federal constitution which would ease their trade and finance, and would serve to protect their common interests. The law of nature faded before the needs of trade and the pressure of common interests. After the exhilaration of the dawn, it faded into the common day. There was no declaration of rights attached to the constitution of 1787; and when a declaration was added, by the first ten amendments of 1791, it was largely a recital of the old English common-law rights.

[1] See below, p. 334, for the reason why the idea of fundamental law may be regarded as less operative, in the sphere of the state constitutions and during the period of their making, than the idea of natural law.

VI

1. *The State Constitutions.* Before we deal with the foundation of the new state constitutions in 1776 and afterwards, it is important to notice that even before 1776 there had been a growing movement of opinion in favour of a fixed and written constitution, standing above the legislature and enshrining unalterable fundamentals which were conceived as connected with and proceeding from the law of nature.[1] It has already been noticed that the colonists, in the course of the struggle with Great Britain, attempted to argue that their own charters were unalterable and inviolable compacts, which, as such, were fundamental; but it has also been noticed that this view of the nature of colonial charters was historically and legally untenable.[2] Even more notable—though also untenable—was another theory which the colonists also attempted to urge. This was the theory that the British constitution, like all free constitutions, contained—or ought to contain—a core of unabridgeable rights, which overbore the legislature and formed a body of fundamental law. This theory was expressed in a variety of forms, which it is difficult to disentangle. One of these forms, which is somewhat confused, is based on a philosophy of natural rights, and may be traced in the writings of James Otis and Samuel Adams. Assuming the British constitution as it stands, but idealising it beyond recognition to suit the needs of their case, they argue that the constitution is based on the law of nature and is therefore a body of fundamental and unalterable law. This is an equation which may be expressed in the terms, 'Natural law = fundamental law = the British constitution', or as Samuel Adams wrote, 'The British constitution built its foundation in the immutable laws of nature, and as the supreme legislature...derives its authority from that constitution, it should seem that no laws can be made...that are repugnant to any essential law in nature.' He added that 'in all free states the constitution is fixed'. The

---

[1] On the connection between the notion of natural law and that of the fundamental law of the constitution, see above, p. 316.

[2] Supra, pp. 287–89.

difficulty of this view is that the British constitution was *not* fixed, and that it knew nothing of fundamental law and still less of the immutable laws of nature. But another form of the American theory of the British constitution, in the years before 1776, had a sounder basis. Those who expounded this other form did not assume the British constitution as it stood, nor did they argue that it already contained a fundamental and unalterable core. They thought of a new British constitution, imperial in its scope, which *ought* to be written and fixed, and which *ought* to contain fundamentals. Some of them envisaged 'a "Magna Carta Americana"', which permanently limited the rights of parliament and guaranteed the rights of Americans'.[1] John Adams, who unlike his cousin Samuel placed little reliance on appeals to natural law, and preferred to argue in terms of constitutional principle, was moving in this direction in the papers which he contributed, under the style of Novanglus, to a Boston newspaper during the course of the year 1775. 'Britain', he wrote, 'has been imprudent enough to let colonies be planted, until they are become numerous and important, without ever having wisdom enough to concert a plan for their government.... The consequences are that she has, after 150 years, discovered a defect in her government, which ought to be supplied by some just and reasonable means, that is by the consent of the colonies....She has found out that the great machine will not go any longer without a new wheel....We are willing, if she can convince us of the necessity of such a wheel, to assist with artists and materials in making it.'[2] The 'new wheel' of which Adams writes can only be a new constitution, necessarily written and necessarily containing fundamentals.

[1] J. C. Miller, op. cit. p. 126, referring to a writer in the *Virginia Gazette* of 24 March 1768.
[2] Quoted from S. E. Morison, *Sources and Documents of the American Revolution*, pp. 132–3. R. G. Adams, in his *Political Ideas of the American Revolution*, pp. 92–3, summarises the ideas of John Adams as (1) that the empire was (or should be) an association of equals; (2) that the British constitution was (or should be) a superior law, regulating the relations of its members; and (3) that there should be judicial disallowance of the acts of any of the legislatures which contravened that superior law.

In one form or another, during the years before 1776, the Americans were thus moving towards the idea of a fixed and express constitution, which, as all of them thought, should contain fundamentals limiting the legislature, and, as some of them thought, should be based on the law of nature and the foundation of natural rights. Down to 1776 they had attempted to believe that the British constitution itself either was such a constitution already, as Samuel Adams had argued, or, as his cousin preferred to think, could be made such by American assistance 'with artists and materials'. The scene was changed in 1776. The British constitution was left behind. But the Americans still retained the idea of the fixed and express constitution, standing above the legislature; and compelled by their own independence to erect their own constitutions, they resolved that those constitutions should be based upon that idea. In May 1776, nearly two months before the Declaration of Independence, the continental congress recommended the several colonies to set up governments of their own under the authority of the people. John Adams, bringing no little skill 'to the manufacture of governments', took a leading part in the drafting of state constitutions. If he could not assist the British Empire in making a new wheel for the great machine, he would assist the new states of America in making their own new wheels.

Connecticut and Rhode Island kept their existing constitutions:[1]

[1] The original constitutions of Connecticut and Rhode Island had been framed under the inspiration of two remarkable Cambridge men—Thomas Hooker of Emmanuel and Roger Williams of Pembroke. Hooker and Williams may both be called political theorists; and the writings of both show a similar theory, which proclaims (1) the origin of the state in compact, (2) the sovereignty of the people, and (3) the right of the people, as 'having fundamentally in themselves the root of power', freely to appoint their 'derivatives and agents' and 'to set the bounds and limitations of the power and place unto which they call them'. (V. L. Parrington, The Colonial Mind, pp. 58–61 and 68–73.) The constitution of Connecticut, called the Fundamental Orders, was originally made by the inhabitants in 1639, with a system of representation and a liberal franchise: it has been termed, as has already been noted, 'the first written constitution of modern democracy'. A generous charter, granted by Charles II in 1661, confirmed and even extended the previous form of government, permitting the colonists to erect their own courts and make their own laws;

the other eleven states, ending with Massachusetts in 1780, made new constitutions for themselves. Seven of these eleven, as has already been noticed—they included Virginia, Pennsylvania and Massachusetts—included in their constitutions, or added to their constitutions, a declaration or bill of rights. We may therefore distinguish, in these seven states, two sorts of documents—a declaration or bill of rights, enunciating principles of the law of nature (generally mixed with the old principles of the English common law and the English Bill of Rights); and a 'frame of government', as it was generally called, to 'ordain and declare the future form of government'. Both of these documents are sometimes stated to have been made by a 'convention' (for example the constitution of Pennsylvania is described in its title as 'established by the general convention elected for that purpose'); and the term may suggest a constituent assembly elected *ad hoc* by the people, as their immediate representative, in accordance with the natural-law principle enunciated by Vattel[1] that the constitution is the act and deed of the sovereign people itself. In fact, however, as we shall see presently, both documents generally proceeded from the ordinary colonial legislatures; but we shall also see that in Massachusetts the idea of the special constitutional convention was carefully discussed and eventually adopted.

If the full philosophy of the law of nature and the fundamental law of the constitution, which had been advanced by the colonists against the British legislature before 1776, were now to be put

and this charter served as the constitution of the colony down to 1818. (J. Truslow Adams, *The Founding of New England*, pp. 192–3, 318.) Rhode Island, which had begun its life as a loose group of townships each acting as a pure democracy (with the heads of the families in each meeting fortnightly to discuss and settle common affairs), acquired a single government by a charter of 1644, which still left legislative initiative to the people of each township, who recommended legal proposals to the general assembly. The charter was renewed by Charles II about 1667, on its old liberal lines (but with the additional grant of full toleration for all confessions); and in this form the constitution of Rhode Island remained in force for the next 180 years. (J. Truslow Adams, op. cit. pp. 185–6; 320.) Did the constitutions of Connecticut and Rhode Island, both still in force in and after 1776, affect the building of state constitutions in the other colonies between 1776 and 1780?

[1] Supra, p. 315.

into operation by them *vis-à-vis* their own legislatures, in the constitutions which they were now making at their own will, we should expect those constitutions to contain two sets of provisions. We should expect, in the first place, some provision for making null and void any act passed by a state legislature which contravened the law of nature; at any rate we should expect, where a declaration of rights had been made, some provision for making null and void any act which contravened such principles of the law of nature as were contained in that declaration. In the second place we should expect, in all the new constitutions, some provision disabling a state legislature from altering the constitution or legislating in any way which was contrary to the constitution. These expectations can hardly be said to be fulfilled. The declarations are not expressed as overriding the powers of the legislatures. They contain an enunciation of 'certain natural, inherent, and inalienable rights'; but the enunciation is left in the air.[1] (Perhaps that is the fate of all declarations of human rights. And yet men may be affected by what is floating in the air they breathe.) Pennsylvania, it is true, declares its Declaration of Rights 'to be a part of the Constitution of this Commonwealth...never to be violated on any pretence whatever'; but it is not clear that this adding of declaration to Declaration creates any legal validity, or brings rights down from the air. Nor, again, do the state constitutions contain any rule disabling the legislature—itself, in many cases, the maker of the constitution—from making amendments in it or passing acts contrary to it. Pennsylvania perhaps comes nearest, with its curious 'council of censors' (an antiquarian reminiscence of the *regimen morum* of the Roman censors, or perhaps of the Spartan ephoralty)[2] 'to inquire whether the constitution has been preserved inviolate' and, on the basis of such

---

[1] It may be noted that the declarations of rights made by most of the original thirteen States were copied by the new States which arose in the nineteenth century. (Becker, op. cit. pp. 239-40.) But they were sometimes altered or supplemented. Texas in 1845 altered 'all men are equal' into 'all freemen are equal'. Kansas in 1857 added the supplement, 'The right of property is before and higher than any constitutional sanction.'

[2] See above, p. 117.

inquiry, 'to recommend to the legislative the repealing of laws enacted contrary to the principles of the constitution', and 'to call a Convention' for amending any defective article in it.

These may be said to be matters of form, or at any rate merely of political theory. What is to be said of the substance of the new constitutions, and, in particular, of their social content and the social-economic ideas which they express or imply? It has been suggested by an American historian that 'in general this was true of American revolutionaries—radical as regards American rights against Great Britain, they had no wish to usher in democracy in the United States'.[1] There are facts which support the suggestion. There were those who wished the American Revolution to be a placid and propertied revolution like the English Revolution of 1688. There were Virginians who protested (as Ireton had protested in 1647 against a private soldier of the New Model Army who demanded manhood suffrage as a 'birthright') that men of birth and fortune should have their due power. A property qualification was made the condition of the suffrage in most of the new state constitutions; and town artisans, deprived of a vote, protested their inalienable right to ratify any new laws and to confirm the new constitutions.[2] But there are also facts which go the other way, and suggest that the American Revolution was a social as well as a political revolution. Ejecting the loyalists, who were generally men of substance and standing, the Revolution put into power a new governing class, drawn from a wider area and a poorer social stratum; and it was this new governing class which was destined to work the new constitutions.[3] The South might stand for a combination of political liberty with social inequality; but this was not true of the Northern, or even the Middle, States. The constitution of Pennsylvania is a particularly notable example

[1] J. C. Miller, op. cit. p. 349.   [2] Ibid. p. 353.
[3] In the seventeenth century the suffrage in the colonies had been liberal. During the eighteenth a property qualification began to be required; and this was sometimes high. Pennsylvania, under its old Charter of Privileges, which remained in force from 1701 to 1776, gave the vote only to 8 per cent of the rural and 2 per cent of the urban population. (J. C. Miller, op. cit. p. 44.) The franchise after 1776 was generally less restricted.

of social as well as political radicalism. Drafted by Benjamin Franklin and Tom Paine (the English exciseman who had come to Philadelphia with an introduction from Franklin at the end of 1775), it established a single chamber; it gave the franchise to every freeman, of the age of twenty-one and upwards, who had paid public taxes for a year; it provided for the prefixing of explanatory preambles to laws (in the style of Plato and Jeremy Bentham); and it instituted a supreme executive council directly elected by the people, with rapid rotation among its members and a system of checks on their action imposed by the single chamber. But even Massachusetts, in spite of the urgency of Samuel Adams, preferred a bicameral legislature; and this was the rule in most of the new constitutions. There was still a fear of what was called the 'mobility' (nor was it entirely ungrounded); and a system of two chambers, with the suffrage based on a property qualification, was regarded as the course of safety.

In the matter of substance and social content it would thus appear that the new constitutions, though they were hardly radical or 'populist', were certainly not reactionary. Property still talked in most of the states; but it talked in a lower key. In any case we have to beware of the anachronism of wearing the spectacles of the twentieth century when we look at the ideas and institutions of the eighteenth. What we consider reactionary to-day might be judged as dangerously radical (even by those who called themselves liberal) a century and a half ago.[1] Nor must we, in our modern zeal for the social-economic interpretation of history, allow ourselves to undervalue the solid achievement of the men of 1776–80 in the field of political principles and political form and method. It is true that the idea of natural law, after serving first as a destructive force in the period of resistance and then as a constructive impulse in the period of constitution-making, began to disappear in the sunset-glow of majestic (but perhaps academic) declarations of rights. But it is also true that the idea of a fundamental law of the constitution made quiet if unspectacular conquests. Divorcing itself without any ceremony—and perhaps

[1] See above, p. 253.

without any consciousness that a divorce was taking place—from the idea of natural law with which it had been connected, it solidified itself in solitude as the major rule of political life. Declarations of rights might remain in the air. But the 'frame of government' had a substantial existence; and the constitutional law expressed in such a frame acquired a major validity, overriding the acts of legislatures which drew their being from it, were therefore unable to alter it, and on the contrary were bound to obey it. This was the great achievement of the period of constitution-making: it was perhaps the greatest achievement of the American political genius; and it was an achievement destined to endure.

We must admit that the philosophy of Vattel, which ascribes to the people itself the original establishment of the constitution, was not generally triumphant. Only in two states did the people even ratify the constitution made for them by their representatives.[1] On the other hand, the idea of a constitutional convention, somehow distinct from the legislature, specially elected for the purpose, and specially and immediately representing the people, began to make its appearance. Proclaimed by Tom Paine in his *Common Sense* of January 1776, and announced by Pennsylvania, in the title of its constitution, in September of the same year, it was first clearly expressed by a Concord town-meeting held in the October of that year. This town-meeting (one wonders whether Samuel Adams was present, and whether he inspired its views) gave its reasons for holding that the legislature was 'by no means a body proper to form and establish a constitution', and it proposed instead a convention, elected by all the inhabitants of the age of twenty-one and upwards, which should form a constitution and publish it 'for the inspection and remarks of the inhabitants'.[2] The proposal of the Concord town-meeting was not followed: the existing legislature acted as a convention; but it submitted its draft of a constitution to the people, by whom the draft was rejected,

---

[1] There was, however, an informal submission of constitutions to the people in several other states.

[2] S. E. Morison, *Sources and Documents of the American Revolution*, p. 177.

mainly on the ground that it contained no declaration of rights. A second attempt was made in 1779; and this time a convention *was* chosen, which, after drafting a constitution, submitted it to the people assembled in their town-meetings, and, after considering their votes and suggestions, finally declared it adopted.[1]

It is true that the procedure of Massachusetts was, at the time, unique (though the example was followed soon afterwards by New Hampshire in a revision of its constitution); and it was only gradually that the idea of making constitutions by special popular conventions—and not by the ordinary legislature—struggled into life and effect. We can hardly wonder at this slow growth, when we remember that the period of the making of state constitutions was a period of war and standing emergency. Slowly, however, the idea emerged, and established itself as a practice. With it, and implied in it, we get the theory of what has been called 'the compact-origin of government and the body politic'.[2] Convention implies compact, as compact involves convention: it is in the process, and for the purpose, of 'tying themselves together' by the *compact* of a constitution that men 'come together' in a *convention*, through special representatives who carry the person of all and sundry. The preamble to the Massachusetts constitution (made by special convention and submitted to popular criticism) has an immanent logic when it speaks of 'the social compact by which the whole people covenants with each citizen, and each citizen with the whole people, that all shall be governed by certain laws for the common good'. The social contract is a reality, and not a hypothesis or fiction of scholars, when a constitution is made by this process and in these terms.

While the idea of the making of constitutions by special conventions was thus establishing itself, another and correlative idea began to grow by its side. This was the idea that a constitution so made, and the law of that constitution, necessarily overbore the legislature which it instituted and any law which that legislature made, and that judges accordingly might—or rather should—

---

[1] A. C. McLaughlin, *Foundations of American Constitutionalism*, pp. 94–100.
[2] Ibid. p. 98.

disallow any act of the legislature which contravened the higher law of the constitution. It is true that, during the troubled period of the making of state constitutions, the notion still survived that ordinary assemblies might frame constitutions, and make constitutional law, as well as pass ordinary laws; it is true that, along with it, there might also survive the notion that judges were bound to recognise and enforce *all* acts of legislatures equally, without any discrimination. But just as legislatures began to be ousted by special conventions in the making of constitutional law, so, and *pari passu*, the judges began to assume the power of distinguishing between constitutional law and the ordinary laws of the legislature, as made by two different authorities and possessing two different degrees of validity, and of disallowing the latter if they conflicted with the former. They had to find the law; and therefore, if there were two laws, they had to find which of the two was *the* law. This conception of the power of the judges had already, as we have seen,[1] been urged by Otis as early as 1764; but the distinction on which he had sought to base the power which he claimed for the judges was a distinction between the ordinary law and 'natural law' or 'eternal equity'. It is a different thing— and it remains different even if the idea of 'natural law' is combined or confused (as it was by Samuel Adams, if not by Otis) with the idea of a 'fundamental law' of the constitution—when a written constitution is substituted for natural law as the canon by which a judge may proceed in disallowing legislative acts. Instead of a floating and nebulous idea, you have now a sure and certain document; instead of the sanction of 'feelings of the heart', you have the known and tangible foundation (slowly, but surely, being laid) of convention, compact, ratification. The cloudy idea of the colonists, in the years before 1776, that the British legislature was somehow limited by something, is changed and clarified. It is changed, in the sense that it is now their own legislatures (the British legislature has gone into limbo) which are to be limited. It is clarified, in the sense that the 'something' has become a definite fact—the fact of the written constitution—and the 'somehow' has

[1] Supra, pp. 302–3.

become the definite process of judicial disallowance by courts, instituted and acting under that constitution.

How early does the practice emerge that judges in the new states may disallow acts of their legislatures, and use the rights of judicial review, in the name and authority of their constitutions? 'The idea had grown up in the states,' Lord Acton noted,[1] 'chiefly, I think, in Virginia'; and he quoted what Judge Wythe, one of the leading lawyers of Virginia, had said at Richmond as early as 1782: 'If the whole legislature...should attempt to overleap the boundaries prescribed to them by the people,[2] I, in administering the justice of the country, will meet the united powers at my seat in this tribunal, and, pointing to the constitution, will say to them, "Here is the limit of your authority: hither shall you go, but no further."' The protest of Wythe was effective; and the offending law was repealed by the legislature. The example of Virginia suggests—what other evidence corroborates—that the right of judicial review must not be considered as first developed under the federal constitution of 1787, or as being the achievement ('the usurpation', Jefferson would have preferred to say)[3] of Chief Justice Marshall. It was a right first exercised by state courts; and it was first exercised by them for the simple reason that the states were the first in the field with written constitutions made by the method of convention, based on the principle of compact, and proceeding specially and immediately from the source of the people. In the American air, and with the American background,

[1] *Lectures on the French Revolution*, pp. 35–6.

[2] The constitution of Virginia (which was formed before the Declaration of Independence and served as a general model) was drafted by the provincial assembly acting as a convention. But this, to Wythe, was 'the people'.

[3] Jefferson was opposed to judicial review in the federation, and disliked the federal judiciary. But we have to remember that he was not enamoured of the federation itself, and still less of the Federalist leaders; he believed that true democracy and the true way of social progress were to be found in the constitutions and policies of the states. He felt that the people who had made the constitution were its true interpreters, and that judicial interpretation might be a restrictive interpretation. The feeling long survived, and is perhaps active even to-day, in the party which he inspired. But it is not clear that Jefferson's opposition to judicial review *in the federation* extended to judicial review as practised in Virginia and the other states.

such a written constitution, and the law of that constitution, removed itself, and distinguished itself, from other law; it inevitably put to the judges the question: 'What will you do if there is a discrepancy, and which will then be *the* law?' It is the written constitution—*any* written constitution—and not the particular federal variety, which (again in American air, and with the American background) produces judicial review.

The final implication of the whole period of the making of state constitutions may be expressed in a single phrase—'the sovereignty of the constitution'. Convention, compact, limitation of the legislature, the right of judicial review—everything culminated in the sovereignty of the constitution. What is involved in that phrase? To find an answer we must go back to the philosophy of Locke.[1] Locke, it may be said, had made the legislature sovereign; and he certainly speaks of it as 'the supreme power'. This was a view which might suit the British; it did not suit the Americans. But Locke, it may also be said, had a second sovereign in reserve. He had also spoken of the contracted and covenanted people as being the supreme power, and he had regarded the legislature as deriving from it a 'fiduciary' power to be exercised under an implied deed of 'trust'. The Americans, thinking in terms of Locke's philosophy, could thus choose between two sovereigns— either the legislature or the people. But this was not all. Locke had still in reserve yet another sovereign—a third sovereign. This was the law of nature, 'which stands as an eternal rule to all men, legislators and others'. The American could thus choose, in the last resort, among three sovereigns—legislature; people; law of nature. Which did they actually choose?

We may say that they chose none of them, but a *quartum quid*. They paid some homage to the people—as authors through a convention of the compact and frame of government; they paid

---

[1] The writer would refer to some pages in his introduction to *The Social Contract* (a volume in the World's Classics) which deal with Locke's philosophy (pp. xxxii–iv). It is noticed there that Locke's idea of sovereignty is an oscillating idea, and that the needle of his compass can point in three different directions— sovereignty of the legislature; sovereignty of the community; sovereignty of natural law.

some homage to natural law—as expressed in declarations of rights. But they gave their final homage to the sovereign constitution. We may imagine them turning, first to Locke's covenanted and contracted people, next to his 'trustee' legislature acting under its implied trust, and finally saying, with a shake of the head: 'We are plain men, and we want to have things made plain. We are not content with an implied trust: we want something explicit. We like this idea of a covenanted people: it is in our bones; it is part and parcel of our religious history; but we should like to see the actual covenant, and to see it set down in writing. So this is what we propose to do. We, the people, will set our own representatives, assembled in a convention, to draft for our acceptance a written compact, which we will call a constitution; and we will impose this compact or constitution on the legislature, not as a sort of trust-deed, but as a specific and binding body of instruction. This means that we propose to insert the constitution between your covenanted people and your trustee legislature. We will not have merely a tacit consent "to make one community or government", such as you suggest; we will have an actual and written compact. We will not have merely a sort of trust-deed; we will have a real memorandum of instructions, which will be found in that same contract. That being so, we shall not talk of the sovereignty of the legislature, or of the people (though we ourselves are the people), or even of natural law (though we make our bow to that in our declarations of rights); we shall talk instead, and we shall talk only, of the sovereignty of the constitution. That is what we prefer. It is something in black and white; and it tells us where we are. The legislature will know where *it* is: it is under the constitution. The judges will know where *they* are: they are there to vindicate the sovereignty of the constitution, and to recognise and enforce such laws, and such only, as are made "in pursuance thereof". The constitution, as we see the matter, is "the supreme law of the land"; and the sovereign of sovereigns which we prefer is law—definite, black and white, law.'[1]

[1] This is expressed in Article VI 2 of the federal constitution of 1787 (if we lift the words used from their immediate application to a wider significance):

2. *The Federal Constitution of* 1787. The Constitution of 1787 belongs to a new epoch of ideas. It also belongs to the sphere of internal American development, in which contact and conflict with Britain is no longer a drag—or an inspiration. It can only be treated here so far as it shows some survival, and is moved by some after-swell, of the ideas which had heaved and tossed during the period of the Revolution. The great generalities and the universal appeal of the Declaration of Independence, and of the state constitutions with their accompanying declarations of rights, are succeeded by an era of practical problems and particular solutions. Lord Acton spoke of the difference 'between the revolutionary epoch and the constituent epoch that succeeded'. Remembering the great constituent activity of the revolutionary epoch itself, in the years between 1776 and 1780, we may prefer to speak of the difference between two different periods of constituent activity—the first or state-founding period, which was contemporaneous with the War of Independence, and the second or federation-founding period, which succeeded the war. In this second period one of the ideas which had still been active in the first (though less active, even then, than it had been in the years which preceded the Declaration of Independence) has faded and disappeared. This is the idea of natural law. There is no declaration of rights in the constitution of 1787. (The thought occurs that, even if there had been, it should logically have been of a different type from the declarations in the state constitutions of the first period of constituent activity. In view of the fact that the parties contracting in 1787 were states rather than individual men—states that were making a new federal super-state of which they were

'this constitution and the laws...made in pursuance thereof...shall be the supreme law of the land.'

Paine, at the end of *Common Sense* (published in January 1776), had already written: 'Where...is the King of America? I will tell you, friend.... Let a day be solemnly set apart for proclaiming the charter (the charter of the united colonies, answering to what is called the Magna Carta of England); let it be brought forth, placed on the divine law, the law of God; let a crown be placed thereon, by which the world may know that so far we approve of monarchy [i.e. sovereignty] that in America *the law is king*.'

units and individual members—it may be argued that logic would have dictated a declaration of the rights of the individual states, rather than a declaration of the rights of individual men.) True, such a declaration of rights was proposed in the first Federal Congress of 1789. True, ten articles, often termed by the name of the Bill of Rights, were added by way of amendment in 1791. But these articles are mainly recitals of old English common-law rights, and the rights they recite can hardly be held to involve any ideas of natural law, unless Article IX, with its reference to 'rights...retained by the people', may be held to involve that idea.

But if the idea of natural law thus faded in the second constituent period, the other idea which since 1764 had attracted the minds of the colonists—the idea of a fundamental law expressed and enshrined in a constitution—attained a new and signally important development. It had, indeed, already attained a large recognition in the state constitutions. There, however, it was still connected with the logic of the school of natural law; and there the idea of a fundamental law expressed and enshrined in a constitution could still be regarded as flowing from the principle that peoples have a *natural* right to make their own constitutions and impose them as a *ne plus ultra* on the powers of legislatures. Here, in the constituent period of 1787, the idea of fundamental law expressed in a constitution appears in a new connection. It is linked with federalism, and not with nature: it is connected, not with the natural right of men to form a frame and compact of government, but with the rights and duties of states in forming and sustaining a compact of federation.

The essential problem in a federal union is that of division of powers between the federal authority of the union and the several and separate authorities of the states which it unites. We may say, if we take a broad view, that this problem had been agitating America for the quarter of a century before 1787; and we may proceed to trace three phases or periods in the course of that agitation. In the first period, which lasts down to 1774 (the year of the meeting of the Continental Congress which eventually issued in the Confederation of 1777–87), there is already a *de facto* federal union, which goes by the name of the British Empire. That Empire, in a confused sort of way, gives an answer to the problem; but it does not afford a solution. Great Britain acts as the federal authority, and confronts as such the several legislatures of the colonies. Acting as the federal authority, Britain is generous in practice, but she becomes restrictive in theory. 'In practice', an American historian has said, 'they [the colonies] actually had a federal system, wherein powers of government were fairly well separated, where Parliament and colonial legislatures exercised their proper quotas of authority and kept within their spheres, except for the disputed right of parliament to exact money for imperial use.'[1] But if this was the British practice, British theory

[1] Van Tyne, *England and America*, p. 106. The same point is made by A. C. McLaughlin (*Foundations of American Constitutionalism*, p. 145): 'the principles of federalism were in reality embodied in the practice of the old Empire... colonies did exist, and had long existed, in possession of governments of their own with many powers and with actual authority.' The fact here noted by both historians—the fact of the federal practice of the old British Empire—leads them both to conclude that the American constitution of 1787 was a formulation *de jure* of the principles of that practice. 'Except for the disputed right of Parliament, the central authority, to exact money directly from the colonists for imperial use, the scheme of distribution of powers which, a generation later, was to be embodied in the American Federal constitution, was already the practice of the British Empire.' (Van Tyne, *The Causes of the War of Independence*, p. 221.) 'The American federal state was the child of the old British Empire, because the Americans gave legal and institutional reality to the practice of diversification of powers, and thus crystallized a system much like that under which the colonists had grown to maturity.' (McLaughlin, op. cit. p. 140.)

But perhaps these historians prove too much. There must have been something wrong, and even badly wrong, in a situation which produced the result that the expression of British practice in an American 'crystallisation' could only be achieved by war and secession. Four considerations occur to the mind: (1) The theory of Great Britain, as suggested in the text, was an irritation, even if her practice was not ungenerous; and if it was a case of the British bark being worse than the British bite, mere barking can be an annoyance. (2) The federal authority of the British Parliament, however fairly it might be practised, had a unilateral basis; there was no bilateral agreement between the colonists and the British, set down in an 'express convention'. ('All that was needed', Van Tyne remarks, 'was a working legal basis, an acknowledgement of the practice in the theory of the constitution'; but this *unum necessarium* was never achieved.) (3) Even in practice, the federal authority of the British parliament contained

was sadly different. It was a theory—more and more explicit after the Declaratory Act (1766)—of a unitary state which recognised, as such, no regular division of powers; and the colonists, annoyed by the theory, were led by a natural contagion to criticise even the practice. More and more they began to assert the principle of division of powers—to specify the powers which they claimed for themselves as parts, and to restrict the powers (more especially the power of 'exacting money for imperial use') which they were willing to accord to the federal authority of the British Parliament. In this way, and by this assertion of the principle of division, they were laying the foundations of the future: they were suggesting *sans le savoir* (and at the time *sans le vouloir*) the ideas on which they would ultimately build a federal constitution of their own. At the time they were only trying to find a *modus convivendi* with Britain. But they could not agree with Britain—or rather Britain could not agree with them—on a method of division; and failing to achieve division they took the path of secession. A second period ensued; and the colonies substituted, for the space of some dozen years, a confederation of their own, with the congress of that confederation acting as federal authority in lieu of displaced Britain. A natural reaction against the claims of federal authority, as exemplified by Britain, made even their own congress weak. This was not logical, for a congress of their own was something different from a British parliament; but it was natural. Weak even in war, the confederation was still weaker, after 1783, in peace.

no element of colonial representation: the federal authority of the American Congress under the Constitution of 1787 was based, especially in the Senate, on a full representation of the states. (4) In practice too, as suggested above on p. 292, n. 2, the actual division of powers between the British parliament and the colonial legislatures was not well calculated; and the colonial legislatures, faced by a British governor bound to act under his instructions, had an insufficient control of their own colonial affairs. By 1787 the colonies, now become states, had given themselves constitutions of their own, under which they enjoyed a larger control of their own affairs than they had ever enjoyed when they were connected with Britain; and on this basis it was possible to achieve in 1787 a new and more equitable division of powers between the federal authority and the authorities of the states than would ever have been possible under the conditions of 'the old empire'.

Just as, before the making of the state constitutions in 1776 and afterwards, there was something of a chaos of individual liberty, with each individual going his own way,[1] so there was now something of a chaos of state liberty, with the confederated states unwilling to fulfil the obligations incumbent upon them. Division of powers had indeed been achieved in the Confederation; but the division was inequitable, giving too much to the states and too little to the federal authority, and it was certainly insecure. The Confederation has been called a magnificent failure; and the great reason of its failure was an inequitable division of powers, and especially a refusal of the parts to give to the central authority the essential powers (the power of taxing and the power of regulating commerce) which the Americans had denied, with some justice, to Britain, continued to deny, with far less justice, to the central authority of their own confederation, and were ultimately compelled to concede, alike by the logic of equity and the pressing compulsion of security, to the central authority of the federation established in 1787.[2]

[1] Supra, p. 327.

[2] This summary account of the reasons leading to the federal constitution of 1787 may be called traditional, or even old-fashioned. It is couched in political terms; and a more modern version, followed by a number of recent American writers, is couched in terms of 'the economic interpretation of the constitution'. V. L. Parrington, for instance (*The Colonial Mind*, pp. 267 seqq.), regards the states of the Confederation as standing for the higher democracy of 'populism' and the juster economics of agrarianism; and he conceives them as defeated by 'a close working alliance of property and culture for the purpose of erecting a centralised state with coercive powers' (p. 274). Alexander Hamilton figures as the head of the alliance; and he accordingly becomes the hero less of American federalism than of American capitalism—or rather of American federalism acting as the agent of American capitalism. He and his colleagues, we are told, discovered a new fundamental law in 'the interest of the money-economy'; they 'discarded the revolutionary doctrines', and 'were done with natural rights and romantic interpretations of politics'.

It hardly becomes an English writer to take any side on an issue which would appear to be connected with the American party politics of the twentieth century. It may be noted, however, that Professor Parrington, after having made 'property and culture' instal 'a centralised state with coercive powers', proceeds in a later passage (p. 282) to argue that it was not Montesquieu, but 'considerations of economic determinism', that produced the system of checks and balances (between the federal legislature and the federal executive)

The third period was accordingly a return to the practice (but not to the theory) of the old British Empire—a return on a higher level, in the sense that it took the form of a negotiated agreement about division of powers. The essence of the federal constitution, achieved in this third period, was not so much (as is often said), the 'great compromise' which combined the equal representation of states in the Senate with their proportionate representation in the House of Representatives: it was rather the clear division and the exact enumeration of the rights belonging to the federal congress in contradistinction to the rights left to the states. The pivot of the constitution was the section of the first article which recited the eighteen powers of the Congress, and included among them, in the first three, the power 'to lay and collect taxes' for the common use and the power of regulating commerce with foreign nations and among the states. Here at last is the black and white of an acknowledged and agreed division of powers, clear to both sides and accepted by both.

But such an agreed and acknowledged division demands, as the colonists had argued when they were opposing Great Britain, a fundamental and unchallenged law based on the principle of compact. It must be expressed beyond a doubt and secured beyond a peradventure. Once more—but now on the new federal ground of the necessity of a binding division of powers—we return to the American principle of the sovereignty of the constitution and the law contained in the constitution; and with it we return again to the idea of the compact—the written, pledged, and inviolable compact. Just as a fundamental law, based on the idea of compact, had been established *in* each state by the making of the state

which imposed restraints upon the expression of majority will. 'Economic determinism' would appear to produce two contrary effects if it issues both in 'a strong centralised state with coercive powers' and in a system of checks and balances which tends to enfeeble those powers. In any case the system of checks and balances, if it be understood to mean the mutual check and balance of President and Congress, may best be interpreted as the product neither of Montesquieu nor of 'economic determinism', but of a traditionalism which perpetuated the old diarchy of the colonial governor and the colonial assembly (supra, p. 292), or rather installed it afresh in the shape of the new diarchy of President and Congress.

constitutions between 1776 and 1780, so now, in 1787, a further fundamental law, based on the same idea, was established *between* the states by the making of the federal constitution. These two acts of establishment not only succeed one another: they are also logically connected; and the first is the condition and the presupposition of the second. You could not have had the fundamental law of the whole federal state, unless each and all of the federal states had been limited in advance by the fundamental law of their own state constitutions.[1] You must have each state itself under compact before you can have a federal system of states which is equally under compact. We may therefore say that the fact of Massachusetts having spoken, in the preamble to her own constitution of 1780, of 'the social compact' between the people and each citizen 'to be governed by certain laws', is the reason, the indispensable reason, why Massachusetts could also speak, in adopting the Constitution of 1787, of 'the people of the United States... entering into an explicit and solemn compact with each other by assenting to and ratifying a new constitution'.[2] Indeed, that new constitution *was* a compact: we may even call it 'the great compact' (rather than 'the great compromise')—the great compact which sealed and ratified, as 'the supreme law of the land', a system of division of powers between the federal authority and the authorities of the states. The idea of the social contract was still operative to the last; and if that idea be regarded as a part of the philosophy of natural law, may we not argue that natural law too was still operative to the last, and had not, after all, entirely faded or disappeared in 1787.[3]

[1] See A. C. McLaughlin, op. cit. p. 163.
[2] Ibid. p. 77, and see above, p. 320.
[3] It may be argued that the right of judicial review by the federal judiciary, or the power of the supreme court to disallow acts contrary to the constitution, flowed logically and inevitably from the nature of the constitution as a compact. Compacts must be kept (at any rate in the thought of the men of 1787, if not in the more dynamic and evolutionary thought of a later age): *fides est servanda*, and men must obey the rule *pactum serva*. If pacts are to be kept, and faith observed, the judges must be able to say what the pact means, whether it has been kept, or whether faith has been broken. *Legally*, it might be necessary to put together two articles of the constitution (III 2 (3) and VI 2) in order to justify

VII

What were the ultimate issues of a quarter of a century's ferment of ideas, and what were the lasting effects of the leaven of the idea of natural law, which had played so large a part in the ferment? The immediate result was the emergence (to repeat Lord Acton's phrase) of 'the international extra-territorial universal Whig'. In other words it was the emergence of European Liberalism, already foreshadowed by the thought of France, but now made active and living by the actual experience and the bold construction of America. The American state declarations of rights, which begin with the Virginia Bill of Rights of 12 June 1776, are the precursors of the French declaration *des droits de l'homme et du citoyen* prefixed to the constitution of 1791, as that in turn is the precursor of the later declarations prefixed to the French constitutions of 1793, 1795, and 1848. Whether the American state declarations were the sources of the French, or were only precursors and precedents, is a question in dispute; but even if they were only precedents, they were still an effective influence.[1] That influence is still operative, even in the middle of the twentieth century. The declaration of human rights, which it is now proposed that the United Nations should frame and proclaim, has a long

judicial review by the federal judiciary; and even so Chief Justice Marshall might be accused of usurpation. *Logically*, it was inevitable that a constitution based on compact should be supported by a judicial authority competent to interpret and enforce the compact.

In any case, as has already been noticed, the power of judicial review was already being exercised in the states; and that exercise was a precedent and a presumption in favour of its use in the federation. But just as judicial review in the states helped to produce judicial review in the federation, so, vice versa, judicial review in the federation helped ultimately to strengthen judicial review in the states. The sovereignty of the state constitutions, even when supported by the power of judicial review, might have suffered from the impact of popular will and majority pressure if it had not been buttressed by the sovereignty of the federal constitution, similarly supported by a like power. This is part of the general interlocking between the state systems and the federal system.

[1] See A. Esmein, *Éléments de droit constitutionnel* (ed. 1927), vol. I, p. 594, n. 61.

ancestry; and it may count Thomas Jefferson among its progenitors. But above and beyond declarations of rights the Americans also gave to Europe, and to the cause of European Liberalism, the idea and practice of the written constitution, made by convention, expressed as a compact, and serving as the ultimate sovereign of the life of each people and nation. That too was a prolific and fecund idea; and that too has had a long line of descent. But the two constructive ideas of the written declaration of rights and the written constitution were not the only contributions made by America to European Liberalism. The destructive ideas of revolutionary theory and revolutionary technique were also carried across the Atlantic, to join the examples provided by Geneva[1] and the initiatives of the people of Paris. 'What the French took from the Americans', it has been said, 'was their theory of revolution, not their theory of government—their cutting, not their sewing.' But the law of nature, as the course of the argument has shown, has always had this double edge—the one edge critical, revolutionary, destructive of the past: the other edge positive, progressive, constructive of the future.

In America itself the natural-law philosophy continued to linger in the nineteenth century. Still present, in the form of the idea of compact, at the birth of the Federal Constitution of 1787, it was also present two generations later—but now in the form of the idea of the natural right of *all* men to life, liberty, and the pursuit of happiness—at the birth of the abolitionist cause and the launching of the crusade against negro slavery. It was in the spirit of 1776[2] that Dr Channing (pastor of a Boston congregation, and

---

[1] On Geneva, see above, p. 238 and n. 1.

[2] 'In the spirit of 1776'—for Jefferson included in his original draft of the Declaration of Independence an accusation against George III (which was also, as John Adams called it, a philippic against negro slavery) that 'he has waged cruel war against human nature itself, violating its most sacred rights of life and liberty in the persons of a distant people who never offended him...and carrying them into slavery in another hemisphere'. (Quoted by Becker, *Declaration of Independence*, p. 212, as is also the passage from Dr Channing's *Slavery*, p. 242.) Jefferson's accusation against George III is rhetoric rather than history; but the share of Great Britain in the slave-trade and slavery *is* history. On the other hand, it is only fair to add that Great Britain had declared through Mansfield,

heir to the best traditions of the Boston clergy) protested, in his book on slavery, that 'man has rights by nature...in the order of things they precede society, lie at its foundation, constitute man's capacity for it, and are the great objects of social institutions'. The struggle against negro slavery issued in a civil war—the second in American history (for the War of Independence had also been in the nature of a civil war)—but it was the nature of the federal union, and the sanctity of 'the great compact', rather than the natural rights of the negro or the principle of abolition, which lay at the heart of that war. Less momentous than that great struggle, which was waged on the field of constitutional law, was another and more peaceful struggle which was engaged in the field of ordinary or civil law. The United States of America, in seceding from Great Britain and establishing a separate body of constitutional law, had still retained—and indeed may be said to retain to this very day—the rules and the procedure of the ordinary English common law. English decisions continued to be cited as authorities in American courts; and the American system of jurisprudence remained essentially the same as the English. But though there was this similarity, which came very near to identity, between the two systems of law, it was also natural that the courts of an independent America, in the early and formative phase of their history, should adopt an independent attitude towards the English courts and the law of those courts. The two systems might be connected; but should not a country which had just won its freedom on one field vindicate it also on the other? Accordingly, as Professor Gutteridge has noted, 'the formative period of the law was tinged by hostility to all that was English, with a consequent trend in the direction of natural law which was sought for mainly in the writings of the French jurists'. Instead of relying

in 1772, that slavery cannot exist in England, and that the British Parliament passed a resolution against the slave-trade in the very year of the Declaration of Independence (1776). The final British repentance comes later; but the slave-trade went in 1807; slavery was abolished in all the British Dominions in 1833; and one of Dr Channing's last acts, two months before his death in 1842, was to deliver an address commemorating the emancipation of slaves in the British West Indies, which he had studied and admired.

solely upon English jurisprudence, American lawyers turned to France: they began to compare what they found in French law-books with what they found in the English; and the result (in a phrase which Professor Gutteridge quotes from the writings of Dr Roscoe Pound) was the 'conception of an ideal of comparative law as declaratory of natural law, a conception which is especially manifest in the writings and judgments of Kent and Story'.[1]

The words of Dr Roscoe Pound suggest a train of reflection with which the argument of this essay may naturally end. He speaks of 'an ideal of comparative law'. What is comparative law, and in what sense does it suggest, or contain, an ideal? In itself it is a comparison—a process or method of comparison (and not a body of law)—applied to the different bodies of existing positive law. Does the process stop at comparison, and is it an end in itself; or has it an end beyond itself, and does it proceed to a further goal? It is only the further development of the comparative study of law which can give an adequate answer. But it is perhaps permissible to guess, from the signs and indications which have already been given, that students who begin in comparison will proceed to distillation—the distillation of the common ideal which the different bodies of positive law are attempting, in different ways, to express. If the comparative study of law should thus extend its scope, may we not say that it will be proceeding—or returning—to the conception of natural law? True, if it should thus return, it will do so, as the philosophers say, on à higher level. It will attain the conception in a better way (the way of comparison between, and distillation from, the existing bodies of positive law) than the old way followed by the jurists of the school of natural law, who were content to draw upon one body of law—the civil law of Rome—and to illuminate what they drew from it by their own *a priori* reasoning. But this return on a higher level seems already to have begun. Already we may find French jurists of the new school of comparative law arguing that it is the function of their study to distil the principles common to all civilised systems of

---

[1] See Professor Gutteridge's *Comparative Law*, ch. I and II, and especially p. 13.

positive law, and contending that these principles constitute a model law which may be called *droit idéal relatif*.[1] Others prefer to speak of the disengaging of what they term 'international common law', taking the view that the substance of such law consists of the rules which are applicable to the needs of all societies that have attained a similar standard of civilisation.[2] It is possible to regard such views as mere speculations, seductive indeed, but also dubious. Yet it is to be noticed that an article of the Statute of the Permanent Court of International Justice directs the court to apply, along with other rules, 'the general principles of law recognised by civilised nations'. The conclusion of the matter would seem to be that 'nature', expelled by the pitchfork of the positive lawyer, has a habit of returning. The saying of Gierke recurs to the mind: 'the undying spirit of Natural Law can never be extinguished.'

The vision of an ideal is something which is always needed—even in law. We may dismiss natural law as a vision. It *is* a vision; but we cannot dismiss it because it is. *Tamen usque recurret.* In one form or another—comparative law, *droit idéal relatif*, international common law, the general principles of law recognised by civilised nations, a Declaration of Human Rights framed by the United Nations—it will always return.

And so a theme of the first essay has recurred, or returned, in the last. That theme is the common law of all men, which is also the law 'conformable to nature'. Alexander and Zeno, the Macedonian conqueror and the Stoic philosopher from Cyprus, had stood together by the cradle of this common law, the one its armed but unconscious vindicator, the other its unarmed but conscious prophet. Plutarch had recognised the conjunction when he wrote, in a treatise celebrating the fortitude of Alexander, that 'the admired polity of Zeno, the founder of the Stoic school, was directed to this single conclusion, that. . .we should count all men fellow-citizens, and be as one flock on a common pasture feeding

---

[1] Saleilles, in Gutteridge, op. cit. p. 5.
[2] Lambert, in Gutteridge, op. cit. pp. 16, 18.

together by a common law'—the 'conclusion' which Alexander had sought to enforce. A little more than two thousand years later Washington and Jefferson, the general of armies and the master of ideas, stood together in a similar conjunction, similarly engaged in the same fundamental cause of the common law of humanity and the common rights of men under that law. There is a long line of connection in the tradition of civility which runs from the end of the fourth century B.C. to the end of the eighteenth century of our era.

INDEX